DEVELOPING DATABASES

FOR THE WEB & INTRANETS

DEVELOPING DATABASES

FOR THE WEB & INTRANETS

John Rodley

CORIOLIS GROUP BOOKS

Publisher	Keith Weiskamp
Project Editor	Scott Palmer
Copy Editor	Marianne Krcma
Cover Artist	Gary Smith
Cover Design	Anthony Stock
Interior Design	Nicole Birney
Layout Production	Dorothy Bungert
Proofreader	Kathy Dermer
Indexer	Caroline Parks

The Coriolis Group, Inc.
14455 N. Hayden Road, Suite 220
Scottsdale, AZ 85260
Phone: (602) 483-0192
Fax: (602) 483-0193
Web address: http://www.coriolis.com

ISBN 1-57610-051-0: $39.99

Printed in the United States of America

10 9 8 7 6 5 4 3 2 1

This book is dedicated to Claire and Joe, who taught me to read.

Contents

Acknowledgments

Throughout most of the process of writing this book, I worked propped in a chair nursing a very broken leg and wallowing in self-pity. I would like to take this opportunity to thank all the people who kept me fed, medicated, and entertained while my body cooked up a new tibia. In particular, I owe a debt of thanks to Howie, Judy, and Holly, who made food and mowed the lawn without once accusing me of being a baby.

Two virtual thumbs-up to my virtual co-workers, Dennis and Larry who kept me in stitches with their Dilbertian tales of life in the real work world. Also to project editor Scott Palmer for not laughing at me every time I turned in a new schedule. And to Richard Scothern, whose Herculean data collection efforts resulted in the Newf database. I am also deeply indebted to Roger Erickson of Rose Partners for his assistance. Without it, this book would not have been possible.

Finally, and forever, to my wife Heather, without whom I would not have started writing in the first place.

Introduction

With the explosive growth in the use of local area networks in the 1980s, many PC programmers were dragged, kicking and screaming, into the world of client-server programming. Well, if the LAN rush was an explosion, the Web rush is a nuclear blast. Thousands of coders who've been happily hand crafting pretty, little, standalone Windows programs now find themselves thrust onto the Web, where millions of clients and servers are packed cheek by jowl jostling for attention. It's an exciting place. It's also an environment where none of the old magic works anymore.

Not only does the old magic not work anymore, but the path from user to application is full of potholes. In fact, at first glance, the whole process of linking an Internet user sitting at his browser to an application back at corporate central reeks of something that was hacked together over a couple of weeks by a group of guys who didn't really like each other very much. Even experienced programmers venturing onto the Web for the first time often get very far into the process before finding out they've forgotten some really important piece.

If this little rant strikes a chord, then this book is for you. It's a Web programming adventure, taking three different paths to putting a business application up on the World Wide Web. First, in Chapters 1 through 4, we'll do it the hard way, putting up a simple database with some query screens and a bit of data entry using C, CGI and a standalone multi-user database. The Newfoundland Dog Database will use today's technology, limiting the database transaction to the server, and passing all communications through the HTTP server. Along the way, we'll construct an SQL Server database from scratch, build a complete CGI database access program in C, and draw up the HTML documents that link the whole thing together. When we're done with Chapter 4, we'll have a complete Web database application (and one that you can check out on the Web today at http://www.channel1.com/users/ajrodley).

In Chapter 5, we'll get a little fancier, using tools like Java to present an active interface to a typical business application: the ubiquitous stock price application. Active Web content is the hot topic among Websters today, and here we'll take a radical step: linking active content to useful data.

Chapter 6 gets fancier still, building one of today's hot applications, an Internet store. This chapter looks at some of the thornier issues of Web application development, such as authentication and state maintenance using the new Jeeves Web server from JavaSoft.

In Chapters 7 and 8, we'll look back at our three applications and talk in more depth about some of the specific issues that arise with each and how to deal with them. In chapter 7, it's security, in chapter 8, database issues—operational and otherwise.

The entire field of Web application development is like a speeding merry-go-round. There's no convenient time or place to get on, and boarding is guaranteed to hurt. It's also no picnic just trying to stay on the ride. Solutions that make sense today will look dated or even stupid tomorrow. That's just the way it goes. I have no doubt that at least some of the contents of this book will be a little stale by the time you read it. But the whole trick in safely boarding this merry-go-round is getting up to speed *before* you jump on. Hopefully, this book can get you moving rapidly in the right direction.

This book is written for programmers. It covers a lot of ground, using a lot of different tools. As such, it is packed with code examples and advanced discussions of database and programming issues. Most of our base technologies are given little, if any, introduction. In most cases, I just leap right in. In particular, to get the full benefit of this book, you should have some familiarity with C programming, SQL and basic relational database systems. I hesitate to require familiarity with Java, because so few people have it, but in truth, it would be extremely helpful. Again, if you're a competent C/C++ programmer, anything written in Java will look familiar and probably be readily understandable, at least syntactically. In any case, you won't see any Java until the second half of the book, when we've already built a working Web database.

We use a lot of HTML code here, but in-depth knowledge of HTML, in my opinion, is not necessary to use this book. If you know enough C to get along here, then you can easily pick up HTML in a half-hour playing with one of the HTML editors (my favorite is HotMetal from SoftQuad).

Tools And Portability

Listed below are the tools I used for this book, and the ones on which the examples are based. These are the tools I use, and the only ones for which the code examples will compile and run without modification. Many of you face situations where, for historical or other reasons, you must use tools and platforms other than the ones I've used here. My experience tells me that for the examples used here, switching tools would not be especially difficult, but, as we all know, easy to do is easy to say. Thus, presented below are the tools/platforms and my personal read on what portability problems their use introduces. If you're unsure whether this book will be applicable to your configuration, check here.

The Browser: Netscape Navigator

The whole premise of Web application development is to present something useful no matter what browser the user is running. Thus, having the wrong browser is no excuse for not buying this book.

The Web Servers: Jeeves, IIS, And Netscape Commerce Server

This is a little more problematic. I went with these three because they're popular now and I had to use something. Some of the more advanced features like Secure Socket Layer will not be available on other servers. However, most of the servers I've used (O'Reilly, Apache...) support the basic CGI functionality necessary to run the Newf database.

The Database Server: Microsoft SQL Server

Again, slightly problematic. Much of the configuration information I present is absolutely specific to SQL Server. However, the basic concepts behind these configuration issues are common to all multiuser, relational database management systems. I try to explain each issue in enough depth that the concept behind it can be applied to other platforms. However, doing so will probably require sitting down with the manuals. Manual-phobics should not try to port this code to other database platforms.

The Embedded SQL Preprocessor And Libraries: MS ESQL/C

The choice of Microsoft's ESQL/C is dictated by the choice of SQL Server as database platform. However, this tool is absolutely the least of your worries when it comes to ports. The embedded SQL code is completely vanilla, in fact, no different from the embedded SQL I've written for Sybase and IBM's DB2/2.

The C Compiler: Microsoft Visual C++

Ditto for the C compiler. I do *not* use Microsoft Foundation Classes or any of the GUI libraries that might make these programs a real pain in the neck to port. The applications are command-line only, and as such, a reasonably experienced programmer should be able to port them to any modern operating system, even Unix, without a great deal of hair-pulling. The one spot that might cause trouble is the tiny bit of exception handling code in the main function for newfq.exe. Once you understand what it does, however, it should be easy to work around.

The Operating System: Windows NT 3.51 & 4.0

To be perfectly honest, I would rather have used Unix for much of this project. In fact, I've felt that way about nearly every project I've worked on since the late 70's. Unix multitasking is, and always has been, superior to the competition, and nearly all the really neat programming ideas in use today have been ported from the Unix world. Unfortunately, there's always a *really* good reason (or two or three) not to use Unix, in this case cost. Everything is too expensive in the Unix world. So we go with Windows NT as the only cost-effective way to present the ideas we have to present. Again, my experience in the Unix world tells me that the code we've written here would be an easy port, as I try to stay away from operating-system specific calls and tools.

Java

The Java code we use in the stock ticker application and the shopping cart app is, by definition, portable. If there's a Java interpreter for your operating system (and most of them have one now) then this Java code should work without modification (or even a recompile). It's produced using Symantec's Café to the 1.02 specification of the JDK.

JDBC

Some of the Java examples rely on having a JDBC driver and class libraries installed. I used Weblogic's jdbcKona/MSSQLServer. There are, undoubtedly, other implementations that would work. JDBC is a very young standard right now. As such, it remains to be seen how compatible various implementations will be.

Technical Support For This Book

As readers of my other books know, I go to great lengths to support what I write. If you have any questions about what I've written here, you should feel free to write me. If you don't understand something, or can't get it to work, don't seethe in silence - email me. In my experience, most problems go away with the exchange of a couple of emails over the course of a couple of days. The best way to reach me is via email at:

john.rodley@channel1.com

I can also be contacted through the publisher's Web site at:

http://www.coriolis.com

The errata for this book, along with downloadable copies of the latest version of all the book's example code, can be found at either

http://www.rodley.com

or:

http://www.channel1.com/users/ajrodley

In addition, these sites will also be running versions of the example code. So, for instance, you can log into rodley.com and do searches against the Newfoundland Dog Database.

Over the course of reading this book, I would suggest that you check into the support site once or twice. Readers frequently bring up important points, which, while they might or might not be bugs, are still serious "qualifications" of whatever was said in the book. Seeing what others have gotten, or quibbled with, from the book will give you important perspective on what's said here.

part one

Chapter 1

Getting Started

CHAPTER 1

Getting Started

The World Wide Web has finally gotten down to business. After going through brief flirtations with, among other things, personal home pages, animation, sound, and a host of other cool but unprofitable ventures, the Web has figured out what it's best at: presenting lots of useful information in a pleasing and timely manner. And lots of information can mean only one thing: lots of database programming. That's where we come in.

Putting a Web face on a database is not rocket science, but it's not trivial either. Over the course of this book, we'll develop three Web database applications:

- The Newfoundland Dog Database
- A stock price-quote system
- An online store

Each of these applications affords us a different perspective on the Web database problems, and we'll use a range of tools to solve them.

Before we get down to the nitty-gritty problems of actually programming our database, we have to establish our assumptions—the hardware we'll be running on, the type of connection we have to the Net, and the software services we need to have running on our Net machine. When we're done, we'll have a set of fairly loose requirements that describe what a Web database server looks like.

If you already have a Net-connected machine ready to go, you might want to skip the brief sections on hardware and Net connections. If you already have a good handle on basic database programming, you might want to skip the last half of this chapter. And, if you who just plain don't have any patience, you might want to go straight to Chapter 2 to start coding.

Why Publish?

Many of us are making a fine living putting databases up on the Web. Every information hoarder on Earth is hiring a crew to put their little corner of the library of human knowledge up for all the world to see. In that environment it may sound heretical, perhaps even stupid, to question the wisdom of putting up Web databases. After all, The Net is A Good Thing, and The Web is An Even Better Thing. However, it can't hurt to go over just why webbing databases is Such A Good Thing. At heart, there are three obvious attractions to putting databases up on the Web:

- *A built-in potential audience of millions of Internet-connected users.* This is the one that has led to the land-rush aspect of Web database development. The users are out there, and once your database is accessible via a network URL, all you need to do is to get the users to look at it (no small feat). It is a tantalizing prospect, although it often sounds distressingly similar to the "billions of Chinese" syndrome that throughout this century has led thousands of businesses to waste years of effort and millions of dollars chasing a billion Chinese buyers who have yet to materialize. The potential of Web databases can be realized, though. The Newfoundland Dog Database, for example, has reached thousands of users in dozens of countries, including such unlikely places as Finland and Estonia. Other, equally unlikely applications have achieved equally satisfactory results.
- *A standardized, highly capable, user-interface shell: the Web browser.* While HTML has serious limitations, the existence of a standard, any standard, is crucial to any effort that attempts to reach users whose hardware and software configurations are not under our control. Up to

now, many of us in the database application-development business have worked under the luxurious assumption that we can specify the software that the user runs to interface with our database. This is no longer the case. We can, however, assume that the user's software understands HTML.

- *A ready-to-use pipeline from the database machine to the user's browser.* Many, many distributed applications still being sold today rely on proprietary software packages that dial each other up via the telephone and relay information via some proprietary, or perhaps just obscure, protocol. With the advent of widespread, low-cost Internet access, such solutions are, for the most part, obsolete. Users can often be relied on to connect themselves to the Net, reducing the database provider's problem to one of simply putting the database on the Net. In many companies, most workers are already networked.

To reach those millions of Web users, though, we must figure out how to connect our database machines to the Net, and how to communicate successfully with HTML-compliant browsers. The first step is setting up Web-capable hardware.

The Hardware

A Web database machine has many requirements in common with any database server machine. In general, it needs to be big, fast, and ultra-reliable. Lots of RAM and hard disk space are essential. DBMSs are expensive processes. Today's products generally use lots of threads and processes, which are all costly in terms of memory and CPU time. The hard disk space required will generally depend on the amount of data you intend to store.

Reliability is another important factor. A database that loses data is a contradiction in terms. In order to minimize the chances of losing data, you have to consider the following possibilities:

Power Loss

What happens if the power goes out? This is an easy one to fix, since uninterruptible power supplies (UPSs) with automatic shut-down features have been available for years. The one thing to pay attention to is that the shut-down process terminates the DBMS properly.

Hard Disk Failure

All hard disks crash eventually. Sad but true. No hardware lasts forever. There are a number of ways to deal with the disk crash problem. At the top end of the scale, you can implement a RAID disk array with data redundancy and hot swapping for nonstop operation. At the other end of the scale is the much more common solution of regularly scheduled tape backups. This is an absolute minimum for any database server—regular (as in weekly) tape backups.

Software Error

This is a tough one to get a grip on, but it has to be acknowledged. Your DBMS, operating system, network OS, firmware, video driver, tape backup software—all of them have bugs. Occasionally, one of those bugs will pop up and trash a machine. Again, the only practical protection against buggy software is to keep a fairly long trail of regular backups.

We've briefly outlined a couple of steps you can take to guard against data disasters—a plan. A plan, however, is no good if it's executed poorly. How do you know that your data protection plan will work? That's easy. You test it.

The UPS is the easiest to test. Pull the UPS plug out of the wall and see if the system shuts down and comes back up properly.

The tape back-up test is just as simple, although a lot more work. Shut the system down unexpectedly, then restore from the last backup. If it works, you're all set.

This may sound like such incredibly basic, commonsense stuff that it's not worth talking about. Maybe so, for you, but I've gone to any number of clients who had elaborate disaster plans that nobody had ever tested. Nobody had the time to try it. I've even had clients who backed up their systems faithfully for years (never testing any of the tapes) only to discover that, because of a procedural mistake, none of the tapes had anything written on them. Don't let it happen to you. Plan well, execute religiously, and test early and often.

Our database machine must be big and fast, with at least an uninterruptible power supply, tape backup, and possibly a RAID array to ensure data integrity and maximum availability.

The Network Connection

Connecting this big, ultra-reliable database server to the Net is, for the most part, no different than connecting any machine to the Net. Figure 1.1 shows the basic problem. Users get themselves connected to the backbone. In order to reach them, you must connect your database machine to the backbone. In most cases, this means buying a connection to an Internet Service Provider (ISP). This connection most often consists of one of the following:

- A leased or dialup line, connected via a 28.8Kbps modem, running SLIP or PPP to make a TCP/IP connection

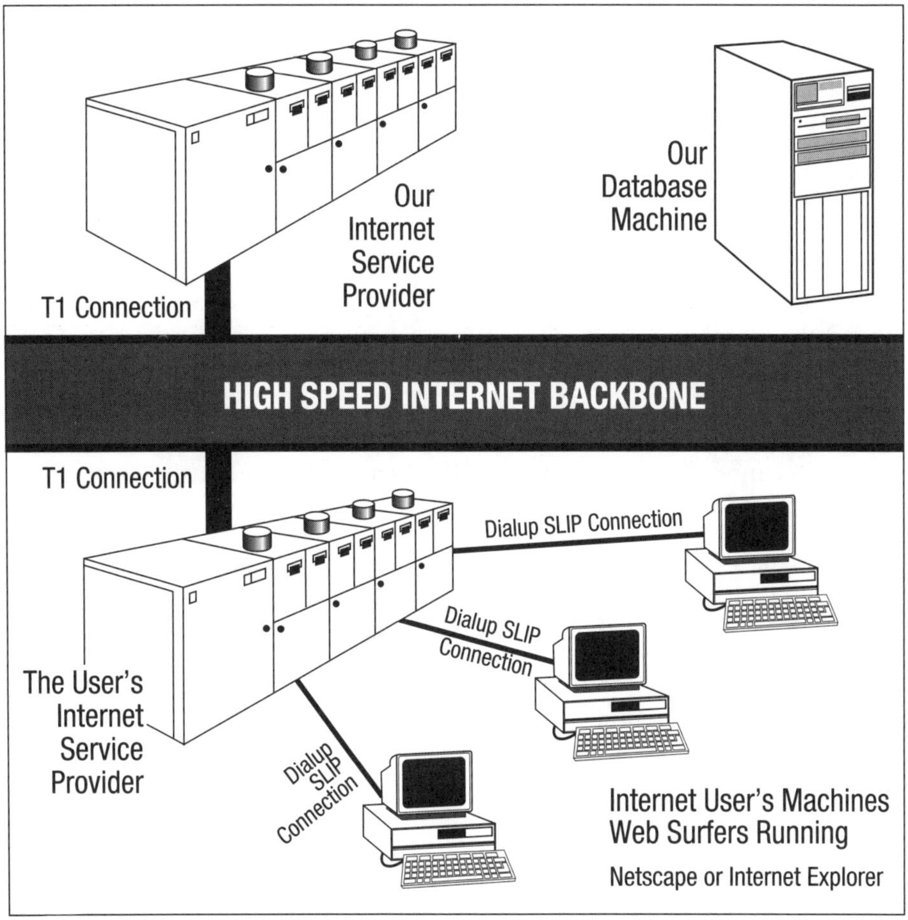

Figure 1.1 Connecting a machine to the Net.

- An ISDN line, connected via an ISDN modem at 64Kbps or 128Kbps, running PPP to make the TCP/IP connection
- A fractional T1 using specialized hardware to make the TCP/IP connection to the backbone

What you want is a machine running TCP/IP over some sort of hardware connection to the backbone. The TCP/IP connection that you end up with is actually to your Internet Service Provider. The ISP provides your machine with a unique IP address. Once you have that IP address, your machine can be reached by any other machine on the Internet simply by accessing that IP address.

The IP address is the door to your Web castle. Your IP address is exactly analogous to your regular mail address. If you send mail to 50 Otis Street, you know it will get through to me. If an application connects to IP address 199.9.1.13, it knows it will be getting through to my ISP. We're all used to hearing URLs like http://www.channel1.com, but what happens underneath is that, via a mechanism known as *DNS* (domain name service), the site name www.channel1.com gets translated into an IP address such as 199.9.1.13.

This IP address-lookup is a key to deciding what kind of Net access you need. A basic PPP or SLIP connection often assigns a semi-random IP address to every caller. Thus, if you have a cheap, dialup, PPP connection to your ISP, you will have a different IP address from one call to the next. This obviously makes it impossible for others to find you.

This gives us two more requirements for our Web database machine:

- A TCP/IP connection to the backbone
- A fixed IP address

Firewalls

While a full-fledged discussion of firewalls is beyond the scope of this book, they deserve a mention because a firewall is almost always part of any Internet-connected database server setup. A firewall aims to keep your internal network safe from malicious traffic generated outside your internal network.

The firewall is generally a single machine running firewall software. All traffic to and from the Internet goes through this single machine. There are a number of techniques any firewall uses to keep dangerous traffic off your internal network. Most of them involve inspecting each and every packet to tell where it comes from, where it's going, and what it does, then making a decision on whether or not to allow the packet based on those parameters.

Since the Web server is designed to use a large amount and wide variety of potentially dangerous network traffic, it will usually be installed on the firewall machine itself. Thus, the firewall does not protect the Web server.

If the database machine is part of an internal network, then there must be a firewall between the internal net and the Internet.

The HTTP Server

In order to put a database up on the Web, you have to make a number of components work together. Figure 1.2 shows a block diagram of a Web server that serves only HTML documents.

Web service is a little more complicated than that, though. A user can actually cause a program to execute on the server, by accessing it via a CGI

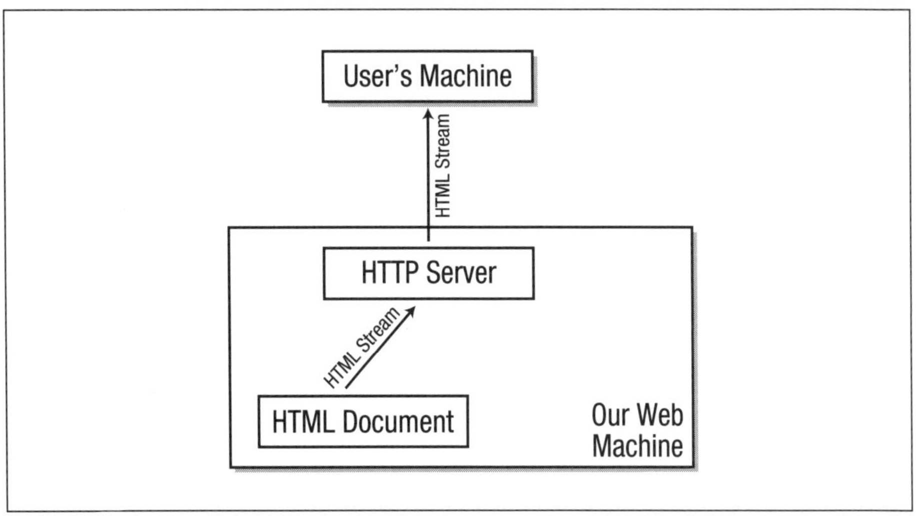

Figure 1.2 Web server serving HTML documents.

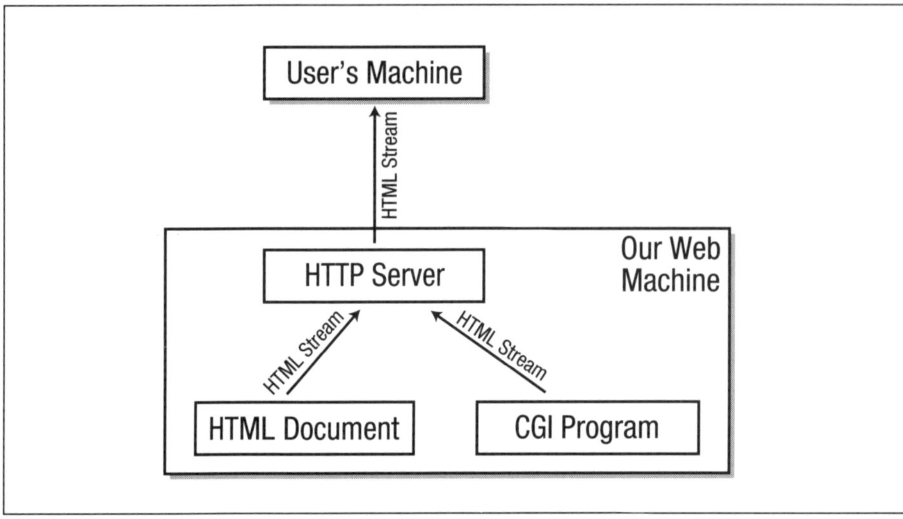

Figure 1.3 Web server serving HTML documents and CGI programs.

URL. CGI programs create HTML documents on the fly, and the Web server passes that dynamic HTML back to the browser. Adding CGI gets us the block diagram of Figure 1.3.

Now to the good stuff. Let's add a database to the mix. Figure 1.4 adds a database to our Web server machine.

What we need to concentrate on is getting information out of the database through the Web server and into the user's browser. Figure 1.3 clearly shows a couple of obvious ways to get database data out to the user's browser—by creating static HTML documents, or creating dynamic HTML via a CGI program.

The HTTP server (Web server) has a very simple job description. It sends documents to any browser that requests them. In more technical terms, it listens to a particular port for requests for HTML documents, and then sends those documents out over that port to the browser that requested them. Here's the process:

1. Server sits listening to a port.
2. Browser connects to that port.
3. Browser asks the server for a document.
4. Server sends that document to the browser.

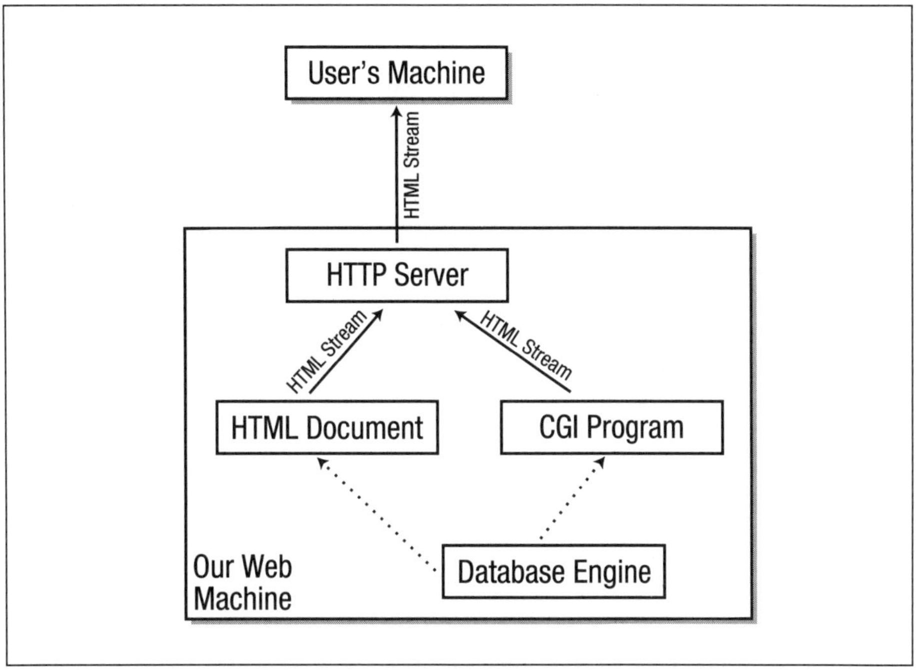

Figure 1.4 Web server serving HTML documents, CGI programs, and a database.

To take a concrete example, say that you want to look at my old home page. So you enter the URL http://www.channel1.com/users/ajrodley/index.html into your browser, and tell it to go there. The browser takes the site information (http://www.channel1.com) and sees two important bits of information. The first is the site name, www.channel1.com. Via your DNS server, the browser turns this into the IP address, 199.1.13.9. Second, the *HTTP* protocol tells it to use port 80, because that is the default port for HTTP servers. This is all the browser needs to know to make the physical connection: the IP address and port number.

By connecting to IP address 199.1.13.9, port 80, the browser now has an open, two-way channel to the HTTP server at my ISP. The browser then passes the rest of the URL, /users/ajrodley/index.html, to the server as a document request. The server responds by sending the document /users/ajrodley/index.html back to the browser. As index.html arrives on the browser over the network connection, the browser interprets the HTML code and displays the document on the screen.

To see how simple a bare-bones HTTP server really is, take a look at Patrick Naughton's *Java Handbook*. He includes source for a basic HTTP server that uses less than 300 lines of Java code. Where Web servers tend to differ are in the areas of security, nonstandard datatypes, CGI support, process control, and database integration.

Security

Security deserves, and gets, a chapter all its own, but we need to take just a quick look at it here. There are two types of security the Web server can provide—authorization and link encryption.

Authorization is the process of requiring a password to access a page, the same user-name/password process many of us go through every day to log onto our own systems. Some servers, like Netscape, can protect individual pages, or entire directories, with authorization screens.

Link encryption is the process of encrypting data sent between the browser and the Web server. This protects the transaction from being understood by anyone who might be surreptitiously viewing the transaction as it flows back and forth over the Internet. Netscape has promulgated a standard, which many browsers and servers now support called *SSL*, for Secure Sockets Layer. Once a browser and server are connected via an SSL connection, all data transferred is encrypted. For most Internet transactions, this level of link security should be sufficient.

CGI Support

Another feature of HTTP servers is their ability to support a standard known as *Common Gateway Interface*, or CGI. CGI is a standard that defines how executable programs invoked from within an HTML document interact with the Web server. Most Web servers support the concept of a CGI directory (often called cgi-bin) where any URL that points to that directory is assumed to be a CGI program. Assume that I've configured my Web server to use /cgiDir as my CGI directory. If a browser requests the document http://www.myserver.com/cgiDir/AProgram.exe, then instead of reading the file Aprogram.exe and sending all the bytes to the browser, the Web server will execute the program Aprogram.exe and send the program's standard output to the browser.

This is a very powerful mechanism that allows you almost unlimited freedom in creating dynamic HTML. It is the mechanism we will use in The Newfoundland Dog Database when creating a page from the results of a user query.

Our Web server must support CGI, page-level security, and possibly link encryption.

CGI itself is a lot more complicated than this, of course. We will talk about CGI in depth in a later chapter.

The Database Engine

The database engine is one of the most important parts of any Web database site. It is the mechanism that actually stores the data, and allows you to query and update it.

In Appendix A, we discuss some of the virtues and vices of individual DBMS packages on the market today. For the most part, our examples in later chapters will use Microsoft's SQL Server. We will try, however, to avoid using any mechanisms that are specific to this product. The hope is that whatever we write here is easily modified to use whatever database package you have available.

The first thing to think about when evaluating a database engine for Web service is the multiuser question. That is, your database needs to be able to handle multiple, concurrent users. There are ways around this, as we will discuss later, but, as a rule of thumb, the database engine needs to support some number of multiple, concurrent accesses.

To further simplify, we're going to add two more restrictions to the list of DBMSs we'll consider:

- It must be relational.
- It must support the SQL/92 language spec.

These are not really such terrible restrictions. Many of the most popular database packages available today meet these criteria. Appendix A lists some of them.

Concurrent Database Connections

We've already specified multiple concurrent connections as a requirement for our database engine. This is not optional. And since the number of concurrent connections to the database is a rough indicator of how many people are using it, most RDBMS vendors price their products by the number of concurrent connections to the database they'll allow. Prices of $1,000 per concurrent connection are not uncommon. This makes the calculation of how many connections we actually need critically important. It also gives us a great incentive to minimize the number of concurrent connections.

Unfortunately, connection calculation is a very difficult equation. You have to take into account:

- Average and maximum elapsed transaction time
- The amount of time users are willing to wait for transaction results
- Average and maximum number of users trying to do transactions concurrently

If you try to quantify any of these parameters, you quickly realize how difficult this problem is.

Average And Maximum Elapsed Transaction Time

This is probably the easiest variable to deal with, because you can test it. Set up a test database. Create a test suite using a representative mix of the transactions users are likely to run. Measure the elapsed time of each transaction. Calculate the average and maximum from these results.

There are a number of problems with this test. The mix of transactions, for one, is necessarily a guess. For some applications where users create their own queries, this guess may be completely useless. For another thing, it's impossible to mimic under test conditions what will happen when the machine is under an operational load. Transactions that took 5 seconds on the test bed could take 50 in some operational cases. The best you can hope for is a number that's generally correct in most cases.

Amount Of Time Users Are Willing To Wait For Transaction Results

Why does this number have any impact on the number of concurrent connections? To answer that, we have to answer another question, namely, "What happens when we have more concurrent users than concurrent connections?" FTP servers, for example, typically tell users to go away and come back later if their maximum concurrent connection limit is exceeded. We can't do that, at least not as a first option, for any business application I can think of. Customers who are turned away once generally don't come back.

What applications like the ones in this book need to do is queue users waiting for database connections, and service them, in order, as connections become available. As we will discuss later, with a system like this, you can provide fewer concurrent connections than concurrent users, as long as the end-to-end elapsed time (transaction time plus the amount of time the user spends on the queue waiting for a connection) does not exceed the amount of time the user is willing to wait.

How long will users wait? Obviously, that depends on the user. Someone migrating from a batch mainframe environment might be willing to wait several hours. Your average PC programmer, on the other hand, will probably cancel any transaction that lasts longer than 30 seconds. I think a good rule of thumb out on the Web is that anything over 60 seconds is probably pushing it. Remember, most users are logging on to our Web application from a PC where their standalone applications typically bring up new windows in a matter of one or two seconds. If, like most users, they are unclear on the technical difference between Web and standalone applications, then their tolerance is likely to be fairly low.

Average And Maximum Number Of Users Trying To Do Transactions Concurrently

Here again, we're in a quandary. Theoretically, every Web user on earth could be looking at our page, and they could all hit the Update button all at once. Then, our maximum number of users is limited by our connection bandwidth and the Web server, most of which impose their own limits on the number of concurrent users. But again, guessing at this number is next to worthless.

There is a way to get a useful number here, but you have to ask the question a little differently—average and maximum number of concurrent transactions. One number that any project *should* have a reasonable guess at (via market research, or asking the guy in the next cubicle) is how many transactions you expect to process per day and how many you want to account for in the extreme case. If you combine these numbers with your average and maximum transaction times, a little statistical analysis can give numbers for average and maximum transactions that will be valid for some huge percentage of cases.

Let's take an example. Say our parameters are as follows:

parameter	average	maximum
transactions per day	10000	20000
transaction time	3 seconds	20 seconds

It's obvious that if you spread 10,000 3-second transactions (30,000 total) evenly over the 86,000 seconds in the day, you'd get an average load of less than one connection. It's equally obvious that if you spread 20,000 20-second transactions (400,000 seconds total) evenly over the 86,000 seconds in the day, you'd get an average load of a little less than five connections.

This is far too simple, assuming that users magically spread their database accesses evenly over the entire day. What we need to do is refine and fill out this flat usage graph a little further with some educated guessing. If our clients are primarily U.S.-based, we can eliminate the hours when everyone here is asleep—about 1 AM to 8 AM Eastern time (10 PM to 5 AM Pacific). Then, we install a little bit of usage when one coast is awake, but the other asleep. Build to a crescendo in the middle of the workday (taking into account that the West coast generally works an earlier day to "line up" with the East coast), then taper off as the East coast leaves work. When both coasts are off work but still awake, we have some activity, then it tapers to nothing as everyone nods off. Figure 1.5 shows the usage graph we come up with using this fairly generic set of assumptions.

The curve itself plots how many transactions are happening at any one instant. The area under the curve is the total number of transactions. The area within the box labeled "peak volume period" is the number of transactions that happen during peak volume period. The area of that box is obviously the peak transaction volume multiplied by the length of the peak volume period.

Using our earlier example, with an average of 10,000 transactions per day at an average of 3 seconds apiece, let's say that half of them occur during our peak period, which lasts for 4 hours (4*60*60=14400 seconds). This leads us to an average of 15,000 seconds of connection time over 14,400 seconds. Thus, on average, we could get by easily with two concurrent connections. If we use the maxima, 20,000 transactions at 20 seconds each,

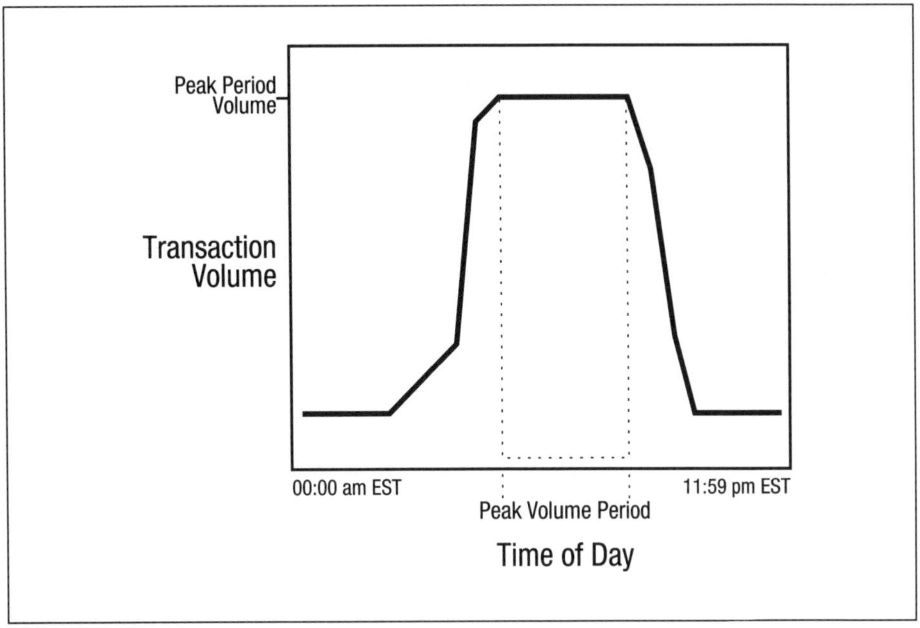

Figure 1.5 Projected-usage graph using generic assumptions.

then we end up with 200,000 seconds of transaction time over 14,400 seconds. Thus, at specified maxima, we'd need 14 concurrent connections to squeeze all the peak transactions into the peak period.

Now, say that we implement a system using these calculations, purchasing 14 concurrent connections for maximum volume. Say also that usage fits our projection exactly, with 200,000 seconds of transaction time during peak periods on the worst days. Does that mean that nobody ever has to wait for a connection during the peak period? Not necessarily, because our definition of the peak period is still an average.

What happens if we purchase connections to handle the average volume, and we run into the maximum volume? Okay, two connections trying to handle 10,000 20-second transactions over 14,400 seconds, meaning 200,000 seconds of transaction over 28,800 seconds of available transaction time. It doesn't work. In fact, two connections can't handle 200,000 transactions in a whole day, since two connections times 86,000 seconds only gives us 172,000 seconds of transaction time in the entire day. If, however, you say that those transactions are only average length (3 seconds), then you only need 30,000 seconds of transaction time, which isn't really that much more than the 28,800 seconds available to us with two connections. By this reckoning, two connections seems like a pretty fair bet. If you think about it, all we've done is reduce the problem to one of defining the length of your peak volume period and how much of your total volume happens within that peak period.

We can also reduce the number of connections we need by queuing concurrent users who exceed the number of concurrent connections. In our example above, we decided to buy 28,800 seconds of connection time to cover 30,000 seconds of transaction. That leaves us with 1,200 seconds of overflow transactions. At 3 seconds per transaction, that amounts to 400 instances of a user trying to get into our system when there's no connection available. If we implement a queuing system where users wait for an open connection, then what should happen is that the peak volume period will simply be extended by that 1,200 seconds. Those 400 transactions will each take longer than our specified 3 seconds, but they will happen. As long as we keep a reasonable limit on the amount of time users spend in the connection queue, we should be able to handle the expected volume.

This is a necessarily brief rehash of the old bank teller problem. How many tellers do you provide to account for the lunch-time rush without having tellers sitting around unused for the rest of the day? It's also the same problem that multi-user operating systems deal with when they have 1,000 terminals trying to use a system that only allows 200 concurrent users. You can get as involved as you want with these calculations (and it's really beyond the scope of this book to go there), but the key to making a successful transition from a development database to a production database is to collect appropriate usage data and analyze it to see how your development estimates match reality. If you keep track of the type and number of transactions as well as their tendency to cluster around certain times of day, you can get more and more accurate estimates of average and peak database loads and adjust the number of concurrent connections as needed.

Our database engine must allow enough concurrent connections to handle the expected transaction volume.

Why Database Vendors Love Client-Server

When database vendors talk about Web-based, client-server database, they usually have a particular model of computing in mind. This model has the client (a user at a browser) opening a connection to the database, and keeping it open for as long as he or she is "in" the database access program. Let's take a concrete example. Say our user logs into our application, queries a set of database rows, and sits there deciding whether to update any of that data. By this model, the entire time the user is thinking (and with some users this could be a big chunk of time), the application is holding a database connection open.

This dramatically and needlessly lengthens the average transaction time, as we've defined it. The practical effect of this lengthening? An equally dramatic rise in the number of concurrent connections you need to purchase to handle the same volume.

There are many simple ways around this, some of which we will discuss later on. It is, however, something to look out for when evaluating Web database tools. How do they manage database connections?

DBMS-Level Security

All of the database packages in Appendix A enforce some system of username/password access control within the database itself. That is, the database system has its own list of users, with their own passwords, and each user is assigned an access profile that defines exactly what he or she can and can't do within the database. This security layer is there because, in many applications, these products still operate as standalone packages, unprotected by either the operating system or an authorizing Web server.

When you put a database on the Web, this extra level of security might seem redundant. After all, you can keep unauthorized users away from the database simply by password-protecting the HTML forms that allow input/update/delete. However, it does have its uses. For one thing, there are ways (like ODBC) to connect to a network-accessible database that are entirely outside the Web framework we're trying to build. For another thing, we may want to have different levels of access for users of different pages.

Object Databases

I can almost hear the object-oriented purists grinding their teeth as I write yet another book about relational databases. This frustration is understandable. The programming world has completely bought into the notion of object-oriented programming, yet we still write allegedly OO programs littered with horrid sequences of SELECT, FETCH, GET COLUMN, GET COLUMN, GET COLUMN. Dozens of lines of code wasted each time we want to access an object within the database.

Object databases fix this problem. Usually with a very few lines of code, you can create an object, or a vector of objects, initialized based on the values stored in a database.

However, object databases have a couple of problems that make them unsuitable for this discussion. First and foremost, they're not that widely used at present. I could write a great book about them, but nobody would read it. More importantly, though, the current crop of OODBMSs are a heterogeneous lot, each implementing things completely differently around the ODMG-93 standard. This lack of agreement on what an OODBMS should be would make any example-based discussion entirely dependent on one vendor's vision.

The relational databases, on the other hand, support a fairly standard set of features, all organized around a very well-understood standard access language, SQL-92. Also, many, perhaps a majority, of us are "stuck" with RDBMSs that the company has bought into for reasons having nothing to do with current Web projects. Thus, the relational versus OODBMS debate is really no debate at all. For now, relational rules.

What Other Daemons Should We Run?

More and more Web development is being done online, that is, by people who are not physically in the same building (or logically on the same net) that the Web server is running on. This is one of the things the Net is good at: empowering telecommuters. In order to do remote Web database development, the developer needs to be able to get files back and forth from the Web server, and be able to run programs on the Web server. To do this, we need to run two more daemons: FTP and Telnet.

FTP, file transfer protocol, is the Internet standard protocol for getting files from one place to another. An FTP server is simply a program that listens to a particular IP socket, and allows FTP file transfers over that socket. When our Web server machine has an FTP server running, an FTP client anywhere out on the Net can simply open the socket (usually 21) and start transferring files. FTP servers always provide username/password level security. Thus, a client wishing to transfer files must provide a username and password. Some sites allow what is called *anonymous FTP*, where the username is typically "guest" and the password can be anything. Enabling anonymous FTP is a bad idea in general, and particularly so for a Web server.

Telnet is another Internet standard service, this one for allowing remote login to a character-mode shell. Much like the FTP server (or any other Internet server), the Telnet server sits listening to a particular port. When a remote client opens that port, the Telnet server starts up a command shell and redirects the standard input and standard output to that port. Thus, the client on the other end of that socket connection "sees" a command line on which to execute programs, and see the results as if he or she were working on the Telnet server machine.

Both the FTP and Telnet servers present a certain amount of security risk. Malevolent souls spend a lot of time figuring out how to break them. Telnet is obviously more of a risk than FTP, but for machines running in production mode, either of these is a risk.

You can mitigate the risk somewhat by using the standard username/password security measures (non-obvious passwords, frequently changed). You can also protect against casual attack by moving them from their usual ports. FTP clients expect to find the server at port 21, Telnet at port 23. Simply by moving them to another port, you force any attacker to search the entire range of possible ports for your server, something most hackers are unwilling to do. Also, a good system administrator can often detect the fact that someone is hitting all the ports and "close the gates" before a break-in.

A Web server under remote development should run FTP and Telnet servers but with the following caveats: standard username/password security, no anonymous FTP, and both servers on nonstandard ports.

The Programming Interface

As you saw back in Figure 1.1, Web programmers need to make the connection from database to Web server. In order to do this, we need two development tools: a programming language to write our programs in, and an API to call that will get information into and out of the database.

C, C++, Java, And The Scripting Languages

There are literally hundreds of programming languages that we could use. The ones that we will use almost exclusively in this book are C, C++, and Java. There are good reasons for this. C and C++ are mature, extremely popular, and have extensive function and class libraries. Also, most database engines are accessible via C-callable APIs.

Java, on the other hand, is new and untested, but already very popular for Internet applications. It includes a very simple and powerful Internet class library, and has just recently become database-accessible via third-party JDBC drivers.

Three other languages that are often used to provide CGI access to databases are Perl, Rexx, and shell script. All are extremely capable, high-level languages that are arguably easier to program in than either C or Java. We do not use them in any of the examples in this book.

Native Calls Vs. ODBC

The second piece of our database program is the database API. Every database engine comes with a set of libraries (*dynamic link libraries*, or *DLLs*, under Windows NT) that allow applications to connect to and use that database engine. An application that directly calls those dynamic link libraries is said to be using *native calls*. That is, the call is native to (specific to) that particular database product.

Using native calls within, for example, a C program requires a couple of pieces above and beyond the C compiler and the database engine. Specifically, you need the dynamic link libraries that supply the native calls, and the development library that gives your program the native-call entry point.

Listing 1.1 shows a bare native-call implementation of a select statement for an SQL Server database.

Listing 1.1 A bare native-call implementation of a select statement.

```
sqlastrt((void far *)pid, (void far *)0,
   (struct tag_sqlca far *)sqlca);
sqlaaloc(1, 4, 10, (void far *)0);
sqlasetv(1, 0, 462,(unsigned short)sizeof(temp_name),
   (void far *)&temp_name, (void far *)0,0L);
```

```
sqlasetv(1, 1, 462,(unsigned short)sizeof(temp_sire),
   (void far *)&temp_sire, (void far *)0,0L);
sqlasetv(1, 2, 462,(unsigned short)sizeof(temp_dam),
   (void far *)&temp_dam, (void far *)0,0L);
sqlasetv(1, 3, 462,(unsigned short)sizeof(yob),
   (void far *)&yob, (void far *)0,0L);
sqlaaloc(2, 1, 10, (void far *)0);
sqlasetv(2, 0, 462, (unsigned short)strlen(sought_name),
   (void far *)sought_name, (void far *)0, (void far *)0L);
sqlxcall(24, 10, 2, 1, 75, (char far *)" SELECT NAME, SNAME, \
   DNAME, DOB2 FROM shortdog WHERE name = @p1      ");
if(sqlca->sqlcode < 0) {
   sqlastop((void far *)0L);
   ErrorHandler() ;
}
   sqlastop((void far *)0L);
```

By definition, native calls are specific to a particular database. The native calls of Listing 1.1 are specific to SQL Server. They cannot access an Oracle or Informix database. In order to implement the same SELECT statement for an Oracle database, you would have to start over from scratch. The end result might look similar, but not similar enough.

As you can see from Listing 1.1, native calls by themselves are also pretty messy things. The single SQL statement we're trying to run requires 14 lines of fairly ugly C code. Fortunately, there's a generally accepted method that helps automate the process of turning SQL statements into native calls—*Embedded SQL.*

As the name implies, Embedded SQL is a method for allowing you to embed bare SQL statements in a C program. The theory is that, instead of writing piles of native-call code such as that in Listing 1.1, you simply write the corresponding SQL statement, as shown in Listing 1.2.

Listing 1.2 Listing 1.1 as Embedded SQL.

```
EXEC SQL
 SELECT NAME, SNAME, DNAME, DOB2
    INTO :temp_name, :temp_sire, :temp_dam, :yob
    FROM shortdog
    WHERE name = :sought_name;
```

It's obvious to any C programmer, though, that the code of Listing 1.2 will not compile. After all, no C compiler understands SELECT. In order to compile an Embedded SQL program, you need to run it through a preprocessor. In SQL Server, the embedded SQL preprocessor is called *esqlc*. In order to create an executable program that uses our database, we run esqlc against our embedded SQL source program. This produces a C source file. We then run our C compiler against the C source file, and that creates our executable. Thus, there's one extra step to developing an embedded SQL program. We'll talk a lot more about Embedded SQL in Chapter 2 and later on when we develop the Newfoundland Dog Database.

There's an alternative to native calls known as *ODBC*. ODBC, which stands for *open database connectivity*, is an application programming interface (API) for accessing databases. Its primary advantage over Embedded SQL is that ODBC programs are not database- or db-engine-specific. ODBC achieves this by inserting a driver manager between the application program and the particular database. Each database engine registers its unique ODBC driver with the driver manager. The driver manager passes ODBC-compliant SQL requests from the application program to the unique driver, which then translates the request into native calls. Figure 1.6 shows two application programs accessing an Oracle database, one via a native call, and the other via an ODBC call.

JDBC

Java is an increasingly important language for Internet development. On top of the Java applets that spice up Web pages, it also provides a great platform for developing portable, standalone, Internet- and WWW-aware applications. One of the hotbeds of recent Java development has been in the area of database connectivity. For any new language, this is a predictable development, since a language that can't connect to databases isn't much use to anyone (and is certainly no use to us).

In the race to make Java a useful language, Sun gave Java a headstart by specifying a standard, database access API for Java programs: *JDBC*. JDBC stands for *Java Database Connectivity*. As you might expect, like ODBC, it is an API that specifies how Java programs interact with databases. It makes no assumptions about the underlying technology. In this sense, JDBC is much like ODBC. The main difference is that JDBC is aimed at a single, object-oriented language. Thus, instead of specifying a set of functions, JDBC mandates a set of Java objects and Java interfaces that the JDBC driver must provide in order to be JDBC compliant.

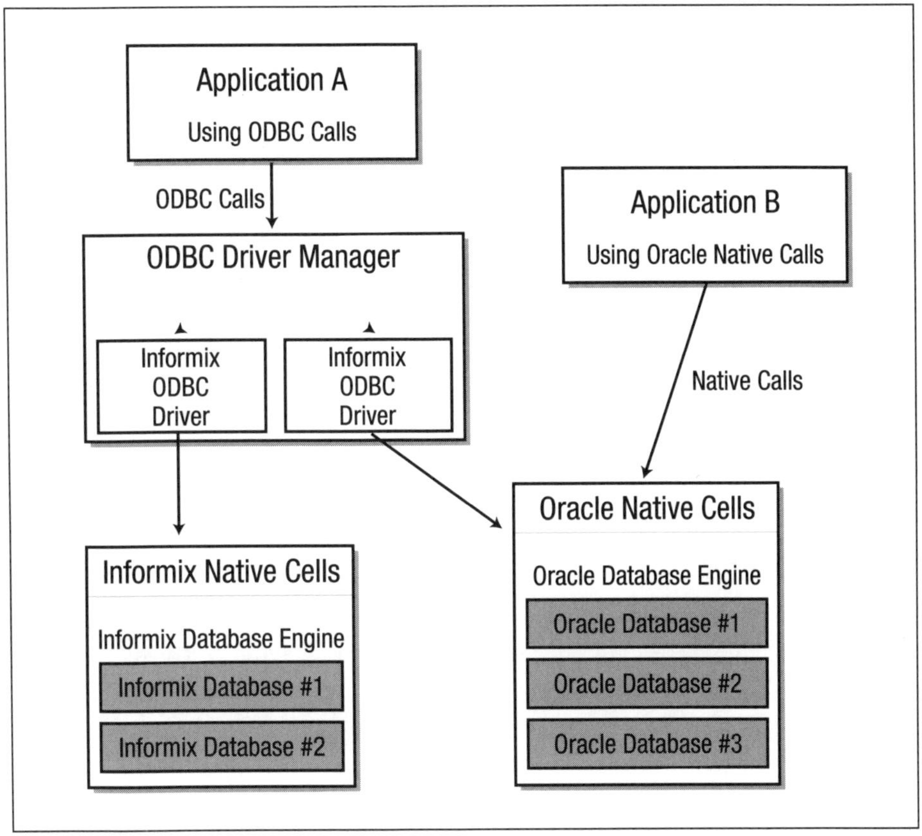

Figure 1.6 Applications using ODBC and native calls for database access.

In fact, JDBC drivers are often implemented on top of ODBC. In that situation, your Java program is going through three different APIs—JDBC, ODBC, and native calls—to get to the database.

We'll talk more about Java and JDBC in later chapters, especially when we write our own Web Watcher, a database of Web-page URLs automatically linked to items of interest.

The database engine must allow programmatic access via either ODBC, JDBC, or a native call library.

Proprietary Turnkey Solutions

Up to now, we've talked about do-it-yourself solutions to the database programming problem—taking a database engine from here, and a Web server from there, and making them work together with custom programs. There are, however, other, perhaps easier ways to get the job done.

Most of these solutions rely on proprietary Web-server/database-engine combinations. Instead of writing database access programs in C or Java, you embed database commands in your HTML code. Instead of passing the HTML code straight through to the browser, the Web server interprets the HTML code, digging the database commands out, executing them, and then sending the results of the database command to the browser.

These types of turnkey solutions are effective, but they generally rely on proprietary tools, and nonstandard, nonportable HTML documents. Along the way, we'll talk about this approach, and some of these tools from time to time, but our focus will be on mixing and matching off-the-shelf components.

Conclusion

Through the course of this chapter, we've seen what a Web-connected database looks like, what hardware it runs on, and what software it runs. We've come up with a number of requirements for our database machine as well as for the Web server, and database engine software and the network connection:

- Our database machine must be big and fast, with at least an uninterruptible power supply, a tape backup, and possibly a RAID array to ensure data integrity and maximum availability.
- It must have a TCP/IP connection to the backbone, with a fixed IP address.
- If the database machine is part of an internal network, then there must be a firewall between the internal net and the Internet.
- Our Web server must support CGI, page-level security, and possibly link encryption.
- The database engine must allow programmatic access via either ODBC, JDBC, or a native call library.
- Our database engine must allow enough concurrent connections to handle the expected transaction volume.

- A Web server under remote development should run FTP and Telnet servers, but with the following caveats: standard username/password security, no anonymous FTP, and both servers on nonstandard ports.

We've shown that the crucial link in Webbing a database is the connection between the database engine and the Web server. We've seen how such tools as straight HTML, CGI, ODBC, JDBC, and native calls all help bridge this gap. We've also talked a little bit about proprietary solutions, such as Microsoft's IIS/SQL Server combination. In short, we've outlined the problem. Now let's look at some of the solutions.

Webliography

JDBC

- http://www.javasoft.com — The Javasoft home page, with JDBC specs
- http://www.weblogic.com — Third party JDBC drivers

ODBC Vs. Native Calls

- http://www.casahl.com/bnchmk. — HTML A discussion of ODBC performance

Object Databases

- http://scitsc.wlv.ac.uk/~c9584315/oodb.html — A discussion of OODBMSs
- http://www.jcc.com/sql_stnd.html — A page of SQL standards information
- http://www.odmg.org — A page maintained by the ODMG database vendor consortium that details its effort to develop Object Database standards including ODMG-93
- http://www.odi.com — Object Design Inc.

- http://www.versant.com — Versant ODBMS
- http://www.objectivity.com — Objectivity
- http://www.o2tech.fr — O2 ODBMS

Proprietary Turnkey Solutions

- http://www.w3spider.com — Spider Technologies NetDynamics Web application development tool

Database Engines

- http://www.microsoft.com — Microsoft SQL Server
- http://www.oracle.com — Oracle 7 RDBMS
- http://www.sybase.com — Sybase RDBMS and SQL Anywhere
- http://www.informix.com — Informix RDBMS
- http://www.borland.com — Dbase RDBMS

Web Servers

- http://home.mcom.com — Netscape Web servers
- http://website.ora.com — O'Reilly's WebSite Web server
- http://www.ncsa.uiuc.edu — NCSA's Web server
- http://www.w3.org/pub/WWW/Daemon — CERN's Web server
- http://www.apache.org — Apache Web server

The Programming Interface

- http://www.javasoft.com — The Java language, development kit and Java workshop
- http://www.microsoft.com — Microsoft Visual C/C++
- http://www.symantec.com — Symantec's Café Java development environment

Chapter 2

Presenting A Passive-View, Read-Only Database

CHAPTER 2

Presenting A Passive-View, Read-Only Database

We've taken a brief survey of the issues surrounding Web database development—the benefits, the challenges, and some of the components you need to meet those challenges. Now that we know just enough to be dangerous, let's dive in and write a Web database.

In this chapter, we'll look at a real, live Web database, the Newfoundland Dog Database. First, we'll create the database itself, the tables and fields, indexes, and any DBMS configuration we might need. Then we'll talk about forms, the HTML element that allows us to construct database queries. From there, we'll cover CGI, the mechanism that gets our query from the browser to our Web server machine. Finally, we'll write a C program that runs the user's query on the server and creates a stream of HTML output that displays the results of that query on the browser.

When we're done, we'll have a completely functional, end-to-end implementation of a queryable Web database, where users can enter queries in their browsers and have the results show up on their browsers.

The Newfoundland Dog Database

The purpose of the Newfoundland Dog Database is to store the genealogy of a particular breed of dog, the Newfoundland. The current version of the database is viewable at **http://www.channel1.com/users/ajrodley/NewfDB.html**. It currently houses records on 62,508 dogs from all over the world and will soon expand to over 100,000 dogs.

The Newfoundland Dog Database has a single main table, SHORTDOG, with 35 fields that describe the dog and some of its history. Table 2.1 shows the structure of the SHORTDOG table, along with a description of each of the fields.

Many of these fields, such as HIPS, HEARTGRADE, and OFANO, are numerical ratings of particular aspects of the dog's health and are primarily of interest only to breeders. Others, such as DIED, DOB, and SEX, are more easily understood.

Three of the fields, NAME, SNAME, and DNAME, deserve further explanation. NAME, as you might expect, is the name of the dog—no surprise there. SNAME is the name of the dog's father (the *S* in SNAME stands for sire, or father). DNAME is the name of the dog's mother (the *D* in DNAME stands for dame, or mother). As you can see, there's an opportunity here for linkage within the database, and that's exactly what we've provided for by making NAME, SNAME, and DNAME compatible data types—62 char varchars. Later on, we'll create a family-tree display function which, given a single dog, creates a five-generation family tree. For now, though, all we're interested in is getting the information for a single dog out of the database.

Table 2.1 The structure of the SHORTDOG table.

Field Name	Data Type	Length	Nulls allowed?
NAME	varchar	(62)	null
QUOTENO	varchar	(7)	null
CHANGEDATE	datetime		null
CHANGETEXT	varchar	(100)	null
REGNO	varchar	(30)	null

continued

Table 2.1 The structure of the SHORTDOG table (continued).

Field Name	Data Type	Length	Nulls allowed?
COUNTRY	varchar	(20)	null
TITLES	varchar	(40)	null
CHDATE	datetime		null
JWOB	varchar	(30)	null
JWDATE	datetime		null
DOB	datetime		null
DOB2	varchar	(12)	null
SEX	varchar	(1)	null
SNAME	varchar	(62)	null
DNAME	varchar	(62)	null
COLOUR	varchar	(40)	null
RECESSIVE	varchar	(40)	null
OWNER	varchar	(62)	null
KENNEL	varchar	(30)	null
BREEDER	varchar	(62)	null
REMARKS	varchar	(200)	null
HIPTOT	varchar	(3)	null
HIPR	varchar	(2)	null
HIPL	varchar	(2)	null
DIED	datetime		null
HDCERT	varchar	(1)	null
HIPS	varchar	(25)	null
OFANO	varchar	(15)	null
OVCNO	varchar	(15)	null
KCBVAEYE	varchar	(10)	null
TATTOO	varchar	(15)	null
HEARTGRADE	varchar	(9)	null
SOURCE	varchar	(30)	null
SB	varchar	(4)	null
WORKAREA	varchar	(20)	null

Our Access Profile

The table structure is fairly straightforward. However, we can't stop there. If we simply created this table with no other refinements, we'd end up with a database that worked, but slowly. Remember that the Web itself introduces a large amount of delay. In some dialup cases, we're already trying the user's patience before his query even runs on the server. Remember also from our discussion of database connections in Chapter 1 that the average transaction time directly affects the number of concurrent connections we have to buy from our DBMS vendor. Thus, we have ample incentive to try to minimize that average transaction time.

Fortunately, there are ways to speed up database access. The easiest is to define indexes into the database. An index is a list of pointers into the indexed table. For example, if we index our SHORTDOG table by the KENNEL field, there will be one record in the KENNEL index for each record in the table. Suppose a user searches the table by KENNEL, as in:

```
SELECT * FROM SHORTDOG WHERE KENNEL='STORMWATCH'
```

Instead of stepping through the table looking at each KENNEL field, the DBMS will search the KENNEL index and get a pointer directly to the proper record. Each record in our hypothetical KENNEL index contains two fields: one field containing the value of the KENNEL field for one of the SHORTDOG records, and the other field containing a pointer to the SHORTDOG record. Figure 2.1 illustrates the example.

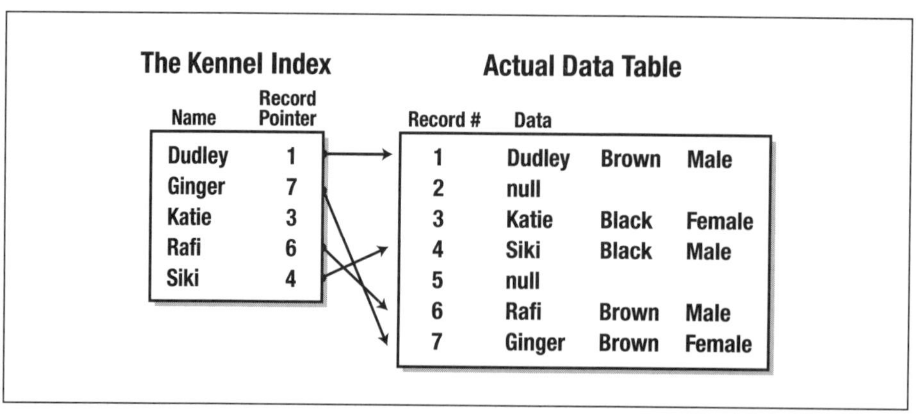

Figure 2.1 A hypothetical, single-level KENNEL index.

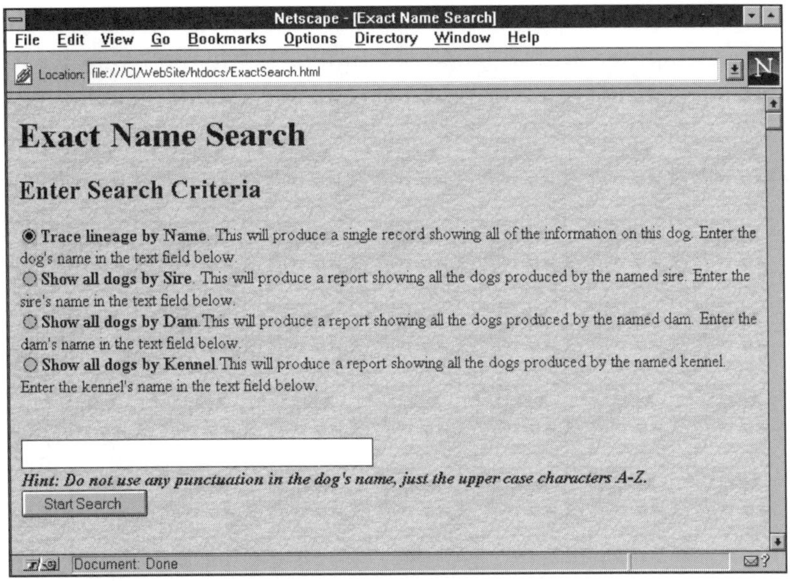

Figure 2.2 The Exact Name Search query screen.

If we think about what queries we're going to run, we can create indexes on the appropriate fields that will dramatically speed up access via those fields. The queries we have in mind at this point are:

- All dogs by kennel
- All dogs by dame
- All dogs by sire
- All dogs by name
- All dogs by name and country

In fact, Figure 2.2 shows the Exact Name Search query screen that we'll eventually use. Thus, our database should have five indexes on the SHORTDOG table.

Clustered Vs. Non-Clustered Indexes

SQL Server provides two types of indexes: clustered and non-clustered. According to the SQL Server documentation, "A clustered index is one in which the physical order of rows is the same as the indexed order of rows. The bottom, or leaf, level of a clustered index contains the actual data pages." That is, the actual data rows of the table will be ordered according to the order defined in the clustered index. Remember that earlier, we defined an index as essentially a list of pointers into the database. Well, a clustered index is more than that, because it defines the ordering of the database as well.

For example, if we defined a clustered index on SHORTDOG based solely on the COUNTRY field, then within our database, all the rows of dog data that had COUNTRY='USA' would be clustered together. In other words, a clustered index on a table determines the actual physical order of rows within the table. Obviously, then, there can only be a single clustered index defined on any one table.

A non-clustered index is a simple index, a list of pointers into the table. It has no effect on the physical order of records in the table. You can define any number of non-clustered indexes on a single table.

How do we decide which of our indexes should be clustered, and non-clustered? The real trick is to decide if any of our indexes should be clustered. There are three questions to ask:

- *Is there a searchable field which has a small set of unique values?* In our example, the COUNTRY field would be a perfect example of this. If we were allowing search-by-country, then it might make sense to physically cluster the table by country. There is a small set of countries, about 100, but the set is not so small that it unduly burdens the insert process. If the set of clusters is very small, then insert/update transactions will have to move a lot of data for each transaction.
- *Is there a field where we will be searching for a range of values?* This one is a little less obvious. Say that one of our primary searches was:

  ```
  SELECT * FROM SHORTDOG WHERE DOB>='1/1/1966' AND DOB<='1/1/1990'
  ```

  In this case, where we're searching for all dogs born in the years between 1966 and 1990, clustering the physical table according to the DOB field might make sense.
- *Is there a query that will return a large result set?* This is really the index of last resort. Say, for example, that our main search is something like:

  ```
  SELECT * FROM SHORTDOG WHERE NAME LIKE 'S%'
  ```

This would return all rows where the dog's name starts with the letter *S*, obviously a huge set. In that case, it would make sense to cluster on the NAME field.

Thus, given the searches we've defined—KENNEL, NAME, SNAME, DNAME, NAME-and-COUNTRY—we can make the following statements:

- Clustering on anything other than the five search fields would be useless.
- SNAME and DNAME are out, since they are nearly unique, and they are also not searchable by fragment, which, of course, would decrease their uniqueness.
- KENNEL might be a good choice, since it is searchable and has a low hit-rate of around 3 percent (2042 unique kennels out of 62,508 records). However, a characteristic of our dataset is that KENNEL is not a well-maintained field, and some large percentage of records (33,996 out of 62,508) have no kennel at all.
- COUNTRY would be an excellent choice but it suffers the same operational problem as KENNEL—a large percentage of the records (22,731 out of 62,508) have a null COUNTRY field.
- NAME would be a good choice since (in the NAME and COUNTRY search) we are allowing searches on six-character name fragments. However, we need to look at the actual SQL statement describing this search. If we were searching on "POUCH COVE" for example, the select statement reads like this (simplified):

```
SELECT * FROM SHORTDOG WHERE NAME LIKE '%POUCH COVE%'
```

The construction "WHERE NAME LIKE %POUCH COVE%" returns all records where POUCH COVE occurs *anywhere* within the NAME field. Thus, clustering by NAME won't help this search. If we changed the construction to "POUCH COVE%"—where NAME *begins* with POUCH COVE—then clustering by NAME would make more sense.

The choice for clustering comes down to COUNTRY and KENNEL. In operation, the search-by-name-and-country query has proven much more popular than search-by-kennel. COUNTRY also has a much better data rate and set distribution. So, in the end, we decide to cluster on COUNTRY.

Indexes are not an unvarnished benefit. While they speed up SELECTs, they slow down INSERTs and UPDATEs. Just think about it. Especially for a clustered index, the DBMS might have to move a large amount of data just to get a single record into the right spot. In most cases, though, the benefits far outweigh the costs. For us, SELECTs far outnumber INSERTs and UPDATEs, in any conceivable case. For this application, more and better indexes are the way to go.

Building The Database In SQL Server

Now that we know what structure we want, we need to actually build it and populate it. In order to do that, we have to go through seven steps.

Step 1: Design the database structure

We've already designed our main table, although we'll add more later on. We've also designed indexes into our main table that are appropriate to our dataset and the queries we intend to implement.

Step 2: Calculate the appropriate size for the database and log

Calculating the table size is a little tedious, and very specific to the DBMS in use, in our case SQL Server. (Refer to the SQL Server Administrator's Companion, Appendix B, for more details.)

In order to make this problem manageable, we break it into two logical pieces: the actual table data size and the index size. Table data size is a fairly straightforward calculation, consisting mostly of adding up all the field sizes, adding a little overhead, and multiplying the result by the total number of records. You should also include a fudge factor to account for variable-sized fields. Where it gets really complicated is when you try to calculate the size of the indexes.

While an in-depth discussion of indexes is beyond the scope of this book, in order to properly size our indexes, we have to take a quick look at just what an index is. An SQL Server index (clustered or non-clustered) is a balanced tree. Figure 2.3 shows an example using a table of animals.

The root level of an SQL Server index is made up of a single page of index records. Each index record contains a key value indicating which values that particular branch of the tree contains, and a pointer to another index page

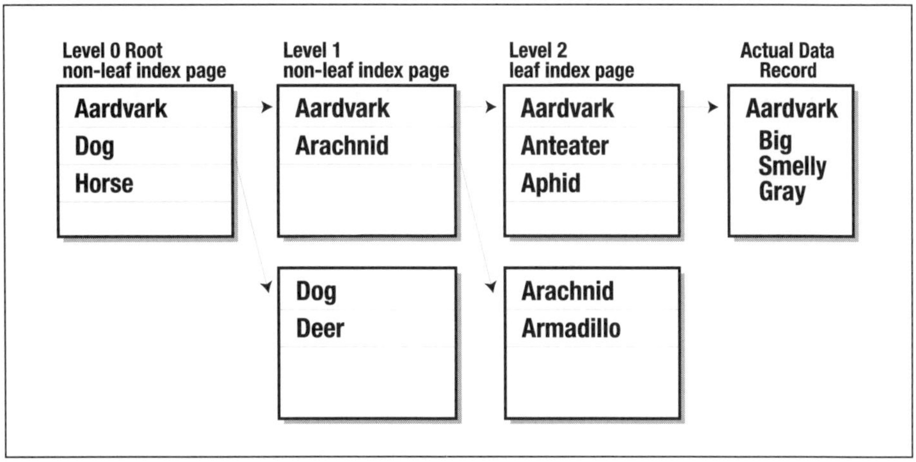

Figure 2.3 The balanced-tree index of animal records.

that contains the next level in the tree. In order to search an index, the DBMS starts at the root and narrows the search successively by level until it reaches a record in a leaf page (a page in the lowest level). The leaf record contains a pointer to an actual data record, rather than to another index page.

How SQL Server traverses this tree is not really important to us right now. What is important is the number of levels in the tree. This number determines how many page-reads the DBMS has to do to find a single record in the non-clustered index. For purposes of efficiency, each node in the tree is a single page, and each page is filled. At each level of the index tree, we cut the database into smaller and smaller pieces. At the root level, we're looking at the whole database. At level 1, we're looking at half the database, and so on, until at the leaf pages we're looking at a single record.

A non-leaf page contains a number of non-leaf records. Each non-leaf record contains a key value and a pointer to another index page. The key value tells the DBMS the range of key values that exist in the index page this record points to.

A leaf page contains a number of leaf records. Each leaf record contains a key value and a pointer to an actual physical data record. (Note: One difference between a clustered index and a non-clustered index is that there are no leaf pages in a clustered index; the leaf level is actual data records.)

In Figure 2.3, suppose we're selecting where name='AARDVARK'. In order to reach the actual record through our non-clustered index, we need to do three page-reads: the read of the root page, the level 1 page, and the level 2 page. Then we need to do another page-read to get the actual record; so in a three-level index, you can get any record through the index in only four page-reads.

When we calculate the number of pages needed for a non-clustered index, we have to work back from the leaf level. The size of a leaf page is fixed at 2016 bytes (2048 - 32 bytes overhead). The number of leaf pages we need will be the total number of records in the database, divided by the number of records we can fit in that leaf page. The size of our leaf page record is the size of the key we're using, plus whatever overhead SQL Server imposes.

Now that we have the number of leaf pages, we go through the same exercise to determine how many non-leaf pages we need at the next level up, to point to the leaf pages. The number of non-leaf index records per page will be 2016 divided by the size of the non-leaf record, all minus 2. The number of non-leaf pages at this level will be the number of leaf pages divided by the number of non-leaf index records per page.

We repeat this process of calculating levels of necessary non-leaf pages until we reach a level where there is only one page needed. This is the root level, and we need go no further.

There are a couple of things to note. The first, and most important, is that our record, as defined, has a maximum size of 1051 bytes (without overhead), while SQL Server accesses its logical devices in 2K (2048 byte) pages. Therefore, if all our variable sized fields are filled, we can only fit a single record on a page, with almost half the page left as wasted space. In practice, most of these variable-sized fields will be *much* smaller than the specified maximum, and we'll get much more than one record per page. The practical effect of this 1051-byte record, then, is to make our calculated database size perhaps twice as large as it will actually turn out to be.

This outsized estimate is acceptable for now, as it establishes a reasonable maximum database size. We can adjust the database size in operation, and there are a number of other adjustments we'll have to make along the way.

in any case. If we were free to redesign the schema, we would undoubtedly try to reduce the maximum record size such that, even at maximum, two records would fit on a page.

Calculating log size is another story altogether. Again, by way of background, MS SQL Server keeps a log of all transactions against the database. This is a data-integrity feature that inoculates our database against corruption via incomplete transactions. Before running a transaction, the DBMS "logs" the transaction itself in the transaction log. Suppose you tried to run this transaction:

```
UPDATE SHORTDOG SET NAME='XXX' WHERE NAME='YYY'
```

The DBMS would first save that SQL statement in the transaction log. Then, suppose the system goes down (somebody unplugs it) before you commit that transaction. To you, that transaction appears finished, yet without the COMMIT, it hasn't been written to disk. When the system comes back up, the DBMS can reconstruct the database, including your UPDATE, using the information in the transaction log.

The actual amount of useful data in the transaction log at any future point in time is incredibly difficult to predict. It depends on a number of factors, including:

- The rate of logged transactions (insert, delete, update)
- The amount of data modified by logged transactions
- The amount of time between checkpoints

Microsoft's documentation recommends reserving a log sized at approximately 20 percent of the database size as a starting point. We need to monitor the log as the database is in operation to ensure that it doesn't overflow. Later on, in Chapter 8, we'll set up an automatic process for truncating overlarge transaction logs. For now, though, we'll assume an initial transaction log size of 146MB * 20%, or 30MB.

Step 3: Create A Database Device For The Data

SQL Server allows us to create logical devices that can contain one or more databases. (Databases can also span devices.) These logical devices are actually disk files on our local hard disk.

Step 4: Create a Database Device for the Log

By default, SQL Server places the transaction log for a database on the same device as the database itself. However, we want to be able to back up the transaction log separately from the database, so we create another device strictly to contain the transaction log. See the Backup section in Chapter 8 for more details.

Step 5: Create a Database on the Device with Its Log on a Separate Device

SQL Server contains a "master" database that maintains a set of overall state information for the entire SQL Server installation. The master database contains, for instance, a table listing all the databases on this server. Thus, we still need to "create" our database as a database entity that has some claim on the two logical devices we've created. Listing 2.1 shows the isql command file we use to create a logical device to hold our database, and a transaction log device.

Listing 2.1 The isql command file to create the devices and database.

```
disk init
   NAME='NEWFDATA',
   PHYSNAME='c:\sql60\data\NEWFDATA.DAT',
   VDEVNO=101,
   SIZE=71346
go
disk init
   NAME='NEWFLOG',
   PHYSNAME='c:\sql60\data\NEWFLOG.DAT',
   VDEVNO=102,
   SIZE=14649
go
create database NEWF ON NEWFDATA = 146 LOG ON NEWFLOG = 30
go
```

Step 6: Create the Tables within the Database

Now that we have registered our database with the master, and have physical disk space allocated to our database and transaction log, we can structure the database with the tables and indexes unique to our application. Listing 2.2 shows the isql command file we use to create our database tables.

Listing 2.2 The isql command file to create Newf DB tables.

```
create table shortdog (
NAME         varchar(62) null
QUOTENO      varchar(7) null
CHANGEDATE   datetime null
CHANGETEXT   varchar(100) null
REGNO        varchar(30) null
COUNTRY      varchar(20) null
TITLES       varchar(40) null
CHDATE       datetime null
JWOB         varchar(30) null
JWDATE       datetime null
DOB          datetime null
DOB2         varchar(12) null
SEX          varchar(1) null
SNAME        varchar(62) null
DNAME        varchar(62) null
COLOUR       varchar(40) null
RECESSIVE    varchar(40) null
OWNER        varchar(62) null
KENNEL       varchar(30) null
BREEDER      varchar(62) null
REMARKS      varchar(200) null
HIPTOT       varchar(3) null
HIPR         varchar(2) null
HIPL         varchar(2) null
DIED         datetime null
HDCERT       varchar(1) null
HIPS         varchar(25) null
OFANO        varchar(15) null
OVCNO        varchar(15) null
KCBVAEYE     varchar(10) null
TATTOO       varchar(15) null
HEARTGRADE   varchar(9) null
SOURCE       varchar(30) null
SB           varchar(4) null
WORKAREA     varchar(20) null

)
go
```

```
create index idx_sname on shortdog (SNAME)
go
create index idx_dname on shortdog (DNAME)
go
create index idx_kennel on shortdog (KENNEL)
go
create clustered index idx_country on shortdog (COUNTRY)
go
```

We keep this separate from the database-creation command file of Listing 2.2 because we might want to re-create the tables without creating new logical devices.

Step 7: Import the Data into the Database Using BCP

The data for the Newf database already exists. In fact, it was originally entered into a dBASE III database on a DOS machine. So what we have for data is a set of field-delimited text files that have been exported from dBASE. SQL Server provides a utility called *bcp* (*Bulk CoPy*) that allows us to import data into the database. Listing 2.3 shows the bcp command we use to import the data into the database.

Listing 2.3 The bcp batch file to load the Newf DB.

```
bcp NEWF..rinmap in newf.dat -U sa -S katie /m 99 /a 4096 /P /c
```

There are a couple of items to note in our bcp batch file. SQL Server logs every INSERT transaction. If we try to insert 62,508 records in one shot, we're going to build a transaction log with 62,508 records in it. This will obviously overrun the transaction log. Instead, within the batch file, we need to *commit* the transactions. When we commit a set of transactions (write them to disk), SQL Server marks the log records for those transactions as inactive (checkpointed). However, SQL Server does not automatically flush inactive transactions from the log. Thus, at the top of our batch, we set a flag within SQL Server that tells it to flush inactive transactions.

There are other database setup and configuration issues we'll deal with later, but for now, these steps are enough to get us up and running. Now that we've dealt with the largely administrative task of creating our database, let's look at how we might construct a query against this database out on the user's browser.

Why Are Web Database Interfaces So Ugly?

One of the conveniently overlooked truths of the WWW gold rush is that Web application interfaces are, at present, uglier, less functional, less efficient, and harder to use than their standalone counterparts. Anyone who's spent any time surfing or programming for the Net has already run into this. In short, the Web is full of applications whose flow and screen design just don't seem to make any sense. Why is this?

The short answer is that Web interfaces are much harder to write than standalone interfaces. A standalone Windows, X-Windows, or OS/2 programmer has a vast array of user-interface elements available that are not available to Web programmers. Combo-boxes, scrollbars, even the ubiquitous File dialog—all of these are unavailable to Web coders.

But that's not even the worst part of the Web interface design problem. The Web has grown up around the idea that scrolling through, and jumping between, hyperlinked documents is the primary Web activity. This is all well and good if all you're trying to do is transmit static information to the user. However, once you add user interaction to the mix, as in searching a database, the Web's scrolling-document paradigm is woefully ill-suited to the task. If you want to test this assertion, simply bring up your favorite Web application, then bring up a polished Windows application like Quicken. Which one is easier to use?

Web tool developers are working feverishly on a range of solutions to this problem, from HTML 3.0 to JavaScript to ActiveX to Java, which we'll use later. However, at present, the only way to interact with a Web user is through the user interface toolset provided by the Web browser, *i.e.,* HTML.

HTML Forms

Windows programmers spend a large part of their work life creating *dialog boxes,* pop-up windows that interact with the user, and then go away when the user presses a button. Dialog boxes are a great way to reach out and get some information without necessarily disrupting the user's idea of where he is in the application.

HTML, however, does not understand the idea of a dialog box. In HTML, the only way to get input from the user is via the **<<FORM>>** element. A form differs from a dialog box in several important ways:

- It provides a severely limited set of controls, as shown in Table 2.3
- It does not allow you to position controls absolutely on the screen
- It does not pop up over the current application screen, but rather replaces whatever was on the screen
- It does not provide the ability to do field-by-field validation. Validation can only be done on an entire form. Correcting invalid data is significantly more difficult
- It is generally used to pass variables from one form to another.

There are two schools of thought on form design. One says that you should try to impose a standalone, dialog-box look on your form. In theory, that means limiting the information on the page to a single screen (no scrolling), and limiting the actions to Okay and Cancel (Forward and Back).

Table 2.3 The list of FORM elements.

HTML Name	Description
SELECT	A selectable list, either multiline or pulldown, multi-select or single select.
TEXTAREA	A multiline text input field.
INPUT Type=FILE	A text input box, with a browse button. A filename can be entered in the text input, and hitting the browse button brings up a standard file dialog.
INPUT Type=BUTTON	A button.
INPUT Type=TEXT	A single-line text input field.
INPUT Type=PASSWORD	A single-line text input field where characters are echoed as * to preserve privacy.
INPUT Type=CHECKBOX	A checkbox, either checked or not.
INPUT Type=RADIO	A radio button, part of a group of buttons where checking one unchecks all the others.
INPUT Type=SUBMIT	A button that automatically causes the form to be 'submitted'.
INPUT Type=RESET	A button that automatically causes the form to be cleared.
INPUT Type=IMAGE	An image.
INPUT Type=HIDDEN	A field that is named and valued but not seen.

The other school of thought, the Web school, says that the Web has its own style, and that there's nothing inherently wrong with scrolling dialogs. In theory, these forms will scroll vertically and are loaded with explanatory text. They may also have hyperlinks to other pages that do not represent some sort of linear progression through the application.

In practice, most Web forms are some combination of the two schools. Limiting yourself to a single page just because that's what Windows dialogs do is clearly silly. However, when tabbing through the fields in a form, you can only tab through the fields that are currently visible on the screen, so there is that to consider. There's also the confusion factor. When you allow more than Okay and Cancel actions on a form, you run the risk (in fact, the certainty) of confusing the user, so limiting the possible actions is also clearly desirable. This is also, however, where I break from the dialog-box model. Dialogs in standalone applications never contain enough explanatory text in-line, usually requiring the user to click a Help button to figure out what to do. There's no reason not to include plenty of explanatory text in an HTML form.

Figure 2.4 shows the basic name-fragment search form for the Newf DB. We provide two fields to search on, name-fragment and country. We also

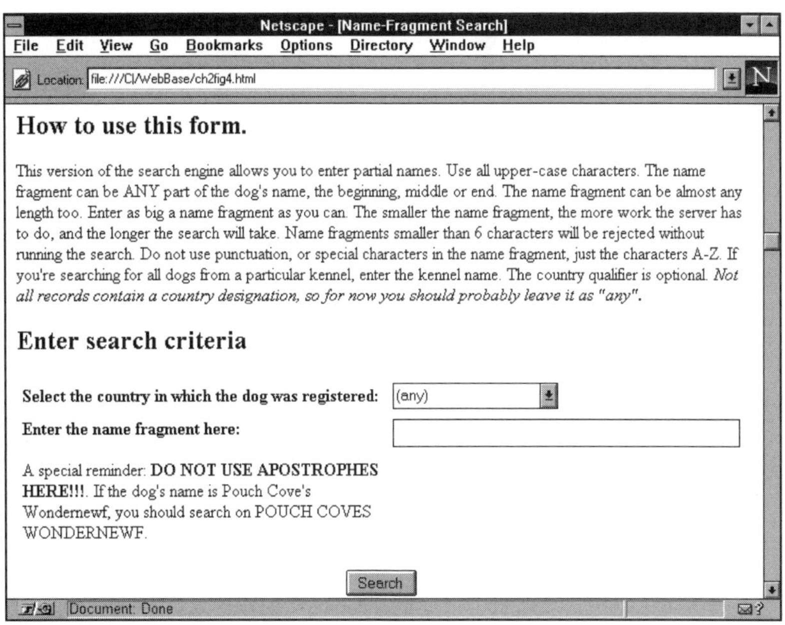

Figure 2.4 The name-fragment search form.

only provide a single action the user can perform, search. Listing 2.4 shows the HTML source for this page.

Listing 2.4 The source for the name-fragment search form.

```
<!DOCTYPE HTML PUBLIC "-//SQ//DTD HTML 2.0 HoTMetaL + extensions//EN">
<HTML>
<HEAD>
<TITLE>Name-Fragment Search</TITLE></HEAD>
<BODY BGCOLOR="white">
<H1>Name-Fragment Search</H1>
<H2>How to use this form.</H2>
<P>This version of the search engine allows you to enter partial names.
Use all uppercase characters. The name fragment can be ANY part of the
dog's name, the beginning, middle, or end. The name fragment can be
almost any length, too.  Enter as big a name fragment as you can. The
smaller the name fragment, the more work the server has to do, and the
longer the search will take. Name fragments smaller than 6 characters
will be rejected without running the search. Do not use punctuation or
special characters in the name fragment, just the characters A-Z. If
you're searching for all dogs from a particular kennel, enter the kennel
name. The country qualifier is optional.  <I>Not all records contain a
country designation, so for now you should probably leave it as
&quot;any&quot;.</I></P>
<H2>Enter search criteria</H2>
<FORM ACTION="http://katie/newf/newfq.exe">
<TABLE ALIGN="CENTER">
<TR>
<TD><B>Select the country in which the dog was registered:</B></TD>
<TD>
<SELECT NAME="country">
<OPTION VALUE="any">(any)</OPTION>
<OPTION VALUE="AUSTRALIA">AUSTRALIA</OPTION>
<OPTION VALUE="AUSTRIA">AUSTRIA</OPTION>
<OPTION VALUE="BELGIUM">BELGIUM</OPTION>
<OPTION VALUE="CANADA">CANADA</OPTION>
<OPTION VALUE="CANDA">CANDA</OPTION>
<OPTION VALUE="CANDAD">CANDAD</OPTION>
<OPTION VALUE="CZECHOSLOVAKIA">CZECHOSLOVAKIA</OPTION>
<OPTION VALUE="DENMARK">DENMARK</OPTION>
```

```
<OPTION VALUE="EIRE">EIRE</OPTION>
<OPTION VALUE="FINLAND">FINLAND</OPTION>
<OPTION VALUE="FRANCE">FRANCE</OPTION>
<OPTION VALUE="GEMANY">GEMANY</OPTION>
<OPTION VALUE="GERMAN">GERMAN</OPTION>
<OPTION VALUE="GERMANY">GERMANY</OPTION>
<OPTION VALUE="HOLLAND">HOLLAND</OPTION>
<OPTION VALUE="ITALY">ITALY</OPTION>
<OPTION VALUE="LUXEMBURG">LUXEMBURG</OPTION>
<OPTION VALUE="NEW ZEALAND">NEW ZEALAND</OPTION>
<OPTION VALUE="NEWFOUNDLAND">NEWFOUNDLAND</OPTION>
<OPTION VALUE="NORWAY">NORWAY</OPTION>
<OPTION VALUE="POLAND">POLAND</OPTION>
<OPTION VALUE="RUSSIA">RUSSIA</OPTION>
<OPTION VALUE="SOUTH AFRICA">SOUTH AFRICA</OPTION>
<OPTION VALUE="SOUTH AFRICA?">SOUTH AFRICA?</OPTION>
<OPTION VALUE="SWEDEN">SWEDEN</OPTION>
<OPTION VALUE="SWITZERLAND">SWITZERLAND</OPTION>
<OPTION VALUE="UK">UK</OPTION>
<OPTION VALUE="USA">USA</OPTION>
<OPTION VALUE="USASA">USASA</OPTION></SELECT></TD>
<TD></TD></TR>
<TR>
<TD><B> Enter the name fragment here:</B>
<P>A special reminder:
<B>DO NOT USE APOSTROPHES HERE!!!</B>.
If the dog's name is Pouch Cove's Wondernewf, you should
search on POUCH COVES WONDERNEWF.</P></TD>
<TD VALIGN="TOP" ALIGN="LEFT">
<INPUT NAME="dog.text" SIZE="40"></TD>
<TD></TD></TR>
<TR>
<TD ALIGN="CENTER" COLSPAN="2">
<INPUT TYPE="SUBMIT" VALUE="Search"></TD>
<TD></TD></TR></TABLE>
<P ALIGN="LEFT">
<INPUT TYPE="HIDDEN" NAME="QueryType" VALUE="partial">
<BR>
<INPUT TYPE="HIDDEN" NAME="db" VALUE="newf">
<INPUT TYPE="HIDDEN" NAME="tbl" VALUE="shortdog">
```

```
<INPUT TYPE="HIDDEN" NAME="server" VALUE="katie">
<INPUT TYPE="HIDDEN" NAME="user" VALUE="sa">
<INPUT TYPE="HIDDEN" NAME="base" VALUE="http://katie">
<BR>
</P>
</FORM>
<HR>
<P><A HREF="NewfDB.html">Return to Newf DB top level</A>
</P></BODY></HTML>
```

While an exhaustive description of HTML is beyond the scope of this book, a little background is appropriate here. Any HTML document is made up of a number of nested elements, most of which have a begin tag (*i.e.*, **<BODY>**) and an end tag (*i.e.*, **</BODY>**). The all-encompassing element is the **<HTML>** element which describes the document as HTML. Then there's the **<HEAD>** element, containing the title and other meta-information. This is followed by the **<BODY>** element. The **<BODY>** element encompasses all the information that will actually appear in the document window.

Within the body, you can have any of dozens of different visual elements. Our search page's body starts off with a paragraph of explanatory text, delineated by the **<P></P>** tag pair. Then comes our form. All of our user-input elements must appear between the **<<FORM>></<FORM>>** tags.

Tables

Within the **<<FORM>>** element, we then define a **<TABLE>** element. Remember, earlier we said that you can't absolutely position your controls within a form. This is true. You can't, for example, tell the browser "place this text field 100 pixels from the right, and 123 pixels up from the bottom." This makes it very difficult to line up a user-input element with the prompt that describes that element. That's where tables come in.

A table is just a grid. You define each cell in the grid, left to right, top to bottom. Thus, we define three rows in our table. In the first two rows, the left-hand cell contains the input prompt, and the right-hand cell contains the input element itself. Listing 2.5 shows only the table portion of our search-screen HTML document.

Listing 2.5 The table of <FORM> input elements.

```
<TABLE ALIGN="CENTER">

<TR><TD><B>Select the country in which the dog was registered:</B></TD>
<TD>
<SELECT NAME="country">
<OPTION VALUE="any">(any)</OPTION>
<OPTION VALUE="AUSTRALIA">AUSTRALIA</OPTION>
<OPTION VALUE="AUSTRIA">AUSTRIA</OPTION>
<!--..... a bunch of selections-->
<OPTION VALUE="USASA">USASA</OPTION></SELECT></TD>
<TD></TD></TR>

<TR><TD><B> Enter the name fragment here:</B>
<P>A special reminder:
<B>DO NOT USE APOSTROPHES HERE!!!</B>.
If the dog's name is Pouch Cove's Wondernewf, you should
search on POUCH COVES WONDERNEWF.</P></TD>
<TD VALIGN="TOP" ALIGN="LEFT">
<INPUT NAME="dog.text" SIZE="40"></TD>
<TD></TD></TR>

<TR><TD ALIGN="CENTER" COLSPAN="2">
<INPUT TYPE="SUBMIT" VALUE="Search"></TD>
<TD></TD></TR>
</TABLE>
```

Here, we've purposely set off each table row with a blank line. Notice that in the third row of our table, something interesting happens. We want our Search button to be centered beneath the two input fields. To do this, we describe the only cell in the third row as center-aligned, spanning two columns, and containing a single button:

```
<TR><TD ALIGN="CENTER" COLSPAN="2">
<INPUT TYPE="SUBMIT" VALUE="Search"></TD></TR>
```

Notice that all we do here is describe the alignment in general terms, and the browser takes care of lining it up for us no matter how the user sizes her browser.

The list of countries in our choice element points up another limitation of static HTML forms. This list is supposed to represent the list of countries for which there are actually records in the database. Obviously, in order to keep this list current, we'd have to regenerate the form every time a country was added. We'll talk about ways to deal with this later in the chapter, but for now, it's just something to think about.

Preformatted Text

Tables are a Netscape enhancement to HTML 2.0, and thus theoretically are not supported in all browsers. How do we deal with this? The other, very popular way to create formatted forms, where the elements of the form line up vertically and retain their relative positions, is to use the Preformatted Fixed-Pitch Text element, defined by the **<PRE></PRE>** tag pair. Listing 2.6 shows our input form rewritten to use preformatted text rather than a table. Figure 2.5 shows Netscape viewing our new form.

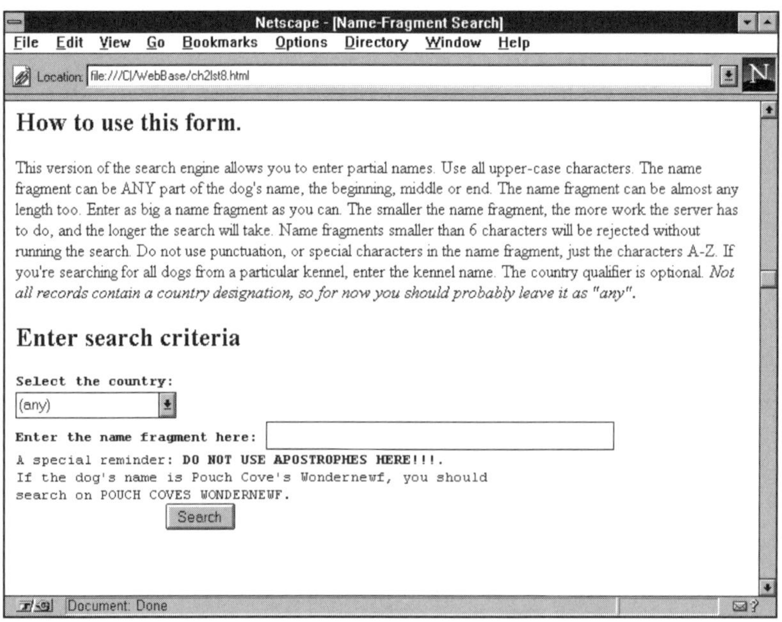

Figure 2.5 The preformatted text version of the form, viewed in Netscape.

Listing 2.6 The partial search form rewritten to use preformatted text rather than tables.

```
<!DOCTYPE HTML PUBLIC "-//SQ//DTD HTML 2.0 HoTMetaL + extensions//EN">
<HTML>
<HEAD>
<TITLE>Name-Fragment Search</TITLE></HEAD>
<BODY BGCOLOR="white">
<H1>Name-Fragment Search</H1>
<H2>How to use this form.</H2>
<P>This version of the search engine allows you to enter partial names.
Use all uppercase characters. The name fragment can be ANY part of the
dog's name, the beginning, middle, or end. The name fragment can be
almost any length too.  Enter as big a name fragment as you can. The
smaller the name fragment, the more work the server has to do, and the
longer the search will take. Name fragments smaller than 6 characters
will be rejected without running the search. Do not use punctuation or
special characters in the name fragment, just the characters A-Z. If
you're searching for all dogs from a particular kennel, enter the kennel
name. The country qualifier is optional. <I>Not all records contain a
country designation, so for now you should probably leave it as
&quot;any&quot;.</I></P>
<H2>Enter search criteria</H2>
<FORM ACTION="http://katie/newf/newfq.exe">
<PRE><B>Select the country:</B>
<SELECT NAME="country" SIZE="1">
<OPTION VALUE="any">(any)</OPTION>
<OPTION VALUE="AUSTRALIA">AUSTRALIA</OPTION>
<OPTION VALUE="AUSTRIA">AUSTRIA</OPTION>
<OPTION VALUE="BELGIUM">BELGIUM</OPTION>
<OPTION VALUE="CANADA">CANADA</OPTION>
<OPTION VALUE="CANDA">CANDA</OPTION>
<OPTION VALUE="CANDAD">CANDAD</OPTION>
<OPTION VALUE="CZECHOSLOVAKIA">CZECHOSLOVAKIA</OPTION>
<OPTION VALUE="DENMARK">DENMARK</OPTION>
<OPTION VALUE="EIRE">EIRE</OPTION>
<OPTION VALUE="FINLAND">FINLAND</OPTION>
<OPTION VALUE="FRANCE">FRANCE</OPTION>
<OPTION VALUE="GEMANY">GEMANY</OPTION>
<OPTION VALUE="GERMAN">GERMAN</OPTION>
<OPTION VALUE="GERMANY">GERMANY</OPTION>
<OPTION VALUE="HOLLAND">HOLLAND</OPTION>
<OPTION VALUE="ITALY">ITALY</OPTION>
<OPTION VALUE="LUXEMBURG">LUXEMBURG</OPTION>
```

```
<OPTION VALUE="NEW ZEALAND">NEW ZEALAND</OPTION>
<OPTION VALUE="NEWFOUNDLAND">NEWFOUNDLAND</OPTION>
<OPTION VALUE="NORWAY">NORWAY</OPTION>
<OPTION VALUE="POLAND">POLAND</OPTION>
<OPTION VALUE="RUSSIA">RUSSIA</OPTION>
<OPTION VALUE="SOUTH AFRICA">SOUTH AFRICA</OPTION>
<OPTION VALUE="SWEDEN">SWEDEN</OPTION>
<OPTION VALUE="SWITZERLAND">SWITZERLAND</OPTION>
<OPTION VALUE="UK">UK</OPTION>
<OPTION VALUE="USA">USA</OPTION>
<OPTION VALUE="USASA">USASA</OPTION></SELECT>
<B>Enter the name fragment here:</B> <INPUT NAME="dog.text" SIZE="40">
A special reminder: <B>DO NOT USE APOSTROPHES HERE!!!</B>.
If the dog's name is Pouch Cove's Wondernewf, you should
search on POUCH COVES WONDERNEWF.
                  <INPUT TYPE="SUBMIT" VALUE="Search"></PRE>
<P ALIGN="LEFT"><INPUT TYPE="HIDDEN" NAME="QueryType"
VALUE="partial"><BR><INPUT
TYPE="HIDDEN" NAME="db" VALUE="newf"><INPUT
TYPE="HIDDEN" NAME="tbl" VALUE="shortdog"><INPUT
TYPE="HIDDEN" NAME="server" VALUE="katie"><INPUT
TYPE="HIDDEN" NAME="user" VALUE="sa"><INPUT
TYPE="HIDDEN" NAME="base" VALUE="http://katie"><BR></P></FORM>
<HR>
<P><A HREF="NewfDB.html">Return to Newf DB top level</A></P></BODY></
HTML>
```

As you can see, the **<PRE>** version of our form is virtually identical to the table version. Why use one over the other? Well, for quick and dirty forms, **<PRE>** versions are generally quicker to write and should work with all browsers. On the other hand, tables can be aligned both vertically and horizontally within the resizeable browser window. Tables can have borders around the cells. They also automatically align columns. This is especially important when you start building larger forms. Preformatted forms of a certain complexity become almost impossible to maintain.

Naming Elements

Now that we've seen, in general terms, how we get the form to look the way we want, let's take a closer look at the individual elements of the form, and see how they store the data we need to make this a functional form. Listing 2.7 shows the source for our two input elements and the Search button.

Listing 2.7 The two input elements and the Search/Submit button.

```
<SELECT NAME="country" SIZE="1">
<OPTION VALUE="any">(any)</OPTION>
<OPTION VALUE="UK">UK</OPTION>

<!--.... a bunch of OPTIONs -->

<OPTION VALUE="USA">USA</OPTION>
<OPTION VALUE="USASA">USASA</OPTION></SELECT>

<INPUT NAME="dog.text" SIZE="40">

<INPUT TYPE="SUBMIT" VALUE="Search">
```

As you can see, each of our input elements has a name. The **<SELECT>** element is named "country" while the **<INPUT>** element is named "dog.text". The **<SELECT>** element also has a set of values, all the countries from the database. The **<INPUT>** element has no **VALUE** attribute (although it could). When the form is processed, the browser creates a series of name/value pairs. So for our form, the browser will create two name/value pairs. If, for example, we chose IRELAND as our country, and SIKI as the dog's name, the browser would create the following strings:

```
country=IRELAND
dog.text=SIKI
```

In programming terms, the process of naming an element is very much like declaring a variable. Here, we've declared two variables, country and dog.text. The browser simply sets the value of the variable. When the form gets processed, the value of these variables can be queried.

How does the form get "processed"? By pressing the Search button, of course. The Search button is a specialized type of **<INPUT>** element, of type **SUBMIT**. All forms have a Submit button, although the text in that button can be anything you want. The values that the user has entered into the form's various fields are not read until the Submit button has been pressed. The Submit button is the browser's cue to create the name/value pairs from the information the user has entered in the fields.

We've now reached an important place in our understanding of forms. We know how to create a form, and how to name our input elements such that we can tell what value a user has entered for a particular variable. All we need to see now is what exactly "processing" a form means.

Using The Common Gateway Interface To Construct Queries

To see what happens when we press the Search button in our form, we have to look back at the **<FORM>** tag:

```
<FORM ACTION="http://katie/newf/newfq.exe">
```

As you can see, our **<FORM>** tag has only a single attribute, **ACTION**. This **ACTION** is the URL of a CGI program that gets executed when we press the Search button. What happens at the lower levels is that the browser tries to access a URL, in this case **http://katie/newf/newfq.exe**, passing along our two name/value pairs. When the browser passes this URL to the Web server, the Web server recognizes it (by one of a few different methods) as a CGI request, starts the CGI program, and directs the output of that program back to the browser. Thus, instead of looking at a static HTML document, the browser is instead looking at the output of a program running on the Web server. The browser relies on that program to produce proper HTML.

The mechanism that describes this interaction is *CGI, Common Gateway Interface.* What is CGI? In short, it's a description of how a Web page can cause a program to execute on a server, and how the browser and Web server can get information into and out of that executing program. The theory behind all CGI interactions is that you set the program running by accessing a particular URL. The program then generates, as its output, a stream of HTML code that the Web server passes to the browser for display.

In this sense, clicking our form's Search button is exactly like clicking on a hyperlink (an **<A>** element in HTML). The browser gets the stream of HTML residing at the URL described by the hyperlink element. For a CGI reference, the HTML doesn't actually exist until you access the URL (in this case, **http://katie/newf/newfq.exe**). The Web server creates it by starting up the program (newfq.exe) and passing the program's HTML output back to the browser. The browser, though, doesn't care where its HTML comes from, just that it's proper HTML.

We'll talk more about the interaction between the browser, the Web server, and the CGI program later. For now, it's enough to know that simply by accessing the URL of the CGI program (hitting the Search button), a user can set the CGI program running and expect to see the output of that program in the browser window.

Getting Form Information Into A CGI Program

Back in Chapter 1, Figure 1.3, we showed the two paths HTML can take to the browser: from a static HTML document, or from a CGI program. In reality, though, the CGI process is a two-way communication, with form variables (our two name/value pairs) going to the CGI program, and HTML coming back from the program. Figure 2.6 shows Figure 1.3 modified to reflect this fact.

As you can see from Figure 2.6, there are two paths down that the browser can send information to our CGI program: the **POST** path and the **GET** path. Most programming languages today understand the concept of "standard input" and "standard output." Standard input is simply a stream of data that goes into the program. The program can read from standard input, and receive whatever data the calling program pushes into that stream. The program can also write to standard output, confident that that data will go somewhere. The standard I/O concept is a powerful one. Originating in the Unix world, it allows programs to be piped together in very long chains, where the standard output of one program goes to the standard input of another program, thus implementing a rudimentary form of interprocess communication. Our use of standard I/O can be summarized as follows:

- The standard output will always contain HTML code that ultimately appears in the browser as the output of our program.
- If the form is of type **POST**, the standard input of the CGI program will contain the name/value pairs from our form.

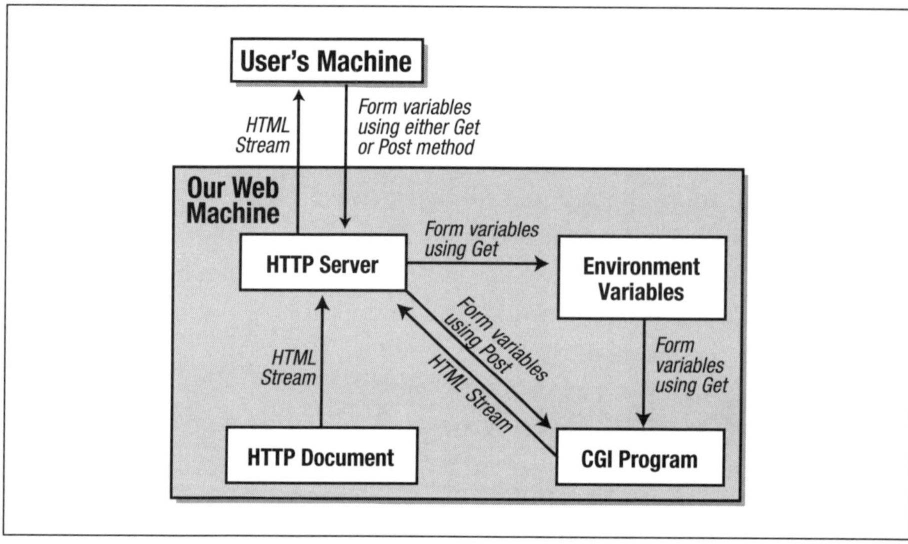

Figure 2.6 The flow of information from Web server to browser and back.

- If the form is of type **GET**, the standard input will contain nothing. In that case, instead of pushing the name/value pairs into the standard input stream, the Web server sets an environment variable (QUERY_STRING) that itself contains our name/value pairs. For a **GET**-style form, the CGI program must query the operating system for the environment variable QUERY_STRING in order to get the name/value pairs.

Let's look at how our CGI program, newfq.exe, gets its name/value pairs from the various forms it uses. The newfq.exe program allows both **POST** and **GET** forms. It can do this because the Web server sets another environment variable, **REQUEST_METHOD**, that tells the CGI program whether the form is **GET** or **POST** style. Listing 2.8 shows the name/value-pair processing code from the C program newfq.exe.

Listing 2.8 Argument processing in newfq.exe.

```
/************** ARGUMENT PROCESSING CODE ****************/

// The maximum number of arguments we'll accept
#define MAX_ARGS        50

/* Grab all the input we can from standard input, stuff it
into a string, then pass that string to ProcessArgs. */
```

```
void PostArguments() {
   int length;
   char *qs;
   char buffer[1024];
   int i;

   // Find the length of the stream coming in over stdin
   qs = getenv( "CONTENT_LENGTH" );
   if( qs == NULL )
      return;
   length = atoi( qs );

   // Read the appropriate number of bytes from stdin
   for( i = 0; i < length; i++ )
      buffer[i] = getchar();
   // Don't forget to null terminate the string.
   buffer[i] = '\0';

   // Now buffer looks just like it would have if
   // we had gotten it via getenv("QUERY_STRING")
   // so send it to ProcessArgs.
   ProcessArgs( buffer );
}

/* Determine which type of input we're getting, GET or POST.
If it's POST, call PostArguments to get the standard in,
otherwise, get the string from QUERY_STRING and pass it
in to ProcessArgs. */
void SetArguments() {
   char *qs;

   // Figure out whether this is a GET or POST by querying
   // REQUEST_METHOD.
   qs = getenv( "REQUEST_METHOD" );
   if( qs == NULL )
       return;

   if( strcmp( qs, "POST" ) == 0 )
      PostArguments();
   else {
      qs = getenv( "QUERY_STRING" );
      if( qs == NULL ) {
        // no arguments is a fatal error
         fprintf( errfp, "no query_string\n" );
         exit( 1 );
```

```
      }
    // Here's where the real argument processing happens
    ProcessArgs( qs );
    }
  }

/* Process the string of arguments passed in via the qs
   argument. */
void ProcessArgs( char *qs ) {
   char *key[MAX_ARGS];
   char *ptr, *ptr1, *qs1;
   char *value[MAX_ARGS];
   char achar[3];
   int srcindex = 0;
   int destindex = 0;
   int i,j,k;
   int index = 0;

   // Convert all the special chars into their actuals
   ptr1 = FixString( qs );
   if( ptr1 == NULL ) {
      fprintf( errfp, "bad strdup\n" );
      exit( 1 );
      }

   qs1 = ptr1;

   // Null out the entire value array.
   for( i = 0; i < MAX_ARGS; i++ )
      value[i] = NULL;

   // March through the name/value-pair string, replacing
   // any instance of '&' or '=' with a string terminator.
   // Since the string is of the form:
   //    key=value&key1=value1&key2=value2
   // this algorithm can quickly turn the string into
   // two arrays of character pointers, one array for keys
   // and one for values.
   for( i = 0; i < MAX_ARGS; i++ ) {
      key[i] = qs1;
      ptr = strchr( qs1, '=' );
      if( ptr == NULL )
         break;
      *ptr = '\0';
      ptr++;
```

```
   value[i] = ptr;

   ptr = strchr( ptr, '&' );
   if( ptr == NULL )
      break;
   *ptr = '\0';
   ptr++;
   qs1 = ptr;
   }

index = 0;
for( j = 0; j < MAX_ARGS; j++ ) {
   if( key[j] == NULL || (value[j] == NULL ))
      continue;
   if( strlen( value[j] ) == 0 )
      continue;

   if( strcmp( value[j], "any" ) == 0 )
      continue;

   // The application enforces certain rules for dog
   // names, so we call NormalizeName to deal with
   // the incoming dog name.
   if( strcmp( key[j], "dog.text" ) == 0 ) {
      NormalizeName( sought_name, value[j] );
      continue;
      }
   if( strcmp( key[j], "NAME" ) == 0 ) {
      NormalizeName( NAME, value[j] );
      strcpy( sought_name, NAME );
      StripChar( NAME, '\'' );
      continue;
      }
   if( strcmp( key[j], "QUOTENO" ) == 0 ) {
              strcpy( QUOTENO, value[j] );
              continue;
              }
      if( strcmp( key[j], "CHANGEDATE" ) == 0 ) {
              strcpy( CHANGEDATE, value[j] );
              continue;
              }
      if( strcmp( key[j], "CHANGETEXT" ) == 0 ) {
              strcpy( CHANGETEXT, value[j] );
              continue;
              }
```

```
if( strcmp( key[j], "REGNO" ) == 0 ) {
        strcpy( REGNO, value[j] );
        continue;
        }
if( strcmp( key[j], "COUNTRY" ) == 0 ) {
        strcpy( COUNTRY, value[j] );
        continue;
        }
if( strcmp( key[j], "TITLES" ) == 0 ) {
        strcpy( TITLES, value[j] );
        continue;
        }
if( strcmp( key[j], "CHDATE" ) == 0 ) {
        strcpy( CHDATE, value[j] );
        continue;
        }
if( strcmp( key[j], "JWOB" ) == 0 ) {
        strcpy( JWOB, value[j] );
        continue;
        }
if( strcmp( key[j], "JWDATE" ) == 0 ) {
        strcpy( JWDATE, value[j] );
        continue;
        }
if( strcmp( key[j], "DOB" ) == 0 ) {
        strcpy( DOB, value[j] );
        continue;
        }
if( strcmp( key[j], "DOB2" ) == 0 ) {
        strcpy( DOB2, value[j] );
        continue;
        }
if( strcmp( key[j], "SEX" ) == 0 ) {
        strcpy( SEX, value[j] );
        continue;
        }
if( strcmp( key[j], "SNAME" ) == 0 ) {
  NormalizeName( SNAME, value[j] );
  StripChar( SNAME, '\'' );
        continue;
        }
if( strcmp( key[j], "DNAME" ) == 0 ) {
  NormalizeName( DNAME, value[j] );
  StripChar( DNAME, '\'' );
```

```
        continue;
        }
if( strcmp( key[j], "COLOUR" ) == 0 ) {
        strcpy( COLOUR, value[j] );
  if( strcmp( COLOUR, "Landseer" ) == 0 )
      strcpy( COLOUR, "WH&BL" );
        continue;
        }
if( strcmp( key[j], "RECESSIVE" ) == 0 ) {
        strcpy( RECESSIVE, value[j] );
        continue;
        }
if( strcmp( key[j], "OWNER" ) == 0 ) {
        strcpy( OWNER, value[j] );
        continue;
        }
if( strcmp( key[j], "KENNEL" ) == 0 ) {
        NormalizeName( KENNEL, value[j] );
  StripChar( KENNEL, '\'' );
        continue;
        }
if( strcmp( key[j], "BREEDER" ) == 0 ) {
        strcpy( BREEDER, value[j] );
        continue;
        }
if( strcmp( key[j], "REMARKS" ) == 0 ) {
        strcpy( REMARKS, value[j] );
        continue;
        }
if( strcmp( key[j], "HIPTOT" ) == 0 ) {
        strcpy( HIPTOT, value[j] );
        continue;
        }
if( strcmp( key[j], "HIPR" ) == 0 ) {
        strcpy( HIPR, value[j] );
        continue;
        }
if( strcmp( key[j], "HIPL" ) == 0 ) {
        strcpy( HIPL, value[j] );
        continue;
        }
if( strcmp( key[j], "DIED" ) == 0 ) {
        strcpy( DIED, value[j] );
        continue;
        }
```

```
if( strcmp( key[j], "HDCERT" ) == 0 ) {
        strcpy( HDCERT, value[j] );
        continue;
        }
if( strcmp( key[j], "HIPS" ) == 0 ) {
        strcpy( HIPS, value[j] );
        continue;
        }
if( strcmp( key[j], "OFANO" ) == 0 ) {
        strcpy( OFANO, value[j] );
        continue;
        }
if( strcmp( key[j], "OVCNO" ) == 0 ) {
        strcpy( OVCNO, value[j] );
        continue;
        }
if( strcmp( key[j], "KCBVAEYE" ) == 0 ) {
        strcpy( KCBVAEYE, value[j] );
        continue;
        }
if( strcmp( key[j], "TATTOO" ) == 0 ) {
        strcpy( TATTOO, value[j] );
        continue;
        }
if( strcmp( key[j], "HEARTGRADE" ) == 0 ) {
        strcpy( HEARTGRADE, value[j] );
        continue;
        }
if( strcmp( key[j], "SOURCE" ) == 0 ) {
        strcpy( SOURCE, value[j] );
        continue;
        }
if( strcmp( key[j], "SB" ) == 0 ) {
        strcpy( SB, value[j] );
        continue;
        }
if( strcmp( key[j], "WORKAREA" ) == 0 ) {
        strcpy( WORKAREA, value[j] );
        continue;
        }
if( strcmp( key[j], "SRCADDRESS" ) == 0 ) {
        strcpy( SRCADDRESS, value[j] );
        continue;
        }
```

```
  if( strcmp( key[j], "SRCEMAIL" ) == 0 ) {
          strcpy( SRCEMAIL, value[j] );
          continue;
          }
  if( strcmp( key[j], "FAMILIAR" ) == 0 ) {
     strcpy( FAMILIAR, value[j] );
     continue;
     }
  if( strcmp( key[j], "SITE" ) == 0 ) {
     strcpy( SITE, value[j] );
     continue;
     }
  if( strcmp( key[j], "URL" ) == 0 ) {
     strcpy( URL, value[j] );
     continue;
     }

  if( strcmp( key[j], "COMMENTS" ) == 0 ) {
     strcpy( COMMENTS, value[j] );
     continue;
     }

// QueryType has a bunch of values and actions
// associated with them. QueryType tells us what
// we're going to do with all this data, insert
// it in newdog, query by name kennel, create
// a pedigree chart, or whatever.
  if( strcmp( key[j], "QueryType" ) == 0 ) {
     if( strcmp( value[j], "update" ) == 0 ) {
             sprintf( table_caption, "updating " );
             QueryType = QUERY_UPDATE;
             }
     if( strcmp( value[j], "insert" ) == 0 ) {
             sprintf( table_caption, "adding " );
             QueryType = QUERY_INSERT;
             }
     if( strcmp( value[j], "Dam" ) == 0 ) {
             sprintf( table_caption, "All dogs from dam " );
             QueryType = BY_DAM;
             }
     if( strcmp( value[j], "Pedigree" ) == 0 ) {
             sprintf( table_caption, "Pedigree chart for " );
             QueryType = BY_PEDIGREE;
             }
```

```
        if( strcmp( value[j], "Sire" ) == 0 ) {
                sprintf( table_caption, "All dogs from sire " );
                QueryType = BY_SIRE;
                }
        if( strcmp( value[j], "Kennel" ) == 0 ) {
                sprintf( table_caption, "All dogs from kennel " );
                QueryType = BY_KENNEL;
                }
        if( strcmp( value[j], "Name" ) == 0 ) {
                sprintf( table_caption, "All dogs named " );
                QueryType = BY_NAME;
                }
        if( strcmp( value[j], "partial" ) == 0 ) {
                sprintf( table_caption, "All dogs named " );
                QueryType = BY_NAME_PARTIAL;
                }
        if( strcmp( value[j], "new" ) == 0 ) {
                sprintf( table_caption, "New dogs " );
                QueryType = QUERY_NEW;
                }
        if( strcmp( value[j], "rbinsert" ) == 0 ) {
                sprintf( table_caption, "Newf Lawn " );
                QueryType = QUERY_RBINSERT;
                }
        }
// These are a bunch of hidden variables in the
// form that I use to switch between my
// development machine and my production system.
// They allow me to switch my database machine
// name and various other things from within
// the calling HTML rather than in the C code.
  if( strcmp( key[j], "base" ) == 0 )
    strcpy( documentbase, value[j] );
  if( strcmp( key[j], "server" ) == 0 )
        sprintf( servername, "%s", value[j] );
  if( strcmp( key[j], "cgi" ) == 0 )
      sprintf( cgi_directory, "%s", value[j] );
  if( strcmp( key[j], "db" ) == 0 )
        sprintf( dbname, "%s", value[j] );
  if( strcmp( key[j], "country" ) == 0 )
        sprintf( country, "%s", value[j] );
  if( strcmp( key[j],"user" ) == 0 )
        sprintf( username, "%s", value[j] );
  if( strcmp( key[j], "tbl" ) == 0 ) {
        sprintf( tblname, "%s", value[j] );
```

```
        }
    }
  sprintf( table_caption, sought_name );
  free( ptrl );
  }
```

In the main function of our C program, almost the first thing we do is call **SetArguments**. **SetArguments**' job is to set up a series of variables that describe the job the user wants the program to do. The first thing **SetArguments** has to do is find out where its name/value pairs are coming from, either standard-in **(REQUEST_METHOD=POST)** or from the environment variable **(REQUEST_METHOD=GET)**.

If the **REQUEST_METHOD** is **GET**, **SetArguments** calls **getenv** to read the environment variable **QUERY_STRING**. Getenv is a run-time library call that calls out to the operating system. The variable qs, which we get back from getenv, will read something like this:

```
country=IRELAND&dog.text=SIKI
```

Notice that the name/value pairs are concatenated into a single string, separated by an ampersand (the & character). **SetArguments** then calls **ProcessArgs**, passing this concatenated string.

If the **REQUEST_METHOD** is **POST**, **SetArguments** calls **PostArguments** to read the name/value pairs from standard input. Before reading standard-in, **PostArguments** first reads another environment variable, **CONTENT_LENGTH**. This tells us how many bytes of standard input we should read. We *must* read exactly **CONTENT_LENGTH** bytes from standard input, no more and no less, or the CGI process will not work. Once we've read **CONTENT_LENGTH** bytes into our character array buffer, we have a string of exactly the same form as the one we would get via the **GET** method:

```
country=IRELAND&dog.text=SIKI
```

Once we have a name/value string of the proper form, we pass it to **ProcessArguments**. This is where the values from this amorphous string get plucked out as discrete items and copied into C variables of the appropriate type. But before we can dig out the values and start using them, we have to deal with a quirk of HTTP—it doesn't like some ASCII characters. In fact, it doesn't like some characters so much that it turns them into other characters. Spaces get turned into the plus sign, and other interesting characters get turned into strings of the form %<hex ascii>. For example, percent signs get turned into %27. We need to turn those changed characters back into the regular old ASCII they started out as, so we implement the functions **FixString** and **hatoi**, as in Listing 2.9, and call **FixString** against our query string before we try to decompose it.

Listing 2.9 FixString and hatoi help un-HTTP a query string.

```
// hatoi - turn a string representing a hex number into
// an integer version of that number.
int hatoi( char *anum ) {
   int byte0, byte1, iret;

   if( anum[0] >= '0' && anum[0] <= '9' )
      byte0 = anum[0] - '0';
   else
      byte0 = (toupper( anum[0] ) - 'A') + 10;
   iret = byte0*16;
   if( anum[1] >= '0' && anum[1] <= '9' )
      byte1 = anum[1] - '0';
   else
      byte1 = (toupper( anum[1] ) - 'A') + 10;
   iret += byte1;
   return( iret );
   }

// FixString - Fix a string that has been webbified to
// turn interesting characters into %XX style strings.
// Return a new, malloced, string that represents the
// unwebbed version of the input string.
char *FixString( char *pi ) {
   char *p;
   int len;
   int i, index;
   char thenum[3];

   len = strlen( pi );
   p = malloc( len+1 );
   if( p == NULL )
      return( NULL );
   index = 0;
```

```
    for( i = 0; i < len; i++ ) {
       if( pi[i] == '%' && ((i+3) <= len )) {
          i++;
          thenum[0] = pi[i++];
          thenum[1] = pi[i];
          thenum[2] = '\0';
          if( hatoi(thenum) == '&' )
             p[index++] = ' ';
          else
             p[index++] = hatoi(thenum);
          }
       else
          {
          if( pi[i] == '+' )
             p[index++] = ' ';
          else
             p[index++] = pi[i];
          }
       }
    p[index] = '\0';
    return( p );
    }
```

When the string has been fixed, we march through it, nulling out any occurrence of either an ampersand or an equals sign. By alternating name/value as we march through, we can quickly set up parallel arrays of name and value strings. Once these parallel arrays are set up, it's a simple matter to march back through those arrays, inspecting the names and acting appropriately on them.

The long series of statements starting at

```
if( strcmp( key[j], "dog.text" ) == 0 )
```

merely sets a number of host variables to whatever value the user has entered back at the form. Most of these values are used in an insert statement that we haven't talked about yet. The only ones used in the query statements we've discussed so far are dog.text, KENNEL, SNAME, DNAME, and COUNTRY.

SetArguments' use of the environment variable **CONTENT_LENGTH** brings up an important point about CGI processes in general. Even if we use the **POST** method, the Web server will still store an abundance of useful information in environment variables. Later on, we'll make use of some of the other CGI environment variables to do usage tracking and browser-capability-based content modification.

We've talked now about **POST** and **GET** style forms, but not how you set up your form to be one or the other. Well, it's quite simple. In fact, let's look back at our simple form tag from the query screen:

```
<FORM ACTION="http://katie/newf/newfq.exe">
```

We could modify this to say this

```
<FORM ACTION="http://katie/newf/newfq.exe" TYPE="GET">
```

and it would work exactly the same way because **GET** is the default form type. If we wanted to modify this to be a **POST** form, we'd simply say this:

```
<FORM ACTION="http://katie/newf/newfq.exe" TYPE="POST">
```

The way we've written newfq.exe, it would work exactly the same either way.

Why use one method and not the other? **GET** is a little easier to implement, since you don't have to do that byte-by-byte read of standard-in. However, **POST** is a better long-term solution, for the simple reason that most operating systems limit the number of bytes you can store in an environment variable, while the number of bytes you can pass by standard-in is unlimited. Remember, all the name/value pairs from your form get concatenated into a single string. Later on, we'll implement a record input screen that takes advantage of **POST**'s unlimited data-carrying capacity.

The Rest Of The CGI Spec

The CGI specification, currently at version 1.1 is, in fact, quite simple. We've already covered most of it. It won't kill us, though, to spend a little bit of time looking at the rest of the spec. For our purposes, it can be split into three parts: environment variables, standard I/O, and the command line.

Environment Variables

Table 2.3 shows the entire list of environment variables defined for CGI 1.1.

The meaning of **SERVER_SOFTWARE, SERVER_NAME, SERVER_PROTOCOL**, and **SERVER_PORT** are all fairly obvious. **GATEWAY_INTERFACE**, for its part, tells you what you can expect from the Web server in the way of a CGI implementation.

Table 2.3 The list of environment variables available under CGI 1.1.

Environment Variable Name	Description	Example
SERVER_SOFTWARE	The name and version of the Web server software.	Netscape Commerce Server/1.0
SERVER_NAME	The server's hostname.	www.channel1.com
SERVER_PROTOCOL	The name and revision of the protocol of this request.	http/2.0
SERVER_PORT	The IP port number that received this request.	Usually 80.
GATEWAY_INTERFACE	The revision of CGI this server implements.	CGI/1.1
REQUEST_METHOD	The method of the request - GET, HEAD, or POST.	
QUERY_STRING	The name/value pairs from the form.	See text.
CONTENT_TYPE	The content type of the data being supplied to the CGI program.	
CONTENT_LENGTH	The number of bytes of information being supplied to the CGI program via either QUERY_STRING or standard input.	
SCRIPT_NAME	The virtual path to the CGI program.	
REMOTE_HOST	The hostname of the machine the browser is running on.	katie.channel1.com
REMOTE_ADDR	The IP address of the machine the browser is running on.	199.1.200.25
REMOTE_USER	The username of the person operating the browser.	
REMOTE_IDENT	The username via RFC 931.	
AUTH_TYPE	The protocol-specific authentication method used to validate the user.	
PATH_INFO	The extra path information.	See text.
PATH_TRANSLATED	PATH_INFO translated by the server.	See text.

We've already talked at length about **QUERY_STRING**, **CONTENT_LENGTH**, and **REQUEST_METHOD**—the variables that define where our name/value pairs are, how much data is in them, and what that data is. **CONTENT_TYPE** will be set to the MIME type of the incoming data stream.

SCRIPT_NAME is the relative path on this server to the CGI program being executed. For instance, if the base directory for Web documents is /**http/docs**, and the CGI program being executed is **/http/docs/cgi-bin/counter.cgi**, then **SCRIPT_NAME** will be set to **"/cgi-bin/counter.cgi"**.

REMOTE_USER, REMOTE_IDENT, REMOTE_HOST, and **REMOTE_ADDR** deserve some explanation. **REMOTE_USER** and **IDENT** are both intended for usernames. If the server authenticates via a username/password dialog box, then the username should appear in **REMOTE_USER**. If the server uses RFC931 identification, then the username will appear in **REMOTE_IDENT**. **REMOTE_HOST** *should* hold the hostname of the machine the browser is running on. In practice, it is *very* rare to get a value from **REMOTE_HOST**. Why? The vast majority of Internet users are connecting to the Net via ISPs like America Online or CompuServe that randomly assign IP addresses to dialup users. In that case, the IP address can't resolve to a host name via DNS. The closest you can get is the domain name of the ISP. **REMOTE_ADDR** is, in my experience at least, always set. If you have the determination, you can dig out the domain name from the masked IP address.

The last environment variables to consider, and ones that will prove useful later, are **PATH_INFO** and **PATH_TRANSLATED**. In short, you can tack extra information onto the URL of the CGI program you want to execute (and many applications do). For example, if our CGI program's URL is **http://www.john.com/cgi/prog.exe**, then we can point our browser at the URL **http://www.john.com/cgi/prog.exe/extra/info**, and the server will still execute prog.exe. The extra information will be stuffed into **PATH_INFO**. The server will also "translate" this extra information and put that translation into **PATH_TRANSLATED**.

Standard I/O

We've already said almost all there is to say about standard I/O in a CGI program. Standard input is either the name/value pairs from the form (**POST**), or nothing (**GET**). Standard output, though, is a little more complicated.

If you recall our little diagram of Figure 2.6, we show the standard output of the CGI program going through the Web server on its way back to the browser. This is an important point. The server gets to look at everything the CGI program sends back to the browser. In fact, our CGI program can use standard output to communicate with the server. There are cases where you might want to take advantage of this communication, allowing the server to do in one command what it would take your CGI program many lines of code to accomplish. The most important of these CGI-program-to-server communication dodges is *Server Side Includes*, or *SSIs*, where in one command our CGI program can tell the server to use a particular file as our output. We'll cover SSIs, as well as some other cases, as we go along.

The Command Line

The command line is the only other method of communicating with our CGI program. Fortunately for us, command-line arguments (**argc** and **argv** to all you C fans out there) are only used with an **ISINDEX** query. **ISINDEX** is beyond the scope of this book.

Conclusion

In this chapter, we've covered a lot of ground. We've defined and built a simple database containing dog-pedigree information, then built a form to query a single record from that database. We looked in detail at a couple of ways (table and preformatted) to create business-like query forms using HTML. Then we followed the trail that leads from the user interacting with this form through the CGI program (in this case, a C program) that actually uses the form information. Finally, we looked in detail at the CGI specification, and talked a little bit about how this specification interacts with the HTTP protocol.

There's an intricate chain of execution, from the user sitting in front of our query form, to the results of that query appearing in the browser window. At this point, we've built half of that chain of execution, from the user designing a query on the browser, to the CGI program executing that query. Let's move on now to look in detail at the other half of that chain of execution: creating and transmitting the HTML stream that will appear in the user's browser as the results of his query.

Webliography

• Common Gateway Interface	http://hoohoo.ncsa.uiuc.edu/cgi/
• HTTP 1.0 protocol specification	http://www.w3.org/pub/WWW/protocols/HTTP1.0/draft-ietf-http-spec.html
• HTTP 1.1 protocol specification	http://www.w3.org/pub/WWW/protocols/HTTP1.0/draft-ietf-http-v11-spec-07.html

Chapter 3

Creating HTML On The Fly

CHAPTER 3

Creating HTML On The Fly

In Chapter 2, we scraped the surface of our CGI database access program, looking into how the Web server invokes and passes arguments into the CGI program. Now we have enough to consider the entire program on its own. In this chapter, we'll build the rest of our C CGI program. Along the way, we'll do SELECTs and INSERTs into our database, catch and handle both SQL errors and fatal C exceptions, and create, on the fly, HTML output suitable for viewing in a Web browser. When we're done, we'll have an end-to-end Web database application with query and insert capability.

Before we dig into the bits and bytes of our CGI program, let's go over some of the logistics peculiar to our installation. As explained in the introduction, our development tools consist of a C compiler (Microsoft Visual C/C++) and an embedded SQL preprocessor (ESQL/C). Our CGI program itself is made up of C source files (with an extension of .c), C source files with embedded SQL (.sqc), and header files (.h). Table 3.1 shows the list of source files.

Table 3.1 The list of files in our CGI program.

File name	Description
newfqmain.c	The main function; calls into newfq.sqc
newfq.sqc	The body of the CGI program; contains all queries
newfq.h	Header file for newfq.sqc
globals.sqc	Some SQL utilities, including error handling
globals.h	Header file for globals.sqc
html.c	Some utilities for emitting HTML code to stdout
html.h	Header file for html.c; mostly function prototypes
gcutil.c	Miscellaneous utilities
gcutil.h	Header file for gcutil.c

The details of using Microsoft Visual C++ to create, compile, and link a project is beyond the scope of this book. However, the SQL preprocessor deserves a brief look.

In Microsoft's ESQL/C, the SQL preprocessor is a program called nsqlprep. When we run it against newfq.sqc, as in

```
nsqlprep newfq.sqc
```

nsqlprep creates a file named newfq.c. We then compile and link newfq.c into our application exactly like any other C source file.

We will cover the contents of each of the source files in detail later on in this chapter. By using the project and source files included on the CD-ROM, you should be able to quickly pick up the basics of developing in this environment.

Dealing With Fatal Errors

One of the first things to think about when designing any application is how to protect the users from your own mistakes. After all, every program has bugs; the only difference between a good and bad program is the number and severity of them. Bugs in C code are especially difficult to deal with since they are often caused by wild pointers marching off into protected memory space, blowing out of the program entirely and invoking operating-system error-handling mechanisms.

Gracefully handling potentially fatal errors is even more important for a CGI program than for standalone, shrink-wrapped applications because a CGI program generally runs on a mostly unattended server. You can't rely on there being someone sitting in front of the machine to click the OK button when a Unrecoverable Application Error dialog pops up. In fact, that Windows error dialog *must* be suppressed. Should that dialog pop up and linger on the screen, any open files (like the log file) will remain locked, and any new instance of our CGI program will fail when it tries to open them. If that fatal error happens in the wrong spot, we may also leave a database connection open, with transactions uncommitted. This will cause us to quickly run out of both open connections and log device space.

The big problem with handling fatal errors is catching them in the first place. Microsoft C provides a method, *structured exception handling*, that gives us this functionality. Borrowed from the world of object-oriented programming, structured exception handling allows you to attach an exception-handling block to any block of C code. You simply enclose your C block in a **_try-_except** structure. Any fatal errors occurring within the C block are caught, and execution resumes at the head of the exception-handling block. Listing 3.1 shows the main function for our CGI program.

Listing 3.1 The main function and its exception handlers.

```
/* main - The main function for newfq.exe.  Splits
the program into three parts: setting up the query,
running the query, and ending the query.  Each part
gets its own exception-handling block, and main
prints a different HTML error message for each
possible failure point.
*/
int main (
    int argc,
    char** argv,
    char** envp)
{
   StartStream();

   _try {
```

```
      if( StartQuery()) {
         BlankDoc();
         return( 1 );
         }
      }
   _except( EXCEPTION_EXECUTE_HANDLER ) {
      BlankDoc();
      ShowException();
      return( 0 );
      }

   _try {
      DoQuery();
      }
   _except( EXCEPTION_EXECUTE_HANDLER ) {
      printf( "<P>This query has caused an internal error.\n" );
      printf( "This error has been logged.  System administrators ");
      printf("closely monitor the system, so the error will be dealt ");
      printf("with as quickly as possible.\n" );
      printf( "You can retry your search using different search terms,");
      printf(" or wait a day or two and retry using the same search");
      printf("terms.\n" );
      printf( "We apologize for any inconvenience this error may have ");
      printf("caused.\n</P>\n" );
      ShowException();
      EndQuery();
      return( 0 );
      }

   _try {
      EndQuery();
      }
   _except( EXCEPTION_EXECUTE_HANDLER ) {
      ShowException();
      return( 0 );
      }

   return( 0 );
}
```

The first line of our program, **StartStream**, we'll talk about later when we look at the HTML output stream. **StartStream** itself is just a function from our HTML output library. After that call, the function splits into three **_try-_except** blocks. The way the **_try-_except** construct works is that the code within the **_try** block is executed

```
if(StartQuery()) {
   BlankDoc();
   return(1);
   }
```

and if any fatal error occurs (such as a protection fault), the **_except** block following it is executed. Say, for instance, that we had a wild pointer somewhere in **StartQuery**. At the point where the wild pointer caused a protection fault, our program would stop executing and "blow out" to some operating-system error handler. Under normal circumstances, that operating-system error handler would put up a dialog box saying "general protection fault" or some such message. But because we've surrounded that error with a **_try** block, instead of executing the dialog box, the operating system will instead execute our **_except** block. So when our wild pointer faults, the next statement to run in our program will be

```
BlankDoc();
```

BlankDoc, shown in Listing 3.2, simply prints a tiny HTML stream stating that there's been an error. **ShowException**, also shown in Listing 3.2, logs the exception to our error log.

Listing 3.2 BlankDoc and ShowException.

```
/* BlankDoc - print out an HTML error message that says the
system is having internal difficulties.
*/
void BlankDoc() {
   printf( "<HTML><BODY><P>Due to technical difficulties,\n" );
   printf( "the system is currently unavailable.\n" );
   printf( "Please try again later\n</P></BODY></HTML>\n" );
   }

/* ShowException - An operating-system-level exception has
occurred.  Report it to stderr. */
void ShowException() {
        char szdate[256];
        char sztime[256];
```

```
        _strdate( szdate );
        _strtime( sztime );

    // display error information from SQLCA
    fprintf(errfp,"%s - %s - exception with QUERY_STRING=%s\n",
      szdate, sztime, getenv( "QUERY_STRING" ) );
  }
```

If the exception occurs while we're running the query itself, we print a slightly wordier HTML document. If the exception happens after we've already run the query, we simply log it, without displaying an error message on the user's browser. Why? Because, for one thing, the query succeeded. More importantly, though, the HTML document describing the results of the query has already been sent to the user's browser at that point. The channel to the browser is not "open" anymore because we've already sent the </HTML> tag, which ends our results document.

SQL Errors

Most implementations of embedded SQL allow you to set up a function that will be called automatically whenever there is an SQL error. This is a neat feature, as all SQL errors have certain things in common, including the SQL error code and SQL error message, that we might want to do something with.

In globals.sqc, we define a function called **ErrorHandler** that reports all the things that might help us in debugging. For our implementation, these include application-specific information like the names of the server, database, table, and CGI directory, as well as generic SQL information like the error code and error message. Listing 3.3 shows **ErrorHandler**.

Listing 3.3 Our SQL error-handler function.

```
/* ErrorHandler -  Called on Embedded SQL for C error,
displays fields from SQLCA. */
void ErrorHandler (void)
{
      EXEC SQL BEGIN DECLARE SECTION;
      char dumplog[81];
      EXEC SQL END DECLARE SECTION;
```

```
        extern char insertstmt[];
        extern char inputline[];
        char szdate[256];
        char sztime[256];

        _strdate( szdate );
        _strtime( sztime );

    // display error information from SQLCA
    fprintf(errfp,"%s - %s - SQL Error Handler called.\n",
      szdate, sztime );
    fprintf(errfp,"\tSQL Code = %li\n", SQLCODE);
    fprintf(errfp,"\tSQL Server Message %li:'%Fs'\n",
      SQLERRD1, SQLERRMC);
    fprintf(errfp,"\tQUERY_STRING=%s\n",getenv("QUERY_STRING"));
    fprintf(errfp,
       "\tservername %s\n\tserverdatabase %s\n\tusername \
        %s\n\tdbname %s\n\ttblname %s\n\tdocumentbase %s\n",
        servername,
        serverdatabase,
        username,
        dbname,
        tblname,
        documentbase );

   if( SQLCODE == -1105L ) {
      fprintf( errfp, "Transaction log is full.  \
                     Dumping transaction with NO_LOG!\n" );
      sprintf( dumplog, "DUMP TRANSACTION NEWF WITH NO_LOG" );
      EXEC SQL EXECUTE IMMEDIATE :dumplog;
      }

}
```

The first thing we do is grab the date and time via **_strdate** and **_strtime** (both Microsoft-specific nonportables), and report that. Then we deal with the three SQL error indicators—**SQLCODE**, which is just a negative integer error code, **SQLERRD1**, the positive version of **SQLCODE**, and **SQLERRMC**, a text message explaining the error.

The variables **servername**, **serverdatabase**, **username**, **dbname**, **tblname**, and **documentbase** are all global variables that are set in **main** and **SetArguments**. Most of them are set to a value that comes from hidden

<INPUT> elements in our HTML query form. They determine, in general, where the components of our system are located. For example, on my internal LAN, these variables have the following values:

documentbase=http://katie	A base URL to which all relative URLs generated by the CGI program can be appended.
servername=katie	Our server's DNS name.
dbname=NEWF	The SQL Server database name.
serverdatabase=katie.NEWF	A simple concatenation of servername and dbname.
tblname=SHORTDOG	The name of the table within the db.
username=webuser	The name of the database user. Defined by the database administrator.

We talked about the environment variable QUERY_STRING back in Chapter 2. The value here determines the type of query we're trying to run. Thus, in our error log, we've reported what the CGI program was trying to do, and the structure of the system it was trying to work within.

The last bit of code in **ErrorHandler** is also worth looking at. Remember back in Chapter 1 we talked about how SQL Server logs all transactions? In Chapter 2, we created a log device to hold these transaction log records. That device has a fixed size. If we simply insert records into the database without ever checkpointing, our log device will overflow, generating an SQL error with error code 1105. From that point on, inserts and updates will always fail with SQLCODE=-1105. For now, it will suffice to say that we need to free up some log device space, and the way to do that is to dump the transaction log.

How does **ErrorHandler** ever get invoked? Let's take a walk through the code, starting at **main**, and find out. In Listing 3.1, **main** calls a function called **StartQuery** to set up the system to run a query. Listing 3.4 shows the source for **StartQuery**.

Listing 3.4 StartQuery sets up SQL error-handling.

```
/* StartQuery -
      Open a log file
      Process the incoming arguments
```

```
      Output an HTML header so the browser doesn't timeout.
      Connect to the database.
   return 0 if successful, 1 if error
*/
int StartQuery() {
   int nRet;           // for return values
   int i, j;

   /* The log must be open before any SQL statements
      are called since they report to errfp. */
   FILE *fp = NULL;
   fp = fopen( "newfq.log", "a+" );
   if( fp != NULL )
        errfp = fp;

   // install Embedded SQL for C error handler
   EXEC SQL WHENEVER SQLERROR CALL ErrorHandler();
   // set Embedded SQL for C options
   EXEC SQL SET OPTION LOGINTIME 10;
   EXEC SQL SET OPTION QUERYTIME 100;

   /* These are simply defaults for variables that
   should be set via hidden fields in the form.  */
   sprintf( servername, "katie" );
   sprintf( username, "sa" );
   sprintf( dbname, "newf" );
   sprintf( tblname, "shortdog" );
   sprintf( documentbase, "http://katie" );
   // hack
   sprintf( cgi_directory, "/cgi-bin" );
   //      sprintf( cgi_directory, "/newf" );

   // Read the incoming arguments and set global vars.
   SetArguments();

   sprintf( query_args,
    "server=%s&user=%s&db=%s&tbl=%s&base=%s",
     servername, username, dbname, tblname,documentbase );
   sprintf( serverdatabase, "%s.%s", servername, dbname );

   // Write out HTML and HEADER tags.
   StartDoc( table_caption );

   // Write out a BODY tag.
   sprintf( buffer, "%s/images/background.jpg", documentbase);
```

```
StartBody( "blue", "magenta", "red", "black", buffer );

// Write out a 1st-level header tag.
Header( 1, table_caption );

// Check if this is an invalid partial search.
if( QueryType == BY_NAME_PARTIAL
        && strlen( sought_name ) < 6 )
   {   return( 0 );   }


// attempt connection to SQL Server
EXEC SQL CONNECT TO :serverdatabase
     USER :username;
if (SQLCODE == 0)
   {
   // fprintf(errfp,
   //     "Connection to SQL Server established\n");
   }
else
   {
   // problem connecting to SQL Server
   ErrorMsg();
   fprintf(errfp,
       "ERROR: Connection to SQL Server failed\n");
   return (1);
   }
return( 0 );
}
```

StartQuery performs the following functions:

- Opens a log file for our application.
- Sets up SQL to call **ErrorHandler** on any SQL error.
- Processes the incoming arguments from either QUERY_STRING or standard input.
- Outputs the HTML code that starts our query results document.
- Opens a connection to the database.

As you can see in Listing 3.4, we open a file called newfq.log to hold our debugging output. Then we make three embedded SQL statements:

- The SET OPTION statements simply set reasonable timeouts for logging in, and for queries.
- The WHENEVER statement sets up **ErrorHandler**.
- The CONNECT TO statement at the bottom of **StartQuery** generates the C source code shown in Listing 3.5.

Listing 3.5 The generated C source for the CONNECT statement.

```
sqlastrt((void far *)pid, (void far *)0,
   (struct tag_sqlca far *)sqlca);
sqlaaloc(2, 2, 3, (void far *)0);
sqlasetv(2, 0, 462, (unsigned short)strlen(serverdatabase),
     (void far *)serverdatabase, (void far *)0, (void far *)0L);
sqlasetv(2, 1, 462, (unsigned short)strlen(username),
    (void far *)username, (void far *)0, (void far *)0L);
sqlxcall(30, 3, 2, 0, 46,
   (char far *)"  CONNECT TO @p1              USER @p2     ");
if(sqlca->sqlcode < 0) {
   sqlastop((void far *)0L);
   ErrorHandler()  ;
   }
```

The C source is all generated by the single CONNECT statement. Notice the call to **ErrorHandler**. That's the result of our WHENEVER statement. The embedded SQL preprocessor generates the **if** block (**sqlca->sqlcode** will be negative if there's an error), and inserts the call to **ErrorHandler** because we specified it in a WHENEVER statement. Thus, if the call to **sqlxcall** sets **sqlca->sqlcode** to a negative number, **ErrorHandler** gets invoked.

Moving down in **StartQuery**, we've already talked a lot about **SetArguments**, so I'll leave that alone for now. **StartDoc**, **StartBody**, and **Header** are all functions in our library of HTML creation functions, which we'll talk about a little later. Each prints one or more HTML tags to stdout.

Finally, we come to an actual bit of interaction with the database, the CONNECT statement. Earlier in the function, we created a database name (**serverdatabase**) by combining the servername and the database name.

Here, we tell ESQL to open a connection to that database, returning 0 if it works and 1 if there's an error.

Our program is now set up to run a query. We've configured the parameters of the query via **SetArguments**, configured SQL via WHENEVER and SET OPTION, and opened a connection to the database that will service the query. We are now ready to run a query and deal with the results.

Querying The Database

Back in Listing 3.1, our **main** function split newfq's functionality into three chunks—**StartQuery**, **DoQuery**, and **EndQuery**. **StartQuery**, as we've just seen, leaves us on the edge of doing some useful work. Let's get to it.

DoQuery encompasses the heart of what this program is trying to accomplish. Within **DoQuery**, we run queries against the database and format the results into useable HTML. Listing 3.6 shows the source for **DoQuery**.

Listing 3.6 DoQuery counts the possible matches and prepares the HTML page for results.

```
/* DoQuery - All the arguments have been read, and all the
global variables defining what we must do have been set,
so now we can go and do the work.
*/
void DoQuery() {
   int i;
   int numrecords = 0;
   struct tm *today;
   time_t long_time;
   char *where_clause;

   char szdate[256];
   char sztime[256];

   // If this is a name-fragment search, make sure they've
   // provided at least 6 chars so we don't return the
   // entire database.
   if( QueryType == BY_NAME_PARTIAL && strlen(sought_name) < 6 ) {
      StartPara();
      printf( "<B>NAME FRAGMENT MUST BE GREATER THAN \
          6 CHARACTERS IN LENGTH.</B>\n" );
```

```
  EndPara();
  return;
  }

// Set the cursor type and declare a cursor
EXEC SQL SET CURSORTYPE CUR_BROWSE;
EXEC SQL DECLARE C1 CURSOR for stmt1;

// Save the information provided in CGI's
// environment variables, like REMOTE_HOST ...
SaveUserData();

// Setup the select command based on the initialized
// format string and the variable table name.
sprintf( select_cmd, select_cmd_fmt, tblname );

// Do a different query based on the value of QueryType
// which, of course, came from our search form.
switch( QueryType ) {
   case QUERY_UPDATE:
      strcat( select_cmd, " WHERE QUOTENO='" );
      strcat( select_cmd, QUOTENO );
      strcat( select_cmd, "'" );
      EXEC SQL PREPARE stmt1 FROM :select_cmd;
      EXEC SQL OPEN C1;
      EXEC SQL FETCH C1 INTO
         :NAME,:QUOTENO,:CHANGEDATE,:CHANGETEXT, :REGNO,
         :COUNTRY,:TITLES, :CHDATE, :JWOB, :JWDATE, :DOB,
         :DOB2, :SEX, :SNAME, :DNAME, :COLOUR, :RECESSIVE,
         :OWNER, :KENNEL, :BREEDER, :REMARKS, :HIPTOT,
         :HIPR, :HIPL, :DIED, :HDCERT, :HIPS, :OFANO,
         :OVCNO, :KCBVAEYE, :TATTOO, :HEARTGRADE, :SOURCE,
         :SB, :WORKAREA;

      FillInEntryTemplate();
      EXEC SQL CLOSE C1;
      return( 0 );
      break;
   case QUERY_INSERT:
      if( VerifyInput() == 0 ) {
         StartPara(); printf(
            "Record failed verification at item %s=%s.\n",
            failed_item, failed_data );
         printf( "Remember that only the following date \
               formats are supported:<BR>\n" );
```

```
    printf( "mm/yyyy (e.g. 12/1996 for December \
            1996)<BR>\n" );
    printf( "mm/dd/yyyy (e.g. 12/1/1996 for December \
            1996)<BR>\n" );
    printf( "mmm dd yyyy (e.g. Dec 1 1996 for December \
            1996)<BR>\n" );
    printf( "mmm dd yyyy hh:mmam/pm (e.g. Dec 1 1996 \
            09:01am)<BR>\n" );
    EndPara();
    fprintf(errfp,"ERROR: Can't save newdog record \
            failed at item %s=%s.\n",
       failed_item, failed_data );
    ErrorMsg();
    return( 0 );
    }
_strdate( szdate );
_strtime( sztime );

time(&long_time);
today = localtime( &long_time );
strftime( szdate, sizeof( szdate ),
   "%b %d %Y %I:%M:%S%p", today );
sprintf( dtime, "%s", szdate );
EXEC SQL BEGIN TRAN
INSERT INTO newdog VALUES ( :NAME,
 :QUOTENO, :dtime, :CHANGETEXT, :REGNO, :COUNTRY,
 :TITLES, :CHDATE, :JWOB, :JWDATE, :DOB,
 :DOB2, :SEX, :SNAME, :DNAME, :COLOUR,
 :RECESSIVE, :OWNER, :KENNEL, :BREEDER, :REMARKS,
 :HIPTOT, :HIPR, :HIPL, :DIED, :HDCERT,
 :HIPS, :OFANO, :OVCNO, :KCBVAEYE, :TATTOO,
 :HEARTGRADE, :SOURCE, :SB, :WORKAREA, :SRCADDRESS,
 :SRCEMAIL, :COMMENTS )
COMMIT TRAN;

if (SQLCODE == 0) {
   StartPara();
   printf( "%s %s, from %s, sired by %s in the year \
           %s has been successfully added to the database. \
           Hit your browser's <B>BACK</B> key to enter another
           record.\n",
   SEX[0]=='D'?"Dog":"Bitch", NAME, DNAME, SNAME, DOB2);
   EndPara();
   }
else {
```

```
      // problem connecting to SQL Server
      StartPara();
      printf( "Record failed verification.  \
               Hit your browser's <B>BACK</B> key to fix the
               problem.\n" );
      EndPara();
      fprintf(errfp,"ERROR: Can't save newdog record\n");
      ErrorHandler();
      }
   return( 0 );
   break;
case BY_KENNEL:
   strcat( select_cmd, " WHERE KENNEL='" );
   strcat( select_cmd, sought_name );
   strcat( select_cmd, "'" );
   break;
case BY_NAME:
   strcat( select_cmd, " WHERE NAME='" );
   strcat( select_cmd, sought_name );
   strcat( select_cmd, "'" );
   break;
case BY_SIRE:
   strcat( select_cmd, " WHERE SNAME='" );
   strcat( select_cmd, sought_name );
   strcat( select_cmd, "'" );
   break;
case BY_DAM:
   strcat( select_cmd, " WHERE DNAME='" );
   strcat( select_cmd, sought_name );
   strcat( select_cmd, "'" );
   break;
case QUERY_NEW:
   strcat( select_cmd,
      " WHERE CHANGEDATE>'May 1 1996 12:00AM'" );
   break;
case BY_NAME_PARTIAL:
   strcat( select_cmd, " WHERE " );
   if( strlen( country ) > 0 ) {
      strcat( select_cmd, " COUNTRY='" );
      strcat( select_cmd, country );
      strcat( select_cmd, "'" );
      strcat( select_cmd, " AND " );
      }
   strcat( select_cmd, " NAME LIKE '%" );
   strcat( select_cmd, sought_name );
```

```
        strcat( select_cmd, "%'" );
        break;
    case BY_PEDIGREE:
        StartUnorderedList();
        PedigreeSearch( sought_name );
        EndUnorderedList();
        return (0);
        break;
    }

    fprintf( errfp, "preparing: %s\n", select_cmd );
    if(( where_clause = strstr( select_cmd, " WHERE " ))
            == NULL ) {
        fprintf( errfp, "NO WHERE CLAUSE IN %s\n",select_cmd);
        return;
        }

// Count how many records in the shortdog table
// meet the criteria. If there are a large number
// of dogs that meet the criteria, this number
// will appear long before all the individual
// records, giving the user a chance to bail
// out of an over-long transaction.
sprintf( count_cmd, "SELECT COUNT (*) FROM %s %s",
    tblname, where_clause );
EXEC SQL DECLARE C2 CURSOR for count_stmt;
EXEC SQL PREPARE count_stmt FROM :count_cmd;
EXEC SQL OPEN C2;
EXEC SQL FETCH C2 INTO :verified_record_count;
fprintf( errfp, "verified_record_count = %d\n",
    verified_record_count );
EXEC SQL CLOSE C2;

// Do the same count for the newdog table
sprintf( count_cmd, "SELECT COUNT (*) FROM %s %s", "newdog",
    where_clause );
EXEC SQL PREPARE count_stmt FROM :count_cmd;
EXEC SQL OPEN C2;
EXEC SQL FETCH C2 INTO :unverified_record_count;
EXEC SQL CLOSE C2;

// Emit the HTML that displays the two counts.
// This will pop up in the user's browser the moment
// we send it.
```

```
StartPara();
printf( "Found %d verified and %d unverified records.",
   verified_record_count, unverified_record_count );
EndPara();

// If there are any records, tell the user
// how to use them.
if( verified_record_count > 0
     || unverified_record_count > 0 ) {
   Header( 2, "What to do on this page." );
   StartUnorderedList();
   printf( "<LI>Scroll right to see the rest \
            of the data.</LI>\n" );
   printf( "<LI>Click on the dog's name to see a chart with \
            %d generations of genealogy.</LI>\n", MAX_DEPTH );
   printf( "<LI>Click on the Dam or Sire to see its \
            individual record.</LI>\n" );
   printf( "<LI>Click on the Kennel to see all dogs from \
            that kennel.</LI>\n" );
   printf( "<LI>Click on the <B>U</B> button in the first \
            column to go to the data entry screen and update the
            record \for that dog.</LI>\n" );
   printf( "<LI>%s</LI>\n", jr_email_link );
   printf( "<LI>%s</LI>\n", rs_email_link );
   EndUnorderedList();
   printf( "<HR>\n" );
   }

// Emit the table of shortdog records
if( verified_record_count > 0 ) {
   Header( 2, "Verified Records" );
   Query(VERIFIED);
   }

// Emit the table of newdog records
if( unverified_record_count > 0 ) {
   Header( 2, "Unverified Records" );
   // now do the unverified records
   sprintf( select_cmd, select_cmd_fmt, "newdog" );
   strcat( select_cmd, " " );
   strcat( select_cmd, where_clause );
   Query(UNVERIFIED);
   }
}
```

The first substantive bits of code in **DoQuery** are the SQL cursor statements, **SET CURSORTYPE** and **DECLARE CURSOR**. As a bit of relational database background, cursors are simply pointers into the database. A cursor is associated with a set of rows in the database. So for all the SELECT statements we want to run, there will be an associated cursor.

Let's skip for now the next two lumps of code in **DoQuery**—the call to **SaveUserData** and the **QUERY_UPDATE** case in our **QueryType** switch. Each will be explained in more detail later on.

Instead, let's look at the remainder of the cases in our **QueryType** switch. Each case appends a different WHERE clause onto an existing SELECT statement, **select_cmd**. This variable has been loaded right above the switch with the value of **select_cmd**, shown in Listing 3.7.

Listing 3.7 The initial value of select_cmd_fmt, from which a SELECT statement is constructed.

```
char select_cmd_fmt[] = "select \
      NAME, QUOTENO, CHANGEDATE, CHANGETEXT, REGNO, \
      COUNTRY, TITLES, CHDATE, JWOB, JWDATE, \
      DOB, DOB2, SEX, SNAME, DNAME, \
      COLOUR, RECESSIVE, OWNER, KENNEL, BREEDER, \
      REMARKS, HIPTOT, HIPR, HIPL, DIED, \
      HDCERT, HIPS, OFANO, OVCNO, KCBVAEYE, \
      TATTOO, HEARTGRADE, SOURCE, SB, WORKAREA \
         from %s ";
```

When we load the first part of **select_cmd** with **select_cmd_fmt**, we also insert the name of the table we're selecting against. Remember that **tbl** is one of the values that is tucked into a hidden <INPUT> element in our search form. So when we hit any of the cases in the **QueryType** switch, **select_cmd** looks something like this:

```
select NAME, QUOTENO, .... SB, WORKAREA from shortdog
```

Each case (except for **QUERY_UPDATE**) then appends a more or less complicated WHERE clause onto this base SELECT statement. When we exit the switch, the important fact is that we have a valid SQL SELECT statement in **select_cmd**. As an example, let's say the user specified an exact-name search on the dog "Stormwatchs Yacht Katrina". When we exit the switch, **select_cmd** will be set to:

```
select NAME, QUOTENO, .... SB, WORKAREA from shortdog where NAME=
      'Stormwatchs Yacht Katrina'
```

Right after exiting the switch, we do an interesting thing. We pluck that carefully constructed WHERE clause back out of **select_cmd**, and construct another SELECT statement with it. This SELECT statement takes the following form:

```
select count(*) from <table> where <where_clause>
```

And there are two instances of this statement, one for the SHORTDOG table and one for the NEWDOG table. What we're trying to do is generate a count of the records that match our SELECT statement, so that, long before they see any actual result data, users can know that the system has found something for them. This is one of the ways that we can increase the amount of time users are willing to wait for results. If they know that something is forthcoming, they'll wait longer to see it through.

The entire sequence—DECLARE, PREPARE, OPEN, FETCH, CLOSE—is all dedicated to getting that single value, the count of records matching the SELECT. You can think of a cursor as a variable SELECT statement. Like any variable, you have to DECLARE it, and to use it, you have to initialize it, via PREPARE.

When we OPEN the cursor, SQL Server builds a temporary table containing the set of rows described by the SELECT statement. We then get the values of an individual row from the cursor by using FETCH. And finally, we close the cursor via CLOSE. Once we have our counts, we output an HTML paragraph describing these counts, using **StartPara** and **EndPara**.

Here we've used cursors to retrieve the count of matching rows, but cursors are actually much more capable than simply as single-row SELECT mechanisms. They are actually more like full-fledged database tables. You can update, delete, and insert against cursors, and these actions will be reflected back against the tables that the cursor selected from.

DoQuery encompasses all the queries, but they don't actually happen there. Most of our queries (again, except **QUERY_UPDATE**) occur within the function **Query**, shown in Listing 3.8.

Listing 3.8 Query runs the query and emits the records found as HTML.

```
/* Query - Run the actual query to retrieve data
from the db and emit HTML results based on that
data.
*/
void Query(int style) {
   int i = 0;
   int numcolumns;

   // Prepare the statement and open a cursor
   EXEC SQL PREPARE stmt1 FROM :select_cmd;
   EXEC SQL OPEN C1;

   // Records from shortdog (VERIFIED) have one more
   // field (the update button) than records from
   // newdog. This sets up an array of table column
   // data fields for our HTML output function to use.
   // The HTML row output function uses the values
   // in the variables pointed to by the cols array
   // to fill in the table. So here, we set up the
   // array to point to our host variables.
   if( style == VERIFIED )
      cols[i++] = update_link;
   cols[i++] = plink;
   cols[i++] = description;
   cols[i++] = headstone;
   cols[i++] = slink;
   cols[i++] = dlink;
   cols[i++] = BREEDER;
   cols[i++] = OWNER;
   cols[i++] = REGNO;
   cols[i++] = COUNTRY;
   cols[i++] = TITLES;
   cols[i++] = CHDATE;
   cols[i++] = JWOB;
   cols[i++] = JWDATE;
   cols[i++] = DOB2;
   cols[i++] = RECESSIVE;
   cols[i++] = kennel_link;
   cols[i++] = REMARKS;
   cols[i++] = HIPTOT;
   cols[i++] = HIPR;
   cols[i++] = HIPL;
```

```
cols[i++] = DOB;
cols[i++] = DIED;
cols[i++] = HDCERT;
cols[i++] = HIPS;
cols[i++] = OFANO;
cols[i++] = OVCNO;
cols[i++] = KCBVAEYE;
cols[i++] = TATTOO;
cols[i++] = HEARTGRADE;
cols[i++] = SOURCE;
cols[i++] = SB;
cols[i++] = WORKAREA;
cols[i++] = CHANGEDATE;
cols[i++] = CHANGETEXT;
cols[i++] = SEX;
cols[i++] = COLOUR;
cols[i++] = QUOTENO;
numcolumns = i;

// Make all column data centered.
for( i = 0; i < MAX_COLUMNS; i++ )
   alignments[i] = "CENTER";

// Go through all the rows, fetching the data
// and outputting HTML to represent it.
rownum = 0;
while (1) {
   EXEC SQL FETCH C1 INTO
      :NAME :null_NAME,
      :QUOTENO :null_QUOTENO,
      :CHANGEDATE :null_CHANGEDATE,
      :CHANGETEXT :null_CHANGETEXT,
      :REGNO :null_REGNO,
      :COUNTRY :null_COUNTRY,
      :TITLES :null_TITLES,
      :CHDATE :null_CHDATE,
      :JWOB :null_JWOB,
      :JWDATE :null_JWDATE,
      :DOB :null_DOB,
      :DOB2 :null_DOB2,
      :SEX :null_SEX,
      :SNAME :null_SNAME,
      :DNAME :null_DNAME,
      :COLOUR :null_COLOUR,
      :RECESSIVE :null_RECESSIVE,
```

```
    :OWNER :null_OWNER,
    :KENNEL :null_KENNEL,
    :BREEDER :null_BREEDER,
    :REMARKS :null_REMARKS,
    :HIPTOT :null_HIPTOT,
    :HIPR :null_HIPR,
    :HIPL :null_HIPL,
    :DIED :null_DIED,
    :HDCERT :null_HDCERT,
    :HIPS :null_HIPS,
    :OFANO :null_OFANO,
    :OVCNO :null_OVCNO,
    :KCBVAEYE :null_KCBVAEYE,
    :TATTOO :null_TATTOO,
    :HEARTGRADE :null_HEARTGRADE,
    :SOURCE :null_SOURCE,
    :SB :null_SB,
    :WORKAREA :null_WORKAREA;

if (SQLCODE == 0) {
   strcpy( l_QUOTENO, QUOTENO );
// Create the headstone - born/died
if( NullDate( DOB, null_DOB ) && NullDate( DIED, null_DIED ))
   sprintf( headstone, "-" );
else {
   buffer[0] = '\0';
   buffer1[0] = '\0';
   if( NullDate( DOB, null_DOB ) == 0 ) {
      sprintf( buffer, DOB );
      if( strlen( buffer ) > 8 )
         buffer[strlen(buffer)-8] = '\0';
      }
   if( NullDate( DIED, null_DIED ) == 0 ) {
      sprintf( buffer1, DIED );
      if( strlen( buffer1 ) > 8 )
         buffer1[strlen(buffer1)-8] = '\0';
      }
   if( NullDate( DOB, null_DOB ) == 1 )
      sprintf( headstone, "Died %s", buffer1 );
   else {
      if( NullDate( DIED, null_DIED ) == 1 )
         sprintf( headstone, "%s", buffer );
      else
         sprintf( headstone, "%s to %s", buffer, buffer1 );
      }
```

```
   }
// End the headstone
if( strlen( NAME ) == 0 )
   sprintf( NAME, "-" );
if( NullString( COLOUR, null_COLOUR ) == 1 )
   sprintf( COLOUR, "-" );
else {
   if( strcmp(COLOUR,"WH&BL" ) == 0 )
      sprintf( color, "Landseer" );
   else
      sprintf( color, COLOUR );
   }
if( NullString( SEX, null_SEX ) == 1 )
   sprintf( SEX, "-" );
else {
   if( SEX[0] == 'D' )
      sprintf( description, "%s dog", color );
   else {
      if( SEX[0] == 'B' )
         sprintf( description, "%s bitch", color );
      else
         sprintf( description, "%s %c", color, SEX[0] );
      }
   }
if( strlen( headstone ) == 0 )
   sprintf( headstone, "-" );
if( strlen( slink ) == 0 )
   sprintf( slink, "-" );
if( strlen( dlink ) == 0 )
   sprintf( dlink, "-" );
if( NullString( BREEDER, null_BREEDER ) == 1 )
   sprintf( BREEDER, "-" );
if( NullString( OWNER, null_OWNER ) == 1 )
   sprintf( OWNER, "-" );
if( NullString( REGNO, null_REGNO ) == 1 )
   sprintf( REGNO, "-" );
if( NullString( COUNTRY, null_COUNTRY ) == 1 )
   sprintf( COUNTRY, "-" );
if( NullString( TITLES, null_TITLES ) == 1 )
   sprintf( TITLES, "-" );
if( NullDate( CHDATE, null_CHDATE ) == 1 )
   sprintf( CHDATE, "-" );
if( NullString( JWOB, null_JWOB ) == 1 )
   sprintf( JWOB, "-" );
if( NullDate( JWDATE, null_JWDATE ) == 1 )
```

```
    sprintf( JWDATE, "-" );
if( NullString( DOB2, null_DOB2 ) == 1 )
    sprintf( DOB2, "-" );
if( NullString( RECESSIVE, null_RECESSIVE ) == 1 )
    sprintf( RECESSIVE, "-" );
if( NullString( KENNEL, null_KENNEL ) == 1 ) {
    sprintf( KENNEL, "-" );
    sprintf( kennel_link, "-" );
    }
else
    {
    // If there's kennel data, make it a hyperlink to a
    // new query that brings up all records with that
    // kennel name.
    sprintf( buffer, KENNEL );
    for( i = 0; i < strlen( buffer ); i++ )
        if( buffer[i] == ' ' )
            buffer[i] = '+';
    sprintf( kennel_link, "<A HREF=\"%s%s/newfq.exe?\
            dog.text=%s&QueryType=Kennel&%s\">%s</A></P>",
        documentbase, cgi_directory, buffer,
         query_args,KENNEL );
    }
if( NullString( REMARKS, null_REMARKS ) == 1 )
    sprintf( REMARKS, "-" );
if( NullString( HIPTOT, null_HIPTOT ) == 1 )
    sprintf( HIPTOT, "-" );
if( NullString( HIPR, null_HIPR ) == 1 )
    sprintf( HIPR, "-" );
if( NullString( HIPL, null_HIPL ) == 1 )
    sprintf( HIPL, "-" );
if( NullDate( DOB, null_DOB ) == 1 )
    sprintf( DOB, "-" );
if( NullDate( DIED, null_DIED ) == 1 )
    sprintf( DIED, "-" );
if( NullString( HDCERT, null_HDCERT ) == 1 )
    sprintf( HDCERT, "-" );
if( NullString( HIPS, null_HIPS ) == 1 )
    sprintf( HIPS, "-" );
if( NullString( OFANO, null_OFANO ) == 1 )
    sprintf( OFANO, "-" );
if( NullString( OVCNO, null_OVCNO ) == 1 )
    sprintf( OVCNO, "-" );
if( NullString( KCBVAEYE, null_KCBVAEYE ) == 1 )
    sprintf( KCBVAEYE, "-" );
```

```
if( NullString( TATTOO, null_TATTOO ) == 1 )
   sprintf( TATTOO, "-" );
if( NullString( HEARTGRADE, null_HEARTGRADE ) == 1 )
   sprintf( HEARTGRADE, "-" );
if( NullString( SOURCE, null_SOURCE ) == 1 )
   sprintf( SOURCE, "-" );
if( NullString( SB, null_SB ) == 1 )
   sprintf( SB, "-" );
if( NullString( WORKAREA, null_WORKAREA ) == 1 )
   sprintf( WORKAREA, "-" );
if( NullDate( CHANGEDATE, null_CHANGEDATE ) == 1 )
   sprintf( CHANGEDATE, "-" );
if( NullString( CHANGETEXT, null_CHANGETEXT ) == 1 )
   sprintf( CHANGETEXT, "-" );
if( NullString( QUOTENO, null_QUOTENO ) == 1 )
   sprintf( QUOTENO, "-" );

// If there's name data, make it a hyperlink to a
// new query that brings up an update screen for that
// dog.
sprintf( update_link, "<A HREF=\"%s%s/newfq.exe?QUOTENO=%s&\
      QueryType=update&%s\"><IMG SRC=%s/images/update.jpg></A>",
   documentbase, cgi_directory, QUOTENO,
      query_args, documentbase );
// Use different column headings depending on whether
// we're using shortdog, or newdog records.
if( rownum == 0 ) {
   if( style == VERIFIED )
      StartTable( "", TRUE, numcolumns, colcaps );
   else
      StartTable( "", TRUE, numcolumns, &colcaps[1] );
   }
rownum++;
if( strlen( BREEDER ) == 0 )
   sprintf( BREEDER, "-" );

sprintf( buffer, NAME );
for( i = 0; i < strlen( buffer ); i++ )
   if( buffer[i] == ' ' )
      buffer[i] = '+';

// Create the pedigree query hyperlink.
if( style == VERIFIED )
   sprintf( plink, "<A HREF=\"%s%s/newfq.exe?dog.text=%s&\
      QueryType=Pedigree&%s\">%s</A></P>",
```

```
            documentbase, cgi_directory, buffer,query_args,NAME );
        else
            strcpy( plink, NAME );
        // Create the sire query hyperlink.
        sprintf( buffer, SNAME );
        for( i = 0; i < strlen( buffer ); i++ )
            if( buffer[i] == ' ' )
                buffer[i] = '+';
        sprintf( slink, "<A HREF=\"%s%s/newfq.exe?dog.text=%s&QueryType=
            Name&%s\">%s</A></P>",documentbase, cgi_directory,
            buffer,query_args,SNAME );
        // Create the dame query hyperlink.
        sprintf( buffer, DNAME );
        for( i = 0; i < strlen( buffer ); i++ )
            if( buffer[i] == ' ' )
                buffer[i] = '+';
        sprintf( dlink, "<A HREF=\"%s%s/newfq.exe?dog.text=%s&QueryType=
            Name&%s\">%s</A></P>",documentbase, cgi_directory, buffer,
            query_args,DNAME );

        // THIS CALL ACTUALLY EMITS THE HTML CORRESPONDING TO
        // THIS RECORD!
        AddRowNoWidth( numcolumns, cols, alignments );
        }
    else {
        if( SQLCODE == 100 ) {
            if( rownum == 0 ) {
                ShowNoRecords();
                }
            }
        else {
            ErrorMsg();
            fprintf( errfp, "bad fetch %d\n", SQLCODE );
            }
        break;
        }
    }
    if( rownum > 0 ) {
        EndTable();
        printf( "<HR>\n" );
        }
    else {
        // Emit two mailto: hyperlinks for mailing the
        // webmaster and data librarian.
        StartPara();
```

```
    printf( "%s<BR>%s\n", jr_email_link, rs_email_link );
    EndPara();
    }

  // Close cursor
  EXEC SQL CLOSE C1;
  }
```

We call **Query** twice from **DoQuery**, once to get all the records from shortdog (the verified records) and once to get all the records from NEWDOG (unverified records). Like our count statements, **Query's** select uses a cursor, the previously declared **C1**. We prepare **C1** using **select_cmd**, then open it, actually building the temporary table containing the selected data. So within the first two lines of an incredibly long function, we've already done most of the work of the function. The rest of the function is a huge **while** loop, fetching the rows of our temporary table into host variables that we can use to create our HTML output.

We haven't talked much about host variables yet, so it's probably worth going over right here. Listing 3.9 shows the top section of newfq.sqc, where all the global and host variables are declared.

Listing 3.9 Variable declarations in newfq.sqc.

```
#include <stddef.h>         // standard C run-time header
#include <stdio.h>          // standard C run-time header
#include <stdlib.h>
#include <io.h>
#include <fcntl.h>
#include "gcutil.h"         // utility header
#include "globals.h"
#include "html.h"
#include <string.h>
#include <time.h>
#include <ctype.h>
#include "db.h"

// GLOBAL VARIABLES

/* The maximum number of columns in our result table. */
#define MAX_COLUMNS 38
```

```
/* The depth of the pedigree chart.  MAX_DEPTH is the
number of generations which we will present in one screen.
Anything more than 5 is prohibitively expensive. */
#define MAX_DEPTH 5

/* This is the depth we're at now.  When this counter
hits MAX_DEPTH, the recursive chart record creation function
returns without recursing. */
   int current_depth = 0;

/* The months of the year.  Used to translate what the user
enters into something SQL Server will accept.  */
   typedef struct xxx {
      char *shortname;
      char *longname;
      } MONTHNAME;

   MONTHNAME months[12] = {
      { "Jan", "January"},
      { "Feb", "February" },
      { "Mar", "March" },
      { "Apr", "April" },
      { "May", "May" },
      { "Jun", "June" },
      { "Jul", "July" },
      { "Aug", "August" },
      { "Sep", "September" },
      { "Oct", "October" },
      { "Nov", "November" },
      { "Dec", "December" }
      };

/* These are the environment strings available to CGI programs.
We use some of them for usage tracking, others for debugging.  Our
debugging function ShowEnvStrings rolls through this array,
calling getenv with each of these as an argument.
*/
   char *envstrings[] = {
      "AUTH_TYPE",
      "CONTENT_LENGTH",
      "CONTENT_TYPE",
      "GATEWAY_INTERFACE",
      "HTTP_ACCEPT",
      "HTTP_REFERER",
      "HTTP_USER_AGENT",
```

```
        "PATH_INFO",
        "PATH_TRANSLATED",
        "QUERY_STRING",
        "REMOTE_ADDR",
        "REMOTE_HOST",
        "REMOTE_IDENT",
        "REMOTE_USER",
        "REQUEST_METHOD",
        "SCRIPT_NAME",
        "SERVER_NAME",
        "SERVER_PROTOCOL",
        "SERVER_PORT",
        "SERVER_SOFTWARE"
        };

/* This file is where we report errors.  Some Web servers redirect
stderr to their own log file.  We generally open our own log file
to use.
*/
   FILE *errfp = stderr;

/* This string is the actual data, from the data the user entered in
the form, which failed verification.
*/
   char *failed_data = NULL;

/* This is the name of the data item that failed verification. The
theory is that the user, given the data item name and the actual data,
can go back to the for and figure out which item was wrong and
how to fix it.
*/
   char *failed_item = NULL;

/* The base URL of all the HTML docs in this system. */
   char documentbase[1024];

/* The URL of the cgi directory for this application. */
   char cgi_directory[1024];

/* The level 1 header displayed in the table of results. */
   char table_caption[1024];

/* The anchor that links the kennel table cell to a new
   CGI query generating a table of dogs from one kennel. */
   char kennel_link[1024];
```

```
/* The anchor that links a dog's record to a CGI query
   allowing you to update the information in that record. */
   char update_link[1024];

/* This variable defines which type of HTML document we're going
to create. It is set to one of the following defines. */
   int QueryType;

// The types of queries.  Should be an enum.
#define BY_DAM 0   // Search for all dogs born of a particular mother
#define BY_SIRE 1   // Search for all dogs born of a particular father
#define BY_NAME 2   // Search for all dogs with a particular name
#define BY_KENNEL 3   // Search for all dogs from a particular kennel

// Search for all dogs whose name contains the fragment
#define BY_NAME_PARTIAL 4
#define BY_PEDIGREE   5      // Construct a pedigree tree for named dog
#define QUERY_INSERT   6   // Insert a new dog record in newdog table
#define QUERY_UPDATE   7   // Insert a record in newdog
#define QUERY_NEW   8      //

/* Here are anchor links to my email address, and the data
librarian's email address. These get inserted into various
HTML docs.*/
   char jr_email_link[] =
"<A HREF=\"mailto:john.rodley@channel1.com\">Click here</A> \
to email the db administrator (e.g. questions about the Web \
site).";
   char rs_email_link[] =
"<A HREF=\"mailto:101503.2063@Compuserve.com\">Click here</A> \
to email the data librarian (e.g. questions about the data \
itself).";

/* These are the headings that will appear as column heads on
the output HTML page. */
   char *colcaps[] = {
      "", "Name", "Description",  "----Lifespan----",
      "Sire", "Dam", "Breeder",
      "Owner", "REGNO", "Country",  "Titles",
      "CHDate", "JWOB", "JWDate",  "DOB2",
      "Recessive", "Kennel", "REMARKS",  "HIPTOT",
      "HIPR", "HIPL","DOB",  "DIED",
      "HDCERT", "HIPS", "OFANO",  "OVCNO",
      "KCBVAEYE", "TATTOO", "HEARTGRADE",  "SOURCE",
```

```
      "SB", "WORKAREA","CHANGEDATE",  "CHANGETEXT",
      "Sex", "Colour","QUOTENO"   };

/* We distinguish between verified records (those from the
shortdog table) and unverified records (those from newdog). */
#define VERIFIED 0
#define UNVERIFIED 1

// Function prototypes.
   void Query(int style);
   void ShowNoRecords();
   int NullString( char *szstring, int null_indicator );
   int NullDate( char *szdate, int null_indicator );
   void NormalizeName( char *OutputName, char *InputName );
   void PrintValue( char *name );
   int VerifyInput();
   int VerifyDate( char *item, char *origdata, int *pYr );
   int VerifyYear( char *szYear );
   int VerifyMonth( char *szMonth );
   int VerifyDay( char *szDay );
   void ShowEnvStrings();
   void SetArguments();
   int fileExists( int index );
   void PedigreeSearch( char *tname );
   void FillInEntryTemplate();
   char *FixedValue( char *buffer );
   void PostArguments();
   void ProcessArgs( char *qs );
   void StripChar( char *p, char c );

/* Here is the SQL select statement we use to retrieve either
shortdog or newdog records. */
   char select_cmd_fmt[] = "select \
      NAME, QUOTENO, CHANGEDATE, CHANGETEXT, REGNO, \
      COUNTRY, TITLES, CHDATE, JWOB, JWDATE, \
      DOB, DOB2, SEX, SNAME, DNAME, \
      COLOUR, RECESSIVE, OWNER, KENNEL, BREEDER, \
      REMARKS, HIPTOT, HIPR, HIPL, DIED, \
      HDCERT, HIPS, OFANO, OVCNO, KCBVAEYE, \
      TATTOO, HEARTGRADE, SOURCE, SB, WORKAREA \
         from %s ";

/* We save all the hidden <INPUT> element values in this
string in order to pass it on to other CGI queries. */
   char query_args[256];
```

```
/* The pedigree CGI query hyperlink. */
   char plink[1024];
/* The sire CGI query hyperlink. */
   char slink[1024];
/* The dame CGI query hyperlink. */
   char dlink[1024];

/* All-purpose buffers used for everything under the sun. */
   char buffer[2056];
   char buffer1[256];

/* We concatenate the dog's death date to his birth date
   in this field. */
   char headstone[1024];

/* Dog's description. */
   char description[256];

/* The dog's color, translated from db abbreviation. */
   char color[256];

/* Each item in this array contains the address of a host
   variable. The FETCH statement sets the value of the host
   variable, then this array is passed to the HTML row-
   creation function, which then runs through this array
   printing out the value of the host variables. */
   char *cols[MAX_COLUMNS];

/* The HTML width of the corresponding table column. */
   int colwidths[MAX_COLUMNS];
/* The alignment of the corresponding table column. */
   char *alignments[MAX_COLUMNS];

/* The row index within the FETCH. */
   int rownum = 0;

/* Now we begin the section of host variables--variables that
ESQL/C will use to store data retrieved from the database. */

EXEC SQL BEGIN DECLARE SECTION;

   char sought_name[1024];
   int id;
   char cmd[] = "select name, id from sysobjects where type='U'";
   char tcmd[] = "select name, type, length from syscolumns where id=?";
```

```
   char objname[256];
   char colname[256];
   int coltype;
   int collength;
   char label[31];


   /* These host variables are used to store dog, sire, and dame
   names as the pedigree search recurses through the db. */
   char temp_name[63];
   char temp_dam[63];
   char temp_sire[63];

/* Variables used for connecting to the database.
server, user, db, table.
*/
   char servername[(SQLID_MAX * 2)+2] = "";
   char serverdatabase[(SQLID_MAX * 2)+2] = "";
   char username[(SQLID_MAX * 2)+2] = "";
   char dbname[(SQLID_MAX * 2)+2] = "";
   char tblname[(SQLID_MAX * 2)+2] = "";

/* The country selected in the name-fragment search
   where you give a dog's name fragment and his
   country.  Usually "any".
*/
   char country[(SQLID_MAX * 2)+2] = "";

/* Number of records retrieved from the shortdog table. */
   int verified_record_count = 0;
/* Number of records retrieved from the newdog table. */
   int unverified_record_count = 0;

/* This is where the actual select statement gets built.*/
   char select_cmd[4192];
/* This is where the count(*) select statement gets built.*/
   char count_cmd[4192];

/* These are null-indicators for each of the possible
   fields selected. */
   int null_NAME, null_QUOTENO, null_CHANGEDATE;
   int null_CHANGETEXT, null_REGNO, null_COUNTRY;
   int null_TITLES, null_CHDATE, null_JWOB;
   int null_JWDATE, null_DOB, null_DOB2;
   int null_SEX, null_SNAME, null_DNAME;
```

```
   int null_COLOUR, null_RECESSIVE, null_OWNER;
   int null_KENNEL, null_BREEDER, null_REMARKS;
   int null_HIPTOT, null_HIPR, null_HIPL;
   int null_DIED, null_HDCERT, null_HIPS;
   int null_OFANO, null_OVCNO, null_KCBVAEYE;
   int null_TATTOO, null_HEARTGRADE, null_SOURCE;
   int null_SB, null_WORKAREA, null_SRCADDRESS;
   int null_SRCEMAIL, null_COMMENTS;

   char l_QUOTENO[8];

/* These are the host variables that values are actually
   fetched into, one for each field in shortdog/newdog. */
   char NAME[63];
   char FAMILIAR[63];
   char SITE[63];
   char QUOTENO[8];
   char CHANGEDATE[27];
   char CHANGETEXT[101];
   char REGNO[31];
   char COUNTRY[21];
   char TITLES[41];
   char CHDATE[27];
   char JWOB[31];
   char JWDATE[27];
   char DOB[27];
   char DOB2[13];
   char SEX[2];
   char SNAME[63];
   char DNAME[63];
   char COLOUR[41];
   char RECESSIVE[41];
   char OWNER[63];
   char KENNEL[31];
   char BREEDER[63];
   char REMARKS[201];
   char HIPTOT[4];
   char HIPR[3];
   char HIPL[3];
   char DIED[27];
   char HDCERT[2];
   char HIPS[26];
   char OFANO[16];
   char OVCNO[16];
```

```
   char KCBVAEYE[11];
   char TATTOO[16];
   char HEARTGRADE[10];
   char SOURCE[31];
   char SB[5];
   char WORKAREA[21];
   char SRCADDRESS[1024];
   char SRCEMAIL[41];
   char URL[1024];
   char COMMENTS[8192];

/* Used to build dates for database insertion. */
   char dtime[512];
EXEC SQL END DECLARE SECTION;
```

We've talked about some of the global variables already, and we'll cover the rest of them as they occur in the source. The host variables are all the variables declared within these lines:

```
EXEC SQL BEGIN DECLARE SECTION;
EXEC SQL END DECLARE SECTION;
```

Any variable that is used directly in an SQL statement must be declared as a host variable. If we look back at the CONNECT statement from **StartQuery**:

```
EXEC SQL CONNECT TO :serverdatabase
       USER :username;
```

SQL Server uses the values from the host variables **serverdatabase** and **username** as the database and user to connect to. For our SELECT statements, we need a host variable for each field that we're going to FETCH a value into, thus the long list of variables corresponding to the **shortdog** and **newdog** fields.

Another interesting set of host variables are those with the **null_** prefix. Back in Chapter 2, we declared many of the fields in our database as "allowing null." This is the default for a field definition in a CREATE TABLE statement. What "allowing null" means in practice is that there is a second place to check for the value of a field.

For example, the FETCH statement in **Query** specifies pairs of host variables for every field. For the **NAME** field, we FETCH into the host variables **NAME** and **null_NAME**. If **null_NAME** is set to 1, then the field is considered null. When we FETCH, if the null indicator is set, then there's no valid value in the corresponding field-value host variable.

Query is a very long function, but much of it is pretty repetitive. The FETCH statement goes into the cursor's temporary table and puts the field values into the host variable and the null indicator.

After we've fetched the field values, the remainder of the function is dedicated to deciding how to display those values in HTML. For most of the values, we simply check whether the value is null, via both the null indicator and the string length. For us, a zero-length string has the same meaning as a null value, so we check both, and set our string to the single character "-":

```
if( NullString( QUOTENO, null_QUOTENO ) == 1 )
        sprintf( QUOTENO, "-" );
```

If the field isn't null, we usually just leave our display string as whatever is in the host variable. (Remember that earlier we loaded our array of display strings with pointers to our host variables.)

Creating HTML On The Fly

We've followed the execution trail of newfq.exe all the way to the point where we've got a set of C strings loaded with values from the database. This is probably as good a time as any to look at the process of creating the HTML output that brings the results up on our user's browser.

Earlier, we glossed over several spots where we already started sending data back to the browser. The first instance of this was the call **StartStream** from our main function. **StartStream**, shown in Listing 3.10, is part of our HTML output module.

Listing 3.10 StartStream letting the browser know we're here.

```
/* StartStream - Tell the browser we're sending back HTML. */
void StartStream() {
   printf( "Content-type: text/html\n\n");
   }
```

What we're really outputting is not strictly an HTML stream, but an HTTP protocol stream—and this content-type is an HTTP header. HTTP allows a number of different headers, some of which we'll discuss later, but for now, content-type is the most important. Here, we're telling the browser that what's coming back is HTML.

Why do we execute this as the first line of our program? Why not group it back with the rest of the output code? We have to respond with this line within a certain amount of time or the browser will time out waiting for it. Once we've sent this line, we have a tight grip on the browser. It will wait for us forever. This is important. We have a number of points in the code where we might conceivably waste time that could time us out, so getting this line out first protects us. The line of text itself *must* be followed by a blank line. This terminates the HTTP header.

After StartStream, the next bit of HTML output is the call to **StartDoc** in **DoQuery**. **StartDoc**, shown in Listing 3.11, simply opens an HTML document and outputs a complete header element, which sets the title to whatever we've supplied as a title argument.

Listing 3.11 StartDoc begins our HTML results document.

```
/* Start the HTML document, printing a header, and leaving
the HTML element (but not body) open. */
void StartDoc( char *title ) {
   printf( "\n" );
   printf( "<HTML><HEAD><TITLE>%s</TITLE></HEAD>\n", title );
   }
```

Our document title, **table_caption**, was set for us way back in **ProcessArgs**, when we decided what kind of query we'd do, and what dog or dogs we'd be searching for. For a straight query-by-name or -name-fragment, the title will usually simply be the dog's name or name fragment.

The next bit of HTML, **StartBody**, comes up immediately after **StartDoc**. In **StartBody**, shown in Listing 3.12, we set the colors of all the HTML anchor types (VLINK, ALINK, and LINK) as well as the background image.

Listing 3.12 StartBody opens a body element.

```
/* Start the body of the HTML document, specifying the color for
all the link types as well as the background image. */
void StartBody( char *vlinkColor, char *alinkColor,
   char *linkColor, char *textColor, char *szFileBackground ) {
   printf( "<BODY VLINK=\"%s\" ALINK=\"%s\" LINK=\"%s\" \
      TEXT=\"%s\" BACKGROUND=\"%s\">\n",
        vlinkColor, alinkColor, linkColor, textColor,
           szFileBackground );
   }
```

We use a bland, light, mottled background JPEG image in a file called background.jpg. This small image will be repeated endlessly over the entire background of the document. Right after **StartBody**, we call **Header**, shown in Listing 3.13, which puts out a complete HTML header element using the specified text.

Listing 3.13 Header puts a heading in our HTML document.

```
/* Header - put out an HTML header at the specified level,
using the specified text. */
void Header( int level, char *text ) {
   printf( "<H%d>%s</H%d>\n", level, text, level );
   }
```

We can specify any level for our header, from 1 to *n*. This will determine the font used for the header—the smaller the number, the bigger the font. For our application, the header text will be the same as the document title, i.e. the dog's name. Note that the header element is complete, that is, it includes the start tag, <H1>, and end tag, </H1>. When **Header** exits, it does not leave its element open. After the call to **StartBody**, though, we do have two open elements in our HTML stream—<HTML> and <BODY>. These will eventually have to be closed with end tags.

The next bits of HTML output, ignoring the **QUERY_UPDATE** case for now, are the verified and unverified record counts. Though we could easily get fancier, we output both of these as simple sentences within a paragraph element via **StartPara** and **EndPara**, shown in Listing 3.14. No mystery to either of these.

Listing 3.14 StartPara and EndPara encapsulate a paragraph.

```
/* StartPara - Begin a paragraph element with a P tag. */
void StartPara() { printf( "<P>\n" ); }
/* EndPara - End a paragraph element with a /P tag. */
void EndPara() { printf( "</P>\n" ); }
```

The next bit of HTML output comes when we get down to **Query**, where we march through the cursor's temporary table of selected rows. After we've decided how to represent all the data values (in **Query**) on the screen, the following code snippet begins the HTML <TABLE> element that will hold the rows of result data:

```
// Use different column headings depending on whether
      // we're using shortdog, or newdog records.
      if( rownum == 0 ) {
         if( style == VERIFIED )
            StartTable( "", TRUE, numcolumns, colcaps );
         else
            StartTable( "", TRUE, numcolumns, &colcaps[1] );
         }
```

Remember that **Query** gets called twice, once for verified records, and once for unverified. We display different column headings depending on whether the records are verified or not. Listing 3.15 shows how StartTable opens up a <TABLE> element.

Listing 3.15 StartTable opens up a <TABLE> element.

```
/* StartTable - Open up a TABLE element, label it with the
supplied caption, and print out all the specified
column headings. */
void StartTable( char *caption, int bBorder,
                      int numcols, char **colcaps ) {
   int i;
   printf( "<TABLE %s ALIGN=\"CENTER\"><CAPTION><B>%s</B>\
     </CAPTION>\n", bBorder?"BORDER=\"BORDER\"":"", caption );
   for( i = 0; i < numcols; i++ )
      printf( "<TH>%s</TH>\n", colcaps[i] );
   }
```

The <TABLE> tag itself is unremarkable. It describes a table centered within the browser page that, according to the **bBorder** argument, may have a border around all the cells. It also provides the specified name as the table's caption. Of more interest are the column captions. We provide an array of strings to the function that defines the column headings. These headings can be seen back in Listing 3.9, where the elements of **colcaps** are set to appropriate values. Each column caption is contained in a table heading element, <TH></TH>.

At this point, we're in **Query** and we've fetched the first row of field values, where rownum==0. The table has been opened by **StartTable**. Our HTML output stream is now ready for a row of result data. We fetch the data into the host variables with the FETCH statement. Then, our call to **AddRowNoWidth**, shown in Listing 3.16, emits that row of result data as a row of the HTML table.

Listing 3.16 AddRowNoWidth outputs a row of field values.

```
/* AddRowNoWidth - Output a row of table data, where each cell
is NOT sized.  Run through the supplied column data printing it
with the attached alignment. */
void AddRowNoWidth( int numcols, char **coldata, char **align ) {
int i;

   printf( "<TR>" );
   for( i = 0; i < numcols; i++ )
      {
      if( align[i] != NULL )
         printf( "<TD COLSTART=\"%d\" ALIGN=\"%s\"><B>%s</B></TD>",
                    i, align[i], coldata[i] );
      else
         printf( "<TD COLSTART=\"%d\">%s</TD>", i, coldata[i] );
      }
   printf( "</TR>\n" );
   }
```

Any HTML table row is made up of a number of elements. The outermost is the table row element, denoted by the <TR></TR> tags. Within the table row element, you can have any number of table data elements enclosed in <TD></TD> tags. The table data element is your actual table cell. At long last, we're right at the spot where result data gets sent to the user's browser.

Our table-data cell has a start number (**COLSTART=*X***) which usually goes from 1 to **numcolumns**. We can align the data within the cell too, using the ALIGN attribute. Most of our cells will be centered. Finally, the actual field data comes as the last item in the table data element. When we break out of the FETCH loop, we end the table with an **EndTable** call. Eventually, in **EndQuery** (Listing 3.17), we close both the open <BODY> and <HTML> elements with **EndBody** and **EndDoc**.

Listing 3.17 EndQuery, EndBody, and EndDoc finish off our conversation with the browser.

```
/* EndQuery - End the current query, closing the BODY and
HTML elements, disconnecting from the db and closing the log. */
void EndQuery() {
    EndBody();
    EndDoc();
    // disconnect from SQL Server
    EXEC SQL DISCONNECT ALL;
        if( errfp != stderr && errfp != NULL )
                fclose( errfp );
    return;
}
/* Close a BODY element. */
void EndBody() {
   printf( "</BODY>\n" );
   }
/* EndDoc - Close the HTML element. */
void EndDoc() {
   printf( "</HTML>\n" );
   }
```

An Example Search

Talk is all well and good, but seeing the program in action is better. Let's look at an example from beginning to end, starting with entering search criteria at a data-entry screen, examining the variables that pass through the system, and finally viewing the HTML output in source and browser form.

Figure 3.1 shows our name-fragment search screen, with a dog's name filled in. When the user clicks the Search button, we end up with the set of name-value pairs shown in Table 3.2.

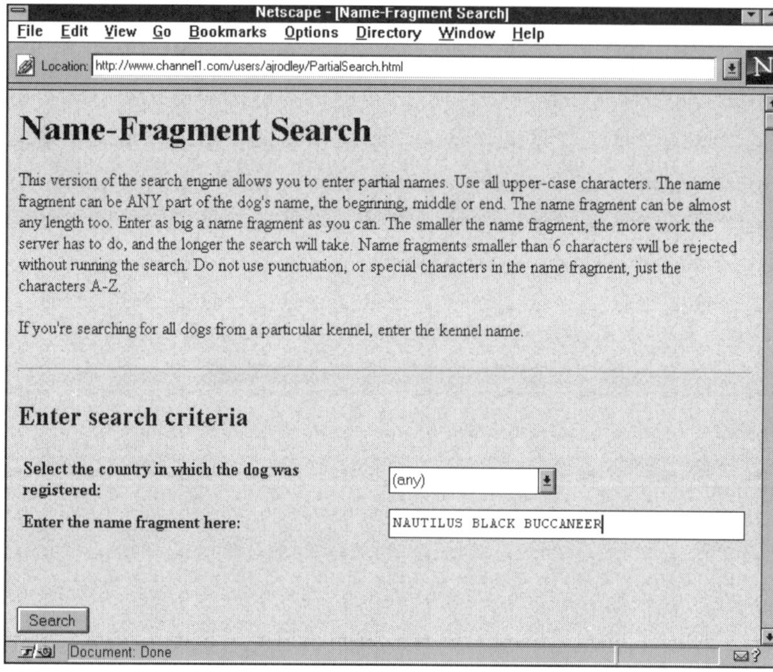

Figure 3.1 Name-fragment search with name filled in.

The important value, from the user's point of view, is **dog.text**, set to the value entered in the search screen. Pressing the Search button causes us to request the CGI URL from the Web server. The Web server launches the CGI program. When the CGI program comes up, it sees the environment set up as in Table 3.3.

Table 3.2 The name-value pairs set from Figure 3.1.

Name	Value
QueryType	Name
dog.text	NAUTILUS+BLACK+BUCCANEER
server	katie
user	webuser
db	newf
tbl	shortdog
base	http://katie

Table 3.3 The environment variables from Figure 3.1.

Variable Name	Value
REQUEST_TYPE	GET
QUERY_STRING	QueryType=Name&dog.text=NAUTILUS+BLACK+BUCCANEER&db=newf&tbl=shortdog&server=katie&base=http://katie&user=webuser

The CGI program takes QUERY_STRING apart in **ProcessArgs**, then goes off to find the dog's record in the specified database table on the specified machine. When the query is done, the CGI program outputs the HTML source code shown in Listing 3.18.

Listing 3.18 The HTML output of the search shown in Figure 3.1.

```
<HTML><HEAD><TITLE>NAUTILUS BLACK BUCCANEER</TITLE></HEAD>
<BODY VLINK="blue" ALINK="magenta" LINK="red" TEXT="black"
BACKGROUND="http://katie/images/background.jpg">
<H1>NAUTILUS BLACK BUCCANEER</H1>
<P>
Found 1 verified and 5 unverified records.</P>
<H2>What to do on this page.</H2>
<UL>
<LI>Scroll right to see the rest of the data.</LI>
<LI>Click on the dog's name to see a chart with 5
generations of genealogy.</LI>
<LI>Click on the Dam or Sire to see its individual record.</LI>
<LI>Click on the Kennel to see all dogs from that kennel.</LI>
<LI>Click on the <B>U</B> button in the first column to go to
the data entry screen and update the record for that dog.</LI>
<LI><A HREF="mailto:john.rodley@channel1.com">Click here</A>
to email the db administrator (e.g. questions about the Web site).
</LI>
<LI><A HREF="mailto:101503.2063@Compuserve.com">Click here</A>
to email the data librarian (e.g. questions about the data itself).</LI>
</UL>
<HR>
<H2>Verified Records</H2>
<TABLE BORDER="BORDER" ALIGN="CENTER"><CAPTION><B></B></CAPTION>
<TH></TH>
<TH>Name</TH>
```

```
<TH>Description</TH>
<TH>----Lifespan----</TH>
<TH>Sire</TH>
<TH>Dam</TH>
<TH>Breeder</TH>
<TH>Owner</TH>
<TH>REGNO</TH>
<TH>Country</TH>
<TH>Titles</TH>
<TH>CHDate</TH>
<TH>JWOB</TH>
<TH>JWDate</TH>
<TH>DOB2</TH>
<TH>Recessive</TH>
<TH>Kennel</TH>
<TH>REMARKS</TH>
<TH>HIPTOT</TH>
<TH>HIPR</TH>
<TH>HIPL</TH>
<TH>DOB</TH>
<TH>DIED</TH>
<TH>HDCERT</TH>
<TH>HIPS</TH>
<TH>OFANO</TH>
<TH>OVCNO</TH>
<TH>KCBVAEYE</TH>
<TH>TATTOO</TH>
<TH>HEARTGRADE</TH>
<TH>SOURCE</TH>
<TH>SB</TH>
<TH>WORKAREA</TH>
<TH>CHANGEDATE</TH>
<TH>CHANGETEXT</TH>
<TH>Sex</TH>
<TH>Colour</TH>
<TH>QUOTENO</TH>
<TR><TD COLSTART="0" ALIGN="CENTER"><B><A HREF="http://katie/cgi-bin/
newfq.exe?QUOTENO=13893&QueryType=update&server=katie&user=sa&db=
      newf&tbl=shortdog&base=http://katie">
      <IMG SRC=http://katie/images/update.jpg></A></B></TD>
<TD COLSTART="1" ALIGN="CENTER"><B><A HREF="http://katie/cgi-bin/
newfq.exe?dog.text=NAUTILUS+BLACK+BUCCANEER&QueryType=
      Pedigree&server=katie&user=sa&db=newf&tbl=shortdog&base=
      http://katie">NAUTILUS BLACK BUCCANEER</A></P></B></TD>
<TD COLSTART="2" ALIGN="CENTER"><B>BLACK - WH MKGS dog</B></TD>
```

```
<TD COLSTART="3" ALIGN="CENTER"><B>Jun 22 1964</B></TD>
<TD COLSTART="4" ALIGN="CENTER"><B><A HREF="http://katie/cgi-bin/
newfq.exe?dog.text=SKIPMIRES+BLACK+SAILOR&QueryType=Name&server=
      katie&user=sa&db=newf&tbl=shortdog&base=http://katie">
      SKIPMIRES BLACK SAILOR</A></P></B></TD>
<TD COLSTART="5" ALIGN="CENTER"><B><A HREF="http://katie/cgi-bin/
newfq.exe?dog.text=SEAWARDS+SEA+RIPPLE&QueryType=
      Name&server=katie&user=sa&db=newf&tbl=shortdog&base=
      http://katie">SEAWARDS SEA RIPPLE</A></P></B></TD>
<TD COLSTART="6" ALIGN="CENTER"><B>LEWANDROWSKI, SEBA K</B></TD>
<TD COLSTART="7" ALIGN="CENTER"><B>GAINES, SEBA K & W ROBERT</B></TD>
<TD COLSTART="8" ALIGN="CENTER"><B>WA 482910</B></TD>
<TD COLSTART="9" ALIGN="CENTER"><B>USA</B></TD>
<TD COLSTART="10" ALIGN="CENTER"><B>AM CH</B></TD>
<TD COLSTART="11" ALIGN="CENTER"><B>Oct 9 1966 12:00AM</B></TD>
<TD COLSTART="12" ALIGN="CENTER"><B>-</B></TD>
<TD COLSTART="13" ALIGN="CENTER"><B>-</B></TD>
<TD COLSTART="14" ALIGN="CENTER"><B>1964</B></TD>
<TD COLSTART="15" ALIGN="CENTER"><B>(WH&BL)</B></TD>
<TD COLSTART="16" ALIGN="CENTER"><B>-</B></TD>
<TD COLSTART="17" ALIGN="CENTER"><B>-</B></TD>
<TD COLSTART="18" ALIGN="CENTER"><B>-</B></TD>
<TD COLSTART="19" ALIGN="CENTER"><B>-</B></TD>
<TD COLSTART="20" ALIGN="CENTER"><B>-</B></TD>
<TD COLSTART="21" ALIGN="CENTER"><B>Jun 22 1964 12:00AM</B></TD>
<TD COLSTART="22" ALIGN="CENTER"><B>-</B></TD>
<TD COLSTART="23" ALIGN="CENTER"><B>-</B></TD>
<TD COLSTART="24" ALIGN="CENTER"><B>-</B></TD>
<TD COLSTART="25" ALIGN="CENTER"><B>-</B></TD>
<TD COLSTART="26" ALIGN="CENTER"><B>-</B></TD>
<TD COLSTART="27" ALIGN="CENTER"><B>-</B></TD>
<TD COLSTART="28" ALIGN="CENTER"><B>-</B></TD>
<TD COLSTART="29" ALIGN="CENTER"><B>-</B></TD>
<TD COLSTART="30" ALIGN="CENTER"><B>-</B></TD>
<TD COLSTART="31" ALIGN="CENTER"><B>-</B></TD>
<TD COLSTART="32" ALIGN="CENTER"><B>-</B></TD>
<TD COLSTART="33" ALIGN="CENTER"><B>Mar 20 1996 12:00AM</B></TD>
<TD COLSTART="34" ALIGN="CENTER"><B>-</B></TD>
<TD COLSTART="35" ALIGN="CENTER"><B>D</B></TD>
<TD COLSTART="36" ALIGN="CENTER"><B>BLACK - WH MKGS</B></TD>
<TD COLSTART="37" ALIGN="CENTER"><B>13893</B></TD>
</TR>
</TABLE>
<HR>
<H2>Unverified Records</H2>
```

```
<TABLE BORDER="BORDER" ALIGN="CENTER"><CAPTION><B></B></CAPTION>
<TH>Name</TH>
<TH>Description</TH>
<TH>----Lifespan----</TH>
<TH>Sire</TH>
<TH>Dam</TH>
<TH>Breeder</TH>
<TH>Owner</TH>
<TH>REGNO</TH>
<TH>Country</TH>
<TH>Titles</TH>
<TH>CHDate</TH>
<TH>JWOB</TH>
<TH>JWDate</TH>
<TH>DOB2</TH>
<TH>Recessive</TH>
<TH>Kennel</TH>
<TH>REMARKS</TH>
<TH>HIPTOT</TH>
<TH>HIPR</TH>
<TH>HIPL</TH>
<TH>DOB</TH>
<TH>DIED</TH>
<TH>HDCERT</TH>
<TH>HIPS</TH>
<TH>OFANO</TH>
<TH>OVCNO</TH>
<TH>KCBVAEYE</TH>
<TH>TATTOO</TH>
<TH>HEARTGRADE</TH>
<TH>SOURCE</TH>
<TH>SB</TH>
<TH>WORKAREA</TH>
<TH>CHANGEDATE</TH>
<TH>CHANGETEXT</TH>
<TH>Sex</TH>
<TH>Colour</TH>
<TH>QUOTENO</TH>
<TR><TD COLSTART="0" ALIGN="CENTER">
<B>NAUTILUS BLACK BUCCANEER</B></TD>
<TD COLSTART="1" ALIGN="CENTER"><B>BLACK dog</B></TD>
<TD COLSTART="2" ALIGN="CENTER"><B>Jun 22 1964</B></TD>
<TD COLSTART="3" ALIGN="CENTER">
<B><A HREF="http://katie/cgi-bin/newfq.exe?
dog.text=SKIPMIRES+BLACK+SAILOR&QueryType=Name&server=katie&
```

```
      user=sa&db=newf&tbl=shortdog&base=http://katie">
SKIPMIRES BLACK SAILOR</A></P></B></TD>
<TD COLSTART="4" ALIGN="CENTER">
<B><A HREF="http://katie/cgi-bin/newfq.exe?
dog.text=SEAWARDS+SEA+RIPPLE&QueryType=Name&server=katie&user=sa&
db=newf&tbl=shortdog&base=http://katie">
SEAWARDS SEA RIPPLE</A></P></B></TD>
<TD COLSTART="5" ALIGN="CENTER"><B>LEWANDROWSKI, SEBA K</B></TD>
<TD COLSTART="6" ALIGN="CENTER"><B>GAINES, SEBA K   W ROBERT</B></TD>
<TD COLSTART="7" ALIGN="CENTER"><B>WA 482910</B></TD>
<TD COLSTART="8" ALIGN="CENTER"><B>USA</B></TD>
<TD COLSTART="9" ALIGN="CENTER"><B>AM CH</B></TD>
<TD COLSTART="10" ALIGN="CENTER"><B>Oct 9 1966 12:00AM</B></TD>
<TD COLSTART="11" ALIGN="CENTER"><B>-</B></TD>
<TD COLSTART="12" ALIGN="CENTER"><B>-</B></TD>
<TD COLSTART="13" ALIGN="CENTER"><B>1964</B></TD>
<TD COLSTART="14" ALIGN="CENTER"><B>(WH BL)</B></TD>
<TD COLSTART="15" ALIGN="CENTER"><B>-</B></TD>
<TD COLSTART="16" ALIGN="CENTER"><B>-</B></TD>
<TD COLSTART="17" ALIGN="CENTER"><B>-</B></TD>
<TD COLSTART="18" ALIGN="CENTER"><B>-</B></TD>
<TD COLSTART="19" ALIGN="CENTER"><B>-</B></TD>
<TD COLSTART="20" ALIGN="CENTER"><B>Jun 22 1964 12:00AM</B></TD>
<TD COLSTART="21" ALIGN="CENTER"><B>-</B></TD>
<TD COLSTART="22" ALIGN="CENTER"><B>-</B></TD>
<TD COLSTART="23" ALIGN="CENTER"><B>-</B></TD>
<TD COLSTART="24" ALIGN="CENTER"><B>-</B></TD>
<TD COLSTART="25" ALIGN="CENTER"><B>-</B></TD>
<TD COLSTART="26" ALIGN="CENTER"><B>-</B></TD>
<TD COLSTART="27" ALIGN="CENTER"><B>-</B></TD>
<TD COLSTART="28" ALIGN="CENTER"><B>-</B></TD>
<TD COLSTART="29" ALIGN="CENTER"><B>-</B></TD>
<TD COLSTART="30" ALIGN="CENTER"><B>-</B></TD>
<TD COLSTART="31" ALIGN="CENTER"><B>-</B></TD>
<TD COLSTART="32" ALIGN="CENTER"><B>May 29 1996  5:01PM</B></TD>
<TD COLSTART="33" ALIGN="CENTER"><B>-</B></TD>
<TD COLSTART="34" ALIGN="CENTER"><B>D</B></TD>
<TD COLSTART="35" ALIGN="CENTER"><B>BLACK</B></TD>
<TD COLSTART="36" ALIGN="CENTER"><B>13893</B></TD>
</TR>
<TR><TD COLSTART="0" ALIGN="CENTER">
<B>NAUTILUS BLACK BUCCANEER</B></TD>
<TD COLSTART="1" ALIGN="CENTER"><B>BLACK dog</B></TD>
<TD COLSTART="2" ALIGN="CENTER"><B>Jun 22 1964</B></TD>
<TD COLSTART="3" ALIGN="CENTER"><B>
```

```
<A HREF="http://katie/cgi-bin/newfq.exe?
dog.text=SKIPMIRES+BLACK+SAILOR&QueryType=Name&server=katie&
user=sa&db=newf&tbl=shortdog&base=http://katie">
SKIPMIRES BLACK SAILOR</A></P></B></TD>
<TD COLSTART="4" ALIGN="CENTER"><B>
<A HREF="http://katie/cgi-bin/newfq.exe?
dog.text=SEAWARDS+SEA+RIPPLE&QueryType=Name&server=katie&
user=sa&db=newf&tbl=shortdog&base=http://katie">
SEAWARDS SEA RIPPLE</A></P></B></TD>
<TD COLSTART="5" ALIGN="CENTER"><B>LEWANDROWSKI, SEBA K</B></TD>
<TD COLSTART="6" ALIGN="CENTER"><B>GAINES, SEBA K   W ROBERT</B></TD>
<TD COLSTART="7" ALIGN="CENTER"><B>WA 482910</B></TD>
<TD COLSTART="8" ALIGN="CENTER"><B>USA</B></TD>
<TD COLSTART="9" ALIGN="CENTER"><B>AM CH</B></TD>
<TD COLSTART="10" ALIGN="CENTER"><B>Oct 9 1966 12:00AM</B></TD>
<TD COLSTART="11" ALIGN="CENTER"><B>-</B></TD>
<TD COLSTART="12" ALIGN="CENTER"><B>-</B></TD>
<TD COLSTART="13" ALIGN="CENTER"><B>1964</B></TD>
<TD COLSTART="14" ALIGN="CENTER"><B>(WH BL)</B></TD>
<TD COLSTART="15" ALIGN="CENTER"><B>-</B></TD>
<TD COLSTART="16" ALIGN="CENTER"><B>-</B></TD>
<TD COLSTART="17" ALIGN="CENTER"><B>-</B></TD>
<TD COLSTART="18" ALIGN="CENTER"><B>-</B></TD>
<TD COLSTART="19" ALIGN="CENTER"><B>-</B></TD>
<TD COLSTART="20" ALIGN="CENTER"><B>Jun 22 1964 12:00AM</B></TD>
<TD COLSTART="21" ALIGN="CENTER"><B>-</B></TD>
<TD COLSTART="22" ALIGN="CENTER"><B>-</B></TD>
<TD COLSTART="23" ALIGN="CENTER"><B>-</B></TD>
<TD COLSTART="24" ALIGN="CENTER"><B>-</B></TD>
<TD COLSTART="25" ALIGN="CENTER"><B>-</B></TD>
<TD COLSTART="26" ALIGN="CENTER"><B>-</B></TD>
<TD COLSTART="27" ALIGN="CENTER"><B>-</B></TD>
<TD COLSTART="28" ALIGN="CENTER"><B>-</B></TD>
<TD COLSTART="29" ALIGN="CENTER"><B>-</B></TD>
<TD COLSTART="30" ALIGN="CENTER"><B>-</B></TD>
<TD COLSTART="31" ALIGN="CENTER"><B>-</B></TD>
<TD COLSTART="32" ALIGN="CENTER"><B>Aug 12 1996 12:45PM</B></TD>
<TD COLSTART="33" ALIGN="CENTER"><B>-</B></TD>
<TD COLSTART="34" ALIGN="CENTER"><B>D</B></TD>
<TD COLSTART="35" ALIGN="CENTER"><B>BLACK</B></TD>
<TD COLSTART="36" ALIGN="CENTER"><B>13893</B></TD>
</TR>
<TR><TD COLSTART="0" ALIGN="CENTER"><B>NAUTILUS BLACK BUCCANEER</B></TD>
<TD COLSTART="1" ALIGN="CENTER"><B>BLACK dog</B></TD>
<TD COLSTART="2" ALIGN="CENTER"><B>Jun 22 1964</B></TD>
```

```
<TD COLSTART="3" ALIGN="CENTER">
<B><A HREF="http://katie/cgi-bin/newfq.exe?
dog.text=SKIPMIRES+BLACK+SAILOR&QueryType=Name&server=katie&
user=sa&db=newf&tbl=shortdog&base=http://katie">
SKIPMIRES BLACK SAILOR</A></P></B></TD>
<TD COLSTART="4" ALIGN="CENTER"><B>
<A HREF="http://katie/cgi-bin/newfq.exe?
dog.text=SEAWARDS+SEA+RIPPLE&QueryType=Name&server=katie&
user=sa&db=newf&tbl=shortdog&base=http://katie">
SEAWARDS SEA RIPPLE</A></P></B></TD>
<TD COLSTART="5" ALIGN="CENTER"><B>LEWANDROWSKI, SEBA K</B></TD>
<TD COLSTART="6" ALIGN="CENTER"><B>GAINES, SEBA K   W ROBERT</B></TD>
<TD COLSTART="7" ALIGN="CENTER"><B>WA 482910</B></TD>
<TD COLSTART="8" ALIGN="CENTER"><B>USA</B></TD>
<TD COLSTART="9" ALIGN="CENTER"><B>AM CH</B></TD>
<TD COLSTART="10" ALIGN="CENTER"><B>Oct 9 1966 12:00AM</B></TD>
<TD COLSTART="11" ALIGN="CENTER"><B>-</B></TD>
<TD COLSTART="12" ALIGN="CENTER"><B>-</B></TD>
<TD COLSTART="13" ALIGN="CENTER"><B>1964</B></TD>
<TD COLSTART="14" ALIGN="CENTER"><B>(WH BL)</B></TD>
<TD COLSTART="15" ALIGN="CENTER"><B>-</B></TD>
<TD COLSTART="16" ALIGN="CENTER"><B>-</B></TD>
<TD COLSTART="17" ALIGN="CENTER"><B>-</B></TD>
<TD COLSTART="18" ALIGN="CENTER"><B>-</B></TD>
<TD COLSTART="19" ALIGN="CENTER"><B>-</B></TD>
<TD COLSTART="20" ALIGN="CENTER"><B>Jun 22 1964 12:00AM</B></TD>
<TD COLSTART="21" ALIGN="CENTER"><B>-</B></TD>
<TD COLSTART="22" ALIGN="CENTER"><B>-</B></TD>
<TD COLSTART="23" ALIGN="CENTER"><B>-</B></TD>
<TD COLSTART="24" ALIGN="CENTER"><B>-</B></TD>
<TD COLSTART="25" ALIGN="CENTER"><B>-</B></TD>
<TD COLSTART="26" ALIGN="CENTER"><B>-</B></TD>
<TD COLSTART="27" ALIGN="CENTER"><B>-</B></TD>
<TD COLSTART="28" ALIGN="CENTER"><B>-</B></TD>
<TD COLSTART="29" ALIGN="CENTER"><B>-</B></TD>
<TD COLSTART="30" ALIGN="CENTER"><B>-</B></TD>
<TD COLSTART="31" ALIGN="CENTER"><B>-</B></TD>
<TD COLSTART="32" ALIGN="CENTER"><B>Aug 12 1996 12:52PM</B></TD>
<TD COLSTART="33" ALIGN="CENTER"><B>-</B></TD>
<TD COLSTART="34" ALIGN="CENTER"><B>D</B></TD>
<TD COLSTART="35" ALIGN="CENTER"><B>BLACK</B></TD>
<TD COLSTART="36" ALIGN="CENTER"><B>13893</B></TD>
</TR>
<TR><TD COLSTART="0" ALIGN="CENTER">
<B>NAUTILUS BLACK BUCCANEER</B></TD>
```

```
<TD COLSTART="1" ALIGN="CENTER"><B>BLACK dog</B></TD>
<TD COLSTART="2" ALIGN="CENTER"><B>Jun 22 1964</B></TD>
<TD COLSTART="3" ALIGN="CENTER">
<B><A HREF="http://katie/cgi-bin/newfq.exe?
dog.text=SKIPMIRES+BLACK+SAILOR&QueryType=Name&server=katie&
user=sa&db=newf&tbl=shortdog&base=http://katie">
SKIPMIRES BLACK SAILOR</A></P></B></TD>
<TD COLSTART="4" ALIGN="CENTER">
<B><A HREF="http://katie/cgi-bin/newfq.exe?
dog.text=SEAWARDS+SEA+RIPPLE&QueryType=Name&server=katie&
user=sa&db=newf&tbl=shortdog&base=http://katie">
SEAWARDS SEA RIPPLE</A></P></B></TD>
<TD COLSTART="5" ALIGN="CENTER"><B>LEWANDROWSKI, SEBA K</B></TD>
<TD COLSTART="6" ALIGN="CENTER"><B>GAINES, SEBA K   W ROBERT</B></TD>
<TD COLSTART="7" ALIGN="CENTER"><B>WA 482910</B></TD>
<TD COLSTART="8" ALIGN="CENTER"><B>USA</B></TD>
<TD COLSTART="9" ALIGN="CENTER"><B>AM CH</B></TD>
<TD COLSTART="10" ALIGN="CENTER"><B>Oct 9 1966 12:00AM</B></TD>
<TD COLSTART="11" ALIGN="CENTER"><B>-</B></TD>
<TD COLSTART="12" ALIGN="CENTER"><B>-</B></TD>
<TD COLSTART="13" ALIGN="CENTER"><B>1964</B></TD>
<TD COLSTART="14" ALIGN="CENTER"><B>(WH BL)</B></TD>
<TD COLSTART="15" ALIGN="CENTER"><B>-</B></TD>
<TD COLSTART="16" ALIGN="CENTER"><B>-</B></TD>
<TD COLSTART="17" ALIGN="CENTER"><B>-</B></TD>
<TD COLSTART="18" ALIGN="CENTER"><B>-</B></TD>
<TD COLSTART="19" ALIGN="CENTER"><B>-</B></TD>
<TD COLSTART="20" ALIGN="CENTER"><B>Jun 22 1964 12:00AM</B></TD>
<TD COLSTART="21" ALIGN="CENTER"><B>-</B></TD>
<TD COLSTART="22" ALIGN="CENTER"><B>-</B></TD>
<TD COLSTART="23" ALIGN="CENTER"><B>-</B></TD>
<TD COLSTART="24" ALIGN="CENTER"><B>-</B></TD>
<TD COLSTART="25" ALIGN="CENTER"><B>-</B></TD>
<TD COLSTART="26" ALIGN="CENTER"><B>-</B></TD>
<TD COLSTART="27" ALIGN="CENTER"><B>-</B></TD>
<TD COLSTART="28" ALIGN="CENTER"><B>-</B></TD>
<TD COLSTART="29" ALIGN="CENTER"><B>-</B></TD>
<TD COLSTART="30" ALIGN="CENTER"><B>-</B></TD>
<TD COLSTART="31" ALIGN="CENTER"><B>-</B></TD>
<TD COLSTART="32" ALIGN="CENTER"><B>Aug 13 1996  4:39PM</B></TD>
<TD COLSTART="33" ALIGN="CENTER"><B>-</B></TD>
<TD COLSTART="34" ALIGN="CENTER"><B>D</B></TD>
<TD COLSTART="35" ALIGN="CENTER"><B>BLACK</B></TD>
<TD COLSTART="36" ALIGN="CENTER"><B>13893</B></TD>
```

```
</TR>
<TR><TD COLSTART="0" ALIGN="CENTER">
<B>NAUTILUS BLACK BUCCANEER</B></TD>
<TD COLSTART="1" ALIGN="CENTER"><B>BLACK dog</B></TD>
<TD COLSTART="2" ALIGN="CENTER"><B>Jun 22 1964</B></TD>
<TD COLSTART="3" ALIGN="CENTER"><B>
<A HREF="http://katie/cgi-bin/newfq.exe?
dog.text=SKIPMIRES+BLACK+SAILOR&QueryType=Name&server=katie&
user=sa&db=newf&tbl=shortdog&base=http://katie">
SKIPMIRES BLACK SAILOR</A></P></B></TD>
<TD COLSTART="4" ALIGN="CENTER"><B>
<A HREF="http://katie/cgi-bin/newfq.exe?
dog.text=SEAWARDS+SEA+RIPPLE&QueryType=Name&server=katie&
user=sa&db=newf&tbl=shortdog&base=http://katie">
SEAWARDS SEA RIPPLE</A></P></B></TD>
<TD COLSTART="5" ALIGN="CENTER"><B>LEWANDROWSKI, SEBA K</B></TD>
<TD COLSTART="6" ALIGN="CENTER"><B>GAINES, SEBA K   W ROBERT</B></TD>
<TD COLSTART="7" ALIGN="CENTER"><B>WA 482910</B></TD>
<TD COLSTART="8" ALIGN="CENTER"><B>USA</B></TD>
<TD COLSTART="9" ALIGN="CENTER"><B>AM CH</B></TD>
<TD COLSTART="10" ALIGN="CENTER"><B>Oct 9 1966 12:00AM</B></TD>
<TD COLSTART="11" ALIGN="CENTER"><B>-</B></TD>
<TD COLSTART="12" ALIGN="CENTER"><B>-</B></TD>
<TD COLSTART="13" ALIGN="CENTER"><B>1964</B></TD>
<TD COLSTART="14" ALIGN="CENTER"><B>(WH BL)</B></TD>
<TD COLSTART="15" ALIGN="CENTER"><B>-</B></TD>
<TD COLSTART="16" ALIGN="CENTER"><B>-</B></TD>
<TD COLSTART="17" ALIGN="CENTER"><B>-</B></TD>
<TD COLSTART="18" ALIGN="CENTER"><B>-</B></TD>
<TD COLSTART="19" ALIGN="CENTER"><B>-</B></TD>
<TD COLSTART="20" ALIGN="CENTER"><B>Jun 22 1964 12:00AM</B></TD>
<TD COLSTART="21" ALIGN="CENTER"><B>-</B></TD>
<TD COLSTART="22" ALIGN="CENTER"><B>-</B></TD>
<TD COLSTART="23" ALIGN="CENTER"><B>-</B></TD>
<TD COLSTART="24" ALIGN="CENTER"><B>-</B></TD>
<TD COLSTART="25" ALIGN="CENTER"><B>-</B></TD>
<TD COLSTART="26" ALIGN="CENTER"><B>-</B></TD>
<TD COLSTART="27" ALIGN="CENTER"><B>-</B></TD>
<TD COLSTART="28" ALIGN="CENTER"><B>-</B></TD>
<TD COLSTART="29" ALIGN="CENTER"><B>-</B></TD>
<TD COLSTART="30" ALIGN="CENTER"><B>-</B></TD>
<TD COLSTART="31" ALIGN="CENTER"><B>-</B></TD>
<TD COLSTART="32" ALIGN="CENTER"><B>Aug 14 1996  9:38AM</B></TD>
<TD COLSTART="33" ALIGN="CENTER"><B>-</B></TD>
```

```
<TD COLSTART="34" ALIGN="CENTER"><B>D</B></TD>
<TD COLSTART="35" ALIGN="CENTER"><B>BLACK</B></TD>
<TD COLSTART="36" ALIGN="CENTER"><B>13893</B></TD>
</TR>
</TABLE>
<HR>
</BODY>
</HTML>
```

This HTML source displays in a browser as shown in Figure 3.2. Some lines have been wrapped to fit in publication. There is only one verified record, and five unverified records for this dog, undoubtedly because he's one of my test dogs.

The record scrolls out of view to the right. We arranged it this way on purpose, so that the less interesting fields were available, but not in the way.

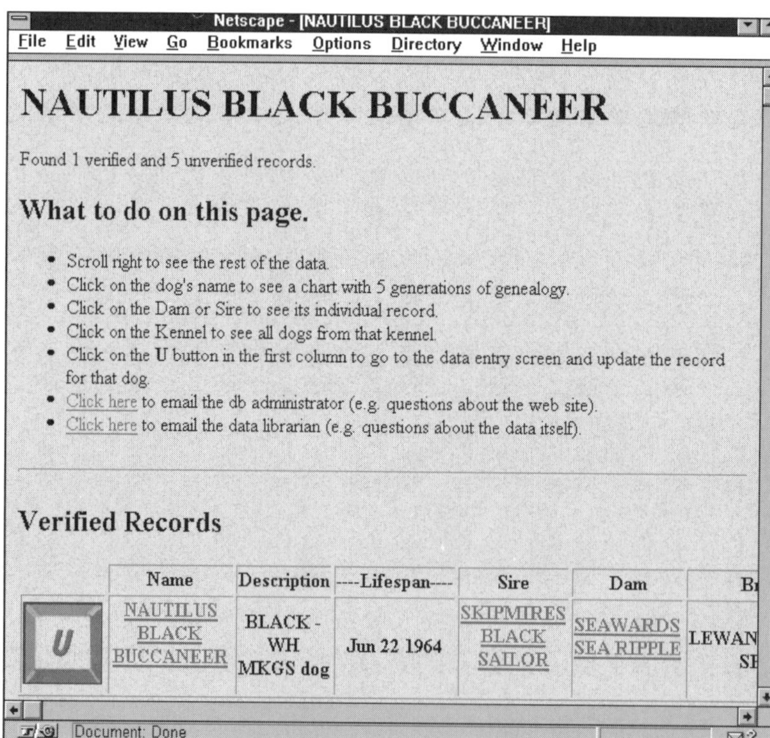

Figure 3.2 The HTML output displayed.

An HTML Template Processor

All along, we've talked about verified and unverified records. One of the operational requirements of the Newfoundland Dog Database is that an expert Newfie historian reviews any data before it becomes part of the database. This is a quality-control issue for us, but it conflicts with the stated goals of the Web version of the database—to acquire as much data as possible and to fill in the gaps in existing data. What we needed was a mechanism to allow users to enter and correct data that didn't necessarily modify existing, verified, records.

The imperfect solution we came up with was to store new and modified records in a completely separate table, NEWDOG. NEWDOG is nearly identical to SHORTDOG, merely adding fields that allow us to identify the person creating the record so that we can get back to them with any questions. Listing 3.19 shows the structure of the NEWDOG table.

Listing 3.19 Structure of the NEWDOG table.

```
NAME        varchar(62) null,
QUOTENO     varchar(7) null,
CHANGEDATE  datetime,
CHANGETEXT  varchar(100) null,
REGNO       varchar(30) null,
COUNTRY     varchar(20) null,
TITLES      varchar(40) null,
CHDATE      datetime,
JWOB        varchar(30) null,
JWDATE      datetime,
DOB         datetime,
DOB2        varchar(12) null,
SEX         varchar(1) null,
SNAME       varchar(62) null,
DNAME       varchar(62) null,
COLOUR      varchar(40) null,
RECESSIVE   varchar(40) null,
OWNER       varchar(62) null,
AFFIX       varchar(30) null,
BREEDER     varchar(62) null,
REMARKS     varchar(200) null,
HIPTOT      varchar(3) null,
HIPR        varchar(2) null,
HIPL        varchar(2) null,
DIED        datetime,
```

```
HDCERT       varchar(1) null,
HIPS         varchar(25) null,
OFANO        varchar(15) null,
OVCNO        varchar(15) null,
KCBVAEYE     varchar(10) null,
TATTOO       varchar(15) null,
HEARTGRADE   varchar(9) null,
SOURCE       varchar(30) null,
SB           varchar(4) null,
WORKAREA     varchar(20) null,
SRCADDRESS   text null,
SRCEMAIL     varchar(40) null,
COMMENTS     text null
```

By itself, NEWDOG is relatively uninteresting. We've already seen how the QUERY functions query both SHORTDOG and NEWDOG for records matching the user's criteria. The interesting part of NEWDOG is that it allows us to address a database issue we've avoided so far—database inserts. There are two ways to insert a record into the NEWDOG table:

- Create a new record from scratch by selecting Add Data from the HTML screen of Figure 3.3.

Figure 3.3 The main screen of the Newfoundland Dog Database, allowing search and add-data.

- Update an existing record by pushing the Update button from Figure 3.2.

Selecting Add Data from the main screen brings you to the empty data-entry screen shown in Figure 3.3. Listing 3.20 shows the HTML source for our data-entry screen.

Listing 3.20 Empty data-entry screen.

```
<!DOCTYPE HTML PUBLIC "-//SQ//DTD HTML 2.0 HoTMetaL + extensions//EN">
<HTML><HEAD><TITLE>Newfoundland DB Data Entry</TITLE></HEAD>
<BODY BACKGROUND="images/background.jpg">
<H1>Newfoundland DB Data Entry</H1>
<P>Use the form below to enter new records for the Newfoundland
database or to correct existing records.  If you don't know what the
value of a particular field is, leave it blank.  The data librarian will
do his best to merge your input with existing data.  Most fields include
a number in parentheses next to the prompt.  This is the maximum number
of characters allowed. Data larger than the maximum will be either
truncated, or rejected. </P>
<P>When you submit a record (by hitting the &quot;add record&quot;
button), the system will try to add the record to the database.  A
message will be displayed indicating whether the record was accepted
or rejected. At that point you can either quit or continue adding records
(using the same source address). If the record was rejected, you can
either quit without saving the record, or go back, edit the record and
resubmit. </P>
<HR>
<H2>Address/Data Source</H2>
<P>You MUST enter a name and either an email or regular mail address.
Each item of data in the newf database is tagged with the source of that
data so that any conflict between two versions of the same data item can
be resolved quickly and correctly.  If there is any question about the
data you've entered, we may use this address to contact you.  These
addresses will be seen only by the Web database administrator, John
Rodley, and the data librarian, Richard Scothern.</P>
<P>Starting now, data entered here WILL show up in searches of the
database. It must still pass through a checking process before being
merged with the verified records.  Currently, newly entered data DOES
NOT show up in pedigrees. I will be working to fix this over the
next few weeks.</P>
<FORM ACTION="http://katie/cgi-bin/newfq.exe" METHOD="POST">
<TABLE><TR><TD
COLSTART="1">Enter your name and postal address here.</TD>
<TD COLSTART="2"><TEXTAREA
```

```
NAME="SRCADDRESS" ROWS="6" COLS="30"></TEXTAREA></TD></TR>
<TR><TD COLSTART="1">Enter your email address here. (40)</TD>
<TD COLSTART="2"><INPUT
NAME="SRCEMAIL" SIZE="20" MAXLENGTH="40"></TD></TR>

</TABLE>
<HR>
<H2>Vital Information</H2>
<H3>Dates</H3>
<P>All dates MUST be entered in one of three ways:</P>
<UL><LI>The four digit year, as in <B>1975</B>, or <B>1833</B>, or
<B>1991</B>.</LI>
<LI>The month and year, as in <B>12/1992 </B>(for December 1992), or
<B>3/1877</B> (for March 1877).</LI>
<LI>The month, day and year, as in <B>12/1/1992</B> (for December
1st, 1992) or <B>3/7/1960</B> (for March 7, 1960).</LI></UL>
<P>All other date formats WILL BE REJECTED.  Like other data items, if
you don't know a date, leave it blank.</P>
<H3>Dog Names</H3>
<P>When entering dog names (Dog Name, Sire, and Dame) don't use
CH prefixes.  So<B>CH Stormwatch's Yacht Katrina</B> would be entered
as <B>STORMWATCHS YACHT KATRINA.</B>  If the dog is a champion,
either enter a valid championship date, or add it as a comment.</P>
<TABLE BORDER="5" CELLPADDING="5" CELLSPACING="4" ALIGN="CENTER">
<TR><TD VALIGN="MIDDLE" ALIGN="RIGHT" COLSTART="1"><P>Dog Name: (62)</
P></TD>
<TD COLSTART="2"><INPUT NAME="NAME" SIZE="30" MAXLENGTH="62"></TD>
<TD VALIGN="MIDDLE" ALIGN="RIGHT" COLSTART="3">
<P>Date of Birth: (MM/DD/YYYY)</P></TD><TD
COLSTART="4"><INPUT NAME="DOB" SIZE="10" MAXLENGTH="10"></TD>
<TD COLSPAN="3" COLSTART="5"></TD></TR><TR><TD
VALIGN="MIDDLE" ALIGN="RIGHT" COLSTART="1"><P>Sex: (1)</P></TD><TD
VALIGN="TOP" COLSTART="2"><SELECT NAME="SEX" SIZE="0">
<OPTION VALUE="D">Dog</OPTION>
<OPTION VALUE="B">Bitch</OPTION></SELECT></TD><TD
VALIGN="MIDDLE" ALIGN="RIGHT" COLSTART="3">
<P>Died: (MM/DD/YYYY)</P></TD>
<TD COLSTART="4"><INPUT NAME="DIED" SIZE="10" MAXLENGTH="10"></TD>
<TD COLSPAN="3" COLSTART="5"></TD></TR><TR><TD
VALIGN="TOP" ALIGN="RIGHT" COLSTART="1"><P>Colour: (40)</P>
<P>Colors other than those listed should be described in the comments
field below.</P></TD><TD VALIGN="TOP" COLSTART="2"><SELECT NAME="COLOUR">
<OPTION SELECTED="SELECTED" VALUE="BLACK">Black</OPTION>
```

```
<OPTION VALUE="Landseer">Landseer</OPTION>
<OPTION VALUE="BROWN">Brown</OPTION>
<OPTION VALUE="GREY">Grey</OPTION></SELECT></TD><TD
VALIGN="MIDDLE" ALIGN="RIGHT" COLSTART="3"><P>Sire: (62)</P></TD><TD
VALIGN="MIDDLE" COLSTART="4">
<INPUT NAME="SNAME" SIZE="30" MAXLENGTH="62"></TD><TD
COLSPAN="3" COLSTART="5"></TD></TR><TR><TD
VALIGN="MIDDLE" ALIGN="RIGHT" COLSTART="1"><P>Recessive: (40)</P></TD>
<TD COLSTART="2"><INPUT NAME="RECESSIVE" SIZE="20" MAXLENGTH="40">
</TD><TD VALIGN="MIDDLE" ALIGN="RIGHT" COLSTART="3"><P>Dam: (62)</P></
TD><TD COLSTART="4"><INPUT NAME="DNAME" SIZE="30" MAXLENGTH="62"></TD><TD
COLSPAN="3" COLSTART="5"></TD></TR><TR><TD
VALIGN="MIDDLE" ALIGN="RIGHT" COLSTART="1"><P>Breeder: (62)</P></TD><TD
COLSTART="2"><INPUT NAME="BREEDER" SIZE="30" MAXLENGTH="62"></TD><TD
VALIGN="MIDDLE" ALIGN="RIGHT" COLSTART="3"><P>Titles: (40)</P></TD><TD
COLSTART="4"><INPUT NAME="TITLES" SIZE="30" MAXLENGTH="40"></TD><TD
COLSPAN="3" COLSTART="5"></TD></TR><TR><TD
VALIGN="MIDDLE" ALIGN="RIGHT" COLSTART="1"><P>Country: (20)</P></TD><TD
COLSTART="2"><INPUT NAME="COUNTRY" SIZE="20" MAXLENGTH="20"></TD><TD
VALIGN="MIDDLE" ALIGN="RIGHT" COLSTART="3"><P>Kennel: (30)</P></TD><TD
COLSTART="4"><INPUT NAME="AFFIX" SIZE="30" MAXLENGTH="30"></TD><TD
COLSPAN="3" COLSTART="5"></TD></TR><TR><TD
VALIGN="MIDDLE" ALIGN="RIGHT" COLSTART="1"><P>OFA NO: (15)</P></TD><TD
COLSTART="2"><INPUT NAME="OFANO" SIZE="15" MAXLENGTH="15"></TD><TD
VALIGN="MIDDLE" ALIGN="RIGHT" COLSTART="3"><P>Owner: (62)</P></TD><TD
COLSTART="4"><INPUT NAME="OWNER" SIZE="30" MAXLENGTH="62"></TD><TD
COLSPAN="3" COLSTART="5"></TD></TR><TR><TD
VALIGN="MIDDLE" ALIGN="RIGHT" COLSTART="1"><P>Heartgrade(9): </P></TD>
<TD COLSTART="2"><INPUT NAME="HEART" SIZE="9" MAXLENGTH="9"></TD><TD
VALIGN="MIDDLE" ALIGN="RIGHT" COLSTART="3"><P>Registration: (30)</P>
</TD><TD COLSTART="4"><INPUT NAME="REGNO" SIZE="30" MAXLENGTH="30"></
TD><TD COLSPAN="3" COLSTART="5"></TD></TR><TR><TD
VALIGN="MIDDLE" ALIGN="RIGHT" COLSTART="1"><P>Hip left: (2)</P></TD><TD
COLSTART="2"><INPUT NAME="HIPL" SIZE="2" MAXLENGTH="2"></TD><TD
VALIGN="MIDDLE" ALIGN="RIGHT" COLSTART="3">
<P>Championship Date (MM/DD/YYYY):
</P></TD><TD COLSTART="4">
<INPUT NAME="CHDATE" SIZE="10" MAXLENGTH="10"></TD>
<TD COLSPAN="3" COLSTART="5"></TD></TR><TR><TD
VALIGN="MIDDLE" ALIGN="RIGHT" COLSTART="1"><P>Hip right: (2)</P></TD>
<TD COLSTART="2"><INPUT NAME="HIPR" SIZE="2" MAXLENGTH="2"></TD><TD
VALIGN="MIDDLE" ALIGN="RIGHT" COLSTART="3"><P>OVCNO: (15)</P></TD><TD
COLSTART="4"><INPUT NAME="OVCNO" SIZE="15" MAXLENGTH="15"></TD><TD
COLSPAN="3" COLSTART="5"></TD></TR><TR><TD
```

```
VALIGN="MIDDLE" ALIGN="RIGHT" COLSTART="1"><P>Hiptotal: (3)</P></TD><TD
COLSTART="2"><INPUT NAME="HIPTOTAL" SIZE="3" MAXLENGTH="3"></TD><TD
VALIGN="MIDDLE" ALIGN="RIGHT" COLSTART="3"><P>Tattoo: (15)</P></TD><TD
COLSTART="4"><INPUT NAME="TATTOO" SIZE="15" MAXLENGTH="15"></TD><TD
COLSPAN="3" COLSTART="5"></TD></TR><TR><TD
VALIGN="MIDDLE" ALIGN="RIGHT" COLSTART="1"><P>Hip scores other than OFA
or UK: (25)</P></TD><TD COLSTART="2"><INPUT NAME="HIPS" SIZE="20"
MAXLENGTH="25">
</TD><TD VALIGN="MIDDLE" ALIGN="RIGHT" COLSTART="3"><P>HD CERT: (1)</P></
TD><TD
COLSTART="4"><INPUT NAME="HDCERT" SIZE="1" MAXLENGTH="1"></TD><TD
COLSPAN="3" COLSTART="5"></TD></TR><TR><TD
VALIGN="MIDDLE" ALIGN="RIGHT" COLSTART="1"><P>Other titles that
appear after the dog's name: (30)</P></TD><TD COLSTART="2"><INPUT
NAME="JWOB" SIZE="30" MAXLENGTH="30"></TD><TD
VALIGN="MIDDLE" ALIGN="RIGHT" COLSTART="3"><P>KCBVA Eye: (10)</P></TD>
<TD COLSTART="4"><INPUT NAME="KCBVAEYE" SIZE="10" MAXLENGTH="10"></TD><TD
COLSPAN="3" COLSTART="5"></TD></TR>
<TR><TD VALIGN="MIDDLE" ALIGN="RIGHT" COLSTART="1"><P>Date of other
titles.
(MM/DD/YYYY): </P></TD><TD COLSTART="2"><INPUT
NAME="JWDATE" SIZE="10" MAXLENGTH="10"></TD><TD COLSTART="3"><P>-</P></
TD>
<TD COLSTART="4"><P>-</P></TD><TD COLSPAN="3" COLSTART="5"></TD></TR>
<TR><TD VALIGN="MIDDLE" ALIGN="RIGHT" COLSTART="1"><P>Comments: </P>
</TD> <TD COLSTART="2" COLSPAN="3" ROWSPAN="2"><TEXTAREA
NAME="COMMENTS" ROWS="4" COLS="60"></TEXTAREA></TD>
<TD COLSPAN="2" COLSTART="5"></TD>
<TD COLSTART="7"></TD></TR>
<TR><TD COLSTART="1"></TD><TD COLSTART="5"></TD><TD COLSTART="6"></TD>
<TD COLSTART="7"></TD></TR>

</TABLE>
<P><BR></P>
<TABLE ALIGN="CENTER"><TR><TD ALIGN="CENTER" COLSTART="1"><INPUT
TYPE="SUBMIT" VALUE="Add This Record to the Database"></TD><TD
ALIGN="CENTER" COLSTART="2">
<INPUT TYPE="RESET" VALUE="Clear the form"></TD></TR>
</TABLE><INPUT TYPE="HIDDEN" NAME="QueryType" VALUE="insert"><INPUT
TYPE="HIDDEN" NAME="db" VALUE="newf"><INPUT
TYPE="HIDDEN" NAME="tbl" VALUE="newdog"><INPUT
TYPE="HIDDEN" NAME="server" VALUE="katie"><INPUT
TYPE="HIDDEN" NAME="user" VALUE="webuser"><INPUT
TYPE="HIDDEN" NAME="base" VALUE="http://katie"></FORM>
```

```
<HR>
<P><A HREF="NewfDB.html">[Return to Newf DB top page]</A></P>
</BODY></HTML>
```

In Listing 3.20, we define an entry field for every field in the NEWDOG record, and, as you might expect, each entry field is named the same as its associated NEWDOG field. The entry screen <FORM> element does have one big difference from the query-description <FORM> tags we've seen up to now—it uses the POST method to get its name/value pairs into the CGI program. Simply looking at the size of the form, you can see why. The massive number of <INPUT> elements, and the potential size of the data entered into those fields, would create a QUERY_STRING far longer than any operating system would allow an environment variable to be. From this form, I've gotten query strings up to 1k in length.

If we look back at Listing 3.6, we can see what happens to an inserted record. When, in the data-entry screen, the user clicks the Add Record button, our CGI program is started up, and, via **ProcessArgs**, **QueryType** is set to **QUERY_INSERT**. Our host variables are also set to the values from the form via **ProcessArgs**. All that remains is for us to insert the record in NEWDOG, which we do in **DoQuery**.

The important thing to note about the record insert in **DoQuery** is that we surround the INSERT statement with a BEGIN TRAN...COMMIT TRAN pair of SQL statements. What this does is define a transaction. Every SQL statement between the BEGIN TRAN and COMMIT TRAN is part of that transaction. When we COMMIT the transaction, SQL Server writes the transaction-log record to disk, so we can be sure that no matter what happens, that transaction-log record will be part of the on-disk representation of the database, i.e. the transaction can be recovered if the database machine crashes right now. What happens if the transaction isn't committed? Uncommitted transactions are kept in memory and can be rolled back via the ROLLBACK TRANSACTION statement.

Updating an existing record is a more interesting problem. What we want to do is take all the data from an existing record and use it to populate a data-entry screen. Back in Listing 3.8, we can see that the Update button in a dog's record is actually a hyperlink to the form.

This CGI invocation sets **QueryType** to **QUERY_UPDATE**, and gives us only a single host variable—**QUOTENO**. Within the SHORTDOG table, **QUOTENO** is a unique identifier. Thus, we can retrieve the dog's record just by searching SHORTDOG on the **QUOTENO** field. The alternative to using the **QUOTENO** key is to stuff all the dog's data into the anchor tag. Instead of just having the single **QUOTENO=*xxx*** name/value pair, we would need all 35 name/value pairs for all the dog data. This is clearly overly complicated.

Looking back at Listing 3.6, the **QUERY_UPDATE** case of the **QueryType** switch fetches the single record corresponding to the supplied **QUOTENO** into the appropriate host variables. Then, all we do before exiting is call the function **FillInEntryTemplate**, shown in Listing 3.21.

Listing 3.21 FillInEntryTemplate and PrintValue implement a simple HTML database template.

```
/* FillInEntryTemplate - Open the template file, read it line
by line, for each line pluck out any field-name surrounded by
% signs and replace the %fieldname% with the value now residing
in that host variable. Everything that is not a %fieldname% is
printed to stdout, the host variable named in fieldname is
printed to stdout as well.  Only works with ONE %fieldname% per
line of HTML in the entry template. */
void FillInEntryTemplate() {
   FILE *fp;
   char *start, *end, *name;
   char buffer[1024];

   sprintf( buffer, "entry.tmp" );
   if(( fp = fopen( buffer, "r" )) == NULL ) {
      fprintf( errfp, "Couldn't open entry.tmp\n" );
      return;
      }

   while( 1 ) {
      if( fgets( buffer, sizeof( buffer ), fp ) == NULL )
         break;
      if(( start = strchr( buffer, '%' )) == NULL )
         printf( buffer );
      else
         {
```

```
        if(( end = strchr( &start[1], '%' )) == NULL )
            printf( buffer );
        else
            {
            *start = '\0';
            *end = '\0';
            name = &start[1];
            printf( buffer );
            PrintValue( name );
            printf( &end[1] );
            }
        }
    }

  fclose( fp );
  }

/* PrintValue - Print the value of the host variable named
in the argument. */
void PrintValue( char *name ) {
        if( strcmp( name, "NAME" ) == 0 ) {
                if( strlen( NAME ) == 0 )
                        printf( "\"\"" );
                else
                        printf( "\"%s\"", NAME );
                return;
                }
        if( strcmp( name, "QUOTENO" ) == 0 ) {
                if( strlen( QUOTENO ) == 0 )
                        printf( "\"\"" );
                else
                        printf( "\"%s\"", QUOTENO );
                return;
                }
        if( strcmp( name, "CHANGEDATE" ) == 0 ) {
                if( strlen( CHANGEDATE ) == 0 )
                        printf( "\"\"" );
                else
                        printf( "\"%s\"", CHANGEDATE );
                return;
                }
        if( strcmp( name, "CHANGETEXT" ) == 0 ) {
                if( strlen( CHANGETEXT ) == 0 )
                        printf( "\"\"" );
                else
```

```
                printf( "\"%s\"", CHANGETEXT );
        return;
        }
if( strcmp( name, "REGNO" ) == 0 ) {
        if( strlen( REGNO ) == 0 )
                printf( "\"\"" );
        else
                printf( "\"%s\"", REGNO );
        return;
        }
if( strcmp( name, "COUNTRY" ) == 0 ) {
        if( strlen( COUNTRY ) == 0 )
                printf( "\"\"" );
        else
                printf( "\"%s\"", COUNTRY );
        return;
        }
if( strcmp( name, "TITLES" ) == 0 ) {
        if( strlen( TITLES ) == 0 )
                printf( "\"\"" );
        else
                printf( "\"%s\"", TITLES );
        return;
        }
if( strcmp( name, "CHDATE" ) == 0 ) {
        if( strlen( CHDATE ) == 0 )
                printf( "\"\"" );
        else
                printf( "\"%s\"", CHDATE );
        return;
        }
if( strcmp( name, "JWOB" ) == 0 ) {
        if( strlen( JWOB ) == 0 )
                printf( "\"\"" );
        else
                printf( "\"%s\"", JWOB );
        return;
        }
if( strcmp( name, "JWDATE" ) == 0 ) {
        if( strlen( JWDATE ) == 0 )
                printf( "\"\"" );
        else
                printf( "\"%s\"", JWDATE );
        return;
        }
```

```
if( strcmp( name, "DOB" ) == 0 ) {
        if( strlen( DOB ) == 0 )
                printf( "\"\"" );
        else
                printf( "\"%s\"", DOB );
        return;
        }
if( strcmp( name, "DOB2" ) == 0 ) {
        if( strlen( DOB2 ) == 0 )
                printf( "\"\"" );
        else
                printf( "\"%s\"", DOB2 );
        return;
        }
if( strcmp( name, "SEX" ) == 0 ) {
        if( strlen( SEX ) == 0 )
                printf( "\"\"" );
        else
                printf( "\"%s\"", SEX );
        return;
        }
if( strcmp( name, "SNAME" ) == 0 ) {
        if( strlen( SNAME ) == 0 )
                printf( "\"\"" );
        else
                printf( "\"%s\"", SNAME );
        return;
        }
if( strcmp( name, "DNAME" ) == 0 ) {
        if( strlen( DNAME ) == 0 )
                printf( "\"\"" );
        else
                printf( "\"%s\"", DNAME );
        return;
        }
if( strcmp( name, "COLOUR" ) == 0 ) {
        if( strlen( COLOUR ) == 0 )
                printf( "\"\"" );
        else
                printf( "\"%s\"", COLOUR );
        return;
        }
if( strcmp( name, "RECESSIVE" ) == 0 ) {
        if( strlen( RECESSIVE ) == 0 )
                printf( "\"\"" );
```

```
        else
                printf( "\"%s\"", RECESSIVE );
        return;
        }
if( strcmp( name, "OWNER" ) == 0 ) {
        if( strlen( OWNER ) == 0 )
                printf( "\"\"" );
        else
                printf( "\"%s\"", OWNER );
        return;
        }
if( strcmp( name, "KENNEL" ) == 0 ) {
        if( strlen( KENNEL ) == 0 )
                printf( "\"\"" );
        else
                printf( "\"%s\"", KENNEL );
        return;
        }
if( strcmp( name, "BREEDER" ) == 0 ) {
        if( strlen( BREEDER ) == 0 )
                printf( "\"\"" );
        else
                printf( "\"%s\"", BREEDER );
        return;
        }
if( strcmp( name, "REMARKS" ) == 0 ) {
        if( strlen( REMARKS ) == 0 )
                printf( "\"\"" );
        else
                printf( "\"%s\"", REMARKS );
        return;
        }
if( strcmp( name, "HIPTOT" ) == 0 ) {
        if( strlen( HIPTOT ) == 0 )
                printf( "\"\"" );
        else
                printf( "\"%s\"", HIPTOT );
        return;
        }
if( strcmp( name, "HIPR" ) == 0 ) {
        if( strlen( HIPR ) == 0 )
                printf( "\"\"" );
        else
                printf( "\"%s\"", HIPR );
        return;
```

```
        }
if( strcmp( name, "HIPL" ) == 0 ) {
        if( strlen( HIPL ) == 0 )
                printf( "\"\"" );
        else
                printf( "\"%s\"", HIPL );
        return;
        }
if( strcmp( name, "DIED" ) == 0 ) {
        if( strlen( DIED ) == 0 )
                printf( "\"\"" );
        else
                printf( "\"%s\"", DIED );
        return;
        }
if( strcmp( name, "HDCERT" ) == 0 ) {
        if( strlen( HDCERT ) == 0 )
                printf( "\"\"" );
        else
                printf( "\"%s\"", HDCERT );
        return;
        }
if( strcmp( name, "HIPS" ) == 0 ) {
        if( strlen( HIPS ) == 0 )
                printf( "\"\"" );
        else
                printf( "\"%s\"", HIPS );
        return;
        }
if( strcmp( name, "OFANO" ) == 0 ) {
        if( strlen( OFANO ) == 0 )
                printf( "\"\"" );
        else
                printf( "\"%s\"", OFANO );
        return;
        }
if( strcmp( name, "OVCNO" ) == 0 ) {
        if( strlen( OVCNO ) == 0 )
                printf( "\"\"" );
        else
                printf( "\"%s\"", OVCNO );
        return;
        }
if( strcmp( name, "KCBVAEYE" ) == 0 ) {
        if( strlen( KCBVAEYE ) == 0 )
```

```
                        printf( "\"\"" );
                else
                        printf( "\"%s\"", KCBVAEYE );
                return;
                }
        if( strcmp( name, "TATTOO" ) == 0 ) {
                if( strlen( TATTOO ) == 0 )
                        printf( "\"\"" );
                else
                        printf( "\"%s\"", TATTOO );
                return;
                }
        if( strcmp( name, "HEARTGRADE" ) == 0 ) {
                if( strlen( HEARTGRADE ) == 0 )
                        printf( "\"\"" );
                else
                        printf( "\"%s\"", HEARTGRADE );
                return;
                }
        if( strcmp( name, "SOURCE" ) == 0 ) {
                if( strlen( SOURCE ) == 0 )
                        printf( "\"\"" );
                else
                        printf( "\"%s\"", SOURCE );
                return;
                }
        if( strcmp( name, "SB" ) == 0 ) {
                if( strlen( SB ) == 0 )
                        printf( "\"\"" );
                else
                        printf( "\"%s\"", SB );
                return;
                }
        if( strcmp( name, "WORKAREA" ) == 0 ) {
                if( strlen( WORKAREA ) == 0 )
                        printf( "\"\"" );
                else
                        printf( "\"%s\"", WORKAREA );
                return;
                }
}
```

FillInEntryTemplate (and its helper **PrintValue**) is a very simple function. It reads a template named "entry.tmp" that contains, for the most part, the original HTML text of the new-record-insert data-entry screen (Listing 3.20) with simple markers to indicate where to insert the current value of the host variables. Listing 3.22 shows the hacked-HTML source for entry.tmp.

Listing 3.22 The update screen template.

```
<H1>Newfoundland DB Data Entry</H1>
<P>Use the form below to enter new records for the
Newfoundland database or to correct existing records.  If you
don't know what the value of a particular
field is, leave it blank.  The data librarian will do his best
to merge your input with existing data.  Most fields include a
number in parentheses next to the prompt.  This is the maximum
number of characters allowed. Data larger than
the maximum will be either truncated, or rejected. </P>
<P>When you submit a record (by hitting the &quot;add
record&quot; button), the
system will try to add the record to the database.  A message
will be displayed indicating whether the record was accepted
or rejected.  At that point you can either quit or continue
adding records (using the same source address).  If the
record was rejected, you can either quit without saving the
record, or go back, edit the record, and resubmit. </P>
<HR>
<H2>Address/Data Source</H2>
<P>You MUST enter a name and either an email or regular mail
address.  Each item of data in the newf database is tagged
with the source of that data so that any conflict between two
versions of the same data item can be resolved quickly
and correctly.  If there is any question about the data you've
entered, we may use this address to contact you.  These
addresses will be seen only by the Web
database administrator, John Rodley, and the data librarian,
Richard Scothern.</P>
<P>Right now, data entered here does NOT show up in a search
immediately.  It must pass through a checking process before
being made publicly available. Future versions of the database
may allow users to view unverified records.</P>
<FORM METHOD="POST" ACTION="http://katie/newf/newfq.exe">
<TABLE><TR><TD
COLSTART="1">Enter your name and postal address here.</TD><TD
COLSTART="2"><TEXTAREA
NAME="SRCADDRESS" ROWS="6" COLS="30"></TEXTAREA></TD></TR>
<TR><TD COLSTART="1">Enter your email address here.
```

```
(40)</TD><TD COLSTART="2"><INPUT
NAME="SRCEMAIL" SIZE="20" MAXLENGTH="40"></TD></TR>

</TABLE>
<HR>
<H2>Vital Information</H2>
<H3>Dates</H3>
<P>All dates MUST be entered in one of three ways:</P>
<UL><LI>The four digit year, as in <B>1975</B>, or
<B>1833</B>, or <B>1991</B>.</LI>
<LI>The month and year, as in <B>12/1992 </B>(for December
1992), or <B>3/1877</B>
(for March 1877).</LI>
<LI>The month, day and year, as in <B>12/1/1992</B>
(for December 1st, 1992)
or <B>3/7/1960</B> (for March 7, 1960).</LI></UL>
<P>All other date formats WILL BE REJECTED.  Like other data items, if
you
don't know a date, leave it blank.
<INPUT TYPE="HIDDEN" NAME="QUOTENO" VALUE=%QUOTENO%>
<INPUT TYPE="HIDDEN" NAME="QueryType" VALUE="insert">
</P>
<TABLE BORDER="5" CELLPADDING="5" CELLSPACING="4" ALIGN="CENTER">
<TR>
<TD VALIGN="MIDDLE" ALIGN="RIGHT" COLSTART="1">
<P>Dog Name: (62)</P></TD>
<TD COLSTART="2">
<INPUT NAME="NAME" VALUE=%NAME% SIZE="30" MAXLENGTH="62"></TD>
<TD VALIGN="MIDDLE" ALIGN="RIGHT" COLSTART="3">
<P>Date of Birth: (MM/DD/YYYY)</P></TD>
<TD COLSTART="4">
<INPUT NAME="DOB" VALUE=%DOB% SIZE="10" MAXLENGTH="10"></TD>
<TD COLSPAN="3" COLSTART="5"></TD></TR>
<TR><TD
VALIGN="MIDDLE" ALIGN="RIGHT" COLSTART="1"><P>Sex: (1)</P></TD>
<TD VALIGN="TOP" COLSTART="2"><SELECT NAME="SEX" SIZE="0">
<OPTION VALUE="D">Dog</OPTION>
<OPTION VALUE="B">Bitch</OPTION></SELECT></TD>
<TD VALIGN="MIDDLE" ALIGN="RIGHT" COLSTART="3">
<P>Died: (MM/DD/YYYY)</P></TD>
<TD COLSTART="4">
<INPUT NAME="DIED" VALUE=%DIED% SIZE="10" MAXLENGTH="10"></TD>
<TD COLSPAN="3" COLSTART="5"></TD></TR>
<TR><TD VALIGN="TOP" ALIGN="RIGHT" COLSTART="1">
<P>Colour: (40)</P><P>Colors other
```

```
than those listed should be described in
the comments field below.</P></TD>
<TD VALIGN="TOP" COLSTART="2"><SELECT NAME="COLOUR">
<OPTION SELECTED="SELECTED" VALUE="BLACK">Black</OPTION>
<OPTION VALUE="Landseer">Landseer</OPTION>
<OPTION VALUE="BROWN">Brown</OPTION>
<OPTION VALUE="GREY">Grey</OPTION></SELECT></TD>
<TD VALIGN="MIDDLE" ALIGN="RIGHT" COLSTART="3">
<P>Sire: (62)</P></TD>
<TD VALIGN="MIDDLE" COLSTART="4">
<INPUT NAME="SNAME" VALUE=%SNAME% SIZE="30" MAXLENGTH="62"></TD>
<TD COLSPAN="3" COLSTART="5"></TD></TR>
<TR><TD VALIGN="MIDDLE" ALIGN="RIGHT" COLSTART="1"><P>
Recessive: (40)</P></TD>
<TD COLSTART="2">
<INPUT NAME="RECESSIVE" VALUE=%RECESSIVE% SIZE="20" MAXLENGTH="40"></TD>
<TD VALIGN="MIDDLE" ALIGN="RIGHT" COLSTART="3"><P>
Dam: (62)</P></TD>
<TD COLSTART="4">
<INPUT  NAME="DNAME" VALUE=%DNAME% SIZE="30" MAXLENGTH="62"></TD>
<TD COLSPAN="3" COLSTART="5"></TD></TR>
<TR>
<TD VALIGN="MIDDLE" ALIGN="RIGHT" COLSTART="1"><P>
Breeder: (62)</P></TD>
<TD COLSTART="2">
<INPUT  NAME="BREEDER" VALUE=%BREEDER% SIZE="30" MAXLENGTH="62"></TD>
<TD VALIGN="MIDDLE" ALIGN="RIGHT" COLSTART="3"><P>
Titles: (40)</P></TD>
<TD COLSTART="4">
<INPUT  NAME="TITLES" VALUE=%TITLES% SIZE="30" MAXLENGTH="40"></TD>
<TD COLSPAN="3" COLSTART="5"></TD></TR>
<TR>
<TD VALIGN="MIDDLE" ALIGN="RIGHT" COLSTART="1"><P>
Country: (20)</P></TD>
<TD COLSTART="2">
<INPUT  NAME="COUNTRY" VALUE=%COUNTRY% SIZE="20" MAXLENGTH="20"></TD>
<TD VALIGN="MIDDLE" ALIGN="RIGHT" COLSTART="3"><P>
Kennel: (30)</P></TD>
<TD COLSTART="4">
<INPUT  NAME="AFFIX" VALUE=%AFFIX% SIZE="30" MAXLENGTH="30"></TD>
<TD COLSPAN="3" COLSTART="5"></TD></TR>
<TR>
<TD VALIGN="MIDDLE" ALIGN="RIGHT" COLSTART="1"><P>
OFA NO: (15)</P></TD>
<TD COLSTART="2">
```

```
<INPUT  NAME="OFANO" VALUE=%OFANO% SIZE="15" MAXLENGTH="15"></TD>
<TD VALIGN="MIDDLE" ALIGN="RIGHT" COLSTART="3"><P>
Owner: (62)</P></TD>
<TD COLSTART="4">
<INPUT  NAME="OWNER" VALUE=%OWNER% SIZE="30" MAXLENGTH="62"></TD>
<TD COLSPAN="3" COLSTART="5"></TD></TR>
<TR>
<TD VALIGN="MIDDLE" ALIGN="RIGHT" COLSTART="1"><P>
Heartgrade(9): </P></TD>
<TD COLSTART="2">
<INPUT  NAME="HEARTGRADE" VALUE=%HEARTGRADE% SIZE="9" MAXLENGTH="9"></TD>
<TD VALIGN="MIDDLE" ALIGN="RIGHT" COLSTART="3"><P>
Registration: (30)</P></TD>
<TD COLSTART="4">
<INPUT  NAME="REGNO" VALUE=%REGNO% SIZE="30" MAXLENGTH="30"></TD>
<TD COLSPAN="3" COLSTART="5"></TD></TR>
<TR>
<TD VALIGN="MIDDLE" ALIGN="RIGHT" COLSTART="1"><P>
Hip left: (2)</P></TD>
<TD COLSTART="2">
<INPUT  NAME="HIPL" VALUE=%HIPL% SIZE="2" MAXLENGTH="2"></TD>
<TD VALIGN="MIDDLE" ALIGN="RIGHT" COLSTART="3"><P>
Championship Date (MM/DD/YYYY):
</P></TD>
<TD  COLSTART="4">
<INPUT  NAME="CHDATE" VALUE=%CHDATE% SIZE="10" MAXLENGTH="10"></TD>
<TD COLSPAN="3" COLSTART="5"></TD></TR>
<TR>
<TD VALIGN="MIDDLE" ALIGN="RIGHT" COLSTART="1"><P>
Hip right: (2)</P></TD>
<TD COLSTART="2">
<INPUT  NAME="HIPR" VALUE=%HIPR% SIZE="2" MAXLENGTH="2"></TD>
<TD VALIGN="MIDDLE" ALIGN="RIGHT" COLSTART="3"><P>
OVCNO: (15)</P></TD>
<TD COLSTART="4">
<INPUT  NAME="OVCNO" VALUE=%OVCNO% SIZE="15" MAXLENGTH="15"></TD>
<TD COLSPAN="3" COLSTART="5"></TD></TR>
<TR>
<TD VALIGN="MIDDLE" ALIGN="RIGHT" COLSTART="1"><P>
Hiptotal: (3)</P></TD>
<TD COLSTART="2">
<INPUT  NAME="HIPTOT" VALUE=%HIPTOT% SIZE="3" MAXLENGTH="3"></TD>
<TD VALIGN="MIDDLE" ALIGN="RIGHT" COLSTART="3"><P>
Tattoo: (15)</P></TD>
<TD COLSTART="4">
```

```
<INPUT  NAME="TATTOO" VALUE=%TATTOO% SIZE="15" MAXLENGTH="15"></TD>
<TD COLSPAN="3" COLSTART="5"></TD></TR>
<TR>
<TD VALIGN="MIDDLE" ALIGN="RIGHT" COLSTART="1"><P>
Hip scores other than OFA or UK:
(25)</P></TD>
<TD  COLSTART="2">
<INPUT  NAME="HIPS" VALUE=%HIPS% SIZE="20" MAXLENGTH="25"></TD>
<TD  VALIGN="MIDDLE" ALIGN="RIGHT" COLSTART="3"><P>
HD CERT: (1)</P></TD>
<TD COLSTART="4">
<INPUT  NAME="HDCERT" VALUE=%HDCERT% SIZE="1" MAXLENGTH="1"></TD>
<TD COLSPAN="3" COLSTART="5"></TD></TR>
<TR>
<TD VALIGN="MIDDLE" ALIGN="RIGHT" COLSTART="1"><P>
Other titles that appear after
the dog's name: (30)</P></TD>
<TD  COLSTART="2">
<INPUT
NAME="JWOB" VALUE=%JWOB% SIZE="30" MAXLENGTH="30"></TD>
<TD VALIGN="MIDDLE" ALIGN="RIGHT" COLSTART="3"><P>
KCBVA Eye: (10)</P></TD>
<TD COLSTART="4">
<INPUT  NAME="KCBVAEYE" VALUE=%KCBVAEYE% SIZE="10" MAXLENGTH="10"></TD>
<TD COLSPAN="3" COLSTART="5"></TD></TR>

<TR>
<TD  VALIGN="MIDDLE" ALIGN="RIGHT" COLSTART="1"><P>
Date of other titles.
(MM/DD/YYYY): </P></TD>
<TD  COLSTART="2">
<INPUT
NAME="JWDATE" VALUE=%JWDATE% SIZE="10" MAXLENGTH="10"></TD>
<TD  COLSTART="3"><P>
-</P></TD>

<TD  COLSTART="4"><P>
-</P></TD>
<TD  COLSPAN="3" COLSTART="5"></TD></TR>

<TR>
<TD  VALIGN="MIDDLE" ALIGN="RIGHT" COLSTART="1"><P>
Comments: </P></TD>
<TD COLSTART="2" COLSPAN="3" ROWSPAN="2"><TEXTAREA
NAME="COMMENTS" VALUE=%COMMENTS% ROWS="4" COLS="60"></TEXTAREA></TD>
```

```
<TD  COLSPAN="2" COLSTART="5"></TD>

<TD  COLSTART="7"></TD></TR>

<TR>
<TD  COLSTART="1"></TD>
<TD  COLSTART="5"></TD>
<TD  COLSTART="6"></TD>
<TD COLSTART="7"></TD></TR>

</TABLE>
<P>
<BR></P>
<TABLE ALIGN="CENTER"><TR>
<TD  ALIGN="CENTER" COLSTART="1">
<INPUT
TYPE="SUBMIT" VALUE="Add This Record to the Database"></TD>
<TD ALIGN="CENTER" COLSTART="2">
<INPUT  TYPE="RESET" VALUE="Clear the form"></TD></TR>
</TABLE>

<INPUT
TYPE="HIDDEN" NAME="db" VALUE="newf">
<INPUT
TYPE="HIDDEN" NAME="tbl" VALUE="newdog">
<INPUT
TYPE="HIDDEN" NAME="server" VALUE="katie">
<INPUT
TYPE="HIDDEN" NAME="user" VALUE="webuser">
<INPUT
TYPE="HIDDEN" NAME="base" VALUE="http://katie"></FORM>
<HR>
<P>
<A HREF="NewfDB.html">[Return to Newf DB top page]</A></P>
```

There's nothing complicated about the template itself. The first thing we need to look at is where we are in the HTML output process when we begin filling in the entry template. **FillInEntryTemplate** is called from **DoQuery**. Thus, we've already executed **StartQuery**, which opens an <HTML> element and a <BODY> element. So our template must exclude both the <HTML> and <BODY> open tags. Notice that the first HTML tag in Listing 3.22 is an <H1> tag. The next thing to think about is closing those open tags. Fortunately for us, our call to **EndQuery** closes these elements automatically. Thus, the last tag in our template is just a hyperlink to the Newfoundland Dog Database home page.

The functional parts of our template are the field names surrounded by percent signs (%). Take a look, for instance, at the entry box for the dog's name:

```
<TD><P>Dog Name: (62)</P></TD>
<TD COLSTART="2">
<INPUT NAME="NAME" VALUE=%NAME% SIZE="30" MAXLENGTH="62"></TD>
```

You see that all we've done is enclose a field name from the SHORTDOG table, **NAME**, in percent signs. **FillInEntryTemplate** reads this file, and scans each line for strings enclosed in percent signs. If the line doesn't have a fieldname on it, we simply print the line out and go on to the next one. If the line does have a fieldname on it, we print out the line up to the first percent sign. Then we pass the %-enclosed field name to **PrintValue**. **PrintValue** figures out which host variable the fieldname corresponds to, and prints out the value of that host variable. Then, **FillInEntryTemplate** prints out the rest of the line after the %-enclosed fieldname. When all the lines in the template file have been processed this way, we return to **main**, which calls **EndQuery** to close the <BODY> and <HTML> elements, and we're done.

It's that simple, and many of the turnkey Web-database solutions implement something very similar, either in a CGI preprocessor as we have, or in the Web server itself.

Conclusion

In this chapter, we constructed an entire CGI database-access program in C. Using structured exception handling, our program catches and handles both SQL errors and fatal C exceptions. It creates, on the fly, HTML output suitable for viewing in a Web browser. And, using a simple template processor, it fills in a customizable template based on the results of a CGI-specified query. In short, we now have a basic beginning-to-end Web database application with query and insert capability. What remains is to analyze its real-world performance and optimize it accordingly.

Webliography

- http://www.snugharbor.com/ — Preferred way to access a running version of the Newfoundland Database. Also contains pointers to errata and updated source for this example application.
- http://www.channel1.com/users/ajrodley/NewfDB.html — Another way to access a running version of the Newfoundland Database. Also contains pointers to errata and updated source for this example application.

part two

Chapter 4

The Example Database In Action

CHAPTER

4

The Example Database In Action

In Chapters 2 and 3, we looked in detail at the construction of a C/CGI Web database application, the Newfoundland Dog Database. In this chapter, we're going to take a long and critical look at how it works, what it looks like in action, and where it falls short. Far from perfect, the database suffers from many shortcomings. Here we'll look at, and sometimes implement, solutions to these problems. When we're done, we'll have closed some of the holes in the original implementation, and, at the very least, we'll have set ourselves up nicely for later chapters where we discuss newer technologies that augment or replace the Web's original HTML/CGI application model.

How It Works

Up to now, we've approached our Newfoundland Dog Database application as a disconnected set of screens and CGI queries. From the screen shots, we've seen that it most emphatically does not look like a traditional application. However, if we look back at it in a more structured fashion, we can see that it is as coherent and self-contained an application as any standalone system. Figure 4.1 shows a block diagram of the Newf database.

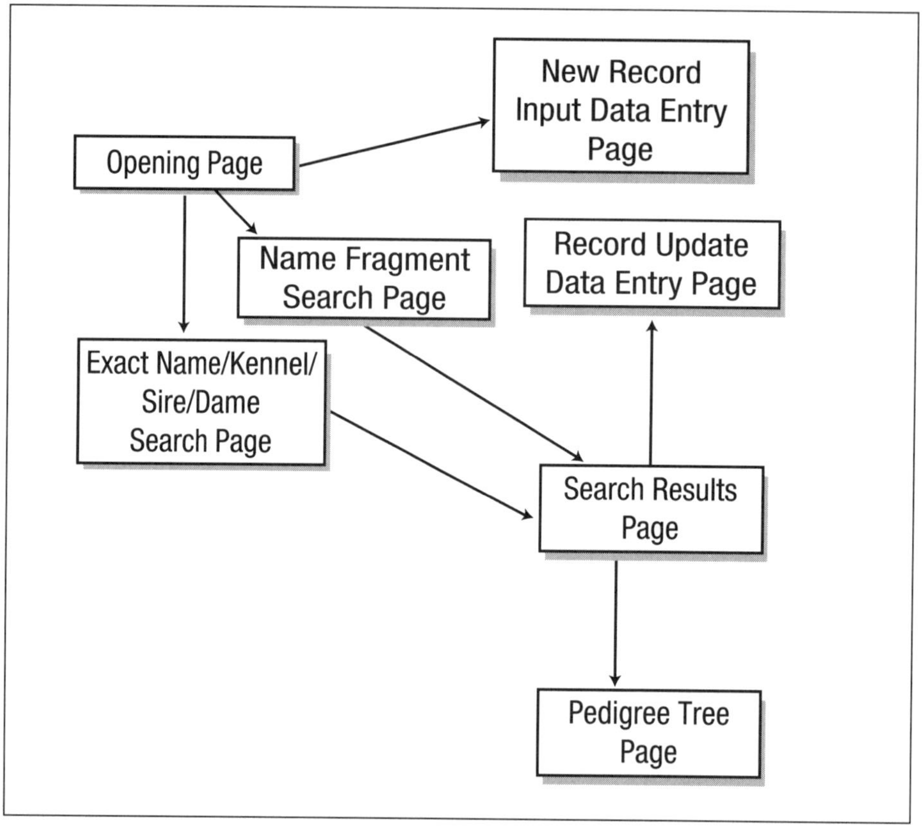

Figure 4.1 The Newf database application block diagram.

From the opening screen, you can go down the search branch or the insert branch. From the search branch, you can do a name-fragment search, or an exact-name search by name, kennel, sire, or dame. Searching either of the search branches takes you to a result screen. At that point, we introduce a certain amount of circularity. From the result screen, you can click on a dog's name and bring up a pedigree tree. From that pedigree tree, you can click on a dog's name and go to that dog's result screen, and so on and so on.

In fact, from any result screen, you can go to any of three different result screens—by kennel, sire, or dame—as well as to the pedigree tree and the update screen. You can think of the result screen as the endpoint of the system, the screen that contains the real information value in this application.

We've already talked about the insert screen. It's essentially a dead end, where you submit the record and receive an acknowledgment. The dead-end nature of the insert screen brings up an interesting design point. Many Web applications try to impose a hierarchical structure by providing a button bar that helps the user keep some idea of the entire application onscreen at one time. A button bar for the Newf database, for example, might provide Home, Search, and Insert buttons. However, after receiving acknowledgment for the most recent insert, a user will often want to insert another new record using many of the same values. For example, one breeder entering one litter might want to insert many records leaving the breeder, kennel, owner, date-of-birth, sire, and dame all the same. If we just slap an Insert button on the insert-acknowledgment screen without embedding the values of these variables in the hyperlinked URL, then the user clicking the Insert button will be dropped back at an empty screen. Instead, we skip the button-bar approach and simply tell the user to click the browser's Back button to go back to the form with the most recent data already filled in.

This is another example of the "stateless" nature of Web applications. This statelessness can be very confusing for users, and anything you can do to alleviate it, including button bars, is worth trying. At all points, however, you have to consider what lengths you are willing to go to in order to preserve state, and what shortcuts might be appropriate.

User Reactions To The Application

While not strictly a programming topic, user reaction to your Web application is worth considering, especially in light of the preceding section on the view from different browsers. The Newf database doesn't work properly under some browsers, as we'll see in the next section. Some browsers don't support tables, others don't support graphics, and some don't support things as silly as the background graphic.

The real difficulty, especially with low-end, mass-market Web sites, is figuring out that users are having a problem at all. There are various rules of thumb to calculate the ratio of loud complainers to silent fumers. Suffice to say that, if your site has a problem, for every user who realizes that it's your site (and not his browser) that's the problem, there are many more users who have simply given up and clicked away, frustrated, angry, and unlikely to return.

In its early days, the Newf database, for example, had a problem on the data-entry screen where perfectly good records were being rejected. At least two dozen users went away stumped before one recognized there was a problem and emailed the (properly embarrassed) administrator. The only real solution to this natural shyness of users is to provide easy, frequent, prominent, and enthusiastic opportunities to email the Webmaster if they run into a problem.

The Drawbacks Of This Approach

The heart of the Newf database's functionality is the user entering data, and our CGI program acting on that input. However, as with any real-world application, there are rules that can cause a user's input to be rejected. On the name-fragment search, the name fragment must be six characters or greater. On the data-entry screen, all dates must be formatted in one of a small set of formats.

Field Validation

What happens when the user, for whatever reason, enters bad data? If you look back at Listing 3.6, you can see a call to the function **VerifyInput**, shown in Listing 4.1. **VerifyInput** has one task, to make sure that the data entered by the user is useable by our CGI program.

Listing 4.1 VerifyInput dealing with data input errors.

```
/* VerifyDate - Take a string date (item) as entered by the user and
make sure that it fits one of our date formats:
  yyyy
  mm/yyyy
  mm/dd/yyyy
  mm/dd/yyyy hh:mm:ss AM/PM

decompose it into parts and reconstruct according to OUR one and
only format
  mm/dd/yyyy hh:mm:ss AM/PM

returns  0 if success - also reformats date into origdata and places
integer year into *pYr.
    1 if error
*/
int VerifyDate( char *item, char *origdata, int *pYr ) {
  int i;
  int component_count = 0;
  char *component[4];
```

```
char data[1024];
char day[3];
char month[3];
char year[5];
char hhmm[80];

strcpy( data, origdata );
failed_data = origdata;
failed_item = item;

if( strlen( data ) <= 0 ) {
  failed_data = NULL;
  failed_item = NULL;
  return( 1 );
  }
component[component_count++] = data;
if( isalpha( origdata[0] )) {
  for( i = 0; origdata[i] != '\0'; i++ ) {
    if( origdata[i] == ' ' ) {
      data[i] = '\0';
      component[component_count++] = &data[i+1];
      }
    if( component_count == 4 ) {
      fprintf( errfp, "component_count rolling over\n" );
      break;
      }
    }
  if( component_count == 3 )
    component[component_count++] = "00:00:04am";
  }
else {
  for( i = 0; origdata[i] != '\0'; i++ ) {
    if( origdata[i] == '/' ) {
      data[i] = '\0';
      if( component_count == 3 )
        return( 0 );
      component[component_count++] = &data[i+1];
      }
    }
  }
switch( component_count ) {
  case 1:    // Year only, MUST be between 1700 and 2000
    strcpy( hhmm, "00:00:01am" );
    strcpy( day, "01" );
    strcpy( month, "01" );
    if( !VerifyYear( component[0] ))
```

```
        return( 0 );
      strcpy( year, component[0] );
      break;
    case 2:    // Month and year
      strcpy( hhmm, "00:00:02am" );
      strcpy( day, "01" );
      if( !VerifyMonth( component[0] ))
        return( 0 );
      strcpy( month, component[0] );
      if( !VerifyYear( component[1] ))
        return( 0 );
      strcpy( year, component[1] );
      break;
    case 3:  // Month, day and year
      if( !VerifyMonth( component[0] ))
        return( 0 );
      strcpy( month, component[0] );
      if( !VerifyDay( component[1] ))
        return( 0 );
      strcpy( day, component[1] );
      if( !VerifyYear( component[2] ))
        return( 0 );
      strcpy( year, component[2] );
      strcpy( hhmm, "00:00:03am" );
      break;
    case 4:
      for( i = 1; i <= 13; i++ ) {
        if( i == 13 )
          return( 0 );
        if( strcmp( component[0], months[i-1].shortname ) == 0 ) {
          sprintf( month, "%d", i );
          break;
          }
        if( strcmp( component[0], months[i-1].longname ) == 0 ) {
          sprintf( month, "%d", i );
          break;
          }
        }
      strcpy( day, component[1] );
      strcpy( year, component[2] );
      strcpy( hhmm, component[3] );
      break;
    }
  sprintf( origdata, "%s/%s/%s %s", month, day, year, hhmm );
  failed_data = NULL;
```

```
  failed_item = NULL;
  *pYr = atoi( year );
  return( 1 );
  }

/* VerifyYear - Verify that provided string is an integer
number between 1700 and 2000 inclusive.
return 1 if success
     0 if error
*/
int VerifyYear( char *szYear ) {
  if( atoi( szYear ) < 1700 || atoi( szYear ) > 2000 ) {
    fprintf( errfp, "bad yy %s\n", szYear );
    return( 0 );
    }
  return( 1 );
  }

/* VerifyMonth - Verify that provided string is an integer
number between 1 and 12 inclusive.
return 1 if success
     0 if error
*/
int VerifyMonth( char *szMonth ) {
  if( atoi( szMonth ) <= 0 || atoi( szMonth ) > 12 ) {
    fprintf( errfp, "bad mm %s\n", szMonth );
    return( 0 );
    }
  return( 1 );
  }

/* VerifyDay - Verify that provided string is an integer
number between 1 and 31 inclusive.
return 1 if success
     0 if error
*/
int VerifyDay( char *szDay ) {
  if( atoi( szDay ) <= 0 || atoi( szDay ) > 31 ) {
    fprintf( errfp, "bad dd %s\n", szDay );
    return( 0 );
    }
  return( 1 );
  }
```

If **VerifyInput** returns an error, the program stops processing the query and displays an HTML document detailing the field and data value that caused the error. Unfortunately, the screen that details bad data entry only comes up once the user has tried to submit the form.

Within CGI, there is literally no way around this. The data entered in a form cannot be analyzed until it reaches the CGI program on the server. In the Newf database, we deal with this as best we can, by putting up a screen that describes the problem as we've diagnosed it, and then prompting the user to click the Back button, which should bring the form back as the user filled it out. The problem diagnosis should point to the problematic field, but this approach is still less than satisfactory. It's clunky, as the user input is no longer onscreen when the problem is described, and the performance stinks, because we've fired up the entire CGI program and gone a long way down the road to doing the whole program before even detecting an invalid field value.

For users of state-of-the-art Windows programs like Quicken or Microsoft Word, this sort of batch field validation is positively barbaric. In Word, for example, my typos get corrected on the fly as I enter them. I don't have to click a button and wait for the whole document to be processed before having the typo even pointed out to me.

Field Validation Using Java

There *are* Web solutions to the field-validation problem. A Java applet, for example, could easily do field validation for us, both batch and field-by-field. In fact, this would be a trivial exercise for a Java programmer. Listing 4.2 shows a simple Java applet with field validation that replaces the Newf database's name-fragment search screen (Figure 3.1).

Listing 4.2 The Java applet for the Newf name-fragment search screen.

```
import java.awt.*;
import java.util.Hashtable;
import java.applet.*;
import java.net.*;

/* NameFragment - A class for presenting a Newf DB name-fragment
```

```
search entry screen to the user and firing off the proper
CGI query when the user hits the button.  Performs both batch
and on-the-fly field validation.
*/
public class NameFragment extends Applet {
  private final String   SEARCH_LINK = "Search";
  private TextField     tfName;
  private Choice       chCountry;
  private Button  bSearch;
  private GenericDialog  dialog;
  String sDB;  // Name of the database we're connecting to.
  String sTbl;  // Name of the db table we're using.
  String sServer;  // Name of the server the DBMS is running on.
  String sUser;  // Name of the db-user we're logging in as.
  String sBase;  // URL of the base directory of the db machine.
  Label errorLabel;  // The text appearing below the search button.
  Panel textPanel;  // The panel the name entry field is in.
  Panel errorPanel;  // The panel the error string is in.

/* constructor - Create all the visual elements and add them
to the container that is this applet.
*/
  public NameFragment() {
// Create a panel for the search button and
// error string.
    Panel bottomPanel = new Panel();
// Set it up as 2 rows, 1 column
    bottomPanel.setLayout( new GridLayout( 2, 1 ));
// Create the search button
    bSearch = new Button(SEARCH_LINK);
    bSearch.setBackground(Color.lightGray);
// Make a panel for it.
    Panel buttonPanel = new Panel();
// Add the button to the button panel
    buttonPanel.add( bSearch );
    bottomPanel.add( buttonPanel );
// Create a panel for the error string
    errorPanel = new Panel();
// Make an initial error string
    errorLabel =
      new Label( "Enter a name, and hit Search to start." );
// Add the error string to the panel
    errorPanel.add( errorLabel );
// Add the error panel to the grid panel
    bottomPanel.add( errorPanel );
```

```
// Set up the applet itself as a BorderLayout window.
    setLayout( new BorderLayout() );
// Add the Search button and error text to the applet
// via their panels at the bottom (South) part of
// the applet.
    add( "South", bottomPanel );
    textPanel = new Panel();
    tfName = new TextField( 40 );
    textPanel.add( new Label( "Name Fragment: " ));
    textPanel.add( tfName );
    add( "Center", textPanel );

// Make a panel to hold the country choice field.
    Panel pTemp = new Panel();
    chCountry = new Choice();
// Add some countries to the choice field.
    chCountry.addItem( "any" );
    chCountry.addItem( "ITALY" );
    chCountry.addItem( "UK" );
    chCountry.addItem( "USA" );
    pTemp.add( new Label( "Country: " ));
    pTemp.add( chCountry );
// Add the choice field to the applet via its panel.
    add( "North", pTemp );

// Configure the entry field.
    tfName.setEditable(true);
    tfName.setBackground(Color.lightGray);
  }

/* init - called when this screen is pulled up for the
first time.  Gets the appropriate parameters from the
HTML page setting servername, username, tablename,
databasename.  Sets the focus to the dog-name-fragment
data-entry field.
*/
public void init() {
   sServer = getParameter( "server" );
   sUser  = getParameter( "user" );
   sBase  = getParameter( "base" );
   sDB    = getParameter( "db" );
   sTbl   = getParameter( "tbl" );
   tfName.requestFocus();
  }
```

```
/* handleEvent - called whenever the user hits a key in
our applet.  Deals with forward and back tab by moving the
focus and calling field-validation routines.  Deals with
the Return key by formulating our CGI query from the
data in the entry fields and using AppletContext.showDocument
to hyperlink to the results of the query.
*/
public boolean handleEvent(Event evt)
  {
    switch (evt.id)
    {
// Here's the Tab key
      case Event.KEY_PRESS:
        if (evt.key == 9)
        {
// If Shift is set, we're back-tabbing
          if (evt.shiftDown())
            tabBack(evt.target);
          else
// Otherwise, we're forward tabbing
            tabAhead(evt.target);

          return true;
        }

// If the Return key is hit, batch validate the fields
        if (evt.key == 10) {
          if( !nameValid(tfName.getText())) {
             showError(
                "Name MUST be at least 6 characters! Try again." );
             tfName.requestFocus();
             }
        else {
// Get the AppletContext (the browser)
           AppletContext ac = getAppletContext();
// Construct the CGI query
           String sURL = new String( "http://katie/cgi-bin/
newfq.exe?country="+chCountry.getSelectedItem()+"&dog.text=
   "+tfName.getText()+
                "&base="+sBase+"&QueryType=partial&db=
                   "+sDB+"&server="+sServer+
                   "&user="+sUser+"&tbl="+sTbl);
// Try executing the CGI query
           try {
              URL uURL = new URL(sURL);
```

```
// Link to the document.  Our applet disappears from screen
// right now.
              ac.showDocument( uURL );
              }
// We should do something more friendly, but for now just
// print a message to stdout if the CGI query fails on
// connection.
           catch( Exception e )
             { System.out.println( "bad URL "+sURL ); }
           }
          return true;
        }

        break;
    }

    return false;
  }

/* nameValid - Check if the supplied string meets our criteria
for dog names in a name-fragment search.  In this case, we only
check for the fragment being greater than 6 chars in length.
*/
public boolean nameValid( String dogName ) {
   if( dogName.length() < 6 )
      return( false );
   else
      return( true );
   }

// tabAhead - Move the focus to the next field in the list.
// If we're on the name field, and it has bad data in it,
// then don't move the focus, just show an error and return
// the focus to the name field.
void tabAhead(Object from)
  {
   if( from == chCountry ) {
      tfName.requestFocus();
      showError( "" );
      }
   if( from == tfName ) {
      if( nameValid(tfName.getText())) {
        bSearch.requestFocus();
        showError( "" );
        }
```

```
        else {
          showError( "Name field MUST be 6 characters or greater" );
          tfName.requestFocus();
          }
        }
    if( from == bSearch ) {
        chCountry.requestFocus();
        showError( "" );
        }
  }

// tabBack - Move the focus to the previous field in the list.
// If we're on the name field, and it has bad data in it,
// then don't move the focus, just show an error and return
// the focus to the name field.
void tabBack(Object from)
  {
    if( from == chCountry ) {
        bSearch.requestFocus();
        showError( "" );
        }
    if( from == tfName ) {
        if( nameValid(tfName.getText())) {
          chCountry.requestFocus();
          showError( "" );
          }
        else {
          showError( "Name field MUST be 6 characters or greater" );
          tfName.requestFocus();
          }
        }
    if( from == bSearch ) {
        tfName.requestFocus();
        showError( "" );
        }
  }

// showError - change the string in the errorLabel under
// the Search button to be the string supplied.
public void showError( String s ) {
  errorLabel.setText( s );
  errorPanel.layout();
  }

// action - handle any button presses in the applet, specifically
// the Search button.
```

```
public boolean action(Event evt, Object obj) {
    if( evt.target instanceof Button ) {
      String label = (String) obj;
      if( label.equals(SEARCH_LINK) ) {
        if( !nameValid(tfName.getText())) {
      showError( "Name MUST be at least 6 characters! Try again." );
           tfName.requestFocus();
           }
        else {
           AppletContext ac = getAppletContext();
// Create a URL for the CGI query and jump to it
           String sURL =
            new String("http://katie/cgi-bin/newfq.exe?country="+
              chCountry.getSelectedItem()+
               "&dog.text="+tfName.getText()+
                "&base="+sBase+"&QueryType=partial&db="+
                 sDB+"&server="+sServer+"&user="+sUser+
                  "&tbl="+sTbl);
           try {
              URL uURL = new URL(sURL);
              ac.showDocument( uURL );
              }
           catch( Exception e )
             { System.out.println( "bad URL "+sURL ); }
           }
        return true;
      }
      else {
// return false if we didn't handle the event.
        return false;
      }
    }
    else {
      return super.action(evt, obj);
    }

  }
}
```

If you look back at our original name-fragment search screen in Figure 3.1, this solution, in Figure 4.2, looks quite familiar. Looking at the HTML source for the screen, Listing 4.3, you can see that the main difference is that it entirely eliminates the HTML **<FORM>** element that used to gather our data.

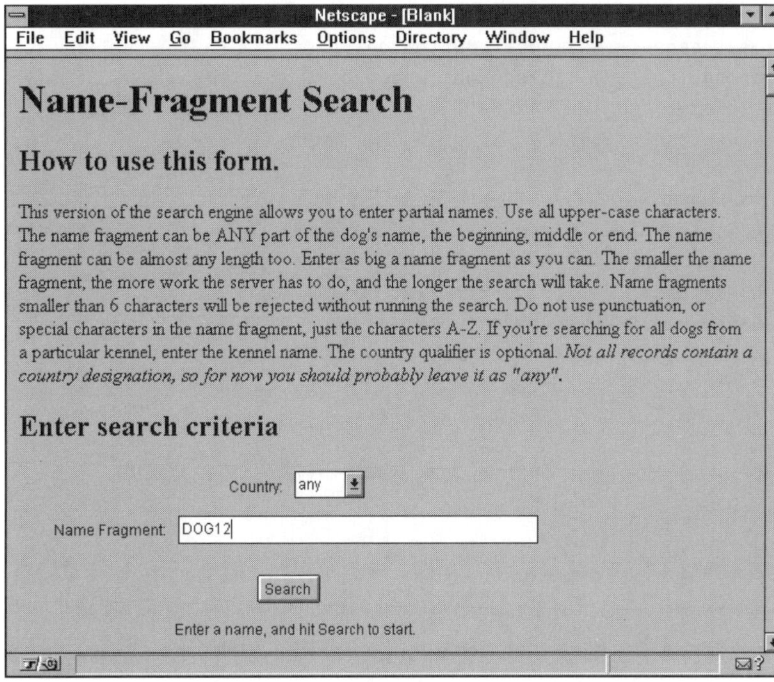

Figure 4.2 The Java field-validating applet in action, before data entry.

Listing 4.3 The new name-fragment HTML source, using a Java applet for validation.

```
<!DOCTYPE
HTML PUBLIC "-//SQ//DTD HTML 2.0 + all extensions//EN" "hmpro3.dtd">
<HTML>
<HEAD>
<TITLE>Blank</TITLE></HEAD>
<BODY BACKGROUND="images/background.jpg">
<H1>Name-Fragment Search</H1>
<H2>How to use this form.</H2>
<P>This version of the engine allows you to enter partial names.
Use all uppercase characters. The name fragment can be ANY part of
the dog's name, the beginning, middle, or end.The name fragment can
be almost any length, too. Enter as big a name fragment as you can.
The smaller the name fragment, the more work the server has to do,
and the longer the search will take. Name fragments smaller than 6
characters will be rejected without running the search. Do not use
punctuation or special characters in the name fragment, just the
characters A-Z. If you're searching for all dogs from a particular
```

```
kennel, enter the kennel name. The country qualifier is optional.
<I>Not all records contain a country designation, so for now you
should probably leave it as &quot;any&quot;.</I></P>

<H2>Enter search criteria</H2>
<P>
<APPLET
   CODE="NameFragment.class" ALT="This browser is not Java enabled!"
   WIDTH="450" HEIGHT="150" ALIGN="MIDDLE" ID="NameFragment">
<PARAM NAME="base" VALUE="http://www.realink.com">
<PARAM NAME="server" VALUE="marconi">
<PARAM NAME="tbl" VALUE="shortdog">
<PARAM NAME="user" VALUE="sa">
<PARAM NAME="db" VALUE="newf"></APPLET></P>
<HR>
<P><A HREF="NewfDB.html">Return to Newf DB top level</A></P>
</BODY></HTML>
```

The **<FORM>** element has disappeared, replaced by an **<APPLET>** element. And what of the information that was inside the **<FORM>** element? The two **<INPUT>** elements, **country** and **dog.text**, as well as the Search button have all disappeared inside our Java applet. The **<ACTION>** attribute that described our CGI query has also been written into the applet. Some of the old **<FORM>** items have remained in the HTML source, though, most notably the five hidden inputs, **base**, **server**, **tbl**, **user**, and **db**. We embedded these in the original form in order to avoid hardwiring them into the C CGI program, and we set them as Java applet parameters here for the same reason, to avoid having to hardwire them into the applet.

Everything else is inside our Java source. The form **<INPUT>** elements have been replaced by Java objects: the Java Button instance **bSearch**, the Java Choice named **chCountry**, and the Java TextField named **tfName**. These are instantiated and positioned within the applet's window by the rather wordy code in the **NameFragment** constructor.

The constructor is more complicated than it probably seems like it needs to be. This is because we need to create multiple Java Panels in order to position our input elements sensibly. We divide the applet window into three Panels:

- The top (or North) Panel contains two elements, the Label **"Country"** and the Choice that contains a list of countries to choose from.

- The bottom (or South) Panel contains two elements, the Search button (**bSearch**) and the error string.
- The middle (or Center) Panel contains two elements, the Label **"Name"** and the text-entry field **tfName**.

Figure 4.3 shows the division of applet window space into panels and elements.

We've already explained the **chCountry**, **tfName**, and **bSearch** objects, but the error string "Enter a name, and click Search to start." is something new. Basically, we've reserved a little window at the bottom of our applet to display messages to the user. When we first come up, the message displayed is "Enter a dog name ...". If, however, the user enters bad data, we can explain that mistake in this window.

There are two points where we perform field validation in this applet—when the user tries to leave the **tfName** text field, and when the user clicks

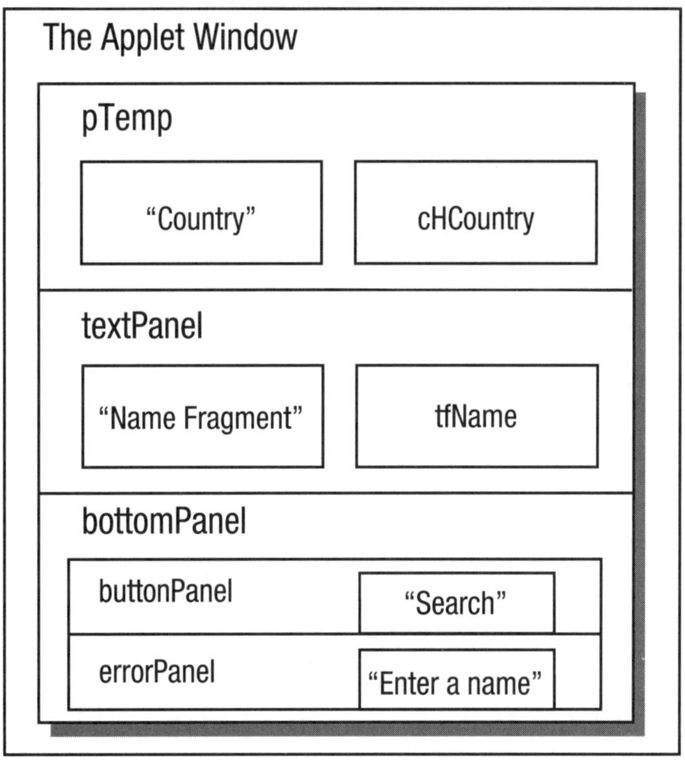

Figure 4.3 The panel and element layout in NameFragment.java.

the Search button. If a user clicks the Search button, the screen of data input does not go away. Instead, Java automatically invokes the action method. Within the action method, we perform a batch validation on the input fields. If the dog-name fragment entered does not meet our validation rule (at least six characters long), we simply display the error string and continue. In that case, the user gets the screen in Figure 4.4, which details the error very quickly, while the bad data remains visible.

In addition to displaying the error message, our field validation also resets the current field to be the field that violated validation, in this case **tfName**. Users are stuck in the invalid field until they correct it or hyperlink away.

If the fields do meet our validation rule, then the applet constructs a CGI URL, then calls **AppletContext.showDocument**, passing that URL. That CGI URL is the same URL that our **<FORM>** tag from Listing 2.4 would access in its ACTION attribute.

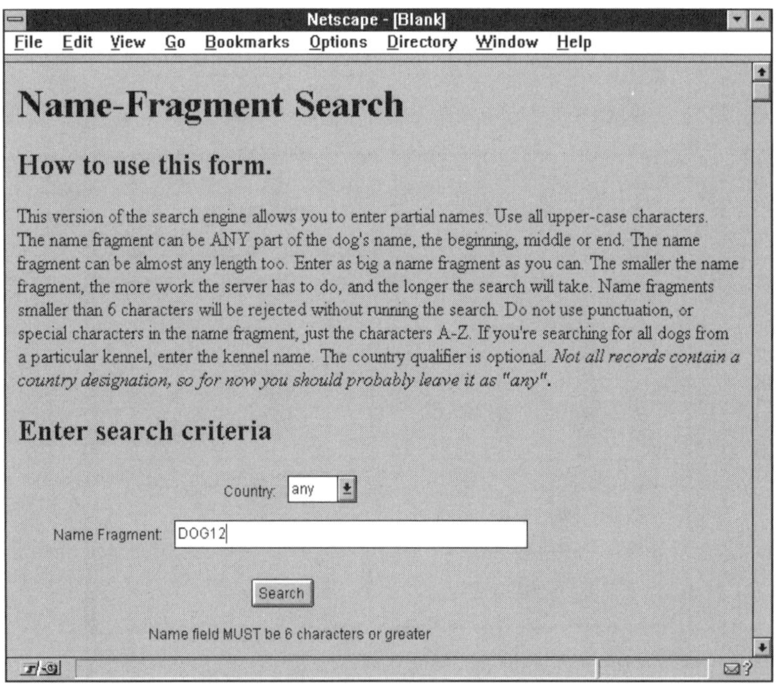

Figure 4.4 Invalid field caught by the Java applet of Listing 4.3.

We go through the same validation/rejection process when the user tries to tab from field to field in our form. When the user presses the Tab (or Shift-Tab) key, Java automatically invokes the **handleEvent** method, where we check to see which key was pressed. For tabs and back-tabs, if the user is in the **tfName** text field and attempts to tab away from there, we check the data in the field. If it is less than six characters, we do not allow the user to leave the field, displaying the error message and remaining in place.

Obviously, with only a single field, this is a simplistic example. However, you can extend it as far as you want, to forms like our data-entry screen, which has 35 fields with dozens of different rules to satisfy. The more field validation you have, and the more immediate it is, the more efficient users will become in filling it out. Efficient users are happy users, and happy users are return customers.

Response Limiting

Another huge problem with the Newfoundland Dog Database, as written, is that it doesn't automatically limit the length of the HTML documents that it tries to send back to users. For instance, a user who does a kennel search on POUCH COVE might get thousands of hits, producing an HTML document well over 1MB in size. This doesn't work. Browsers typically only perform acceptably for documents 100K and under, and at more than 250K, even the heftiest hardware is not enough to bring the entire document onto the screen within the user's lifetime.

A good example of how most Web applications deal with this problem is Digital Equipment Corporation's outstanding Internet search engine, Alta Vista, shown in Figure 4.5.

Alta Vista is a database of Web pages and Usenet messages, indexed so as to be full-text searchable. Users fill in a search form, then kick off a CGI process by clicking the Search button. In the example of Figure 4.5, we've searched on two terms, Java and JDBC, and Alta Vista has found over 200 matches. In order to make the results manageable, Alta Vista arbitrarily limits the results of a search to 200 matches. It also divides those 200 matches into 20 screens of 10. At any one time, the user can only be viewing a single screen of 10 matches. What this means is that, especially if you view listings in "compact" format, all you see is approximately one screen's worth of information.

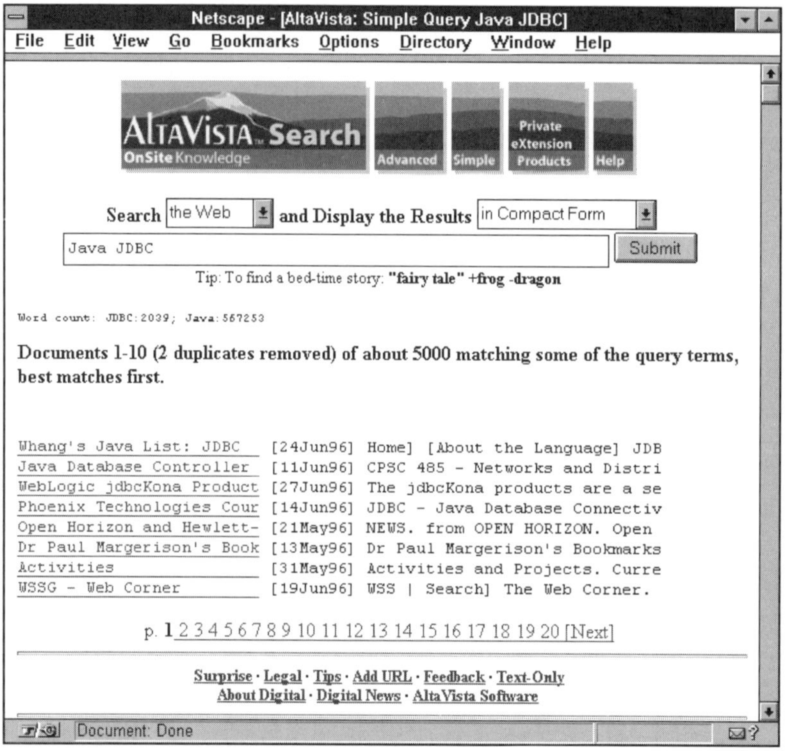

Figure 4.5 Alta Vista presenting a 200-item search result.

The user has a number of action options from any page: going to the next page, going to the previous page, or picking a page at random from the list of available pages. Maintaining this system of search-result page creation is relatively simple. Take, as an example, the CGI query that results if we choose page 3 from the results page of Figure 4.5. The resulting CGI query is:

```
http://altavista.digital.com/cgi-bin/query?pg=q&what=web&stq=
   20&fmt=c&q=Java+JDBC
```

This query has two name value pairs—**q=Java+ODBC&stq=30**—that tell Alta Vista exactly what page of results we want to see. The number of listings per page is set to 10, and the starting item, **startq**, is set to 20. So we get 10 results starting with number 20—page 3. Listing 4.4 shows the HTML source for this screen.

Listing 4.4 The HTML source for the Alta Vista screen of Figure 4.5.

```
<html>
<head>

<title>
AltaVista: Simple Query Java JDBC</title>
</head>
<body  bgcolor="#ffffff"  text="#000000"  link="#0000ee"
vlink="551a8b" alink="ff0000">
<CENTER>
<a href="/cgi-bin/query?pg=about&what=web">
 <IMG src="/av/pix/av-logo.gif" alt="[AltaVista] "
BORDER=0 ALIGN=middle  HEIGHT=73 WIDTH=204>
</a>
<a href="/cgi-bin/query?pg=aq&what=web">
 <IMG src="/av/pix/av-adv.gif" alt="[Advanced Search]  "
BORDER=0 ALIGN=middle  HEIGHT=73 WIDTH=59>
</a>
<a href="/cgi-bin/query?pg=q&what=web">
 <IMG src="/av/pix/av-sim.gif" alt="[SIMPLE QUERY] "
BORDER=0 ALIGN=middle  HEIGHT=73 WIDTH=42>
</a>
<a href=
   "http://altavista.software.digital.com/products/search/choice.htm">
 <IMG src="/av/pix/av-pex.gif" alt="[Private eXtension Products] "
  BORDER=0 ALIGN=middle  HEIGHT=73 WIDTH=65>
</a>
<a href="/cgi-bin/query?pg=h&what=web">
 <IMG src="/av/pix/av-help.gif" alt="[Help with Query]  "
BORDER=0 ALIGN=middle  HEIGHT=73 WIDTH=35>
</a>
</CENTER>
<CENTER>
<FORM method=GET action="/cgi-bin/query">
<INPUT TYPE=hidden NAME=pg VALUE=q>
<B>
Search <SELECT NAME=what>
<OPTION VALUE=web  SELECTED>
the Web<OPTION VALUE=news >
Usenet</SELECT>
 and Display the Results <SELECT NAME=fmt>
<OPTION VALUE="." >
in Standard Form<OPTION VALUE=c SELECTED>
```

```
in Compact Form<OPTION VALUE=d >
in Detailed Form</SELECT>
</B>
<BR>
<INPUT NAME=q size=55 maxlength=200 VALUE="Java JDBC">
<INPUT TYPE=submit VALUE=Submit>
<br>
<FONT size=-1>
Tip: To find a bed-time story: <B>
"fairy tale" +frog -dragon</B>
</FONT>
</FORM>
</CENTER>
<FONT size=-1>
<PRE>
Word count: JDBC:2039; Java:567253<BR>
</PRE>
</FONT>
<P>
<b>
Documents 1-10 (2 duplicates removed) of about 5000 matching
some of the query terms, best matches first.</b>
<br>
<pre>
<a href="http://www.sicc.co.kr/~sjwhang/javalist/lang/jdbc.htm">
Whang's Java List: JDBC  </a>
 [24Jun96] Home] [About the Language] JDB
<a href="http://www.cs.tamu.edu/people/jhamann/jdbc/">
Java Database Controller </a>
 [11Jun96] CPSC 485 - Networks and Distri
<a href="http://www.weblogic.com/products/jdbckona_noframe.html">
WebLogic jdbcKona Product</a>
 [27Jun96] The jdbcKona products are a se
<a href="http://www.phoenixtech.com/JDBC.html">
Phoenix Technologies Cour</a>
 [14Jun96] JDBC - Java Database Connectiv
<a href="http://www.openhorizon.com/pressrel/praesidm.htm">
Open Horizon and Hewlett-</a>
 [21May96] NEWS. from OPEN HORIZON. Open
<a href="http://www-tec.open.ac.uk/design/book.html">
Dr Paul Margerison's Book</a>
 [13May96] Dr Paul Margerison's Bookmarks
<a href="http://www.iei.pi.cnr.it/GRANT/ligonzo/activ.html">
Activities          </a>
```

```
 [31May96] Activities and Projects. Curre
<a href="http://tuna2.berkeley.edu/Webcorner/webcorner.html">
WSSG - Web Corner      </a>
 [19Jun96] WSS | Search] The Web Corner.
</pre>
<CENTER>
      p. <b>
1</b>
<a href="/cgi-bin/query?pg=q&what=web&stq=10&fmt=c&q=Java+JDBC">
 2</a>
<a href="/cgi-bin/query?pg=q&what=web&stq=20&fmt=c&q=Java+JDBC">
 3</a>
<a href="/cgi-bin/query?pg=q&what=web&stq=30&fmt=c&q=Java+JDBC">
 4</a>
<a href="/cgi-bin/query?pg=q&what=web&stq=40&fmt=c&q=Java+JDBC">
 5</a>
<a href="/cgi-bin/query?pg=q&what=web&stq=50&fmt=c&q=Java+JDBC">
 6</a>
<a href="/cgi-bin/query?pg=q&what=web&stq=60&fmt=c&q=Java+JDBC">
 7</a>
<a href="/cgi-bin/query?pg=q&what=web&stq=70&fmt=c&q=Java+JDBC">
 8</a>
<a href="/cgi-bin/query?pg=q&what=web&stq=80&fmt=c&q=Java+JDBC">
 9</a>
<a href="/cgi-bin/query?pg=q&what=web&stq=90&fmt=c&q=Java+JDBC">
 10</a>
<a href="/cgi-bin/query?pg=q&what=web&stq=100&fmt=c&q=Java+JDBC">
 11</a>
<a href="/cgi-bin/query?pg=q&what=web&stq=110&fmt=c&q=Java+JDBC">
 12</a>
<a href="/cgi-bin/query?pg=q&what=web&stq=120&fmt=c&q=Java+JDBC">
 13</a>
<a href="/cgi-bin/query?pg=q&what=web&stq=130&fmt=c&q=Java+JDBC">
 14</a>
<a href="/cgi-bin/query?pg=q&what=web&stq=140&fmt=c&q=Java+JDBC">
 15</a>
<a href="/cgi-bin/query?pg=q&what=web&stq=150&fmt=c&q=Java+JDBC">
 16</a>
<a href="/cgi-bin/query?pg=q&what=web&stq=160&fmt=c&q=Java+JDBC">
 17</a>
<a href="/cgi-bin/query?pg=q&what=web&stq=170&fmt=c&q=Java+JDBC">
 18</a>
<a href="/cgi-bin/query?pg=q&what=web&stq=180&fmt=c&q=Java+JDBC">
 19</a>
<a href="/cgi-bin/query?pg=q&what=web&stq=190&fmt=c&q=Java+JDBC">
```

```
 20</a>
<a href="/cgi-bin/query?pg=q&what=web&stq=10&fmt=c&q=Java+JDBC">
  [Next]</a>
</CENTER>
<CENTER>
<HR>
<FONT size=-1>
<B>
<a href="/cgi-bin/query?pg=s">
Surprise</a>
 &#183;
<a href="/cgi-bin/query?pg=legal">
Legal</a>
 &#183;
<a href="/cgi-bin/query?pg=tips">
Tips</a>
 &#183;
<a href="/cgi-bin/query?pg=addurl">
Add URL</a>
 &#183;
<a href="/cgi-bin/query?pg=fb">
Feedback</a>
 &#183;
<a href="/cgi-bin/query?pg=q&what=web&fmt=c&q=Java+JDBC&text=yes">
 Text-Only</a>
<BR>
<a href="/cgi-bin/query?pg=digital">
About Digital</a>
 &#183;
<a href="/cgi-bin/query?pg=whatsnew">
Digital News</a>
 &#183;
<a href="http://altavista.software.digital.com">
  AltaVista Software</a>
</B>
<hr>
<a href="http://www.digital.com/">
<IMG src=/av/pix/logo22pt.gif alt=" "
BORDER=0 ALIGN=middle  HEIGHT=17 WIDTH=50>
</a>
 <a href="/cgi-bin/query?pg=legal">
Copyright</a>
 &#169; 1996 <a href="http://www.digital.com/">
     Digital Equipment Corporation.</a>
     All rights reserved.
```

```
</FONT>
</CENTER>
</body>
</html>
```

As you can see, all of the hyperlinks from Previous all the way through page 20 to Next are hardwired CGI queries. Now, creating these links by hand would be a daunting task, but doing it programmatically within the CGI query is just a small matter of programming. *Note that the lines in the <PRE> elements have been broken arbitrarily to comply with the publisher's restrictions on line length.*

While the 10-item restriction can be somewhat annoying from a user's perspective, overall, this is excellent Web design, and well worth imitating. Implementing this in the Newf database would require a couple of fairly simple changes. In Listing 2.8, in the function **ProcessArgs**, we'd need to add a variable like Alta Vista's **startq**, to tell us which item to start at. Then, within **Query**, we'd need to output result rows only when we're fetching the right 10 items. And, within the HTML output, of course, we'd need to add hyperlinks to all the other pages, as well as Next and Previous. All in all, not rocket science, but a considerable chunk of code.

Display Limitations

HTML was developed as an easy way to present and link simple types of static data. When you deal with visual items more complicated than static text or black-box image files, HTML quickly becomes unwieldy. A great example of this is the Newfoundland Dog Database's pedigree-tree screen.

The point of the pedigree-tree screen is to present the user with a graphical view of the ancestry of a particular dog going back five generations. This is an important function for breeders to see where various genetic lines intersect and on which side, dame or sire. You reach the pedigree-tree screen by clicking on a dog's name in a search-results screen (such as Figure 3.2). Via a new CGI query, with **QueryType** set to Pedigree, the system will bring up a pedigree tree such as that in Figure 4.6. Listing 4.5 shows the code we use to generate this tree, a single recursive function named **PedigreeSearch**.

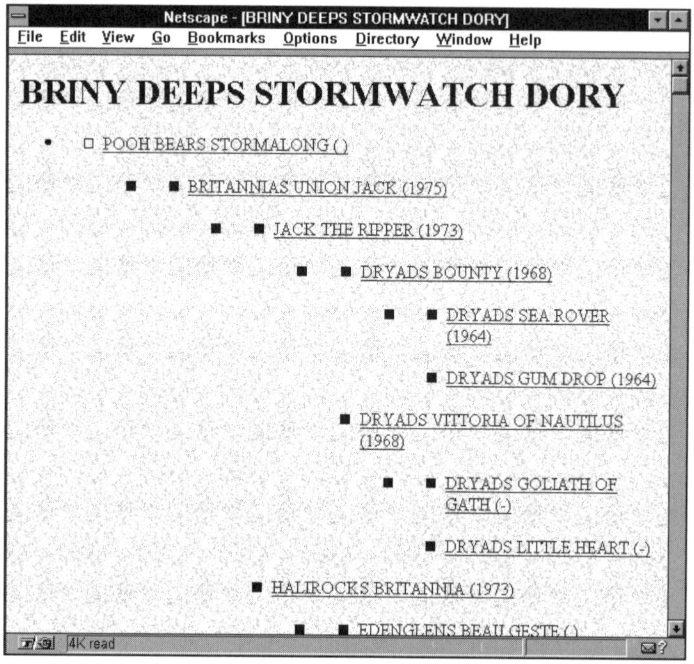

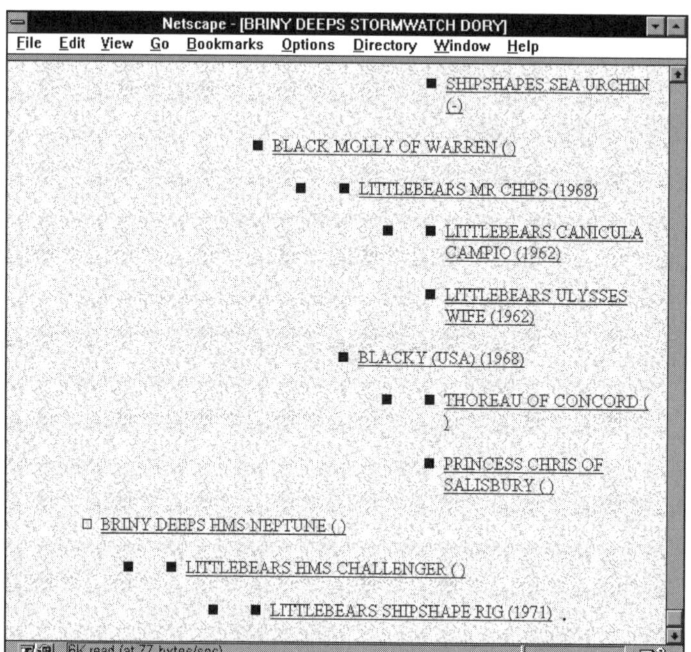

Figure 4.6 A pedigree tree—two screens worth.

Listing 4.5 The pedigree search function.

```
/* PedigreeSearch - Output HTML list items <LI> corresponding
to the sire and dame of the specified dog (tname), then call
this function recursively, specifying the sire and dame.  This
will result in a list of lists where each level of
indentation shows a different generation in the pedigree tree.
If we reach MAX_DEPTH, simply return, cutting off the
recursion at a certain depth.
*/
void PedigreeSearch( char *tname ) {
  int i;
  char sought_dam[256];
  char sought_sire[256];
  char buffer[1024];
  EXEC SQL BEGIN DECLARE SECTION;
  char yob[256];
  EXEC SQL  END DECLARE SECTION;

// If we've reached the maximum recursion, simply return.
  if( current_depth == MAX_DEPTH ) {
    return;
    }
  current_depth++;

// Null our parents out.
  sought_dam[0] = '\0';
  sought_sire[0] = '\0';

// sought_name is a global, set it here, use later.
  strcpy( sought_name, tname );

// Get the sire and dame from the DB.
   EXEC SQL
      SELECT NAME, SNAME, DNAME, DOB2
      INTO :temp_name, :temp_sire, :temp_dam, :yob
      FROM shortdog
      WHERE name = :sought_name;

// Output the sire and dame list items and
// recurse down their branches.
   if (SQLCODE == 0 || SQLCODE == 1 ) {
    if( strcmp( yob, "0" ) == 0 )
      yob[0] = '-';
```

```
// Start the list item for sire.
      printf("<LI><UL>\n" );
    if( strlen( temp_sire ) > 0 )
      strcpy( sought_sire, temp_sire );
    if( strlen( temp_dam ) > 0 )
      strcpy(  sought_dam, temp_dam );
    if( strlen( sought_sire ) == 0 ||
        strcmp( sought_sire, "NOT YET RECORDED" ) == 0 )
      printf( "<LI>unknown</LI>\n" );
    else
      {
        sprintf( buffer, sought_sire );
        for( i = 0; i < strlen( buffer ); i++ )
          if( buffer[i] == ' ' )
            buffer[i] = '+';
    sprintf( slink, "<A HREF=\"%s%s/newfq.exe?dog.text=%s&\
      QueryType=Name&%s\">%s (%s)</A></P>",
        documentbase, cgi_directory, buffer,query_args,
        sought_sire, yob );
      printf( "<LI>%s\n<UL>", slink );
// Recurse down the sire's branch of the tree
      PedigreeSearch( sought_sire );
      printf( "</UL></LI>\n" );
      }
    if( strlen( sought_dam ) == 0 ||
       strcmp( sought_dam, "NOT YET RECORDED" ) == 0 )
      printf( "<LI>unknown</LI>\n" );
    else
      {
        sprintf( buffer, sought_dam );
        for( i = 0; i < strlen( buffer ); i++ )
          if( buffer[i] == ' ' )
            buffer[i] = '+';
      sprintf( dlink, "<A HREF=\"%s%s/newfq.exe?dog.text=%s&\
        QueryType=Name&%s\">%s (%s)</A></P>",
          documentbase, cgi_directory, buffer,
            query_args,sought_dam, yob );
      printf( "<LI>%s\n<UL>\n", dlink );
// Recurse down the dame's branch of the tree.
      PedigreeSearch( sought_dam );
      printf( "</UL></LI>\n" );
      }
    printf( "</UL></LI>\n" );
  }
// If we errored out, output an error message.
  else {
```

```
    if (SQLCODE == 100 )
       printf("Dog (%s) not found!\n", tname);
   else
       ErrorMsg();
   }

// Pop back up a level.
  current_depth--;
}
```

This function is deceptively simple. We get the dog's sire and dame from the database via a simple SELECT. Then, for the sire, we output a list-item giving his name and the year he was bred. Then we call **PedigreeSearch** recursively to do the same thing for the parents of the sire. These recursions continue until **current_depth** reaches **MAX_DEPTH**. This is our generational limit. When **current_depth** reaches **MAX_DEPTH** for the first time, we've followed the male line back **MAX_DEPTH** generations. Thus, the first five lines of the pedigree screen will always be the male line—father, grandfather, great-grandfather....

The pedigree screen shows the two parents of the named dog, then the parents of each of those dogs as indented lists under each of those dogs. HTML coders will instantly recognize this as a brutally simple application of unordered lists. While dyed-in-the-wool C programmers can easily follow the meaning of an indented list like this, it is much less obvious to our target audience—dog people. They're used to a much more explicit graphic, where each dog name is boxed and solid lines lead from one generation to the next.

HTML doesn't provide any built-in element to deal with problems like this; it is beyond the scope. Within a strict HTML framework, items like this should be dealt with by creating an image file. We could deal with it that way. In fact, if we could create a stream of bytes in GIF or JPEG format, then we could simply change our **startStream** function such that it outputs a line that says something like

```
printf( "Content-type: image/gif\n\n");
```

instead of:

```
printf( "Content-type: text/html\n\n");
```

This changes the stream type from **HTML/text** to **GIF/image**, and causes the browser to expect and display a GIF stream. However, within our current, unordered list implementation, the user can click on individual dogs and get the record for that dog. If we output a GIF representation of the tree, then we'd have to create a corresponding image map to make that image clickable. You can see how this exercise quickly becomes unmanageable.

At the point where you're considering outputting a GIF image with a corresponding image map, you're very close in complexity to a Java applet that could take the data and draw the tree by itself, including handling clickable hyperlinks. Factors such as your users' ability to run Java applets should drive this choice, but the trend is clearly away from server-based image processing like the GIF/image-map model and toward client-based graphics via technologies like Java and ActiveX.

Performance

As we've said before, by current industry standards for standalone applications, the performance of the Newfoundland Dog Database is awful, barely tolerable even for those who really, really, want the data and can't get it anywhere else. There are four approaches to improving the real and perceived performance of the Newf database:

- Process creation
- Database connection
- Nonparsed headers
- Table row dimensioning

Process creation is an easy problem to understand. A process is what the operating system calls a running program. Whenever you run a program such as Netscape, you're creating a process. If you run another copy of Netscape, you create another process. Processes are expensive. They take time to create, since the operating system needs to read the file off disk, interpret its header, and set it up to run. Before our CGI program even executes the first line of source, a considerable amount of real time has been spent just loading it into memory.

This is something to think about if you're considering writing CGI programs in an interpreted language like Java. In order to run a Java program, you have to load both the Java interpreter and the Java program itself. Thus, though it may take a lot longer to write, an executable written in C or C++ will almost always load faster than the equivalent Java program.

There are a couple of solutions currently in the works to the process problem: NSAPI and ISAPI. Basically, these solutions require that you write your CGI program as a Dynamic Link Library (DLL) that can then be called by the Web server as NSAPI or ISAPI requests come in. Operating systems treat DLLs differently than executable programs (like our CGI program). A DLL is typically loaded into memory just once, and it stays there forever. Executable programs, like the Web server, can call into the DLL just by using a function name. Thus, we've almost entirely eliminated the process-creation overhead. It remains to be seen which of these technologies will win greatest acceptance.

The database-connection problem is very similar to the process-creation problem. Creating a connection to the database is an expensive operation in terms of real time, often taking up to four or five seconds. Again, under most operating systems, the preferred solution is to use a DLL or a daemon to consolidate the process. The theory is that your DLL opens a connection to the database, then holds that connection open forever. Every time a CGI program or NSAPI function wants to use the database, it uses that open connection, thus eliminating the database-connection time.

This is a solution that most Web database tools like NetDynamics employ. With multiple users calling the database at the same time, this is a trickier problem than it might appear. You must somehow serialize access to the connection such that conflicting operations do not occur at the same time. Under JDBC, for example, if you try to do a new select against a connection while there are still results pending from a previous selection, you'll throw an exception. There are ways to deal with this, especially in Java, but it takes some planning and some work. It is not a simple matter of opening a single connection and handing it out to whatever process asks for it.

Having seen two areas where performance improvement entails a significant amount of work, we now come to a couple of cherries ripe for the picking. Server pass-through is an easy one that would never occur to you if you didn't know how Web servers work. In the **StartStream** function of Listing 3.10, we output a string "Content-type: text/html\n\n". This is a partial HTTP header.

The Web server and the browser speak HTTP protocol to each other, and the HTTP protocol specifies that a header block can have a certain amount of information in it. When we output the string "Content-type: text/html\n\n", what actually goes out over the socket to the browser is something more like this:

```
HTTP/1.0 200 OK
Date: DayOfWeek, DD-Mon-YY nn:nn:nn GMT
Server: Netscape-Communications/1.1
MIME-version: 1.0
Content-type: text/HTML
```

What happens is that the Web server sees (and expects) a partial header, and prepends the other headers to it before sending the whole block off to the browser. This means that the Web server must handle every byte of information flowing back to the browser from the CGI program.

Almost all Web servers allow you to get around this using nonparsed headers. Essentially, with nonparsed headers, your CGI program agrees to send a complete header, and the Web server gives you direct access to the socket connection to the browser. Usually, in order to use nonparsed headers, you have to name your CGI program with a specified sequence. For Netscape, NCSA, and CERN servers, this means starting your program name with the letters nph.

For our CGI program to use nonparsed headers, we'd need to make two changes. First, we'd rename the program from newfq.exe to nph-newfq.exe. We'd then change the ACTION attributes in the forms that call the program to call the new, nonparsed version. Finally, we'd have to have a new version of **StartStream** to output the complete header, as in Listing 4.6. This version outputs various interesting header fields, creating a proper date using **strftime**. We also need to call this version instead of the parsed version from **startQuery** in Listing 3.4.

Listing 4.6 The nonparsed version of StartStream.

```
/* StartStreamNonParsed - Tell the browser we're sending back HTML. */
void StartStreamNonParsed() {
  char szdate[256];
  struct tm *today;
  time_t long_time;

  printf( "HTTP/1.0 200 OK\n" );

  time(&long_time);
  today = localtime( &long_time );
  strftime( szdate, sizeof( szdate ), "%A, %d-%b-%y %H:%M:%S GMT", today
);
  printf( "Date: %s\n", szdate );
  printf( "Server: Netscape-Communications/1.1\n" );
  printf( "MIME-version: 1.0\n" );
  printf( "Content-type: text/html\n\n");
  }
```

Nonparsed headers seem like an unvarnished gain, but they have a downside, mostly related to error handling. In the event of abnormal termination of the CGI program, the server usually deals with it by sending its own error message off to the browser, and logging the error in its log. It can't do this, however, if it doesn't "see" the stream you're sending to the browser. Thus, implementing a nonparsed-header performance enhancement is best reserved for a time when the program has been running successfully for some time and all, or most, bugs have been wrung out.

The other easy picking in the performance arena is not so much an enhancement in performance as an enhancement in perceived performance. Where our last enhancement required a knowledge of Web servers, this one requires an understanding of how browsers work, especially how they process table rows, **<TR>** elements.

Most visual elements in HTML allow you to specify a height and width as an attribute of the element. Thus, for an image **<IMG>** element, you can say **<IMG HEIGHT=200 WIDTH=100>** to tell the browser that the image is 200 pixels high and 100 pixels wide. Why does HTML do this?

Actually, this is one of the best, and least, well understood features of HTML. For our 200 by 100 image, for example, that image may be 100K bytes, and take a full minute to download. Depending on the image type, the browser might have to download a large part of the file before it can know the dimensions of this image. The browser can't render any of the visual elements that follow that image until it knows how big the image is. If it knows how big the image is, it can just reserve a space 200 by 100 pixels, download the image in the background, then continue rendering all the text surrounding and following the image. You've undoubtedly seen this on hundreds of Web pages, where the text appears surrounding a blank box that eventually fills with an image.

In our Newf application, you may notice that even for a query returning hundreds of rows, the browser doesn't display *any* of the data until all the data has been downloaded. This is because table rows operate much the same way as images. If you don't specify the dimensions of the table cells, then the browser scales them on the fly depending on the size of the data within all the cells. Thus, it has to wait for all the cells to be downloaded before it can render *any* of the cells. Netscape, for example, will try to size a column of text cells to be just as wide as needed to hold the single biggest word in any of the cells of that column.

If, however, we size the table cells ourselves, then the browser has no decision to make and can render the row as soon as the data for that row arrives. Table data cells, **<TD>** elements, only allow setting of the width. Thus, if we add a simple attribute, say **WIDTH=100**, to each of our table data cells, our table rows will appear to flow onto the screen one by one, as opposed to appearing all at once in a lump.

Conclusion

In this chapter, we've stepped back a bit and looked critically at the Newfoundland Dog Database as a real-world application. In the process, we've discovered a number of interrelated problems, including performance, input validation, browser incompatibility, display-capacity limitations, and, for the pedigree tree, inadequate display capabilities. Each of these symptoms has a root cause based in the architecture of the Web and its components, the browser, Web server, and CGI program. And for each of these symptoms, there are measures that can be taken to alleviate the problem, as shown in Table 4.1.

Table 4.1 Problems with the Newf application, and possible solutions.

Problem	Possible Solutions
Performance	Nonparsed HTTP headers
	Semi-permanent open database connections
	Statically sized HTML visual elements
	NSAPI
Input validation	Client-side input validation via Java
Browser incompatibility	Least-common-denominator HTML design
	Separate branches of execution based on browser capability
Display capacity limitations	Response limiting via multipart result screens
Inadequate display capability	Client-side graphic processing via Java

Hopefully, through the work of this chapter, we've seen how to take a basic, fairly primitive Web database application and tune it to look and perform more like a halfway-decent standalone application. As tools like Java and ActiveX develop, Web applications should be able to take much better advantage of the client-side capabilities, and thus perform more up to the standard set so far by standalone, graphical applications.

Webliography

- http://www.ncsa.uiuc.edu/SDG/Software/WinMosaic/HomePage.html — NCSA Mosaic browser.
- http://www.cc.ukans.edu/about_doslynx/doslynx.html — About the Lynx browser.
- http://www.microsoft.com/ie/ — Microsoft's Internet Explorer browser.
- http://altavista.digital.com — Digital Equipment's Alta Vista search engine.

- http://www9.netscape.com/newsref/std/server_api.html — An in-depth explanation of Netscape Server API, NSAPI.
- http://www.microsoft.com/infoserv/docs/PROGRAM.HTM#27081 — Microsoft's Win32 extension for its Web server, called Internet Server API (ISAPI).
- http://www.javasoft.com — The Java home page.
- http://www.microsoft.com/activex/actx-gen/awhatis.htm — Microsoft's ActiveX client-side controls technology.

Chapter 5

An Active-View, Client-Server Database

CHAPTER 5

An Active-View, Client-Server Database

We've spent the first four chapters developing static displays of stored data. In this chapter, we'll look at what happens when our data changes in realtime. How can we keep the user's view of the data consistent with what's in the database?

To illustrate the problem, we'll implement a system that keeps track of the last trade price of a set of stocks. The user interface is a single screen that allows the user to pick a stock to follow and then shows the price of the stock in a bar graph.

The Sample Application

Stock-price demo applications are so common that I'm tempted to call this one "The Cliché Server." But there's a reason why they're so popular—they're compelling database applications where changes that happen in realtime must be reflected on client screens in realtime. What we want in this example application is for the user to be able to register a single stock and watch the price change in realtime. As usual, we start with the data. Listing 5.1 shows the schema for our database.

Listing 5.1 Schema for the stock-price database.

```
create table Stock (
Symbol varchar(8),
Description varchar(50),
CurrentPrice float,
LastPrice float
)
create index idx_ticker on stock (Symbol)
```

The Stock table is very simple, containing only the stock-ticker symbol, description, last trade price, and previous trade price. There is also only a single, clustered index into the table, **idx_ticker**, which indexes stocks by their ticker symbol. This is the only way we'll ever query this table.

How the data gets into the table is not really our concern. For testing and demonstration purposes, the CD-ROM contains a simple server that randomly changes the prices at regular intervals. For our purposes here, though, the data in the table changes rapidly, and we don't care how. All we care about is getting these changes out to the Web users who are interested in them.

How Do We Do It?

The solution we've chosen here (and keep in mind that there are many other ways of doing it) has a bunch of parts: a Java applet, a Java server process, a Java native-method DLL, SQL Server triggers, and extended stored procedures. Figure 5.1 shows a block diagram of the system.

The overall design of this solution (though not the "brand" of components used) is literally dictated by our definition of the problem. We must have a client program (our applet) holding an open network connection to a server (our Java server) in order to get fresh data in front of the user. We must have a trigger on the database table to kick off the update process when our data changes. And we must have an extended stored procedure to give our trigger some way to give the Java server its data.

The system works this way:

1. The Java applet is our user interface.
2. The data we retrieve from the database is displayed on the browser by the applet.

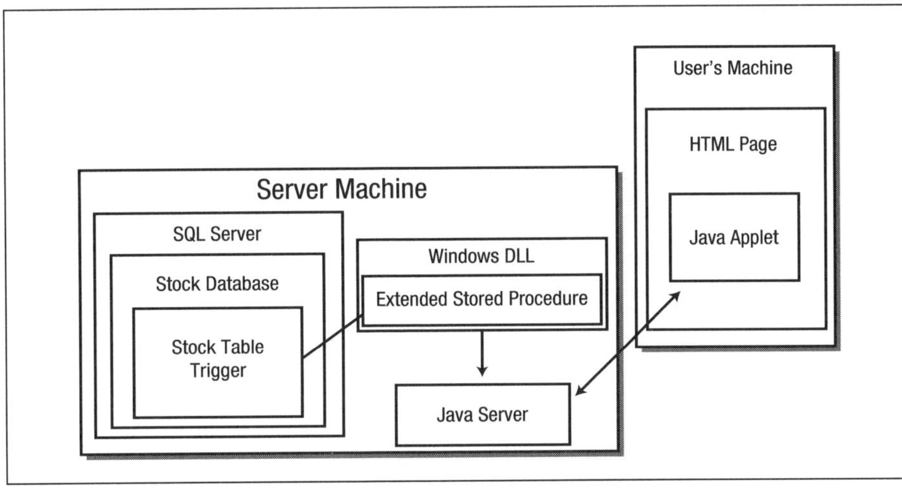

Figure 5.1 This block diagram illustrates the stock-price system.

3. The applet is fed this data over a dedicated network connection that we will set up with our new Java server. The Java server gets the fresh information in two ways. When a user first connects to the site, the Java server queries the database for the initial price of our stock, which it then returns over the network connection to the applet. Independently, we have created a trigger on our stock table. This trigger tells SQL Server to execute a certain extended stored procedure whenever the price of our stock changes. The extended stored procedure, which is itself a DLL, calls our Java server via the native-method DLL.

4. The Java server figures out which applet needs the information, and sends it out to that applet over the network connection.

Triggers

The tricky connection in this whole system is really the one from the extended stored procedure to the Java server, so let's get right to it. In our definition of the problem, we stated that the user would be notified as soon as the price of a stock changed. By defining the problem that way, we've decided that the price-update model would be asynchronous and driven by the data feed, rather than a polling model where the polling interval is determined by the application.

This means that we need some way of knowing when the price changes. The easy way to do this, of course, would be to insert some code somewhere in the data-feed process that updates the database, which would call us whenever a new price comes in. There are, however, many cases where you don't have that kind of access to the data feed. There are also cases where your database gets multiple, independent, incompatible data feeds. It makes no sense to go writing multiple feed-filters when the database itself consolidates these feeds in one place.

Fortunately for us, SQL Server implements a feature known as *triggers*. A trigger allows us to define an action that will be performed whenever something of interest happens within the database. This fits our needs to a *T*. We want to update the display on the user's machine every time the price of our stock changes, so we need to define a trigger that says something like this:

"When a record in the stock table changes, notify the user."

To do that, we use the **create trigger** statement shown in Listing 5.2.

Listing 5.2 This trigger notifies us of changes in the stock table.

```
CREATE TRIGGER symboltrigger ON Stock
   FOR UPDATE
      AS
         DECLARE @symbol varchar(6)
         DECLARE @price float
         SELECT @symbol=i.Symbol, @price=i.CurrentPrice
            FROM inserted i
               if @price = 0.00000
                  BEGIN
                     RAISERROR (50009, 16, 10)
                 END
               else
                  BEGIN
                    execute master..ping @symbol, @price
                 END
```

The first two lines of this statement are easy enough to understand. They simply define the circumstances under which the trigger action is to be performed. In this case, **symboltrigger**'s action is performed whenever there's an update on the table Stock. Everything following the **AS** keyword defines the action to be taken should the trigger condition be met.

In our action statement, we define two variables, **symbol** and **price**. We set these two variables to the values in the "new" record (the record being inserted/updated), then check the price for an invalid value. If the price is zero, we raise an error. If the price is okay, we execute the extended stored procedure, **master..ping**, passing both the price and the symbol as arguments. The trigger itself is as simple as that.

The Extended Stored Procedure

What is **master..ping**? In SQL Server terminology, it's an *extended stored procedure.* Extended stored procedures are simply functions that are registered with SQL Server and conform to a particular API, in this case Microsoft's Open Data Services, ODS, part of the BackOffice SDK. ODS, for its part, merely provides a set of standards and functions for passing data to and from an extended stored procedure. Listing 5.3 shows the code for the **ping** extended stored procedure.

Listing 5.3 This is our extended stored procedure, ping.

```
// Miscellaneous defines
//
#define  XP_NOERROR      0
#define  XP_ERROR      1

RETCODE ping(SRV_PROC *srvproc)
{
   int type;
   int paramnum;
   int paramlength;
   char *symbol;
   double fprice;
   DBCHAR bErrorMsg[MAXLEN];

    // Check number of parameters
    //
    if ((paramnum = srv_rpcparams(srvproc)) != 2) {
        // Send error message and return
        //
```

```
        srv_sendmsg(srvproc, SRV_MSG_ERROR, PING_ERROR, SRV_INFO,
                (DBTINYINT)0,
          NULL, 0, 0, "Error executing extended stored procedure: Invalid
            # of Parameters",
                    SRV_NULLTERM);
        // A SRV_DONE_MORE instead of a SRV_DONE_FINAL must complete the
        // result set of an Extended Stored Procedure.
        //
        srv_senddone(srvproc, (SRV_DONE_ERROR | SRV_DONE_MORE), 0, 0);
    return(XP_ERROR);
    }

    paramlength = srv_paramlen(srvproc, 1);
    symbol = (DBCHAR *)malloc(paramlength);
    if (!symbol) {

        SETERROR("Malloc", bErrorMsg);
        srv_sendmsg(srvproc, SRV_MSG_ERROR, PING_ERROR, SRV_INFO,
          (DBTINYINT)0,
              NULL, 0, 0, bErrorMsg, SRV_NULLTERM);
        // A SRV_DONE_MORE instead of a SRV_DONE_FINAL must complete the
        // result set of an Extended Stored Procedure.
        //
        srv_senddone(srvproc, (SRV_DONE_ERROR | SRV_DONE_MORE), 0, 0);
        return(XP_ERROR);
    }

    // Fetch symbol.
    srv_bmove(srv_paramdata(srvproc, 1), symbol, paramlength);
    symbol[paramlength] = '\0';

    paramlength = srv_paramlen(srvproc, 2);
    srv_bmove(srv_paramdata(srvproc, 2), &fprice, paramlength);
    if( ssnpClientPipe == NULL )
       CreateClientPipe();
    WriteClientPipe( symbol, fprice );
    DestroyClientPipe();
    srv_senddone(srvproc, SRV_DONE_MORE, 0, 0);

    return(XP_NOERROR);
}
```

As defined by our trigger, this function is what gets called whenever the trigger goes off. It may look complicated, but it's actually very simple. To do its job, it uses a number of function calls provided with Microsoft's ODS. These calls are summarized in Table 5.1.

Table 5.1 ODS functions used in ping.

Function name	Description
srv_bmove	Move data to and from SQL Server dataspace.
srv_senddone	Tell SQL Server that we're finished.
srv_rpcparams	Get the number of parameters.
srv_sendmsg	Send an error message to the user.
srv_paramlen	Get the length of the data supplied in the argument to this function.
srv_paramdata	Get a pointer to one of the arguments passed to this function.

The first thing to note with our calls to ODS is that the first argument to each **srv_ call** is **srv_proc**. This is a pointer to the SQL Server process and is also the only actual argument to our DLL call. In our **srv_ calls**, we simply pass this pointer along. It contains within it all the information SQL Server needs to communicate with our DLL call.

Thus, the arguments **symbol** and **price** that we defined in our trigger when we said **"execute master..ping @symbol, @price"** do not come to us as C-style arguments to the extended stored procedure. Instead, they are hidden somewhere within **srv_proc**, and we need to use **srv_ calls** to pry them out.

Our first job within the extended stored procedure is to determine that we've been supplied with reasonable arguments within the trigger. To do this, we call **srv_rpcparams**, passing it our server process, **srv_proc**. This returns the number of arguments that have been supplied. If the number isn't what we expect (two), then we exit. As with any API, though, nothing is that simple. You can't just return from this function as if nothing happened.

When erroring-out of an extended stored procedure, we have three things to do: user notification, server-process notification, and the actual return. In this case, user notification is not strictly necessary, since there is no user on the other end of this transaction. However, it doesn't hurt, it's good practice, and it's also good for the testing that we'll do a little later, so we put it in there. When installing and debugging extended stored procedures like this, we'll often call them from the command line just to test them out, and in that case it's good to have error messages coming back.

Server-process notification is another thing entirely. SQL Server needs to know when we've finished whatever we're doing—simply returning from the call isn't enough. Thus, we need to make a specific call, **srv_senddone**, to tell SQL Server that we're finished. We also use **srv_senddone** to tell SQL Server whether the call worked or not. **Srv_senddone** has four arguments. Of those, **srv_proc** we've already talked about, and **info** is reserved (set to zero). That leaves **status** and **count**.

Status is an indicator of whether the call worked or not. As defined by Microsoft, **status** can have any of the values in Table 5.2. The only values we need, though, are **SRV_DONE_MORE** and **SRV_DONE_ERROR**. If we error-out from the parameter-count check, then we'll use **SRV_DONE_ERROR**. Otherwise, we'll use **SRV_DONE_MORE**. **SRV_DONE_COUNT**, **SRV_DONE_FINAL**, and **SRV_DONE_RPC_IN_BATCH** are, for the most part, used by procedures that return result sets to the user, not procedures like ours that send data out of SQL Server.

Having verified the appropriate number of arguments, we need to get those arguments into local variables where we can use them. **Symbol** is the first argument, a string. To retrieve it, we need to allocate a character buffer for the string, then move those characters from SQL Server dataspace into our new buffer. We call **malloc** to get the buffer. If **malloc** fails, we error-out the

Table 5.2 Possible return values from extended stored procedures.

Return value	Description
SRV_DONE_FINAL	The current set of results is the final set of results.
SRV_DONE_MORE	The current set of results isn't the final set of results.
SRV_DONE_COUNT	The count parameter contains a valid count.
SRV_DONE_ERROR	The current client command received an error.
SRV_DONE_RPC_IN_BATCH	The current set of results is the last set of the currently executing remote stored procedure. This value is used when multiple remote stored procedures are executed in a single batch.

same way we did for bad arguments. Otherwise, we use **srv_bmove** to move the bytes from SQL Server into our local buffer. The interesting part of this call is the source parameter, **srv_paramdata(srv_proc,1)**. This returns a pointer to the first argument, in this case the symbol string. Our **srv_bmove** call simply moves *paramlength* bytes from the argument in SQL Server's dataspace into our local character buffer. We add a null terminator at the end, and *voilá*, our local buffer contains a copy of the string supplied in the trigger action.

We go through the same hoops to get the **price** argument. **Price** does differ though, in that it is a float, not a string. Thus, rather than allocating a new buffer dynamically, we can simply declare a float and copy the argument into that. With the two arguments in hand, all we need to do now is get the **price** argument out to any client that's interested in it.

If you look at the last call to **srv_bmove**, the one that retrieves the price into a local float, you'll see three calls, **CreateClientPipe**, **WriteClientPipe**, and **DestroyClientPipe**. **CreateClientPipe** creates one end of a named-pipe connection. **WriteClientPipe** writes a message containing the symbol and price into that named pipe, and **DestroyClientPipe** terminates that named-pipe connection. We'll talk more about the named-pipe connection later. Suffice to say here that these three calls get our new symbol and price values into the Java server.

Registering The Extended Stored Procedure

At this point, you're probably wondering how SQL Server turns the expression **master..ping** in Listing 5.2 into a call to our extended-stored-procedure DLL. As the argument to an **execute** command, **master..ping** has to be a stored procedure. The first part of our stored procedure name, **master**, is the database in which the stored procedure is registered. The second half of the name, **ping**, is the name under which the DLL function was registered.

To actually register this extended procedure, we must use the **sp_addextendedproc** command:

```
sp_addextendedproc 'ping', 'StockerHelper.dll'
```

This command adds the extended procedure to the database. Listing 5.4 shows the isql batch that registers our stored procedure.

Listing 5.4 Batch file to run the sp_addextendedproc isql command.

```
REM This batch adds the extended proc defined in addproc.sql
REM to the database.  Notice that we connect to the MASTER
REM database and not the STOCK database that will actually
REM use the extended proc.

c:\sql60\binn\isql /U sa /d master /S katie /e /i addproc.sql
```

The **sp_addextendedproc** command is quite simple. The first argument is the function name within the DLL. The second argument is the DLL name. When SQL Server tries to run our extended stored procedure, it merely tells the operating system to load the DLL, StockerHelper.dll. Windows NT looks along the system path to find a file named StockerHelper.dll. Thus, when we've compiled and linked our DLL, we must copy it into one of the directories named in the **PATH** environment variable.

Note carefully that our isql batch file in Listing 5.4 connects to the master database, *not* our Stock database, in spite of the fact that it will only work within the Stock database. This attachment of extended stored procedures to the master database is a requirement of SQL Server.

Now that we've created our extended stored procedure and added it to the database, we need to test it. We don't have all the pieces in place to test it fully, but we can test that the DLL is loadable (with no errors in the image), properly placed along the path and properly registered with SQL Server. To do this, all we need to do is try to call it from the isql command line. Crank up isql and issue this command:

```
master..ping 'xv', 10.0
```

This should execute our procedure, giving it *xv* as the symbol argument and *10.0* as the price. Our procedure does not generate any tabular output that an isql user can see, so we don't really know what the procedure did with the data internally. What we can see here is that the system didn't return an error when trying to run the procedure. This proves that the procedure was registered and loadable, and that it executed without returning an error (or *GPFing*). That's good enough for now.

Extended Stored Procedure To Java Server Communication

If you look back at the block diagram of Figure 5.1, you'll see a line connecting the extended procedure to the Java server. This is the connection we need to make, now that we have good values for **price** and **symbol**. In order to make this connection, we need to look at where things execute. Our extended stored procedure always executes within an SQL Server process. Our Java server is an entirely separate process, running in its own, protected, memory. To get data from one to the other, we need some form of interprocess communication.

There are many ways for processes to communicate under Windows NT. The one I chose to use in this application is named *pipes*. Different operating systems implement other forms of IPC, like shared memory, anonymous pipes, and semaphores. Named pipes, for their part, are as good a mechanism as any and are fairly simple to understand. Listing 5.5 shows the code we use for both ends of the named-pipe connection.

Listing 5.5 Code used for both ends of the named-pipe connection.

```
/* CreateServerPipe - The Java server end-uses this function to create
a named pipe that the extended stored procedure can connect to. */
int CreateServerPipe()
{
LPVOID lpMsgBuf;
       DWORD d;

  /* Create a named pipe for receiving messages */
  ssnpServerPipe=CreateNamedPipe("\\\\.\\pipe\\ssnp1",
    PIPE_ACCESS_INBOUND,
    PIPE_TYPE_MESSAGE | PIPE_WAIT,
    5, 0, 0, 150,
    (LPSECURITY_ATTRIBUTES) NULL);

  /* Check and see if the named pipe was created */
  if (ssnpServerPipe == INVALID_HANDLE_VALUE)
  {
   FormatMessage(
    FORMAT_MESSAGE_ALLOCATE_BUFFER | FORMAT_MESSAGE_FROM_SYSTEM,
```

```
    NULL,
    GetLastError(),
    MAKELANGID(LANG_NEUTRAL, SUBLANG_DEFAULT), // Default language
    (LPTSTR) &lpMsgBuf,
    0,
    NULL
    );

     d = GetLastError();
     printf( "CreateNamedPipe failed 0x%lx %ld %s\n",  d, d, lpMsgBuf );
    return (1);
  }
  return( 0 );
}

/* DestroyServerPipe - destroy the Java server end of the
named-pipe connection. */
int DestroyServerPipe() {
   DisconnectNamedPipe(ssnpServerPipe);
   ssnpServerPipe = NULL;
   return( 0 );
   }

/* ListenServerPipe - Listen on the server end of the named
pipe for a client connecting. Sit in a loop reading messages
until the read fails, meaning the client disconnected.
Cut the message into its two parts, symbol and price, then
send the two parts to the function ShowTrigger for processing.
*/
int ListenServerPipe() {
  char toDisptxt[80];
  DWORD NumBytesRead;
  char *price, *ptr;

if( ssnpServerPipe != NULL )
     DisconnectNamedPipe( ssnpServerPipe );
  if(!ConnectNamedPipe(ssnpServerPipe,
    (LPOVERLAPPED) NULL))
  {
      printf( "connect failed %p\n", ssnpServerPipe );
    return (1);
  }

  /* Repeatedly check for messages until the program
     is terminated */
```

```
  while(1)
  {
    /* Read the message and check to see if read
       was successful */
    if (!ReadFile(ssnpServerPipe, toDisptxt,
      sizeof(toDisptxt),
      &NumBytesRead, (LPOVERLAPPED) NULL))
    {
// The client disconnected, exit
      return (0);
    }
   if(( ptr = strchr( toDisptxt, ';' )) != NULL ) {
      *ptr = '\0';
      price = ptr+1;
      }
   else
      price = "NA";
   showTrigger( toDisptxt, price );
  } /* while */
}

/* CreateClientPipe -  Create the client end of the named pipe
for the extended stored procedure to use. */
int CreateClientPipe()
{
  char pipeName[80];

  sprintf(pipeName, "\\\\.\\pipe\\ssnp1",
    machineName);

  /* Create the named-pipe file handle for sending
     messages */
  ssnpClientPipe=CreateFile(pipeName,
    GENERIC_WRITE, FILE_SHARE_READ,
    (LPSECURITY_ATTRIBUTES) NULL,
    OPEN_EXISTING, FILE_ATTRIBUTE_NORMAL,
    (HANDLE) NULL);

  /* Check and see if the named-pipe file was
     opened, if not terminate program */
  if (ssnpClientPipe == INVALID_HANDLE_VALUE)
  {
    return (1);
  }
  return( 0 );
}
```

```
/* DestroyClientPipe - Destroy the client end of the named pipe. */
int DestroyClientPipe() {
   CloseHandle( ssnpClientPipe );
   ssnpClientPipe = NULL;
   return( 0 );
   }

/* WriteClientPipe - write a new symbol and price message into the
named pipe from the extended stored procedure. */
int WriteClientPipe( char *symbol, double fprice ) {
  char toSendtxt[80];
  DWORD NumBytesWritten;

    /* Write message to the pipe */
   sprintf( toSendtxt, "%s;%f", symbol, fprice );
    if (!WriteFile(ssnpClientPipe,
          toSendtxt, (DWORD) strlen(toSendtxt)+1,
          &NumBytesWritten, (LPOVERLAPPED) NULL))
    {
      CloseHandle(ssnpClientPipe);
      return (1);
    }

}
/* processTriggers - The Java server instantiates the appropriate
classes, then calls this function to process symbol/price messages that
come over the named pipe. */
void Stocker_NativeMethodShell_processTriggers(
      struct HStocker_NativeMethodShell *this) {
      hCurrent = this;
      CreateServerPipe();
      while( 1 )
         if( ListenServerPipe())   // This call runs forever
            break;
      DestroyServerPipe();
      return;
      }

/* showTrigger - a symbol and price have just come over the named
pipe connection. Pass them to the Java method that will transmit
them to any interested clients. */
void showTrigger( char *symbol, char *price ) {
   Hjava_lang_String *hSymbolString;
   Hjava_lang_String *hPriceString;

   hSymbolString = makeJavaString(symbol, strlen( symbol ));
   hPriceString = makeJavaString(price, strlen( price ));
```

```
execute_java_dynamic_method(
  0, (HObject *)hCurrent, "displayOther",
    "(Ljava/lang/String;Ljava/lang/String;)V",
      hSymbolString, hPriceString);
}
```

For this named-pipe connection, there are two sides: the server side where the Java server runs, and the client side where the extended stored procedure runs. Let's look at the server side first to see how the Java server's end of the pipe works.

Through a mechanism we'll discuss later, the Java server calls **Stocker_NativeMethodShell_processTriggers** to read its end of the named pipe and process the messages that come over it. **ProcessTriggers**, on the server side of the pipe, calls **CreateServerPipe**, **ListenServerPipe**, and **DestroyServerPipe**. As we saw back in the code for **ping**, the extended stored procedure on the client side of the named pipe calls **CreateClientPipe**, **WriteClientPipe**, and **DestroyClientPipe**. These calls manage the client side of our named-pipe transaction.

With any named-pipe connection, there are two sides: the side that creates the pipe (the server) and the side that connects to the pipe (the client). On the client side, we treat the pipe like a file. Within **CreateClientPipe**, we open the pipe using **CreateFile**, passing it the pipe name **"\\.\pipe\ssnp1"** as the file to open. Similarly, in **WriteClientPipe**, using the handle we get from **CreateFile**, we call **WriteFile** to push information over the pipe. Finally, when we're done with the pipe on the client side, we call **CloseHandle** to disconnect from the pipe.

Now it's time to look at the server side of the named pipe. The Java server has called **ProcessTriggers**, and through that, **CreateServerPipe**, which returns immediately (assuming that the pipe gets created okay). This creates the server side of the named pipe using, not file I/O calls like **CreateFile**, but the named-pipe-specific call **CreateNamedPipe**. Then, it calls **ListenServerPipe**. **ListenServerPipe** blocks in the call to **ConnectNamedPipe**. This is the connection point between the Java server and the extended procedure. **ConnectNamedPipe** does not return until the client side calls **CreateFile** on our named pipe. When **ConnectNamedPipe** returns, the two sides are connected. Thus, when the extended procedure calls

WriteClientPipe, what is the Java server doing? At the lowest level, it's sitting in the **while** loop of **ListenServerPipe**, trying to read a message over the named pipe.

That takes care of the named-pipe connection—the two sides connect, the client (extended procedure) writes a single message and disconnects, while the server sits in a loop reading the single message. But what happens to that message? Well, what you see in **ListenServerPipe** is the following cryptic code:

```
execute_java_dynamic_method(
     0, (HObject *)hCurrent, "displayOther",
       "(Ljava/lang/String;Ljava/lang/String;)V",
         hSymbolString, hPriceString);
```

The function **execute_java_dynamic_method** is a library call provided by Java to allow C/C++ functions to invoke Java methods. Let's run through the arguments one by one:

- The first argument is the context. Discussion of the context is beyond the scope here; we can just leave it as zero.
- The second argument, **hCurrent**, is the handle of the Java object whose method we want to invoke.
- The third argument, **"displayOther"**, is the name of the method we want to invoke.
- The fourth argument is the method signature, a description of what the method takes as arguments and what it returns. This string says that **displayOther** is a method that takes two **String** arguments (**Ljava/lang/String;Ljava/lang/String**), and returns void (V).
- The last two arguments, **hSymbolString** and **hPriceString**, are the arguments we wish to give to **displayOther**. In this case, they are Java **String** versions of the current symbol and price.

By this method, the message that came over our named pipe ends up as the arguments to a Java method. Where does that Java method execute? It executes in the same process that **processTriggers** executes—within our Java server. The connection between them is the object handle, **hCurrent**.

In the DLL we define a variable, **hCurrent**, which is just a handle to a Java Object. To maintain it, we use the two functions **registerJavaProcess** and **deregisterJavaProcess**, shown in Listing 5.6.

Listing 5.6 The registerJavaProcess and deregister JavaProcess functions.

```
/* registerJavaProcess - Use the Java object supplied as the
only argument to the Java object containing the connection
to the applet. */
void Stocker_NativeMethodShell_registerJavaProcess(
      struct HStocker_NativeMethodShell *this) {
      hCurrent = this;
      return;
      }

/* deregisterJavaProcess - Stop using this Java object as the
applet connection. Destroys the named pipe so there's nobody for
the extended stored procedure to talk to. */
void Stocker_NativeMethodShell_deregisterJavaProcess(
                  struct HStocker_NativeMethodShell *this) {
      hCurrent = NULL;
      DestroyServerPipe();
      return;
      }
```

As you can see, **register** and **deregister** literally do nothing more than set and clear **hCurrent**. **Deregister** also kills the named pipe so that we don't even try to use the NULL **hCurrent** Object handle. These two functions have an interesting facet—they're Java native methods, C DLL functions that can be called from within a Java program.

The picture is probably becoming a little clearer now. The Java server gives our DLL code a handle to itself, and the DLL code uses that handle to call back into the server with the information that came over the named pipe.

The Java Server

We've taken a bit of a back door into the server code. In fact, we've followed a message all the way from its generation in SQL Server's trigger mechanism, through the extended procedure DLL function **ping**, over the named pipe, into the **ProcessTriggers** DLL function, and finally into the Java server via the call to **execute_java_dynamic_method**. It's probably time, then, to go back and cover the Java server itself.

The Java server is a standalone Java application. Like a C program, it has a **main** function (method) that gets invoked automatically at startup and embodies the entire application. When the **main** method returns, the party's over—the application exits.

The Java server consists of a number of elements. The most basic of these is the **Main** class. This class embodies the **main** method that defines the scope of our application. Listing 5.7 shows the **Main** class and its private class, **WaitThread**.

Listing 5.7 Code to create the Main class and its private WaitThread class.

```
package Stocker;

import java.io.*;
import Stocker.*;

/** A shell class for our Stocker Java server. Instantiates the
server class, Stocker, as well as the NativeMethodShell object that the
DLL uses, and the WaitThread class, which actually reads the named
pipe. After all that instantiating, we sit in a blocking read of
the console, so hitting a key should bounce us out of the
application.
@see Stocker.Stocker
@see Stocker.NativeMethodShell
@see Stocker.WaitThread
*/
public class Main {
    static NativeMethodShell hw;
    static Stocker s;

/** The main function for the entire server application.
Instantiate the appropriate classes, then sit listening to the
keyboard. If a key is hit, end the application. */
    public static void main(String[] args) {
    s = new Stocker(args);
    hw = new NativeMethodShell(s);

    WaitThread wt = new WaitThread(hw);
```

```
    s.start();
    wt.start();

    try {
        int x = System.in.read();
        }
    catch( IOException e ) {}
    wt.Die();
    System.exit( 0 );
    }
}

/** A class for processing the messages that come to us over
the named pipe from our extended procedure. It calls into the
DLL via our native methods to register the NativeMethodShell object
as the one to call whenever a message comes in. This is a
daemon thread, so we can kill the whole server without waiting
for this thread to die.
*/
class WaitThread extends Thread {
    NativeMethodShell hw;

/** Save the NativeMethodShell object to give to the DLL, and set
us as a daemon thread. */
    public WaitThread( NativeMethodShell h ) {
        hw = h;
        setDaemon( true );
        }

/** Remove the attachment of the DLL to the NativeMethodShell object. */
    public void Die() {
            hw.deregisterJavaProcess();
            }

/** Attach the DLL to the NativeMethodShell object, then sit in
ProcessTriggers processing messages. */
    public void run() {
        try {
            hw.registerJavaProcess();
            hw.processTriggers();
            }
        finally{
            hw.deregisterJavaProcess(); }
        }
    }
```

The major task of the **Main** class is to instantiate the classes that do all the work, and set them running. In **Main's main** method (the main function for the entire application), it creates a **Stocker**, a **NativeMethodShell**, and a **WaitThread**. It also starts the **Stocker** and **WaitThread**, since those are both **Thread** objects that run independently. Then, our main method sits in a blocking read of the keyboard. Hit a key at the console, and the application exits.

WaitThread's job is equally simple:

- Pass a valid object handle to the DLL via **registerJavaProcess**.
- Call the DLL's named-pipe-handling function, **processTriggers**, to process messages.

Almost all of the work of the **WaitThread** is done within the DLL function **processTriggers**. What **WaitThread** provides is an independent thread for the DLL function to run in. In the declaration of **WaitThread**, we define it as extending **Thread**. Java's **Thread** class provides a method, **start**, which allows us to create a new thread that consists entirely of our run method. When our main method executes the line **wt.start()**, Java creates a new operating-system thread entirely dedicated to running **WaitThread**'s run method, which, of course, simply runs the **processTriggers**' DLL function. This is how we spin the named-pipe message processing off into its own independent thread.

One consideration that will not be obvious unless you've worked with Java for awhile is the importance of maintaining a reference to the **NativeMethodShell** object. Java is a *garbage-collected* language. Objects that do not have references to them will get garbage-collected (*free'd*, in C terminology). If, for instance, we say **"hw = null"** after we call **ProcessTriggers**, then our DLL function will eventually be using a handle to an object that has been garbage-collected.

If you haven't spent a lot of time with Java, you may also be wondering why the DLL functions **registerJavaProcess**, **deregisterJavaProcess**, and **processTriggers** are called the way they are, as **hw.registerJavaProcess**, for example. **Hw**, of course, is the name of our **WaitThread** variable, which we instantiated by saying **"hw = new WaitThread(this)"**. However, we've already seen these functions implemented within the DLL as ***Stocker_NativeMethodShell_***

registerJavaProcess, ***Stocker_NativeMethodShell_*****deregisterJavaProcess**, and ***Stocker_NativeMethodShell_*****processTriggers**. Where does the giant prefix come from?

What we're dealing with here is a scheme similar to C++'s name-mangling scheme. **Stocker** is the Java "package" of which **NativeMethodShell** is a part. **NativeMethodShell** is the class that encapsulates these DLL functions. In Java terminology, these three DLL functions are known as *native methods* of the **NativeMethodShell** class.

Creating The Java Native Methods

We've approached the topic of native methods in a bottom-up fashion, looking at the actual code of the native methods without talking much about how we created that code. Now is as good a time as any to show how native methods are created from scratch.

We start by writing a Java class that encapsulates our native methods, in our case **NativeMethodShell**. Listing 5.8 shows the source for NativeMethodShell.java.

Listing 5.8 Java code for the NativeMethodShell class.

```
package Stocker;
import Stocker.Stocker;

/** A class to encapsulate the native methods for our
stock price notification server. Maintains a handle to
our Stocker object, and calls back to it whenever a
message comes through.
@see Stocker
*/
class NativeMethodShell {

/** The Stocker object that we'll call whenever a watch
message comes through indicating that a client wants
to watch a stock. */
        Stocker st;

/** Save the Stocker handle. */
        public NativeMethodShell(Stocker s) {
            st = s;
        }
```

```
/** Construct with a null Stocker. */
        public NativeMethodShell() {
            st = null;
        }

/** The native methods. */
          public native void registerJavaProcess();
          public native void deregisterJavaProcess();
          public native void processTriggers();

/** The static initialization block. Run once at
instantiation, it merely loads the DLL that our
C native methods live in. */
          static {
              System.loadLibrary("StockerHelper");
              }

/** This is the Java method invoked by the extended stored procedure.
It calls back into the Stocker to transmit the new price to all
interested clients. */
          void displayOther( String symbol, String price ) {
                st.updatePrice( symbol, price );
              }
          }
```

The **NativeMethodShell** object, of which there is only one, maintains a handle to the **Stocker** object, of which there is also only one. When the extended-stored-procedure DLL function, **ping**, receives a new price via the SQL Server trigger, it invokes this **displayOther** method via the library call **execute_java_dynamic_method**. Thus, the new symbol and price arrive in our Java server, passes to our **NativeMethodShell** object first, and from there to our **Stocker** object, where they will be distributed to interested clients.

The other part of our **NativeMethodShell** class is the native methods. **DisplayOther** is not a native method. **RegisterJavaProcess**, **deRegisterJavaProcess**, and **processTriggers** are native methods, as evidenced by the **native** keyword in their declaration. We write these native-method prototypes first, then write the C functions that make up their bodies.

Java native-method C declarations are, to put it mildly, a little obscure, and writing them from scratch is fraught with danger. Fortunately for us, Java provides a tool, **javah**, that automates the process. If we provide **javah** with a Java class file that includes the Java declaration of a native method, it will produce both an include file and a stub C file for all the native methods in that class. Our include file, shown in Listing 5.9, defines the handle to our object, as well as the DLL function prototypes. We used these function prototypes when we first wrote the body of the native methods back in Listing 5.6.

Listing 5.9 Stocker_NativeMethodShell.h.

```
/* DO NOT EDIT THIS FILE - it is machine generated */
#include <native.h>
/* Header for class Stocker_NativeMethodShell */

#ifndef _Included_Stocker_NativeMethodShell
#define _Included_Stocker_NativeMethodShell
struct HStocker_Stocker;

typedef struct ClassStocker_NativeMethodShell {
    struct HStocker_Stocker *st;
} ClassStocker_NativeMethodShell;
HandleTo(Stocker_NativeMethodShell);

#ifdef __cplusplus
extern "C" {
#endif
extern void Stocker_NativeMethodShell_registerJavaProcess(
      struct HStocker_NativeMethodShell *);
extern void Stocker_NativeMethodShell_deregisterJavaProcess(
      struct HStocker_NativeMethodShell *);
extern void Stocker_NativeMethodShell_processTriggers(
      struct HStocker_NativeMethodShell *);
#ifdef __cplusplus
}
#endif
#endif
```

Java does not call our native method directly (nothing is that easy). Instead, it goes through a stub. We need to create this stub (via **javah -stubs NativeMethodShell**), and compile/link it along with the rest of our source files, but we never modify it. As you can see from Listing 5.10, the stub version of **registerJavaProcess** prepends the phrase *Java_* to the native-method name.

Listing 5.10 Stub version of registerJavaProcess.

```
/* SYMBOL: "Stocker_NativeMethodShell/registerJavaProcess()V",
Java_Stocker_NativeMethodShell_registerJavaProcess_stub */
__declspec(dllexport) stack_item
*Java_Stocker_NativeMethodShell_registerJavaProcess_stub(stack_item
*_P_,struct execenv *_EE_) {
    extern void Stocker_NativeMethodShell_registerJavaProcess(void *);
    (void) Stocker_NativeMethodShell_registerJavaProcess(_P_[0].p);
    return _P_;
}
```

The stub function arranges for the proper arguments to be passed to the function, and for a useable value to be returned to the calling Java method.

At this point, we've covered two of the three public classes that make up our Java server. All that's left is the **Stocker** class. The **Stocker** class is responsible for these housekeeping tasks:

- Creating and listening to the socket through which we communicate with clients.
- Retrieving initial values for the stock when a client indicates interest.
- Remembering which client is interested in which stock.
- Distributing new prices to all interested clients.

Listing 5.11 shows the source for the **Stocker** class and its associated private classes.

Listing 5.11 Code for the Stocker class and its private classes.

```
package Stocker;

import java.awt.*;
import java.lang.*;
import java.util.*;
import java.net.*;
```

```
import java.io.*;
import java.sql.*;
import java.util.*;

/** A class for managing the socket connection to the client applet.
Runs a thread that opens and listens to the socket, processing
incoming messages.
@author John Rodley
@version 1.0 12/1/1995
*/
public class Stocker extends Thread {
    Properties prop;
static public boolean bRun = true;
public static Stocker currentStocker;
static String PropertiesFile = "/users/default/.hotjava/properties";

/** The port that the server reads and writes. */
public int port = 2099;

/** The hashtable that attaches symbols to sockets. */
Hashtable Watches;
/** The hashtable that attaches sockets to symbols. */
Hashtable Sockets;
/** Should we report progress? */
public boolean bVerbose = false;

/** The directory that the properties file lives in. */
static String topDirectory;
/** The socket we actually read and write. */
SrvSocket srvsock;
/** The socket at which we accept connections. */
Acceptor acceptor;

/** The connection that all the JDBC calls use. */
public static java.sql.Connection conn;

/** Open the database using the properties in the current properties
file.
Undocumented property "database" sets which database we're using.
@see weblogic.jdbc.dblib.Driver
@see SQLException
@see ClassNotFoundException
*/
void OpenDB() {
    try {
```

```
        Class.forName("weblogic.jdbc.dblib.Driver");
        try {
            if( bVerbose )
               System.out.println(
                  "connecting to jdbc:weblogic:mssqlserver:katie "
                     +prop.getProperty("database") );
           conn = DriverManager.getConnection(
                           "jdbc:weblogic:mssqlserver:katie", prop );
            } catch( SQLException e ) {
                System.out.println( "SQL Error "+e ); System.exit(1); }
        }
    catch( ClassNotFoundException e1 ) {
        System.out.println( "NO Driver "+e1 );
        System.exit(1);}
}

/** A constructor to set up the properties file and create the
hashtables.
@see Acceptor
*/
public Stocker(String argv[]) {

  if( argv.length > 0 ) {
   PropertiesFile = new String( argv[0]+"properties" );
   }
  else
   PropertiesFile = new String( "/users/default/.hotjava/properties" );

    for( int i = 0; i < argv.length; i++ ) {
        if( argv[i].compareTo( "-v" ) == 0 )
            bVerbose = true;
        }

  if( bVerbose )
      System.out.println( "setting properties file to "+PropertiesFile );

    Watches = new Hashtable();
    Sockets = new Hashtable();

  currentStocker = this;

  LoadProperties(); // DB name is in here
  OpenDB();         // Open the db
  setDaemon( false );
  acceptor = new Acceptor( this );  // Listen for clients connecting
```

```
    acceptor.start();
    }

  public static synchronized void SQLExec( String ssql ) throws
  SQLException {
              Statement stmt = Stocker.conn.createStatement();
              stmt.execute(ssql);
      }


  /** The main loop for the AgentServer.  Sits in a loop,
  sleeping for 1 second, then waking up to check whether the user
  interface has been terminated.
  */
  public void run() {
      try {
        while( bRun == true ) {
          try {
            Thread.sleep( 1000 );
              }
          catch( Exception e ) { break; }
          }
      }
    finally {
        acceptor.stop();
        if( bVerbose )
            System.out.println( "out of run loop" );
        System.exit(0);
        }
    }

  /** Read the topDirectory of this application from the properties file.
  */
  void LoadProperties() {
    try {
        prop = System.getProperties();
        prop.load(new FileInputStream(PropertiesFile));
    } catch( IOException e ) {
        System.out.println("properties file exception "+e ); }
    if( bVerbose )
        System.out.println( "system properties "+prop );

      topDirectory = System.getProperty( "Stocker.read" );
      if( topDirectory == null ) {
          System.out.println( "Stocker.read not set in "+PropertiesFile );
```

```
}
    else {
        if( bVerbose )
            System.out.println( "got "+topDirectory+" for Stocker.read");
        }
    }

/** Process a message from the client. If it's a die message,
then kill the socket. Otherwise, decompose the watch message and
attach this socket to the specified symbol and vice versa. If
the socket is already attached to another symbol, remove that
attachment.
@see AcceptedSocket
*/
public void ProcessLine( AcceptedSocket as, String s ) {
    if( bVerbose )
        System.out.println( "Processing "+s );
    if( s.compareTo( "DIEDIEDIE" ) == 0 ) {
        if( bVerbose )
            System.out.println( "received end message from client" );
        String oldsym = (String)Sockets.get( as );
        SymbolWatch sw;
        if( oldsym != null ) {
            sw = (SymbolWatch)Watches.get(oldsym);
            if( sw != null ) {
                if( bVerbose )
                    System.out.println( "Detaching socket from symbol
                      "+oldsym );
                sw.deleteClient( as );
                Sockets.remove( as );
                }
            else
                System.out.println( "Orphan socket on symbol "+oldsym );
            }
        return;
        }
    int k = s.indexOf( ':' );
    byte buffer[] = new byte[k];
    s.getBytes( 0, k, buffer, 0 );
    String s1 = new String( buffer, 0 );
    if( bVerbose )
        System.out.println( "comparing "+s1 );

    buffer = new byte[s.length()-(k+1)];
    s.getBytes( k+1, s.length(), buffer, 0 );
```

```
String Symbol = new String( buffer, 0 );
if( s1.compareTo( "Watch" ) == 0 ) {
    // Is this socket already attached to a symbol?
    String oldsym = (String)Sockets.get( as );
    SymbolWatch sw;
    if( oldsym != null ) {
        sw = (SymbolWatch)Watches.get(oldsym);
        if( sw != null ) {
            if( bVerbose )
                System.out.println( "Detaching socket from symbol
                  "+oldsym );
            sw.deleteClient( as );
            Sockets.remove( as );
            }
        else
            System.out.println( "Orphan socket on symbol "+oldsym );
        }

    // Now see if there's anybody already watching this symbol
    sw = (SymbolWatch)Watches.get( Symbol );
    if( sw == null ) {
        sw = new SymbolWatch( Symbol, as );
        Watches.put( Symbol, sw );
        }
    else
        sw.addClient( as );

    // Attach the socket to the symbol
    if( bVerbose )
        System.out.println( "Attach socket to symbol "+Symbol );
    Sockets.put( as, Symbol );

    // Now update the price for this symbol, writing the new price to
       all watchers
    if( bVerbose )
        System.out.println( "Received watch message" );
    String Price = new String( "0.00" );
    sw.updatePrice( Symbol, Price );
    }

}

/** Update the price for all clients attached to this symbol. */
public void updatePrice( String Symbol, String Price ) {
        // Now see if there's anybody already watching this symbol
```

```
        SymbolWatch sw = (SymbolWatch)Watches.get( Symbol );
        if( sw == null ) {
            return;
            }

        // Now update the price for this symbol, writing the new price to
           all watchers
        if( bVerbose )
            System.out.println( "Received new symbol/price "+Symbol+"/
              "+Price );
        sw.updatePrice( Symbol, Price );
        }
}

/** Handle reading and closing a socket which has already been
accepted.
@see Report
@see Thread
@see AcceptedSocket
@author John Rodley
@version 1.0
*/
class SocketHandler extends Thread {
  Stocker ss;
  public AcceptedSocket as;
  FileOutputStream outputFile;
  boolean bDispatcher = false;
  boolean bContinue = true;

/** Simply saves the Socket that's passed as an argument.
@arg  Socket  This socket is saved and used within the run method to
read from.
@see AcceptedSocket
@see Socket
*/
  public SocketHandler( Socket so, Stocker s ) {
   ss = s;
   as = new AcceptedSocket( so );
  }

/** The run loop for this thread.  Does a single blocking read
from the Socket that was supplied to the constructor for a
maximum of 1024 bytes and then closes the socket and exits the
thread. Passes whatever is read to Report for logging in the
day-file. The small, single read is done for security
```

```
purposes. A malicious app could still flood the log, but it
would have to re-connect every time - an expensive and
dangerous proposition.
@see Report
*/
  public void run() {
    int ret;
    String s;

    while( true ) {
        if(( s = as.readLine()) != null  )
          {
          System.out.println( "read "+ s );
          ss.ProcessLine( as, s );
          }
        else
            break;
        }
    as.close();
    }

}

/** A thread that simply sits in a loop accepting connections
on the port and spawning other threads to read the accepted
socket.
@author John Rodley
@version 1.0
@see SrvSocket
@see SocketHandler
@see Snitch
*/
class Acceptor extends Thread {
  Stocker as;
  SrvSocket s;

/** Constructor - daemonize this thread and save the Snitch
for later use.
*/
  public Acceptor( Stocker a ) {
    setDaemon( true );
    as = a;
    }
```

```
/** The run loop for this thread.  Sits in a loop accepting
connections.  Whenever a client connects, we create a
SocketHandler thread using that accepted Socket, and start the
thread up. Runs until 'stopped' from above.
@see Socket
@see SrvSocket
@see SocketHandler
*/
  public void run() {
    // set up the server socket
    s = new SrvSocket( as.port );
    while( true ) {
      Socket newS = s.Accept();
      SocketHandler a = new SocketHandler( newS, as );
      a.start();
      }
    }
}


/** Class representing a server socket bound to a local port.
@see ServerSocket
@version 1.0 August 1, 1995
@author John Rodley
*/
class SrvSocket {
ServerSocket s;
Socket newS;

/** Constructor creates a ServerSocket bound to a local port.
@arg  port  The integer local port number that this socket will
be bound to.
@see ServerSocket
*/
public SrvSocket( int port ) {
  s = null;
  while( s == null ) {
try {
      s = new ServerSocket( port );
      } catch( IOException e )
        { System.out.println( "exception "+e ); }
    }
  }

/** Accept a connection on this port and return the new
socket.  Swallow any exceptions.
```

```
@see Socket
@see Socket.accept
*/
public Socket Accept() {
  try {
    newS = s.accept();
//    System.out.println( "Accepted on host port" );
    } catch( IOException e )
      { System.out.println( "exception "+e ); }
  return( newS );
  }
}

/** A socket that has been accepted, meaning that there is a
client now attached to it.
@see InputStream
@see OutputStream
@author John Rodley
@version 1.0
*/
class AcceptedSocket {
public InputStream inputStream;
public OutputStream outputStream;
public DataInputStream dis;
Socket s;

/** Constructor - creates input and output streams that read
and write can use.
@arg  so  The accepted Socket, saved for further use.
@see InputStream
@see OutputStream
*/
public AcceptedSocket( Socket so ) {
  s = so;
  try {
    inputStream = s.getInputStream();
    outputStream = s.getOutputStream();
    } catch( IOException e )
      { System.out.println( "exception "+e); }
  }

/** Read a line terminated by one of the usual suspects - \r
and/or \n.  Accomplish this by making a DataInputStream from
our base InputStream.
@see DataInputStream
```

```
*/
public String readLine() {
  String s = new String("");

  try {
    dis = new DataInputStream(inputStream);
    s = dis.readLine();
    if( s == null )
        return( null );
//    System.out.println( "readLine("+s.length()+") "+s );
    } catch( IOException e )
     { System.out.println("exception "+e); return( null );}
  return( s );
  }

/** Read an array of bytes from the socket.
@return The number of bytes read.
*/
public int read(byte buffer[], int length) {
  try {
    return( inputStream.read(buffer));
    } catch( IOException e )
      { System.out.println("exception "+e); return( -1 ); }
  }

/** Write an array of bytes to the socket. */
public void writeLine(String s) {
    new PrintStream(outputStream).println(s);
  }
/** Write an array of bytes to the socket. */
public void write(byte buffer[], int length) {
  try {
    outputStream.write(buffer, 0, length);
    } catch( IOException e )
      { System.out.println( "exception "+e); }
  }

/** Close the socket. */
public void close() {
  try {
    s.close();
    } catch( IOException e )
      { System.out.println( "exception "+e); }
  }
}
```

```
/** A class for managing a collection of client-sockets all
attached to a single stock ticker symbol. Allows updating
all clients interested in a new price with one call.
*/
class SymbolWatch {
/** The symbol that this collection of clients is watching. */
    String symbol;
/** The collection of clients watching the symbol. */
    Vector Sockets;

/** Save the symbol and the original client attached to it. */
    public SymbolWatch( String sym, AcceptedSocket a ) {
        symbol = new String(sym);
        Sockets = new Vector(1);
        addClient( a );
        }

/** Attach a new client to the symbol. */
    public void addClient( AcceptedSocket a ) {
        Sockets.addElement( a );
        }

/** Remove the specified client from the collection. */
    public void deleteClient( AcceptedSocket a ) {
        for( int i = 0; i < Sockets.size(); i++ ) {
            if((AcceptedSocket)Sockets.elementAt(i) == a ) {
                Sockets.removeElementAt(i);
                break;
                }
            }
        }

/** Send the new price for this symbol to all the attached clients. */
    public void updatePrice( String sym, String price ) {
        if( symbol.compareTo( sym ) != 0 )
            return;
        for( int i = 0; i < Sockets.size(); i++ ) {
            AcceptedSocket as = (AcceptedSocket)Sockets.elementAt(i);
            as.writeLine( symbol+":"+price );
            }
        }
    }
```

Stocker.java defines six classes: the public class **Stocker**, and the private classes **Acceptor**, **SrvSocket**, **AcceptedSocket**, **SocketHandler**, and **SymbolWatch**. Let's look first at the public class, **Stocker**.

Back in the static **main** method of the **Main** class, we saw that the application creates a single **Stocker** object. The **Stocker** constructor has a number of small tasks:

- Load the properties file.
- Open the database.
- Create the collections that match clients with ticker symbols and vice versa.
- Create the connection-handling object and set it running.

The constructor first processes the arguments provided to the application. The **String** array provided to the **Stocker** constructor comes straight from the argument to **Main.main** and consists of all the arguments provided on the command line after the class filename. For instance, on my machine, I invoke the Java server by saying ***java Main /webbase/stock/ -v***. When the **Stocker** constructor is called, the **argv String** array consists of two strings—**"/webbase/stock/"** and **"-v"**. The first argument is the location of the properties file. The second argument is a debugging flag which, if set, causes **Stocker** to emit extra debugging information.

The properties file is Java's version of the Windows INI file. It contains values that the application wants to preserve from one session to another. For **Stocker**, the properties file has three values it needs to preserve:

- The database name, in our case **"Stock"**
- The user name (**sa**)
- The password

Listing 5.12 shows our properties file.

Listing 5.12 Properties file for our Java server.

```
#Symantec Cafe 1.0
appletviewer.version=1.0

user=sa
```

```
password=
database=Stock
```

The **database**, **user**, and **password** are the SQL Server database, user, and password that **Stocker** uses to access the database. The constructor doesn't do anything with the properties file. It merely creates a Properties object using that file. We will use the values inside later, when we make a JDBC connection to the database.

After processing the command-line arguments, **Stocker** creates a pair of HashTable objects. We use these HashTables to link stocks with clients and vice versa. A Java HashTable is a keyed collection, where each item has a unique identifier (the key) and a value, which can be anything. There can only be one item in the HashTable with a particular key. **Watches** is the HashTable that attaches from 1 to *n* clients to a particular symbol, while **Sockets** is the HashTable that connects a single client to a single symbol. We'll talk more about these HashTables when we get to the all-important **updatePrice** method.

Finally, the constructor opens a connection to the database via a call to **OpenDB**. **OpenDB** opens a JDBC (*Java DataBase Connectivity*) connection to the database named in our properties file. This requires two calls, **Class.forName** and **DriverManager.getConnection**. A detailed discussion of these two methods is beyond the scope of this book, but we don't really need one to understand what they do for us. **Class.forName**, as you can see, is a static method of the Java class named (confusingly enough) **Class**. It is very similar to the **loadLibrary** method we used earlier to load our native-method DLL, in that it takes the name of a class and tries to load its class file by looking down the **CLASSPATH** for a file of that name. Thus, when we call **Class.forName** with the argument **weblogic.jdbc.dblib.Driver**, we're trying to load the public class named **Driver** from the package **weblogic.jdbc.dblib**. To do this, it looks down the **CLASSPATH** for a file named weblogic\jdbc\dblib\Driver.class. Note that this does not instantiate a **Driver** object. It merely makes that class file available for use later on.

The call to **DriverManager.getConnection** actually establishes the connection to the database that we'll use to establish initial values for our stocks. **GetConnection** takes two arguments: the machine name that the database runs on, and the **Properties** object that contains values for **database**, **username**, and **password**. That's all there is to it. When **getConnection** returns, we have a connection that we can later make JDBC calls against.

The problem we're trying to address with these HashTables is that multiple clients may be interested in a single stock. We want to be able to say "notify all the clients interested in IBM that its new price is 200." To do that, we lump all the clients who are interested in IBM into a collection, then add that collection (an instance of our private class **SymbolWatch**) to the **Watches** HashTable with the symbol **IBM** as the key. Then, whenever we need to update IBM's price, we simply get the **SymbolWatch** attached to **IBM**.

Main also "starts" the **Stocker** object. Since **Stocker** extends **Thread**, invoking **start** against it causes Java to create an independent thread that only runs the **Stocker**'s run method. The run method is basically an endless loop. We sit in the loop sleeping for a second, then testing **bRun** to see if we should keep running. In the future, we could toss some statistical reporting into this loop, such as the number of connections and symbols being watched, but for now, this loop doesn't really do much.

The last two methods in **Stocker**, **ProcessLine** and **updatePrice**, handle the two sides of the socket connection. **ProcessLine** deals with messages that come in from the client, and **updatePrice** sends new price information back out to the client.

Our seat-of-the-pants communication protocol defines only the three message types shown in Table 5.3. **ProcessLine** has to deal with two message types, **DIEDIEDIE** and **Watch**. **DIEDIEDIE**, of course, tells the server that the client is disconnecting. When a client disconnects, we need to detach

Table 5.3 The three message types for the server/applet message protocol.

Message format	Description	Direction
DIEDIEDIE	Kill this connection.	Applet to Server.
Watch:<symbol>	Attach this client to the specified symbol.	Applet to Server.
<symbol>:<price>	This symbol just traded at this price.	Server to Applet.

this connection from whatever symbol it's now attached to in both the **Watches** and **Sockets** collections. **Sockets** is a simple HashTable where the key is the actual **AcceptedSocket** over which the client and server are conversing. To detach the socket from the symbol in **Sockets**, we simply call the HashTable method **remove**, with the **AcceptedSocket** as the key argument.

Watches is a little more complicated. **Watches** is a HashTable like **Sockets**, but each item in the **Watches** collection is itself a collection (a **SymbolWatch** object). Now is as good a time as any, I suppose, to talk about **SymbolWatch**.

The purpose of the **SymbolWatch** class is to attach a set of clients (**AcceptedSockets**) to a single symbol, and allow one-call broadcast communication with all of the clients in that set. In the constructor for **SymbolWatch**, we create a Vector to hold our list of clients, and store the symbol these clients are watching. We also add the initial client for this **SymbolWatch**.

Addclient simply adds the specified client (**AcceptedSocket**) to the list of clients watching this symbol, while **deleteclient** removes the specified client from the list of clients watching this symbol. After checking that we're talking about the right symbol, **updatePrice** sends a message to each client notifying them of the new price.

That's it—a very simple class. Combined with our HashTable processing in **Stocker**, this gives us a very easy way to distribute new price information.

Now, let's get back to **Stocker.ProcessLine** in the **DIEDIEDIE** message. As we said, when a **DIEDIEDIE** message comes in, we simply remove the client from the **Sockets** collection. But for the **Watches** collection, we first get the **SymbolWatch** corresponding to the symbol that this client is attached to, then we delete the client from that **SymbolWatch** using **SymbolWatch.deleteClient**. At this point, the client has been wiped away, and we return.

If the message is not a **DIEDIEDIE** message, then it must be a **Watch** message. The first thing we need to do is take the message apart to get the symbol that this client wants to watch. Using **String.indexOf** and **String.getBytes**, we create two new Strings, **s1** and **Symbol**. The **s1** String should contain the word *Watch*, while **Symbol** contains only the symbol portion of the **Watch** message. We do a perfunctory check to make sure that this is a **Watch** message. Then, we check the **Sockets** collection to see if this client is already attached to a **Symbol**. If it is, then using code straight out of the **DIEDIEDIE** message processing, we detach it from both the **Sockets** and **Watches** collections. Next, we check to see if there's already a **SymbolWatch** in existence for this symbol. If there is, we simply add this client to it. If not, we create a new one with this client as the only attachment. Then, we attach this client to this symbol in the **Sockets** collection. Finally, we send this client (and this client only) an initial price for this stock. Further price updates will come from the **updatePrice** method.

After all the hoops we jumped through in **ProcessLine**, **updatePrice** seems tame by comparison. As you may recall, **Stocker.updatePrice** gets called by **NativeMethodShell.displayOther**, which in turn gets called by the native method **ProcessTriggers** whenever a message comes over the named pipe from the extended procedure. All of this just means that **updatePrice** gets called whenever the database trigger goes off, signaling a new price for a stock. All **updatePrice** needs to do, now that the **SymbolWatch** class is in place, is find the proper **SymbolWatch** object in the **Watches** HashTable, then invoke **SymbolWatch.updatePrice** on that object. **SymbolWatch.updatePrice** will send a message to each client attached to this symbol, notifying it of the new price.

At this point, we've covered everything in the Java server except the actual socket-handling code. This is embodied in the four communication classes, **Acceptor**, **SrvSocket**, **AcceptedSocket**, and **SocketHandler**.

In order to understand the communication classes, we need to step back and talk in general terms about IP sockets. What we want to accomplish here is to have our server open a single port number and serve a number of simultaneous clients from that port. This is generally accomplished by having the server create a socket on the port, then sit in a loop "accepting" client connections to that port. The return value from the socket-accept function is a new socket over which the two sides can communicate.

This is what the **Acceptor** class is used for. **Acceptor** extends **Thread**, and can thus run in an independent thread. We create a single **Acceptor** in the **Stocker** constructor and set it running. **Acceptor's** run method, executing in our new thread, creates a socket (**SrvSocket**), then sits in a loop accepting client connections to that socket. Each time a client connects, **Accept** unblocks and returns a new **Socket** as the value for **newS**. When we get this new **Socket** object, we create another thread, in this case a **SocketHandler** threaded object, to handle the communication with that client. Finally, we start up the new **SocketHandler** threaded object, then go back to **Accept** and block until the next client connection.

SrvSocket, the object we use to accept connections, is a simple encapsulation of the Java **ServerSocket** class. **ServerSocket** creates a socket on a port and allows us to accept connections over that port. We never read or write a **SrvSocket**.

SocketHandler and **AcceptedSocket** work together to do the actual communication. **SocketHandler**, as we said, is a threaded object, created and started up by the **Acceptor** whenever a new client connects to our port. The constructor for our **SocketHandler** creates an **AcceptedSocket** from the simple **Socket** that **ServerSocket.Accept** returns and saves for it. The constructor also saves a handle to the **Stocker** object that **Acceptor** passed in. Then, in its run method (which is now running in a new thread), the **SocketHandler** sits in a loop reading the **AcceptedSocket**, and passing each message it reads on the **Stocker** method **ProcessLine**, which we've already discussed. If our message-read method (**AcceptedSocket.readLine**) returns an error, then the client has disconnected, so we break out of the message-reading loop and close the socket.

Our final communication class, **AcceptedSocket**, is a simple encapsulation of the Java **Socket** class. We use it to simplify reading and writing the port according to the particulars of our communication with the client. In Java's **Socket** classes, we can't actually read and write to the socket. We need to get a stream that's attached to the socket and read/write that stream. Thus, the constructor gets an **InputStream** and an OutputStream from the **Socket** for later use by the read and write methods.

In our **AcceptedSocket** class, we define two read methods, **read** and **readLine**, and two write methods, **write** and **writeLine**. The simple encapsulations **read** and **write** aren't used, so we won't waste any time on them. **ReadLine** attempts to read an entire line of text from the socket. The **InputStream** we get from the socket, however, doesn't recognize "lines" of information. It only knows about bytes. So we use this **InputStream** to create another type of Java stream, a **DataInputStream**. **DataInputStreams** know about lines, providing a **readLine** method of their own. We create the **DataInputStream** by instantiating **DataInputStream** and passing our simple **InputStream** as the only argument. This is a common theme in Java stream I/O, creating new and different streams by passing a simple **InputStream** or OutputStream as the constructor argument. In similar fashion, **writeLine** creates a PrintStream from the simple outputStream and uses **PrintStream.println** to send messages to the client.

AcceptedSocket seems like more than it really is. Most of the functions are simple encapsulations or minor modifications of existing **Stream** and **Socket** capabilities. Check the Java documentation on **Stream** and **Socket** for more information about those items.

Why A Java Server?

If you've been paying attention, you've probably already asked yourself, "What is that Java server doing there?" Strictly speaking, we could have simplified this model by writing all the functionality of the Java server into the C DLL. This would have the benefit of eliminating both the named-pipe connection and the Java native method.

Would this simpler model make a better application? This is something of a religious question. Dyed-in-the-wool C programmers would undoubtedly say yes, while wild-eyed Java evangelists would, of course, take the opposite tack. I chose to do it this way because of the following:

- Writing a functional server in Java was quicker, particularly the network communication parts. There may be C/C++ socket libraries that are as easy to use as Java's. I haven't seen them.
- Writing the collections of symbol/socket and socket/symbol objects was much easier than it would have been in C/C++.
- The Java server is portable. Writing the server in Java reduces the Microsoft-specific portion to its absolutely smallest part—the named-pipe connection and extended stored procedure.
- I'm a wild-eyed Java evangelist.

The Java Applet User Interface

With all the work we've done so far, we only have one piece left to go—the user interface. Our database trigger, stored procedure, and Java server put the data on the Net. All we need is a user interface that can present that data to the user.

Because we're creating a Web application, we're constrained in our choice of user interface. Put simply, our user interface must run within a Web browser. Thus, we need an HTML page to at least provide a shell for our data view. Listing 5.13 shows the HTML shell for our active applet.

Listing 5.13 HTML code for our stock-watch application.

```
<!DOCTYPE HTML PUBLIC
"-//SQ//DTD HTML 2.0 + all extensions//EN" "hmpro3.dtd">
<HTML>
<HEAD>
<TITLE>Snug Harbor Stock Watch</TITLE></HEAD>
<BODY BGCOLOR="white"><IMG SRC="SnugHarbor.jpg"
ALT="Snug Harbor Stock Watch">
<P>
<APPLET
CODEBASE="classes" CODE="StockWatch/StockWatch.class"
ALT="This browser is not Java enabled!"
WIDTH="300" HEIGHT="300" ID="StockWatch">
</APPLET></P></BODY></HTML>
```

Within the body of our HTML page, there are only two elements: an image and an applet. The image is simply the Snug Harbor logo. The applet is where the functionality of our user interface is embodied, so let's dive right in and take a look at it. Listing 5.14 shows the source for our Java applet.

Listing 5.14 The StockWatch Java applet.

```
package StockWatch;
import java.applet.*;
import java.io.*;
import java.net.*;
import java.awt.*;

/** A class for presenting the price of a stock as a bar graph
with a numeric value that follows the top of the bar. The ticker
symbol and current price are also displayed centered over the
top of the bar graph. The scale on the left of the graph changes
based on the current price, showing only 12 points at a time.
@see Applet
*/
public class StockWatch extends Applet {
```

```
/** The ip port the Stocker Java server is listening to.  We'll
  open this port on the host, write our symbol of interest into
  it, then read it for the price messages. */
public int port;

/** The name of the host the Stocker Java server is running on. */
public String host;

/** We sit in a loop running until this boolean is set to false. */
public boolean bRun = false;
/** The ticker symbol we're watching right now. */
String currentSymbol = new String( "AMD" );
/** The string price of the current ticker symbol. */
public String currentPrice = new String( "10" );

/** The button that we use to change ticker symbols. */
Button changeButton;
/** The text field where we enter the new ticker symbol. */
TextField symbolText;
/** The area where our bar graph appears. */
public GraphCanvas gp;
/** The Panel that organizes the button and text field
  changing the ticker symbol. */
Panel controlPanel;
/** The panel at the top where the ticker symbol and the
   current price appear. */
Panel labelPanel;
/** The label that displays the current ticker symbol at
   the top of the page. */
Label textLabel;
/** The label that displays the current price at the top
   of the page. */
Label priceLabel;

/** The current price, in sixteenths of a point.  This is
  a simplifying assumption, since obviously stocks can be
  priced in fractions smaller than sixteenths. The price
  is transmitted as a float with plenty of precision, so
  fixing this sixteenths here would get us exact pricing. */
public int price_in_sixteenths = 100;

/** The price, in sixteenths that is the bottom of the scale
  that appears on the left of the bar graph. */
public int bottom=0;
public int top;
```

```
/** The number of sixteenths in each pixel. Not used here,
   but we could change this to make less fine graphs. */
public int sixteenths_per_pixel = 1;
/** The height of our bar graph in pixels. */
public int graph_height_in_pixels = 200;
/** Boolean set when Applet.init runs. */
boolean bInited = false;

/** The port watcher thread. Sits reading the socket for
   price updates.  */
WatcherThread wt = null;

/** Called once to create a socket reader thread. */
public void init() {
    if( bInited == false ) {
        firstTime();
        bInited = true;
    }
}

/** Called once to create visual elements, as well as the
   port reader thread.  */
public void firstTime() {
    top = graph_height_in_pixels*sixteenths_per_pixel;
    try {
    setLayout( new BorderLayout());
    labelPanel = new Panel();
    textLabel = new Label( "XXXXXXXX" );
    priceLabel = new Label( "XXXXXXXXXXXX");
    labelPanel.add( textLabel );
    labelPanel.add( priceLabel );
    add( "North", labelPanel );

    host = getParameter( "host" );
    if( host == null )
        host = new String( "katie" );
    String sport = getParameter( "port" );
    if( sport == null )
        sport = new String( "2099" );
    port = (new Integer( sport)).intValue();
    controlPanel = new Panel();
    changeButton = new Button( "Change symbol" );
    controlPanel.add( changeButton );
    changeButton.show();
    symbolText = new TextField(20);
```

```
        controlPanel.add( symbolText );
        symbolText.show();
        gp = new GraphCanvas(this);
        add( "Center", gp );
        gp.show();
        add( "South", controlPanel );
        controlPanel.show();
        layout();
        } catch( Exception e ) {System.out.println( "exception in init
          "+e ); }
    }

/** Turn the current price in sixteenths into a string that shows the
price as a whole dollar amount with a fraction attached. Reduces the
fraction to the lowest common denominator.
@return String
*/
    String stringPrice() {
        Integer I = new Integer( price_in_sixteenths/16 );
        Integer J = new Integer( price_in_sixteenths%16 );
        String frac = new String( "/16" );
        if( J.intValue()%2 == 0 ) {
            J = new Integer( J.intValue()/2 );
            frac = new String( "/8" );
            if( J.intValue()%2 == 0 ) {
                J = new Integer( J.intValue()/2 );
                frac = new String( "/4" );
                if( J.intValue()%2 == 0 ) {
                    J = new Integer( J.intValue()/2 );
                    frac = new String( "/2" );
                    if( J.intValue()%2 == 0 ) {
                        J = new Integer(0);
                        frac = new String("");
                        }
                    }
                }
            }
        String sprice = new String( I.toString()+" "+J.toString()+frac );
        if( J.intValue() == 0 )
            sprice = new String( I.toString() );
        return( sprice );
    }

/** Change the bottom of the scale based on the current value of
the price. */
    void setScale() {
```

```
        if((( price_in_sixteenths-bottom ) * sixteenths_per_pixel )
             > gp.dim.height || ( price_in_sixteenths < bottom )) {
//            System.out.println( "price too high, rescaling ..." );
            bottom = price_in_sixteenths-(price_in_sixteenths%16);
            if( bottom < 0 )
                bottom = 0;
        }
    }

/** Startup the socket reader thread. */
    public void start() {
        System.out.println( "start" );
        if( bInited == true ) {
            System.out.println( "already inited" );
}


        try {
            System.out.println( "stopping old watcher thread" );
        if( wt != null ) {
            wt.stop();
            wt = null;
            }
            System.out.println( "making new watcher thread" );
        wt = new WatcherThread(this);
        wt.start();
        try {
            Thread.sleep( 1000 );
        } catch( Exception e ) {}
        changeSymbol( currentSymbol );
        } catch( Exception e ) {System.out.println( "exception in start
          "+e ); }
    }

/** Kill the socket reader socket. */
    public void stop() {
        if( wt != null ) {
            wt.killSocket();
            wt.stop();
            wt = null;
        }
    }

/** Handle UI events, the only one of which is the
change symbol button.  */
    public boolean handleEvent(Event e) {
```

```
        if (e.id == Event.ACTION_EVENT) {
           if( e.target instanceof Button ) {
               changeSymbol( symbolText.getText());
              }
           }
        else {
           }
        return false;
    }

/** Send the specified symbol to the Stocker Java
server as the one we're interested in. */
    void SendNewSymbol( String Symbol ) {
        wt.Write( "Watch:"+Symbol );
    }

/** Change from the current symbol to the specified
symbol and send the new symbol to the Stocker server
as the one we want to be updated on. */
    void changeSymbol( String newSymbol ) {
        currentSymbol = new String( newSymbol );
        currentPrice = new String( "0" );
        price_in_sixteenths = 0;
        textLabel.setText( currentSymbol );
        SendNewSymbol( currentSymbol );
    }


/** Update the price the user sees using the one embedded
in this string. The string is of the form
SYMBOL:PRICE
Check the symbol to make sure the server is feeding us the
right data. Force the graph panel to repaint so that the
new price is displayed.
*/
    public void updatePrice( String s ) {
//        System.out.println( "updatePrice "+s );
        int k = s.indexOf( ':' );
        byte b1[] = new byte[k];
        s.getBytes( 0, k, b1, 0 );
        String s1 = new String( b1, 0 );
        if( s1.compareTo( currentSymbol ) != 0 ) {
            System.out.println( "Server sent us the wrong symbol" );
            changeSymbol( currentSymbol );
            return;
```

```
            }
        byte buffer[] = new byte[s.length()-(k+1)];
        s.getBytes( k+1, s.length(), buffer, 0 );
        currentPrice = new String( buffer, 0 );
//        System.out.println( "setting currentPrice to "+currentPrice );
        Float F = new Float( currentPrice );
        F = new Float( F.floatValue()*16.0 );
        price_in_sixteenths = F.intValue();
        priceLabel.setText( stringPrice());
        labelPanel.repaint();
        setScale();
        gp.repaint();
        }

}

/** A class for reading and writing the Stocker server socket
according to the simple protocol we've defined.
@see Thread
*/
class WatcherThread extends Thread {
    Socket s = null;
    DataInputStream dis;
    DataOutputStream dos;
    StockWatch sw;

/** Save a pointer to the Applet so that we can
call back to it to process incoming messages. */
    public WatcherThread( StockWatch swa ) {
        sw = swa;
        }

/** Send the Stocker server a message that tells it we're
about to abandon this connection, so they can kill their
side. */
    public void killSocket() {
            Write( "DIEDIEDIE" );
    }

/** Write a message to the socket. */
    public void Write( String s ) {
        if( s == null ) {
            System.out.println( "s is null" );
            return;
            }
```

```
        if( dos == null ) {
            System.out.println( "can't write, no output stream" );
            return;
            }
        try {
            dos.writeBytes( s+"\r\n" );
        }
        catch( IOException ioe ) {System.out.println( "write ex "+ioe );
}

    }

/** Connect to the host, then sit in a loop reading the socket and
passing the incoming messages back to the applet. */
    public void run() {
        sw.bRun = true;

        // Open the socket connection
        try {
            s = new Socket( sw.host, sw.port );
            }
        catch( IOException ie ) {
            System.out.println( "IOException "+ie+" on
              "+sw.host+":"+sw.port );
            return; }
        try {
            dis = new DataInputStream( s.getInputStream());
            dos = new DataOutputStream( s.getOutputStream());
            }
        catch( IOException ie1 ) {
            System.out.println( "Stream IOException "+ie1+" on
              "+sw.host+":"+sw.port );
            return; }

        String readString;
        // Read the socket connection
        byte buffer[] = new byte[100];
        while( sw.bRun == true ) {
            try {
                readString = dis.readLine();
                if( readString == null ) {
                    System.out.println( "Server disconnected" );
                    break;
                    }
                else {
```

```
                    System.out.println( "dis.read "+readString );
                    sw.updatePrice( readString );
                    }
                }
                catch( IOException ioe1 ) {
                    System.out.println( "ioexception "+ioe1 );
                    break;
                    }
                if( readString != null )
                    sw.ProcessLine( readString );
                }

            // Close the socket connection
            try {
                killSocket();
                s.close();
                s = null;
            }
            catch( IOException ioe2 ) {
                System.out.println( "close ioexception "+ioe2 );
            }
            s = null;
        }
}

/** A class for displaying the price of a stock as a bar
graph.  */
class GraphCanvas extends Canvas {
    StockWatch sw;
    public Dimension dim = new Dimension( 200, 200 );
    public int maxsixteenths;
    public int offset;
    int lastbottom;

    public GraphCanvas( StockWatch s ) {
        sw = s;
    }
    public Dimension preferredSize() {
        return( dim );
    }
    public Dimension minimumSize() {
        return( dim );
    }

    public synchronized void update(Graphics g) {
```

```
Dimension d = size();
int lastoffset = offset;
offset = ( d.width - dim.width )/2;
if( offset != lastoffset )
    g.clearRect( 0, 0, d.width, d.height );
g.translate( offset, 0 );
FontMetrics fm = g.getFontMetrics();
int h = fm.getMaxAscent()+fm.getMaxDescent()+2;
g.setColor( Color.black );

// Draw a box around the graph.
g.drawRect( 0, 0, dim.height-1, dim.width-1 );
g.setColor( Color.red );

// Draw the bar, erasing the empty portion.
// Height of bar is sixteenths/pixel*(price-bottom)
int height = sw.sixteenths_per_pixel*(sw.price_in_sixteenths-
  sw.bottom);
g.fillRect( 100, (dim.height-1)-height, 50, height );
g.clearRect( 100, 1, 50, (dim.height-1)-height );

// Clear the area on the left where the current price
// appears, then draw the current price and the line from
// the current price to the graph.
String sprice = sw.stringPrice();
g.setColor( Color.black );
int y = (dim.height-1)-height;
g.clearRect( 1, 1, 69, dim.height-2 );
g.drawString( sprice, 10, y );
g.drawLine( 10+fm.stringWidth(sprice), y, 69, y );

// Figure out the scale.
g.setColor( Color.gray );
int maxpossible = dim.height/fm.getHeight();
int maxdollars = dim.height/16;
int numbars = maxdollars;
if( lastbottom != sw.bottom ) {
    lastbottom = sw.bottom;
    g.clearRect( 70, 1, 30, dim.height-2 );
    }

// Draw the scale.
for( int i = 0; i < numbars; i++ ) {
    Integer K = new Integer(i+(sw.bottom/16));
    g.drawString( K.toString(), 70, (dim.height-1)-i*(dim.height/
      numbars));
```

```
            g.drawLine( 70+fm.stringWidth(K.toString()), (dim.height-1)-
i*(dim.height/numbars),100, (dim.height-1)-i*(dim.height/numbars));
            }
    }
}
```

The applet consists of three classes, corresponding roughly to the three largest lumps of functionality: server communication, user interface, and, within the user interface, the active bar graph.

The **WatcherThread** class deals with server communications. It opens, reads, and writes the server socket over which our stock-price information travels. It runs in a separate thread from the one the applet itself runs in. The applet creates a single **WatcherThread**.

The **GraphCanvas** class draws the bar graph. An extension of the **Canvas** class, the single instance of **GraphCanvas** that the applet creates takes up the center of the screen in the **StockWatch** applet. It displays the bar graph, current price, and scale, based on values such as the current price, which it reads from the applet.

The **StockWatch** class is the applet itself, an extension of the **Applet** class. It instantiates both the **WatcherThread** and **GraphCanvas**, which do most of the work. It also creates and manages the other two visual elements (besides the **GraphCanvas**) that occupy the top and bottom of the applet's visual space. These are the two Panels that hold the symbol change button and text field on the bottom, and the current symbol and price labels centered on the top. The **StockWatch** also contains the variables that define the state of the application, most notably current symbol and price.

Having talked about these classes in general terms, let's take a closer look at the applet, and see, in detail, how they work together. The first key to understanding this applet is understanding the flow of control—what executes and when. In general, the browser invokes the applet methods in the following order:

- **Applet** constructor
- **Applet.init**

- **Applet.start**
- **Applet.stop**

In our implementation, we don't use the constructor. Instead, everything is jammed into **init**, **start**, and **stop**. In **init**, the first thing we do is set up the current Panel (our applet) as a **BorderLayout** Panel. What this means is that the applet's display space is divided into five areas, **North**, **South**, **East**, **West**, and **Center**, as in Figure 5.2.

With the layout of the window set, we then create the three visual items—the current symbol and price, the bar graph, and the change-symbol text and button—that make up our user interface. The current symbol and price will go in the **North** section, the change-symbol text field and button will go in the **South** section, and the bar graph will go in the **Center**.

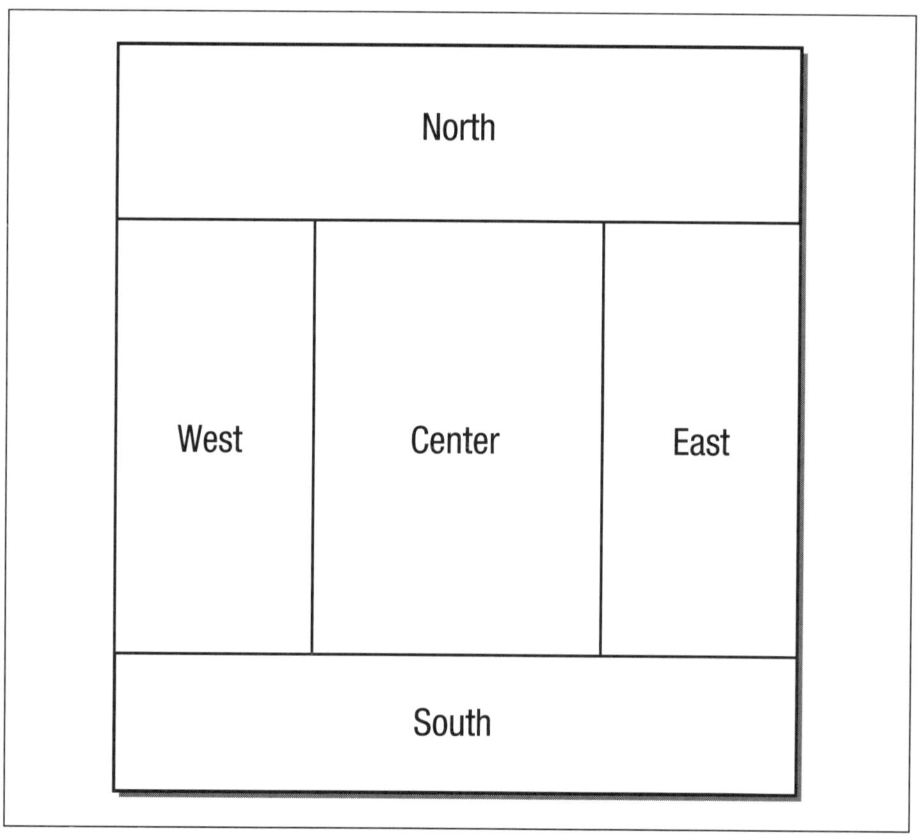

Figure 5.2 The BorderLayout Panel is divided into five areas.

In order to center the two Labels for current symbol and price in the **North** section, we need to create another Panel, add the two labels to that Panel, and then add that Panel to the applet's Panel. That's exactly what these lines accomplish:

```
labelPanel = new Panel();
textLabel = new Label( "XXXXXXXX" );
priceLabel = new Label( "XXXXXXXXXXXX");
labelPanel.add( textLabel );
labelPanel.add( priceLabel );
add( "North", labelPanel );
```

This works because default layout of a Panel is **FlowLayout**, which centers its visual items. Thus, our two Labels appear centered within the **North** section without any extra work on our part. If you look further down, where we create our **changeButton**, you see that we do something similar for the **South** section, creating a separate Panel, then adding the change button and text field to it.

Visually, all that leaves is the **Center** section. To create that, we simply instantiate a **GraphCanvas** and add it to the **Center** section. By definition, the item added to the **Center** section gets any space not claimed by any of the other sections.

The rest of **init** deals with configuring our connection back to the server. What we need to connect to a socket is a hostname (such as www.microsoft.com) and a port number (such as 80, the default HTTP port). We provide these to the applet through parameters defined in the HTML source that invokes this applet in the first place. Listing 5.15 shows the HTML source for the **StockWatch** applet.

Listing 5.15 HTML code to invoke the Java applet.

```
<!DOCTYPE HTML PUBLIC
"-//SQ//DTD HTML 2.0 + all extensions//EN" "hmpro3.dtd">
<HTML>
<HEAD>
<TITLE>Snug Harbor Stock Watch</TITLE></HEAD>
<BODY BGCOLOR="white"><IMG SRC="SnugHarbor.jpg"
ALT="Snug Harbor Stock Watch">
<P>
<APPLET
```

```
CODEBASE="classes" CODE="StockWatch/StockWatch.class"
ALT="This browser is not Java enabled!"
WIDTH="300" HEIGHT="300" ID="StockWatch">
<PARAM NAME="host" VALUE="katie"></PARAM>
<PARAM NAME="port" VALUE="2099"></PARAM>
</APPLET></P></BODY></HTML>
```

As you can see, we define two <PARAM> elements, one for the hostname and one for the port number. Within **init**, we then read these parameters via the **getParameter** method. We'll use these two values later in the **WatcherThread** class.

Start and **stop** are very important methods in an applet's life because we want to make sure that our applet does not use CPU time when it's not on the screen. There's no point—if the user can't see the bar graph, there's no reason to keep reading new values for it. For the applet thread itself, we don't have to worry. However, we *do* need to worry about any other threads we may have created, in our case, the **WatcherThread**.

In **start**, we kill any existing **WatcherThread**, then create a new one and set it running. We sleep for a second to let the **WatcherThread** start up, then send out our current symbol over the now-active socket. In **stop**, we have to try to shut down the socket and thread safely, so we send a **DIEDIEDIE** message to the server to tell it we're going away, then we kill the thread.

The only user input the applet has to deal with is the change-symbol button and text field. These visual controls were created back in **init** (via **firstTime**). Whenever the user presses that change-symbol button, the method **handleEvent** is called. Thus, in our **handleEvent** method, we set up a case for our button. If an event comes in, whose ID is **EVENT_ACTION** and target is an instance of **Button**, then it must be the change-symbol button, since we only have one. If the button is hit, we grab the text from the text field and call **changeSymbol**.

ChangeSymbol sets the current symbol to the new value, the Label to the new symbol, and the price to zero, and then sends the new symbol back to the server as the one we want to watch. If all goes right on the server end, we'll start receiving updates for the new symbol shortly.

StockWatch contains a utility method, **stringPrice**, that takes the current price and turns it into a string-with-fraction for display in the form that stocks customarily use, such as *7 3/16*. We also implement a method, **setScale**, to make sure that the current price is always somewhere on the graph rather than off the scale on the top or bottom. What **setScale** tries to do is set the bottom of the scale to some whole number less than the current price. The **GraphCanvas** class uses that bottom value when it repaints the graph. If it's changed, **GraphCanvas** remakes the scale with the new values.

The last **StockWatch** method, **updatePrice**, does just what its name implies: It updates the current price of our stock. Whenever the **WatcherThread** reads a message over the socket connection from the server, it passes that message to **updatePrice**. Since we've only defined one message that can go from the server to the applet, we assume that all messages are price updates. **UpdatePrice** decomposes the message into its two parts, **symbol** and **price**. After ensuring that the symbol is the one we're interested in, it sets the current price to the new value, changes the price label in the **North** section, sets the scale so that the current price is on-graph, and tells **GraphCanvas** to repaint itself.

What does all this tell us about the flow of execution in the applet? Well, our applet gets constructed, then **init** and **start** get called. What then? Nothing. Our applet exists in memory, but after **start** returns, the **StockWatch** object stops executing, for all intents and purposes. This is an important lesson. **StockWatch** methods only execute because they've been called from the outside. Either the browser calls them as it does the constructor, **init**, **start**, and **stop**, or another independently executing thread calls them, as **WatcherThread** does for **updatePrice**. **StockWatch** is a passive object.

GraphCanvas is also a passive object. As an extension of the **Canvas** class, **GraphCanvas** is a visual element, essentially a rectangular lump of drawable space. Its sole purpose is to draw a "barometer" corresponding to the current price of the stock in the **StockWatch** applet.

For a class with only four methods, three of which are one-liners, **GraphCanvas** gets a lot of work done. The constructor merely saves a pointer back into our applet, so that we can read some public variables; **preferredSize** and **minimumSize** take care of how big our drawable space is; and **update** decides what appears in our drawable space.

As we've already discussed, the screen location of **GraphCanvas** is determined by the code in **StockWatch.init** where we place **GraphCanvas** in the

Center area of our **BorderLayout** applet. The size of our **GraphCanvas** is, however, under our control, via the methods **preferredSize** and **minimumSize**. These two methods are overrides of empty methods in the **Component** class. The applet will try to resize our **GraphCanvas** to fill the **Center** area, but since we've defined **preferredSize** and **minimumSize**, these override whatever resizing the applet might want to do.

GraphCanvas.update is the heart of this class. The update method of any Java Component is the method responsible for drawing that Component on the screen. Our update method must draw three distinct elements—the rectangular bar, which changes size depending on the price; the scale, which remains static unless the current price travels off-scale; and the actual price, which follows the top of the bar.

WatcherThread, is our applet's only active object. In **start**, we create a single **WatcherThread** and start it up. Symmetrically enough, in **stop**, when the user leaves our page, we stop this thread. The constructor for the **WatcherThread** simply saves a handle to the applet itself for later callbacks. All the work of the class is done in the methods **killSocket**, **Write**, and **run**. **KillSocket** merely sends the **DIEDIEDIE** message to the server, telling it this client is about to disconnect. **Write**, for its part, uses the **DataOutputStream dos** to write a message to the server. **Dos** is created further down in run.

The **run** method is the method that reads and processes incoming messages from the server. All the new price messages come through here. It also incorporates a fair amount of initialization code. We start off **run** by creating a client Socket attached to the specified hostname and port (which we got from the <PARAM> elements in the HTML code). Once the Socket is created, we make a set of streams, one **DataInputStream** and one **DataOutputStream** to read and write. Then, much like the **SocketHandler** on the server, we fall into a loop, reading the **DataInputStream** until the **bRun** flag up in the applet is turned off (which happens in **StockWatch.stop**). When a message comes in via **dis.readLine()**, we pass it back up to **StockWatch.updatePrice**. If there's an error, or the **bRun** flag gets cleared, we exit the loop, send the **DIEDIEDIE** message, and return (ending the thread).

Putting It Together

It's been a long haul, but hopefully you've found the trip informative and entertaining. We're now at the finish line, ready to reap the reward for all that hard work. Our reward? A working, soup-to-nuts, active-view database application.

Figure 5.3 shows the output of our application on a user's screen. We've chosen to follow the ticker symbol BGEN. The current price is 1–7/16ths, and both the price display and the accompanying bar chart change as soon as the record in the database changes.

Start up the random price generator and watch the bar graph go up and down as the price changes. Go into the page, then back out, and see which stock you end up tracking. Better yet, check into the sample Web site at http://www.snugharbor.com and see the system at work using a real, live data feed.

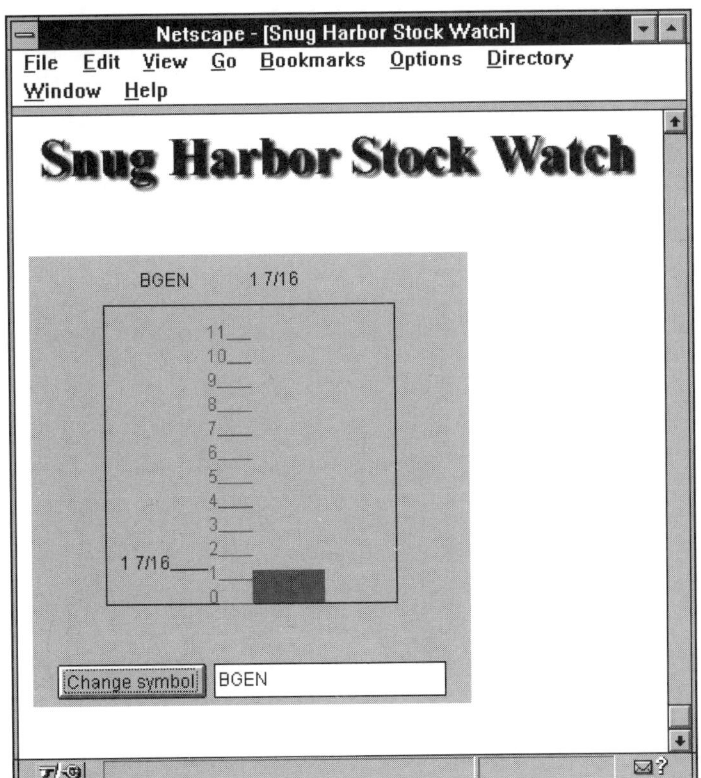

Figure 5.3 Here is the output of the Java applet on the HTML page under Netscape.

Compiling And Linking The Stored Procedure And Native-Method DLL

We all know that writing good code is only half the battle when it comes to programming. The other half is lining up all the libraries, header files, and compiler and linker flags to make the whole thing compile and link. The extended-procedure and Java-native-method functions all live in the same DLL, StockerHelper.dll, but they have distinctly different requirements when it comes to compiling and linking. Consider the extended procedure.

First, the header files. What items in the extended procedure do we need to define that aren't a standard part of the C language? For one thing, we need to define the **srv_** functions that allow us to interface with SQL Server. We also need to define the **SRV_** defines that we use in various **srv_** function calls. Both of these categories of things are defined in srv.h, which is delivered with Microsoft Back Office SDK 1.5.

Listing 5.16 shows the header files for XP.C. As you can see, the only non-standard include file is srv.h.

Listing 5.16 Header files for xp.c.

```
#include <stdlib.h>
#include <stdio.h>
#include <string.h>
#include <ctype.h>
#include <windows.h>
#include <srv.h>
#include <time.h>
#include < windows.h >
#include < iostream.h >
```

That takes care of compiling the function, but we still need to link it. The **srv_** functions are all DLL functions, contained in OpenDS60.DLL. Thus, we need to link with OpenDS60.lib to resolve those calls. We also need to make sure that OpenDS60.DLL is in the path, though installation usually takes care of this.

Those are all the pieces but one. We still need to make our extended procedure, **ping**, accessible to programs outside the DLL. To do this, we define it as an EXPORT from the DLL. This is configured within the DEF file.

Listing 5.17 shows the DEF file to our DLL. Note also that we define the program to be a LIBRARY (a DLL) rather than an executable.

Listing 5.17 The definition file for our DLL.

```
LIBRARY STOCKERHELPER

DESCRIPTION   'SQL Server Extended Stored Procedure DLL'

EXPORTS
   ping
```

Though a pain in the neck to create, our native-method functions are considerably easier to compile and link. As we've seen, our native methods themselves are built from two C source files (NativeMethodShellImp.c and Stocker_NativeMethodShell.c) and one header file (Stocker_NativeMethodShell.h). In addition, we use three more Java header files—StubPreamble.h, interpreter.h, and javastring.h.

Of these three, javastring.h is the easiest to deal with. Remember that back in **showTrigger**, we made two calls to **makeJavaString**. Javastring.h contains this function's prototype. Interpreter.h is a similar case. Right after the two calls to **makeJavaString**, **showTrigger** calls **execute_java_dynamic_method - prototype** in interpreter.h.

StubPreamble.h captures all the other Java definitions that we need to compile. Among these other definitions are object handles (**HObject**...) and the execution environment (**struct execenv**).

When we try to link our DLL, there will be at least two undefined external references to Java functions—**makeJavaString** and **execute_java_dynamic_method**. These functions, like all the accessible Java functions, are defined in the library javai.lib_coff. The *I* in *javai* stands for interpreter, while the *_coff* suffix stands for *common object file format,* the format of the executable/DLL file we're trying to create. Linking with this file gets us all our Java functionality.

Problems With This Approach

This asynchronous approach to updating active views suffers from one huge drawback: There's no upper limit on the amount of bandwidth the application uses. Consider what might happen during something like the stock-market crash of 1987. The trading volume increased so much that the exchange's computers fell hours behind. In our model, there is one message generated from the Java server to the applet for every trade of a particular stock. So, for however many users are logged in, there will be a massive increase in the amount of message traffic. In addition, any crisis draws gawkers, so we'd likely draw two or three times as many simultaneous users as we otherwise might. What you're looking at, then, is some multiple of the average user base, receiving some multiple of the average message traffic. At some point, as volume increases, some link in the data pipeline will be overwhelmed. What happens after that is anyone's guess. As you can see, without any controls, our server functions as a crisis amplifier.

From a network-design standpoint, a much more benign approach would have our Java applet poll the Java server for a new price every 30 seconds or so. That way, our server itself would absorb the increased volume, rather than amplifying it across the net. On a slow day, the polling model might generate many more messages than necessary, but in a volume crisis it would serve to dampen, rather than exacerbate, the bandwidth crunch.

We won't address the bandwidth problem any further here. Polling and/or throttling solutions are well-known and fairly easy to implement. Any programmer of well-behaved network applications must consider implementing such measures before going live and putting the health of the entire network at risk.

Conclusion

In this chapter, we've constructed a simple database and added an active view to it by constructing a pipeline from the database table to the user looking at it. Along the way, we've implemented an extended stored procedure, a database trigger, an active Java applet, and a Java server application, connecting them all with Windows named pipes and IP sockets. This seems like a lot of pieces, and in fact it is, as we saw when we discussed how to eliminate the Java server and named pipes. Though you may encounter higher-level, allegedly easy-to-use active-view tools, any solution that purports to deliver this kind of active-view functionality will necessarily be made up of components much like the ones we've implemented here.

Webliography

• Weblogic, vendor of the JDBC package used in this application.	www.weblogic.com
• The location of this sample application.	www.rodley.com
• Sun's Java native-method tutorial.	www.java.sun.com:80/books/Series/Tutorial/native

Chapter 6

Accepting Input Via The Web

CHAPTER 6

Accepting Input Via The Web

In Chapters 2, 3, and 4, we built an application, the Newfoundland Dog Database, that handles standalone queries which generate standalone result pages. With one small exception, each user interaction with the site stands alone, having no relation to what the user does before or after. In that sense, the Newf DB is like a candy machine dispensing tidbits to anyone who asks, but not remembering anything from one pull of the handle to the next.

In this chapter, we're going to go beyond that and build a real-life application that uses multiple screens to perform complex activities—in this case, that most American of activities: shopping. Along the way, we'll have some cookies, look at a little more JDBC, develop a cool and useful Java applet, and explore the latest in Web server technology: JavaSoft's *Jeeves.*

Maintaining Context

An application running on the Web faces one problem that standalone applications do not: the problem of how to maintain context. HTTP is a stateless protocol. What we mean by this is that requests to an HTTP server are not linked in any way. A browser makes a request and gets a response from the server. If the browser makes another request, the server responds to it as if it had never heard from that browser before. In short, HTTP servers only provide a mechanism for making individual responses to individual requests. If we want to relate those requests to each other, we must build some mechanism on top of the HTTP protocol.

To better understand this problem, let's take a quick look at a hypothetical Web shopping experience. Say you're browsing through the catalog of a computer store. You need a monitor, so you click on the Mag 1495DX. The browser displays a single HTML page describing this monitor. It fits your needs, so you click on the button that adds it to your "shopping cart." Now you need a scanner, so you hyperlink over to the list of scanners. The browser displays a new page that has a list of scanners. There are two bits of information that have to be saved when you hyperlink away from the monitor page: who you are, and what you've bought. HTTP does not provide this mechanism. We have to provide it.

Cookies

One convenient way to deal with the statelessness problem is cookies. Cookies are name/value pairs that a CGI program can store on the user's machine. Typically, these pairs are kept in a file called "cookies.txt." On my development machine, the file is called c:\NS\cookies.txt. Each name/value pair is attached to a domain and path. Cookies are set via an element in the HTTP header stream: **Set-Cookie**. Remember that back in Chapter 2, our Newfoundland DB CGI program sent a single HTTP header line, the Content-type field via the line:

```
printf( "Content-type: text/html\n\n");
```

We should actually consider this line to be two things: the Content-type field and the header terminator "\n." If we wanted to set a cookie for the Newfoundland DB, we could modify the StartStream as follows:

```
printf( "Content-type: text/html\n");
printf( "Set-Cookie: CUSTOMER=JohnRodley;
     path=/; expires=Wednesday, 09-Nov-99 23:12:40 GMT\n" );
printf( "\n" );  // Terminate the header
```

This code sets the "CUSTOMER" cookie for the root directory of this domain to "JohnRodley." It also sets an expiration date/time for the cookie.

For cookie programmers, this is a very important consideration for the simple reason that cookie space is very limited, typically 300 cookies total. When you consider the fact that there are already more than a half-million Web servers connected today, it becomes apparent that one server cannot presume to "claim" 1/300th of the cookie space for any longer than it absolutely needs to. In other words, expire your cookies quickly. When the browser runs out of cookie space, it will expire them for you anyway, so you really haven't saved yourself any programming time by specifying deathless cookies. Notice that the set-cookie line doesn't say anything about the domain. The browser figures out which domain this refers to. If the HTTP server set the domain, it could conceivably meddle with the cookies of other domains.

That, in short, is how the CGI program sets the cookie. But how does it get back to our CGI programs? Whenever the browser makes an HTTP request, it also supplies the cookies for the URL it requested, along with the cookies for every parent directory of that URL within that URL's domain. Thus, if I point my browser at the file www.mydomain.com/John/Stuff/index.html, the browser will include in its HTTP request the cookies attached to www.mydomain.com/, www.mydomain.com/John, and www.mydomain.com/John/Stuff.

Suppose we modify our StartStream program as follows:

```
printf( "Content-type: text/html\n\n");
printf( "Set-Cookie: CUSTOMER=JohnRodley; path=/;
     expires=Wednesday, 09-Nov-99 23:12:40 GMT\n" );
printf( "Set-Cookie: CUSTOMER1=JohnRodley; path=/;
     expires=Wednesday, 09-Nov-99 23:12:40 GMT\n" );
printf( "Set-Cookie: CUSTOMER2=JohnRodley; path=/;
     expires=Wednesday, 09-Nov-99 23:12:40 GMT\n" );
printf( "\n" );  // Terminate the header
```

The first time a browser invokes newfq.exe, these three cookies will be set on the browser machine. The next time this browser invokes newfq.exe it will send these cookies along in the HTTP request, the Web server will use them to set an environment variable, and, finally, the CGI program, newfq.exe, will see the environment variable HTTP_COOKIE set to:

```
CUSTOMER=JohnRodley; CUSTOMER1=JohnRodley; CUSTOMER2=JohnRodley
```

This is very similar to the format of QUERY_STRING, though, of course, not identical to it. Instead of the **&** character separating the name/value pairs, we have ";". Still, it's a simple and functional mechanism.

The Great Cookie Monster

Among users, cookies have an extremely bad image. This is mostly due to the mistaken belief that the cookie concept allows aggressive net.organizations like Microsoft to steal information about the user's machine. Cookies are entirely a result of the user's interaction with CGI programs out on the net. Trust me, when the minions of Microsoft come to get your money, they won't use cookies to do it.

Cookies do, however, have a potential use that might give a reasonable person pause. Up to this point, the Web has been a largely anonymous medium. Users experience the medium as a one-way mirror, where they can see Web pages but the content providers can't see the users. But with cookies, Web sites can track what a particular user does on the site and use that information to whatever purpose the Web site administrators choose. In the best case, a Web site might use this information to memorize preferences or somehow customize the user's interaction with the site, providing a better experience. In the worst case, the site might track user interactions, then sell the data to telemarketers without providing any benefit to the user. In any case, most of us give away data to mass marketers every day, so the malevolent potential of cookies has been vastly overstated.

Hidden Fields

Another, less intrusive way to deal with the statelessness problem is hidden fields. Going back to our monitorbuying example, assume that both the pages in question—the monitor page and the scanners page—are generated by CGI programs. What happens when the user hits the button that says "add this monitor to my shopping cart"? The action associated with this button is a CGI program that regenerates the monitor page. This new monitor page has a subtle difference: a hidden field that assigns an ID number to this user. The CGI program attaches a monitor to that ID and saves that linkage in its database. When the user hyperlinks to the scanner page, this ID follows him via one of the arguments to the CGI program that generates the scanner page. If, from the scanner page, the user decides to check out (pay for the items in his cart), the ID of the shopping cart (embedded as a hidden field in the scanner page) is again passed to the CGI checkout program which knows that there is a monitor attached to that ID.

The hidden-field trick has one flaw. It requires you to generate all action pages on the fly, seemingly eliminating the customized, static HTML pages that usually make for the best product presentations. However, you can get around this by streaming static pages into the CGI-generated document as server-side includes. Also, it is usually impractical to generate static HTML product descriptions for all but the smallest product catalogs. Thus, the dynamic generation requirement is not a big problem for most applications.

We used a hidden field successfully back in Chapter 4 when we needed to load the record update page based on a record ID. This was easy, because it was a simple passing of information between two pages. However, all in all, cookies work much better for frames and other situations in which context must be maintained across a wide range of static HTML pages. Therefore, we will use cookies to maintain context in our Web shopping site.

A Shopping Cart Web Site

Now that we've looked at the key issue in Web shopping applications—maintaining context—let's see how it affects the creation of a real-world application, in this case, a Web shopping site. Our example is a craft business, Doggie Diamonds, that sells various household items custom-imprinted with canine artwork.

Doggie Diamonds' catalog contains a number of categories, and within each category, a dozen or so items. Listing 6.1 shows the schema for our base table, catalog, which contains a single record describing every item we sell.

Listing 6.1 The schema for the catalog table.

```
create table catalog (
   name             varchar(40), -- The name of the item, appears in
                      tables
   image_url        varchar(40), -- The URL of a thumbnail of this item
   style1           varchar(10), -- Style modifiers from imprint
   style2           varchar(10), --
```

```
marketing_info    text,          -- A blurb to advertise it
manufacturer      varchar(40),   -- The manufacturer (Doggie Diamonds)
manufacturer_id   text,          -- How the manufacturer identifies it
category          varchar(40),   -- The category of item
catalog_id        integer,       -- Unique identifier of item
spec_sheet        text,          -- The URL of spec sheet
price             integer,       -- Price in pennies to our customer
ship_wt           integer,       -- Shipping weight in tenths of pound
in_stock          integer,       -- # of items in stock
reorder_point     integer,       -- if in_stock falls below this, reorder
wholesale_price   integer        -- Price we pay for it
)
```

The catalog table is simple, but it gives us a lot of flexibility. When we display the catalog, we'll show the **name**, **marketing_info**, **price**, and a picture (from **image_url**) for each item. Clicking on the name will bring up the spec sheet (from the URL in the **spec_sheet** field) for the item.

The **style1** and **style2** fields allow for modifications of the basic item. Doggie Diamonds products have one of a set of designs imprinted on them, and those designs can be either black-and-white or color. So in **style1** we set the imprint, and in **style2** we set color or black-and-white. Not all items are available in color. Thus, we define a different catalog record for each valid name/color combination.

If we only wanted to show the catalog, those are all the fields we'd really need. However, we want to build a self-contained site, so we need to build in pricing, shipping, and inventory control functions, too. The **price** field holds the customer's retail price while **wholesale_price** contains the price we pay for the item. **Ship_wt** contains the unit shipping weight of the item so that we can calculate the total order shipping weight, and thus the shipping cost. **In_stock** contains the number of these items we have in current inventory. Finally, **reorder_point** allows us to define a value for **in_stock** below which we'll generate an alert to reorder the item.

The imprints table contains a list of all the designs that Doggie Diamonds can print on an item. At some point in the application, the user will view a display of all the available imprints and select one to put on his or her item. The page of imprints is very similar to the page of catalog items. The name and image (from **image_url**) are all that gets displayed. The ID is used in the catalog **style1** field. The imprints are divided by breed so that all the imprints for a particular breed can be displayed on one page. Listing 6.2 shows the imprints table.

Listing 6.2 The imprints table.

```
create table imprints (
   name   varchar(40),          -- The name of the imprint (a style)
   imprint_id   varchar(10),    -- The id of this imprint
   breed   varchar(40),         -- The breed to which this imprint belongs
   image_url   varchar(40)
   )
```

The customer table, shown in Listing 6.3, is fairly standard customer data.

Listing 6.3 The customer table.

```
create table customers (
   customer_id   integer,   -- ID for this customer
   created   datetime,      -- When did we first get him?
   name_first   varchar(20),
   name_middle   char(1),
   name_last   varchar(30),
   street   varchar(40),
   street1   varchar(40),
   city   varchar(40),
   state   char(2),
   zip   varchar(10),
   phone   varchar(10),
   extension   varchar(5),
   fax   varchar(15),
   email   varchar(60)
   )
```

A customer record is not filled in until someone decides to buy. At that point, we put up a form requesting all the customer's information, and when they click the BUY button, we save that information here. The interesting field in this table is the **customer_ID**. This field links a record in the customer table with a record in the shipment table, which in turn points to a series of items in the ship_items table.

The transactions table contains one record for each time a customer buys a set of items. So, if a customer buys a coffee cup, an oven mitt, and a toaster cover in one visit, that transaction generates one record in the transaction table. Each record contains an ID and a link to a customer record for the customer who pays the bill, as well as a link to the customer to whom the items will be shipped. This record contains subtotal and total prices, as well as the shipping weight and shipping cost. It also contains information about the charge card (type, number, and expiration), and the authorization code our credit institution assigned when it authorized the charge. We allow the transaction to be marked void via the void field. Listing 6.4 shows the transactions table.

Listing 6.4 The transactions table.

```
create table transactions (
   transaction_id   integer,      -- Transaction ID
   customer_id   integer,         -- Link to customers table
   web_id       integer,          -- Unique ID used by Web pages
   transaction_date datetime,     -- When was deal made?
   void       integer,            -- Has this transaction been voided?
   subtotal_price   integer,      -- Sum of items cost
   total_weight   integer,        -- Sum ot item weights
   shipping   integer,            -- The projected shipping cost
   total_price   integer,         -- The price charged to card
   charge_type   varchar(10),     -- visa, MC, or AmEx
   charge_id   varchar(20),       -- charge number
   expiration   varchar(10),      -- expiration date
   ship_to_customer_id   char(10)
           -- if ship_to is different, it must be in db
   )
```

The last item in the transactions table is the ID of the Web context that generated this transaction. Every time a customer visits the store, we generate a unique integer ID that identifies that customer's shopping cart. In essence, that identifier *is* the shopping cart. Within our site, we keep that ID and every time the user pushes the "add-to-shopping-cart" button, we add the specified item to that ID. That Web ID is the cookie we will save on the user's machine.

We save the Web ID in the transaction table in order to do a neat bit of traffic analysis. One of the key measures of a store's effectiveness is what percentage of visitors actually buy. If that ratio is too low, then we need to rethink how items are displayed. A low ratio might also be an indicator that the buying mechanism is too awkward. By keeping a sequential Web ID, we can generate this ratio simply by dividing the number of actual transactions by the highest Web ID.

A transaction can be thought of as "a list of items that have to be shipped to the customer." That list of shippable items is kept in the ship_items table, shown in Listing 6.5.

Listing 6.5 The ship_items table.

```
create table ship_items (
   transaction_id   integer,    -- Link to transaction table
   catalog_id   integer,        -- Link to catalog table
   shipment_id   integer,       -- Filled in when order is shipped
   imprint varchar(10),
   number   integer             -- How many of these items do we need?
   )
```

Each item that a customer buys generates a record in the ship_items table. These ship_items are linked together by the **transaction_id**, which also links them to a single transaction in the transaction table. Each item is linked to a catalog item by the **catalog_id**. We also store how many of these items need to be shipped and what imprint appears on them. Finally, we link each item to a record in the shipments table via the shipment_id. Using the shipment_id, we can tell the customer which of his items went out in a single shipment, and which were back-ordered. The shipment_id is not set until an item is actually shipped.

Each shipment of all or part of a transaction is described by a single record in the shipments table, shown in Listing 6.6.

Listing 6.6 The shipments table.

```
create table shipments (
   shipment_id   integer,       -- Our shipment tracking id
   transaction_id   integer,    -- Link to transaction table
   ship_date   datetime,        -- Date shipped
   complete   integer,          -- 1 if any backorders, 0 otherwise
   shipper      varchar(20),    -- Name of shipper
   total_weight   integer,      -- Shipping weight in tenths of pound
   tracking_id   varchar(40)    -- Shippers tracking id
   )
```

The shipments table contains a single record for each shipment of items to a particular address. Theoretically, when we go to ship a customer's order, we'll search the transactions table for an open order, generate a unique shipment_id, generate a list of items in the order, and ship them all out in one lump. However, all the needed items might not be ready. In that case, a single order might generate more than one shipment. Thus, each shipment is linked to a transaction via the **transaction_id**. We also store the shipper's name, the shipper's tracking number, total weight, and whether or not the order was complete.

With that simple set of tables, we've defined the structure of the business's data. What we need to do now is implement a user interface that puts the best face on this data and makes buying as easy as possible.

A Web Server To Serve Us

We could take the easy route here and simply use a plain vanilla HTTP server, serving cookie-ized CGI executables to implement a shopping site. However, we're not going to do that. We've already seen that CGI has limitations that make it less than ideal. For high-volume applications (which all of YOUR shopping sites are going to be, right?), CGI's process creation overhead makes it too slow. We could get around that by using one of the dynamic library APIs, Netscape's NSAPI, or Microsoft's ISAPI. However, since we've already seen a little bit of Java via our StockWatch application in Chapter 5, we might as well go all the way and look at an entirely Java-based HTTP server, Sun's Jeeves.

Instead of replacing CGI executables with calls to dynamic libraries, as NSAPI and ISAPI do, Jeeves implements a concept called servlets that allows HTML code to invoke Java classes that run on the server. So, in the same way that applets are embedded in the HTML page and run on the client, servlets are embedded in the HTML page and run on the server.

In fact, from within the HTML page, the invocation of a Jeeves servlet is indistinguishable from a CGI program. Let's look at the Doggie Diamonds site as an example. Figure 6.1 shows the welcome screen for this site.

In the right hand frame is a welcome message made up of static HTML. In the left hand frame is a set of actions the user can perform. From this frame, the user can view a list of items in a particular category, view the breed imprints

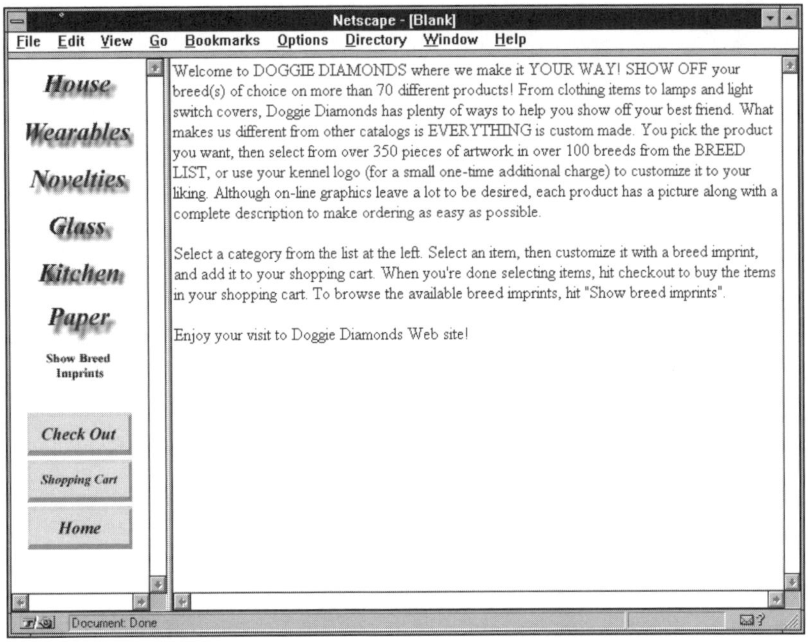

Figure 6.1 The opening screen of the Doggie Diamonds shopping site.

that we use to customize items, go back to the welcome page (Home), view the shopping cart (Shopping Cart), or buy the items in the cart (Checkout). Listing 6.7 shows the HTML source for the Doggie Diamonds action frame.

Listing 6.7 Listing of Categories.html.

```
<!DOCTYPE HTML PUBLIC "-//SQ//DTD HTML 2.0 + all extensions//EN"
"hmpro3.dtd">
<HTML>
<HEAD>
<TITLE>Blank</TITLE></HEAD>
<BODY
BGCOLOR="white" LINK="white" VLINK="white" ALINK="white" LEFTMARGIN="0"
TOPMARGIN="0">
<P ALIGN="CENTER"><A
HREF="http://katie:8080/servlet/CategoryList?operation=display_catalog&
category=wearables" TARGET="Body"><IMG
SRC="images/House.jpg" ALT="House"></A><A
HREF="http://katie:8080/servlet/CategoryList?operation=display_catalog&
category=wearables" TARGET="Body"><IMG
SRC="images/Wearables.jpg" ALT="Wearables"></A><A
HREF="http://katie:8080/servlet/CategoryList?operation=display_catalog&
category=novelties" TARGET="Body"><IMG
```

```
SRC="images/Novelties.jpg" ALT="Novelties"></A><A
HREF="http://katie:8080/servlet/CategoryList?operation=display_catalog&
category=glass" TARGET="Body"><IMG
SRC="images/Glass.jpg" ALT="Glass"></A><A
HREF="http://katie:8080/servlet/CategoryList?operation=display_catalog&
category=kitchen" TARGET="Body"><IMG
SRC="images/Kitchen.jpg" ALT="Kitchen"></A><A
HREF="http://katie:8080/servlet/CategoryList?operation=display_catalog&
category=paper" TARGET="Body"><IMG
SRC="images/Paper.jpg" ALT="Paper"></A><A
HREF="http://katie:8080/servlet/CategoryList?operation=breeds
 TARGET="Body"><IMG
SRC="images/ShowImprints.jpg" ALT="Show Imprints"></A></P>
<P ALIGN="CENTER"><A
HREF="http://katie:8080/servlet/CategoryList?operation=checkout
TARGET="Body"><IMG
SRC="images/Buy.jpg" ALT="Check Out"></A><A
HREF="http://katie:8080/servlet/CategoryList?operation=showcart
TARGET="Body"><IMG
SRC="images/ShoppingCart.jpg" ALT="Check Out"></A><A
HREF="Welcome.html" TARGET="Body"><IMG SRC="images/GoHome.jpg"
     ALT="Home"></A></P></BODY></HTML>
```

Even though they look like CGI calls, each of these links (except Home) is actually a servlet invocation. They all call CategoryList, which is an alias for our servlet, **CategoryServlet.java**. Within the servlet, we distinguish between the various actions with the variable operation, which is set in exactly the same way as a CGI call, by appending "?operation=value" to the servlet URL.

Our Servlet

We've seen how the servlet gets invoked from within the HTML page. Now, it's time to look at the servlet itself.

One of the primary benefits of CGI replacements like servlets or NSAPI/ISAPI is to eliminate the overhead involved with reading the CGI executable file from disk and creating a process. Ideally, you want to load the executable file just once, leave it in memory, and invoke it as often as necessary. This requirement leads us directly to the structure of our servlet.

Our servlet extends the Jeeves class **HttpServlet**, which we'll talk about as we go along. The key method of any servlet is the **service** method. Every invocation of a servlet results in a call to the servlet's **service** method. So, looking back at Figure 6.1, if the user clicks on Wearables, back on our site Jeeves creates a new **CategoryServlet** (if it doesn't exist already). Then it invokes **CategoryServlet.service** passing in all the information that came in through the HTTP request (via the **HttpRequest** parameter). So by the time **service** is invoked, we have in hand the QUERY_STRING environment variable, and all the HTTP_* environment variables. Listing 6.8 shows our service method.

Listing 6.8 The service method and its helper, returnResult.

```
/** Write the result out to ServletOutputStream
@param out The stream this HtmlContainer gets written to.
@param htmlp The HtmlContainer that gets written.
*/
public void returnResult(ServletOutputStream out,
     HtmlContainer htmlp ) {
    try {
        htmlp.write( out );
        }
    catch( IOException ie ) {}
    }

/** Override the service method for servlet.  All the interesting
    request processing happens somewhere beneath this method.  All
    HTTP requests to this servlet start at this method.  From here
    we decide which service routine needs to be used to handle the
    particular request.  Request type is specified by the variable
    "operation".  Its value determines which service routine is
    called.  Also deal with getting and setting the cookie.  Everyone
    who comes through here gets a cookie assigned to them, whether they
    like it or not.
@param req All of the CGI environment is available to us through
this object.
@param res We fill in this object to talk to the browser.
*/
public synchronized void service(HttpServletRequest req,
     HttpServletResponse res)
     throws ServletException, IOException
    {
    Cookie cookie = null;
    boolean noCache = false;

    HtmlPage htmlp = null;
    String lastname = new String("");

    // Set up the cookie.
    try {
        if( req.getHeader( "Cookie" ) != null ) {
```

```
         cookie = new Cookie(req.getHeader("Cookie"));
         System.out.println( "got cookie of "+cookie.toString() );
         }
    else {
         System.out.println( "no cookie" );
         cookie = new Cookie( "cart_number",
            (new Integer( NewCookie())).toString() );
        }

  // This is a giant case statement on the variable operation.
  String operation = req.getParameter("operation");
  if( operation.compareTo( "display_catalog" ) == 0 ) {
    htmlp = DisplayCatalog( req );
    }
  else {
    if( operation.compareTo( "customize" ) == 0 ) {
      htmlp = CustomizeItem( req );
      }
    else {
      if( operation.compareTo( "breeds" ) == 0 ) {
        htmlp = ShowBreeds( req );
        }
      else {
        if( operation.compareTo( "breedimprints" ) == 0 ) {
          htmlp = ShowImprints( req );
          }
        else {
          if( operation.compareTo( "customizeditem" ) == 0 ) {
            htmlp = ShowFinalizedItem( req );
            }
          else {
            if( operation.compareTo( "addtocart" ) == 0 ) {
              htmlp = ShowCart( req, cookie );
              noCache = true;
              }
            else {
              if( operation.compareTo( "clear" ) == 0 ) {
                htmlp = ClearCart( req, cookie );
                noCache = true;
                }
              else {
                if( operation.compareTo( "checkout" ) == 0 ) {
                  htmlp = Checkout( req, cookie );
                  noCache = true;
                  }
                else {
                  if( operation.compareTo( "dotransaction" ) == 0 ) {
```

```
                    htmlp = DoTransaction( req, cookie );
                    noCache = true;
                    }
                  else {
                    if( operation.compareTo( "showcart" ) == 0 ) {
                      htmlp = ShowCart( req, cookie );
                      noCache = true;
                      }
                    }
                  }
                }
              }
            }
          }
        }
      }
    }
  // Set up the cookie for transmission to the browser.
  // Make sure that it expires quickly.
  if( cookie != null ) {
    long tm = System.currentTimeMillis();
    cookie.setExpires(tm + 600000);
    cookie.setPath("/");
    res.setHeader( "Set-Cookie", cookie.toString() );
    System.out.println( "setting cookie to "+cookie.toString() );
    }
  // If this document can't be cached, set it in the header.
  if( noCache == true ) {
    System.out.println( "setting no-cache" );
    res.setHeader( "Pragma", "no-cache" );
    res.setHeader( "Expires", "Wednesday, 27-Dec-95 05:29:10 GMT" );
    }
  // Set the header status to OKAY and content to HTML.
  res.setStatus(res.SC_OK);
  res.setContentType("text/html");

  // Now write the data to the outputstream.
  returnResult((ServletOutputStream) res.getOutputStream(), htmlp);

  } catch (Exception e) { e.printStackTrace(); }
}
```

If you ignore the cookie business for the moment, you can see that service is mostly a giant case statement. It retrieves the value of operation via **HttpServletRequest.getParameter**, which parses QUERY_STRING to find the value associated with the name "operation". Depending on the value of operation, **service** then calls another method to actually create an HTML page from information in the database. Again, ignoring the cookie business, **service** then takes that **HtmlPage** object and writes it to the output stream.

Our servlet relies on three Jeeves classes, **HttpServlet**, its superclass **GenericServlet**, and **Cookie**, and two Jeeves interfaces, **HttpServletRequest**, and **HttpServletResponse**. Tables 6.1 through 6.6 show the public definitions of these classes.

Table 6.1 The HttpServlet class.

Method name	Description
HttpServlet()	
service(HttpServletRequest, HttpServletResponse)	Services a single HTTP request from the client.
service(ServletRequest, ServletResponse)	Services a single request from the client.

Table 6.2 HttpServlet's superclass—GenericServlet.

Method name	Description
GenericServlet()	
destroy()	Destroys the servlet and cleans up whatever resources are being held.
getInitParameter(String)	Gets an initialization parameter of the servlet.
getInitParameters()	Returns a hashtable of the initialization parameters of the servlet.
getServletContext()	Returns the servlet context.
getServletInfo()	Returns a string containing information about the author, version, and copyright of the servlet.
init()	Initializes the servlet.
init(ServletStub)	Initializes the servlet.
log(String)	Logs a message into the servlet log file.
service(ServletRequest, ServletResponse)	Services a single request from the client.

Table 6.3 The HttpServletRequest interface. (From JavaSoft's Jeeves documentation.)

Method	Description
getAuthType()	Returns the authentication scheme of the request, or null if none.
getDateHeader(String, long)	Returns the value of a date header field.
getHeader(int)	Returns the value of the nth header field, or null if there are fewer than n fields.
getHeader(String)	Returns the value of a header field, or null if not known.
getHeaderName(int)	Returns the name of the nth header field, or null if there are fewer than n fields.
getIntHeader(String, int)	Returns the value of an integer header field.
getMethod()	Returns the method with which the request was made.
getPathInfo()	Returns optional extra path information following the servlet path, but immediately preceding the query string.
getPathTranslated()	Returns extra path information translated to a real path.
getQueryString()	Returns the query string part of the servlet URI, or null if none.
getRemoteUser()	Returns the name of the user making this request, or null if not known.
getRequestPath()	Returns the part of the request URI that corresponds to the servlet path plus the optional extra path information, if any.
getRequestURI()	Returns the request URI.
getServletPath()	Returns the part of the request URI that refers to the servlet being invoked.

Table 6.4 The Cookie class.

Method name	Description
Cookie(String)	Constructors
Cookie(String, String)	

continued

Table 6.4 The Cookie class (continued).

Method name	Description
Cookie(String[])	
Cookie(String[], long, String, String, boolean)	
append(StringBuffer, Cookie)	Appends the string value of a cookie to a string buffer.
getCookieNames()	
getValues(String)	Returns a comma separated list of values for a particular name.
setDomain(String)	
setExpires(long)	
setPath(String)	
setSecure()	
toString()	Returns the string value of this cookie.
toString(Cookie[])	Returns a list of cookies as a string.
write(HttpOutputStream)	Writes this cookie to the output stream.

Table 6.5 HttpServletResponse constants.

Constant name	Description
SC_ACCEPTED	Each of these variables corresponds to one of the HTTP response codes. SC_OK and SC_NOT_FOUND are the most commonly encountered. We use only SC_OK.
SC_BAD_GATEWAY	
SC_BAD_REQUEST	
SC_CREATED	
SC_FORBIDDEN	
SC_INTERNAL_SERVER_ERROR	
SC_MOVED_PERMANENTLY	
SC_MOVED_TEMPORARILY	

continued

Table 6.5 HttpServletResponse constants (continued).

Constant name	Description
SC_NO_CONTENT	
SC_NOT_FOUND	
SC_NOT_IMPLEMENTED	
SC_NOT_MODIFIED	
SC_OK	
SC_SERVICE_UNAVAILABLE	
SC_UNAUTHORIZED	

Table 6.6 HttpServletResponse methods (from the Jeeves documentation).

Name	Description
sendError(int)	Sends an error response to the client using the specified status code and no default message.
sendError(int, String)	Sends an error response to the client using the specified status code and detail message.
sendRedirect(String)	Sends a redirect response to the client using the specified redirect location URL.
setDateHeader(String, long)	Sets the value of a date header field.
setHeader(String, String)	Sets the value of a header field.
setIntHeader(String, int)	Sets the value of an integer header field.
setStatus(int)	Sets the status code and a default message for this response.
setStatus(int, String)	Sets the status code and message for this response.
unsetHeader(String)	Unsets the value of a header field.

Let's take them in order. As you've seen, **CategoryServlet** subclasses **HttpServlet**, which subclasses **GenericServlet**. Thus **CategoryServlet** has available to it all the methods and variables of **HttpServlet** and **GenericServlet**. In order to extend those superclasses, **CategoryServlet** has to override two methods: **HttpServlet.service** and **GenericServlet.init**. As we've seen, service contains all the functionality for dealing with a single request.

Init is another story. When Jeeves loads the class from disk, (the first time the class is instantiated), it calls **GenericServlet.init** once, and only once. In an operational setting, a single servlet might stay in memory for weeks. However, **init** will only be called once in all that time. This is similar to applets where **Applet.init** is (theoretically) called only when the applet is first loaded. Listing 6.9 shows our override of **GenericServlet.init**.

Listing 6.9 CategoryServlet.init overrides GenericServlet.init.

```
/** Initialize the servlet. Called once.  Opens the database, a
    debugging log file, and creates a new shopping cart hashTable.
*/
    public void init(ServletStub stub) throws ServletException {
        shoppingCarts = new Hashtable();
        super.init(stub);
        logfile = getInitParameter("logfile");
        switchFiles();
        OpenDB();
        }
```

Aside from those two override methods, **GenericServlet.init** and **HttpServlet.service**, all the rest of the methods are actual utility methods that the superclasses provide to subclasses. The two superclasses are designed to provide a way to interact with the Web server. Thus, methods are provided for logging, retrieving CGI variables, and servicing HTTP requests.

The two parameters to our **service** method are an object which implements the **HttpServletRequest** interface and an object that implements the **HttpServletResponse** interface. Jeeves creates these objects and passes them into the service method. The **HttpServletRequest** is a fully formed object that we simply query to figure out what the user wants us to do. This is apparent just from skimming the class definition which consists solely of a series of "get" methods.

The **HttpServletResponse** on the other hand, is a shell that we have to fill in with interesting values. It contains a set of constants corresponding to HTTP result codes, and a series of "set" methods allowing us to customize our response to the HTTP request. It also contains the key method—**getOutputStream**—that gives us a stream into which we can write the response we've created.

The outline of service then is:

- Find out what the user wants by querying the **HttpServletRequest**.
- Create an **HtmlPage** object that fulfills the request by calling the appropriate method.
- Customize the **HttpServletResponse** with cache, expiration, and cookie values.
- Send the response header and the **HtmlPage** back to the browser.

Now that we've seen the override methods, **service** and **init**, we should take a quick look at the class variables before moving on to the utility methods that service calls to create **HtmlPages**. Listing 6.10 shows the top of our Java class source file.

Listing 6.10 CategoryServlet variables.

```
import java.servlet.*;
import java.servlet.http.*;
import java.servlet.html.*;
import java.io.*;
import java.net.*;
import java.util.*;
import java.sql.*;
import sun.server.http.Cookie;


/** A class for providing service to HTTP requests coming into the
    Doggie Diamonds Web shopping site.
 */

public class CategoryServlet extends HttpServlet {

    static String ServletDirectory =
        "http://katie:8080/servlet/";
    static String DoggieDiamondsDirectory =
        "http://katie:8080/DoggieDiamonds/";
    static String AppletDirectory =
        "http://katie:8080/";
```

```
    static String Server =
        "http://katie:8080";

/*
    static String ServletDirectory =
         "http://207.31.195.11:8080/servlet/";
    static String DoggieDiamondsDirectory =
         "http://207.31.195.11:8080/DoggieDiamonds/";
    static String AppletDirectory =
         "http://207.31.195.11:8080/";
    static String Server =
         "http://207.31.195.11:8080";
*/

    /** The place where all shopping carts get stored,
        keyed on the shopping cart id which is also
        the value of the cookie named cart_number. */
    static Hashtable shoppingCarts;

    /** The initial value of the cookie named cart_number.
        incremented each time a new shopping cart is created. */
    int currentCookie = 0;

    /** The open connection over which all JDBC statements will
        be executed. */
    public static java.sql.Connection conn;
    ServletStub stub;

    /** The name of the log file to which we will write all
        debugging output. */
    String logfile;

    /** The properties we loaded from shoppe.properties. */
    Properties prop;

    /** The location of shoppe.properties. */
    String topDirectory;

    /** The open debugging log file. */
    static File flogfile;

    /** The stream attached to the open debuugging log file. */
    static PrintStream ps;

    /** The full name of the properties file. */
    static String PropertiesFile;
```

We import the standard Java packages, java.net, java.util and java.io. We also need to import the Jeeves class files, java.servlet.*, java.servlet.http, and java.servlet.html, and, of course, the Weblogic JDBC classes, java.sql.*. Then we declare the class **CategoryServlet** as an extension of **HttpServlet**.

Within **CategoryServlet**, we declare a number of class variables. The first set, the **Strings ServletDirectory**, **DoggieDiamondsDirectory**, **AppletDirectory**, and **Server**, all define the first part of URLs that we're going to embed in the HTML pages that we emit within the methods called by service. **conn** is the JDBC database connection we execute our SQL statements against.

shoppingCarts is (essentially, though not precisely) a vector of shopping carts that the **CategoryServlet** maintains. We'll talk a lot more about shopping cart maintenance later on. Suffice to say for now that each shopping cart is a **Vector** of items, and that **CategoryServlet** keeps all those **Vectors** in the **shoppingCarts Vector**. So **shoppingCarts** is a **Vector** of **Vector**s.

Doggie Diamonds Cookies

Now is as good a time as any to talk about cookies. The class variable **currentCookie** is the ID of the next available shopping cart. When a shopping cart is created, we stamp it with the value of **currentCookie**. This value is also used to set the cookie value on the browser. That's how we get a linkage between the user and the set of items the user has selected. There is a cookie on the user's machine, attached to our domain, that says, in essence, "my shopping cart number is 25."

If we look back at the service method, there's a sequence up at the top that says:

```
// Set up the cookie.
    try {
        if( req.getHeader( "Cookie" ) != null ) {
            cookie = new Cookie(req.getHeader("Cookie"));
            System.out.println( "got cookie of "+cookie.toString() );
            }
        else {
            System.out.println( "no cookie" );
            cookie = new Cookie( "cart_number",
               (new Integer( NewCookie())).toString() );
           }
```

What happens is that if the user already has a cookie for our domain and path, then it will be passed in the header, and the call to **HttpServletRequest.getHeader("Cookie")** will return not-null. In that case, the user already has an active shopping cart, so we create a new **Cookie** object initialized to that value. If **req.getHeader** returns null, that means the user did not have a cookie attached to our domain and path, so we assign him a new one using **NewCookie** (shown in Listing 6.11) and create a **Cookie** object using that integer value.

Listing 6.11 NewCookie creates new shopping cart ids.

```
/** Return the value of the next cookie. */
int NewCookie() {
  return( currentCookie++ );
  }
```

The **Cookie** we create in this code is used in all the methods that need access to the user's shopping cart. Thus, if the user wants to look at his shopping cart, **(operation.compareTo("showcart")==0)**, then we pass the new **Cookie** along to the method **showCart** so that **showCart** will know which shopping cart to display. Down at the bottom of the service method, whenever we send a response, we reset the cookie on the user's machine to this value.

A Little JDBC To Go

Before we proceed in taking the application apart, we need to look a little closer at the mechanism that allows us to access the database from Java JDBC (Java DataBase Connectivity). JDBC is actually a specification, not a product, and is designed to allow database vendors to provide standard database access classes and interfaces for Java programmers. We use Weblogic's MSSQLServer JDBC drivers, but in theory packages implementing JDBC should be literally interchangeable.

Back in Chapter 5, we looked briefly at how to connect to a JDBC database, and here in our servlet we use the same method, OpenDB, shown in Listing 6.12.

Listing 6.12 OpenDB opens a connection to our JDBC database.

```
/** Open the database using the properties in the current properties
    file.  Undocumented property "database" sets which database we're
    using.
```

```
@see weblogic.jdbc.dblib.Driver
@see SQLException
@see ClassNotFoundException
*/
void OpenDB() {
    PropertiesFile =  new String(
         "/Program Files/JeevesA2/servlets/shoppe.properties" );
    LoadProperties();
    try {
        Class.forName("weblogic.jdbc.dblib.Driver");
        ps.println( "Before db connection" );
        try {
            if( conn != null )
                conn.close();
            ps.println( "connecting to jdbc:weblogic:mssqlserver "+
               prop.getProperty("database") );
            conn = DriverManager.getConnection(
               "jdbc:weblogic:mssqlserver", prop );
            ps.println( "After db connection "+conn );
            }
        catch( SQLException e ) {
            ps.println( "SQL Error "+e );
            System.exit(1);
            }
        }
    catch( ClassNotFoundException e1 ) {
        ps.println( "NO Driver "+e1 );
        System.exit(1);
        }
    }
```

OpenDB is designed solely to create a useable connection to the database. In order to get a valid connection to an SQL Server database, we need to load a properties file that has the following values set:

- **database:** The name of the database we're connecting to, in our case, Shoppe.
- **server:** The name of the server the database runs on.
- **user:** The username we're using to connect.
- **password:** The password for that username.

We populate the Properties object by loading the properties file, shoppe.properties, within the method LoadProperties shown in Listing 6.13.

Listing 6.13 LoadProperties creates the properties object.

```
/** Load the properties file so that other methods, like OpenDB
    can use the values contained therein.  Set the value of
    topDirectory to Shoppe.read from properties.
*/
void LoadProperties() {
  try {
      prop = System.getProperties();
      prop.load(new FileInputStream(PropertiesFile));
      }
  catch( IOException e ) {
    ps.println("properties file exception "+e );
    }
  ps.println( "system properties "+prop );

  topDirectory = System.getProperty( "Shoppe.read" );
  if( topDirectory == null ) {
    ps.println( "Shoppe.read not set in "+PropertiesFile );
    }
  else
    ps.println( "got "+topDirectory+" for Shoppe.read");
  }
```

The properties file is the equivalent of the Windows.ini file, in that it holds application-specific variables.

Our call to **ClassForName** loads the JDBC driver, while the static JDBC method **DriverManager.getConnection** gets us a JDBC **Connection** object that we can execute SQL statements against. With the **Connection** created, we return to **init**. At that point, we have an open connection to the database stored in the class variable conn.

How do we use this connection? Well, all our SQL statements go through one of the two methods: **SQLExecSelect** and **SQLExecUpdate**. These are our own methods that encapsulate a couple of JDBC calls. We use **SQLExecSelect**, shown in Listing 6.14, to execute any statement that returns a result set (any **SELECT**).

Listing 6.14 SQLExecSelect handles JDBC SELECT statements.

```
/** A method encapsulating the JDBC calls to createStatement
   and executeQuery.
@return The ResultSet that the query created.
*/
```

```
public static synchronized ResultSet SQLExecSelect( String ssql )
        throws SQLException {
    Statement stmt = conn.createStatement();
    stmt.executeQuery(ssql);
    return( stmt.getResultSet());
    }
```

To use SQLExecSelect, we pass it a **String** containing an SQL statement. SQLExecSelect then creates a JDBC Statement using the JDBC method **Connection.createStatement**. Another JDBC call, **Statement.executeQuery** with our string as the argument, actually executes the query. And finally, the JDBC call **Statement.getResultSet** returns another JDBC object, of class **ResultSet,** that we can pry the results from. We create a string query, create a statement, execute the query using the statement, and get the result set from the statement. Very simple and straightforward. Table 6.7 shows the methods implemented within the JDBC **Statement** class as they are documented in the official JDBC documentation.

Table 6.7 The Statement JDBC class.

Method Name	Description
cancel()	Cancel can be used by one thread to cancel a statement that is being executed by another thread.
clearWarnings()	After this call getWarnings returns null until a new warning is reported for this Statement.
close()	In many cases, it is desirable to immediately release a Statement's database and JDBC resources instead of waiting for this to happen when it is automatically closed; The close method provides this immediate release.
execute(String)	Execute a SQL statement that may return multiple results.
executeQuery(String)	Execute a SQL statement that returns a single ResultSet.
executeUpdate(String)	Execute a SQL INSERT, UPDATE or DELETE statement.

continued

Table 6.7 The Statement JDBC class (continued).

Method Name	Description
getMaxFieldSize()	The maxFieldSize limit (in bytes) is the maximum amount of data returned for any column value; it only applies to BINARY, VARBINARY, LONGVARBINARY, CHAR, VARCHAR, and LONGVARCHAR columns.
getMaxRows()	The maxRows limit is the maximum number of rows that a ResultSet can contain.
getMoreResults()	getMoreResults moves to a Statement's next result.
getQueryTimeout()	The queryTimeout limit is the number of seconds the driver will wait for a Statement to execute.
getResultSet()	getResultSet returns the current result as a ResultSet.
getUpdateCount()	getUpdateCount returns the current result, which should be an integer value.
getWarnings()	The first warning reported by calls on this Statement is returned.
setCursorName(String)	setCursorname defines the SQL cursor name that will be used by subsequent Statement execute methods.
setEscapeProcessing (boolean)	If escape scanning is on (the default), the driver will do escape substitution before sending the SQL to the database.
setMaxFieldSize(int)	The maxFieldSize limit (in bytes) is set to limit the size of data that can be returned for any column value; it only applies to BINARY, VARBINARY, LONGVARBINARY, CHAR, VARCHAR, and LONGVARCHAR fields.
setMaxRows(int)	The maxRows limit is set to limit the number of rows that any ResultSet can contain.
setQueryTimeout(int)	

As you can see, **Statement** has a lot of functionality, but you can get a lot of things accomplished using only **getResultSet**, **executeQuery**, and **executeSelect**. We'll restrict our use of this class almost entirely to these methods. As you can also see, JDBC uses separate calls for queries and updates. This is why we implement two different methods: one returns a ResultSet, while the update method, shown in Listing 6.15, returns void.

Listing 6.15 SQLExecUpdate handles non-select statements.

```
/** A method encapsulating the JDBC calls to createStatement
    and executeUpdate.
*/
public static synchronized void SQLExecUpdate( String ssql )
        throws SQLException {
    Statement stmt = conn.createStatement();
    stmt.executeUpdate(ssql);
    }
```

Synchronization And Open Connections

We spent a lot of time back in Chapter 1 talking about open database connections. If you recall, we need a new connection for each simultaneous transaction we wish to process. If we want to be able to handle five users running the same query at the same time, then we need five open connections.

How does the Doggie Diamonds application handle the issue of open connections? Remember that there are two parts to the open connection issue: managing the open connections and handling the case where we need an open connection and there is none.

The ideal way to deal with this is to keep an infinitely expandable pool of open connections. If all the open connections are in use, just create a new one. No one ever lacks for a connection. This solution is not viable in real life, where license restrictions and operating system/dbms limitations put hard limits on the number of open connections you can actually create.

The preferred solution is to open a reasonable number of connections, use them as needed, and make the user wait for one to open up if they're all in use. Keeping a connection pool is a necessity for a high-volume Web site, but it's not clear that Doggie Diamonds will generate that kind of volume (we can monitor this through the server logs). So we're going to punt on the connection pool and use a unique feature of Java to serialize access to our single open connection.

Java implements a feature called synchronization. In essence, a synchronized Java method can only be executing in one thread at any one time. Thread B can not enter a synchronized block until Thread A leaves that synchronized block. You probably already see where this is leading.

The only way for two transactions to attempt to use our open connection at the same time is for two different threads in the Web server, Jeeves, to pass HTTP requests to **service** at the same time. By simply declaring **service** to be **synchronized**, we ensure that there will never be contention for the JDBC connection. Under heavy use, this strategy will undoubtedly cause unreasonable delays, but, in theory, every user should eventually get through even over our single connection.

You may be thinking back and wondering how the Newfoundland Dog Database got around the open connection problem, because there is no connection pooling code there. You have to focus on the key difference between a CGI program and a servlet (and NSAPI/ISAPI). A new copy of our Newf DB CGI program is loaded into memory every time an HTTP request comes in. Each of these copies creates its own connection.

Our servlet is loaded only once, but called many times. In order to mimic the Newf DB strategy of one open connection per request, we'd have to open a new connection every time service is called. However, that would be wasteful and cause a noticeable performance degradation for the average user, whose request, in all likelihood, would not be colliding with some other user's request.

The Structure Of The User Interface

Finally we have enough background to look at the methods that do all the real work in this application, the page-creation methods called by service. The first page-creation method we need to look at is the **DisplayCatalog** method. This is the method that gets called whenever the user presses one of the categories: House, Wearables, Glass, Paper, or Novelties. In Listing 6.7, categories.html, these images are links to **CategoryServlet** with operation set to display_catalog, and category set to house, wearables, glass, paper, or novelties: one of the values that can appear in the category field.

Jeeves receives this key-press as an HTTP request of the form:

```
http://207.31.195.11/servlet/CategoryList?operation=
     &category=wearables
```

Jeeves recognizes /servlet as a servlet directory, and **CategoryList** as an alias for the servlet **CategoryServlet**. So it loads **CategoryServlet**, calls **CategoryServlet.init**, then creates an **HttpServletRequest** containing all the HTTP request data and a (mostly) empty **HttpServletResponse,** and passes both of those to **CategoryServlet.service**. Then, **service** checks the value of operation, sees that the user wants to view a list of items in a particular category, and calls **CategoryDisplay**, passing it the **HttpServletRequest**.

What **DisplayCatalog** needs to do is create an HTML page that shows all the items in a particular category. The easy way to fulfill this requirement would be to show the user a one-record per line page of items from the catalog table. However, if you think of a real-life, hard-copy catalog you realize that the most effective, time-tested presentations don't work that way.

A catalog attempts to draw the reader in by linking an eye-catching visual representation of the sale item with all the information the user needs to make the buying decision. To create those eye-catching visuals, most catalogs group multiple items together in a single picture. In isolation, individual items often look like fish out of water, while grouped with similar items they look much more substantial and "right."

How do we deal with this little complication? Obviously, a one-line per item display isn't going to cut it. Logically, we need to group records in the catalog table by the picture in which the item appears. This grouping becomes clear by looking at the actual data in the catalog table. Each item is linked to the image it appears in via the **image_url** field. Multiple records can have the same **image_url**.

There are two ways to deal with this. The first is represented by the following pseudo-code:

```
Get the set of records for this category
For each record.
   If this is the first record for this image
      Display the image.
   Display the product data.
```

Here we'd build a single SQL statement that says "select * from catalog where category='wearables' order by **image_url**, name." Then we'd have a single **while** loop that runs through the result set building our page, displaying a product image followed by each of the products appearing in that image. While this method is logical and efficient, it poses some problems for us when it comes time to actually create our HTML page.

The second way, and the one that we use, is represented by the following pseudo-code:

```
Get the list of product images for this category.
For each image.
   Display the image.
   Get the products associated with the image.
   For each product.
      Display the product data.
```

This version builds a list of images in memory, then runs through that list getting the products associated with each image. The difference between this version and the first one is the number of SQL statements we need to execute. The first version executes a single SQL statement. This version executes one SQL statement to get the images, plus one SQL statement for each distinct image in the category.

Our version is not as efficient, since one SQL statement is less expensive than a bunch of smaller SQL statements returning the same set of records. It is, arguably, easier to read and debug. If our catalog were bigger, speed concerns would force us to go to the more efficient single SQL statement. Listing 6.16 shows the actual implementation of this method.

Listing 6.16 DisplayCatalog creates an HtmlPage of items in a category.

```
/** Display the catalog page for the specified category.
@param req The HTTP request.
@return An HtmlPage with all the pictures and descriptions
for this category.
*/
HtmlPage DisplayCatalog(HttpServletRequest req) {
    String lastname = new String( "" );
    String category = req.getParameter("category");
    Vector retval;
```

```
  HtmlPage htmlp = new HtmlPage( "Catalog of "+category+" Items" );
  htmlp.setBodyAttributes( "BGCOLOR=\"white\"" );
  Vector vimages = new Vector(1);
htmlp.add( "<H1>Catalog of Doggie Diamonds "+category+" items</H1>" );

  String ssql = new String(
      "select distinct image_url from catalog where category='"+
      category+"'" );
  try {
    ResultSet rs = SQLExecSelect( ssql );
    while( true ) {
      try {
        if( rs.next() == false )
          break;
        vimages.addElement( new String( rs.getString("image_url")));
        }
      catch( SQLException se ) {}
      }
    rs.close();
    }
  catch( SQLException se ) {}

  for( int i = 0; i < vimages.size(); i++ ) {
    ssql = new String( "select name from catalog where image_url='"+
        (String)vimages.elementAt(i)+"' and category='"+category+"'" );
    ps.println( "Getting numitems via "+ssql );
    int numitems = 1;   // start at 1 because the image gets
                        // its own row
  try {
      ResultSet rs = SQLExecSelect( ssql );
      while( true ) {
        if( rs.next() == false )
           break;
           numitems++;
        }
      ps.println( "Got "+numitems+" items" );
      rs.close();
      }
  catch( SQLException sqe ) {
      ps.println( "numitems exception "+sqe );
      continue;
      }

  ssql = new String( "select * from catalog where image_url='"+
      (String)vimages.elementAt(i)+"' and category='"+category+
      "' order by name" );
```

```
try {
    ResultSet rs = SQLExecSelect( ssql );
    htmlp.add( "<HR>" );
    HtmlTable htmlt = new HtmlTable("BORDER=0");
    String ie = new String( "<IMG SRC=\""+DoggieDiamondsDirectory+
        (String)vimages.elementAt(i)+"\">" );
    htmlt.addData( ie, "ALIGN=TOP COLSTART=1 COLSPAN=1 ROWSPAN="+
        numitems );
    while( true ) {
      try {
        if( rs.next() == false )
          break;
        String sname = rs.getString( "name" );
        HtmlRow htmlr = new HtmlRow();

        if( sname.compareTo( lastname ) == 0 ) {
          htmlr.addData( " - ", "COLSTART=2" );
            }
        else {
          String slink = rs.getString( "spec_sheet" );
          String le = new String( "<A HREF=\""+slink+"\"><H2>"+
              sname+"</H2></A>" );
          htmlr.addData( le+"<P><B><I>"+
            rs.getString("marketing_info" )+"</I></B></P>",
            "COLSTART=2");
            }
        lastname = new String(sname);

        String s = rs.getString( "style1" );
        if( rs.wasNull() == true )
          s = new String(" - " );
        String s1 = rs.getString( "style2" );
        if( rs.wasNull() == true )
          s1 = new String(" - " );
        htmlr.addData( s+" "+s1, "COLSTART=3 WIDTH=50");
        String sprice = formatPrice( rs.getInt("price"));

        htmlr.addData( sprice, "COLSTART=4 WIDTH=50" );
    String actionurl = new String( ServletDirectory+"CategoryList" );
        HtmlForm buyForm = new HtmlForm(actionurl,"GET");
        buyForm.addSubmitButton( "Value=Customize" );
    buyForm.addHiddenField( "catalog_id",rs.getString("catalog_id"));
        buyForm.addHiddenField( "operation","customize" );
        htmlr.addData( buyForm, "COLSTART=5 WIDTH=50" );
        htmlt.addRow(htmlr);
        }
```

```
            catch( Exception e ) { break; }
            }

          htmlp.add( htmlt );
          rs.close();
          }
        catch( SQLException sqe ) {}
        }
  return( htmlp );
  }
```

The first part of the method creates an empty **HtmlPage** object with a white background and an appropriate title. Next, an SQL statement and **while** loop builds a **Vector** of images. Then, there's a giant **for** loop that runs through this **Vector**. Within the loop, we create an empty, borderless, **HtmlTable**, and then we count all the products that appear in this image. Why bother counting the products up front? In order to physically cluster the image with the descriptions of the products in the image, in HTML, we need to define the image as starting in column 1 and "spanning" as many rows as there are products. Each of the products, in turn, is defined as starting in column 2. This give us the appearance of the product image left-aligned with the product descriptions abutting it on the right. In order to do this, though, we need to know how many products there are before we define the image element. Once we have the product count, we add a cell to the table via **addData**, that places the image at the left hand side of the new table.

With the product image in place, we just need to add all the product descriptions. So, we execute a new SQL statement selecting all the products for this image. Running through that result set, we create a new row for each product. Since products are unique on name-style (not just name), we need to create a new row for each name-style combination. Since we don't want to re-display the name for each new style, we save the last name displayed, and if the new one is identical, we just display a "-". For each new name-style, we add the name, marketing_info, style, and price as separate cells of our **HtmlRow**.

Finally, we create an **HtmlForm**, **buyForm**, that has as its only element a button labeled "Customize." The form's action is defined to be **CategoryServlet**, operation set to Customize, and **catalog_id** set to the ID of this product. What we want to happen when the user hits the customize button is for a page to come up that allows the user to pick an imprint to put on the product. When the user hits this button, we'll be right back in **CategoryServlet**'s service routine. But that's for later.

The form is the last element in our row, so we add the **HtmlRow** to our **HtmlTable**. We go through this for each product attached to this image. When we've done this for each image in the image **Vector**, we have a complete HTML page. That page contains one table for each image. Each table contains one row for the image, and one row for each product appearing in that image. The result for the **Wearables** category is shown in Figure 6.2.

That takes care of the first five selections in our action frame (House, Glass, Wearables, Paper, and Novelties).

The next selection in the action frame is "Show Breed Imprints." Each item in the Doggie Diamonds product line is decorated with an imprint. The imprints are a big part of the reason that people buy these items. So right up front, we have a button that allows users to browse through the list

Figure 6.2 The catalog page for the Wearables category.

of imprints. Looking back at the source for the action frame in Listing 6.7, we see the link for this button is:

```
http://207.31.195.11/servlet/CategoryList?operation=breeds
```

So again, clicking this button puts us back into **CategoryServlet.service**, with the value of operation set to "breeds." From there, we go into **ShowBreeds**.

ShowBreeds is a much simpler method than our last example, **DisplayCatalog**. All we want to do in **ShowBreeds** is to put up a list of all the dog breeds that are represented in the imprints table. Each "imprint" is some sort of picture of a purebred dog. Thus, each imprint in the imprints table is labeled with a breed. This allows us to mirror how people purchase these items. A poodle owner wants items imprinted with poodle pictures. So we make it easy for shoppers to find the imprints for their particular breed. Many breeds have more than one imprint.

In a traditional, non-Web, standalone application, the breed list would typically be a simple listbox that popped up or dropped down whenever it was needed. However, the Web is a different animal. We could use a Java applet to make this function look and function more like a traditional application, but that would shut out non-Java browsers. So instead, we create a simple HTML page that lists the breeds, one per line, and allows the user to click on one to link to a full page with all of that breed's imprints. Listing 6.17 shows the source for ShowBreeds.

Listing 6.17 ShowBreeds displays a list of breeds represented in the imprints table.

```
/** Create a page that contains the names of all the breeds represented
    in the imprints table, each breed linked back to this servlet's
    ShowImprints method.
@param req The HTTP request.
@return An HtmlPage that contains a list of the breeds.
*/
HtmlPage ShowBreeds(HttpServletRequest req) {
  Vector retval;
  HtmlPage htmlp = new HtmlPage("Doggie Diamonds Breed Imprints List");
  htmlp.setBodyAttributes( "BGCOLOR=\"white\"" );
  Vector vimages = new Vector(1);
  String ssql = new String( "select distinct breed from imprints" );
```

```
  try {
    ResultSet rs = SQLExecSelect( ssql );
    while( true ) {
      try {
        if( rs.next() == false )
          break;
        String s = new String( "<A HREF=\""+ServletDirectory+
          "CategoryList?operation=breedimprints&breed="+
          rs.getString("breed")+"\">"+rs.getString("breed")+"</A><BR>");
        htmlp.add( s );
        }
      catch( SQLException se ) {}
      }
    rs.close();
    }
  catch( SQLException se ) {}
  return( htmlp );
  }
```

After **DisplayCatalog**, this is truly a breeze. We create a new blank **HtmlPage**. Then we select the distinct breeds from imprints. For each distinct breed, we add a line to the **HtmlPage** that gives the breed name as a hyperlink back into **CategoryServlet**, with operation set to **breedimprints** and breed set to whatever breed the user chose. Figure 6.3 shows the breed list.

Just to finish off this branch, we should look at what **breedimprints** gets us. If the user clicks on a breed in the ShowBreeds page, he hyperlinks to the **CategoryServlet** with operation set to **breedimprints**. **CategoryServlet.service** routes this request to the method **ShowImprints**, shown in Listing 6.18.

Listing 6.18 ShowImprints displays all imprints for a particular breed.

```
/** Create a page that contains all the images for the breed
    specified by the "breed" parameter.
@param req The HTTP request.
@return An HtmlPage that contains IMG links to all the images.
*/
HtmlPage ShowImprints(HttpServletRequest req) {
    Vector retval;
    String breed = req.getParameter("breed");
    HtmlPage htmlp = new HtmlPage("Doggie Diamonds "+breed+
        " Imprints List");
    htmlp.add( "<H1>"+breed+" Imprints</H1>" );
```

```
    htmlp.setBodyAttributes( "BGCOLOR=\"white\"" );
    Vector vimages = new Vector(1);
    String ssql = new String( "select * from imprints where breed='"+
        breed+"'" );
    try {
      ResultSet rs = SQLExecSelect( ssql );
      while( true ) {
        try {
          if( rs.next() == false )
            break;
          String s = new String( "<P><IMG SRC=\""+
            DoggieDiamondsDirectory+rs.getString("image_url")+"\">  "+
            rs.getString("marketing_info")+"<BR></P>");
          htmlp.add( s );
          }
        catch( SQLException se ) {}
        }
      rs.close();
      }
    catch( SQLException se ) {}
  return( htmlp );
  }
```

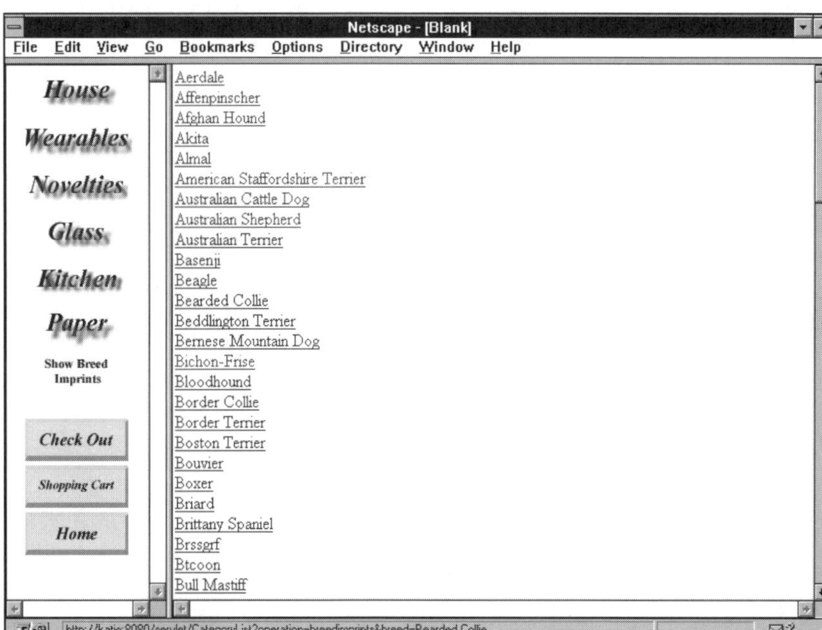

Figure 6.3 The Breed list.

As you can see, this is virtually identical to ShowBreeds. There are two differences. First, instead of selecting distinct breeds, we select all the records where the breed matches the one the user chose. Second, instead of a line naming the breed, each element of the **HtmlPage** here is an image: the image whose URL is named in the **image_url** field of the imprints record.

Next up in the action frame is Checkout: the branch of our application that allows the user to actually pay for the items in the shopping cart. We'll defer that for now, and discuss the customization and purchase processes together in the next section.

Following Checkout in the action frame is Show Shopping Cart. This button is linked to our servlet with operation set to "showcart." When we hit this button, **CategoryServlet.service** gets a new request, sees that operation is set to showcart, and invokes the method **ShowCart**, shown in Listing 6.19.

Listing 6.19 ShowCart displays items in the user's shopping cart.

```
/** Return an HtmlPage showing the current contents of the
    user's shopping cart.  If we've been called from the Customize
    applet, then add the item specified by catalog_id to the cart
    before displaying the contents.
@param req The HTTP request.
@param cookie The Cookie for this user.
@return An HTML page containing all the shopping cart items.
*/
HtmlPage ShowCart(HttpServletRequest req, Cookie cookie) {
    HtmlPage htmlp = new HtmlPage(
        "Your Doggie Diamonds Shopping Cart" );
    htmlp.setBodyAttributes( "BGCOLOR=\"white\"" );
    String scatalog_id = req.getParameter( "catalog_id" );
    if( scatalog_id != null ) {
      String squantity = req.getParameter( "quantity" );
      String simprint = req.getParameter( "imprint" );
      Vector v = GetCart( cookie );
      ShoppingCartItem sci = new ShoppingCartItem( scatalog_id,
            squantity, simprint );
      v.addElement( sci );
      }
    AddTheCart( req, htmlp, cookie );
    return( htmlp );
  }
```

This method actually does multiple duty. We need to display the shopping cart in three different places: here when the user selects ShowCart, later when the user adds an item to the shopping cart, and finally when the user selects Checkout. After all, we can hardly expect the user to fork over his credit card number without seeing what he's buying.

So we create a blank new page, then do a little bit of sorting out. The hyperlink from "Show Shopping Cart" only specifies that operation=showcart. Thus, the three calls to **getParameter** (**catalog_id**, **quantity**, and **imprint**) all return null. These parameters are only set when the user is adding an item to the cart, a case we'll talk about a little later on. So we fall through to the misnamed, **AddTheCart**, shown in Listing 6.20

Listing 6.20 AddTheCart displays the shopping cart.

```
/** Fill in the HtmlPage with the items in the shopping cart
    specified by the supplied cookie.
@param req The HTTP request.
@param htmlp The HtmlPage that needs to be filled.
@param cookie The Cookie identifying the shopping cart.
*/
void AddTheCart(HttpServletRequest req, HtmlPage htmlp, Cookie cookie) {
  int bigsum = 0;


    Vector v = GetCart( cookie );
    if( v.size() == 0 ) {
       htmlp.add( "<H1>Your shopping cart is empty.</H1>" );
      return;
      }

    htmlp.add( "<H1>Your shopping cart now contain these "+v.size()+
        " items.</H1>" );
    HtmlTable htmlt = new HtmlTable("BORDER=0");
    for( int i = 0; i < v.size(); i++ ) {
      try {
        ShoppingCartItem scit = (ShoppingCartItem)v.elementAt(i);
        String ssql = new String(
            "select * from catalog where catalog_id="+scit.catalog_id );
        ResultSet rs = SQLExecSelect( ssql );
        if( rs.next() == false )
          break;
        HtmlRow htmlr = new HtmlRow();
```

```
        htmlr.addData( "<IMG WIDTH=100 SRC=\""+DoggieDiamondsDirectory+
            rs.getString("image_url")+"\">", "COLSTART=1 WIDTH=100" );
        htmlr.addData( rs.getString( "name" ), "COLSTART=2 WIDTH=100" );
        htmlr.addData( "<IMG WIDTH=100 SRC=\""+DoggieDiamondsDirectory+
            "images/"+scit.imprint+".gif\"", "COLSTART=3 WIDTH=100" );
        htmlr.addData( scit.quantity, "COLSTART=4 WIDTH=100" );

        int quantity = (new Integer(scit.quantity)).intValue();
        int price = rs.getInt( "price" );
        int subtotalprice = price*quantity;
        bigsum += subtotalprice;
        htmlr.addData( formatPrice( price ), "COLSTART=4 WIDTH=100" );
        htmlr.addData( "<P><B>"+formatPrice( subtotalprice )+"</B></P>",
            "COLSTART=5 WIDTH=100" );
        htmlt.addRow( htmlr );

        rs.close();
        }
      catch( SQLException sqe ) {
          System.out.println("add error "+sqe );
          }
      }
    HtmlRow htmlr = new HtmlRow();
    int shipping = TotalShipping( req, cookie );
    if( shipping != 0 ) {
      htmlr.addData(
          "<P><B>Total price of all items in shopping cart including ("+
          formatPrice(shipping)+") shipping via UPS: "+
          formatPrice(bigsum+shipping), "COLSTART=1 COLSPAN=6" );
          }
    else {
      htmlr.addData( "<P><B>Total price of all items in shopping cart \
        not including shipping: "+formatPrice(bigsum), "COLSTART=1
        COLSPAN=6" );
    htmlt.addRow( htmlr );

    htmlr = new HtmlRow();

    String actionurl = new String( ServletDirectory+"CategoryList" );
    HtmlForm buyForm = new HtmlForm(actionurl,"GET");
    buyForm.addSubmitButton( "Value=\"Clear the Shopping Cart\"" );
    buyForm.addHiddenField( "operation","clear" );
    htmlr.addData( buyForm, "COLSTART=1 COLSPAN=6 ALIGN=CENTER" );
    htmlt.addRow(htmlr);
```

```
    htmlp.add( htmlt );
    htmlp.add( "<P><BR><BR></P>" );
  }
```

This is a relatively long method, but there's more formatting than function involved. It's a little easier to understand in pseudo-code:

```
Get the shopping cart.
Create an HTML table.
For each item in the shopping cart.
   Create a row.
   Retrieve the catalog record for this item.
   Add the product image to the row.
   Add the name, product image, quantity, imprint image, unit price, and
     subtotal price.
   Add the row to the HTML table.
Add the table to the page.
Add a Clear button to the page.
```

The first call, **GetCart**, gets our cart from the **Hashtable shoppingCarts**. **GetCart** retrieves this user's shopping cart by passing the current cookie to the method **Hashtable.get**. **GetCart**, shown in Listing 6.21, deserves a little bit of explanation.

Listing 6.21 GetCart returns the shopping cart associated with a particular user.

```
/** Get the shopping cart identified by the specified Cookie
    argument.  If there is no cart, create a new one.
@param Cookie   The cookie that identifies this shopping cart.
@return Vector  The Vector of ShoppingCartItems for this user.
*/
Vector GetCart( Cookie cookie ) {
    Vector v = (Vector)shoppingCarts.get(
        cookie.getValues("cart_number") );
    if( v == null ) {
      v = new Vector(1);
      shoppingCarts.put( cookie.getValues("cart_number"), v );
      }
    return( v );
}
```

Remember that a cookie is a name/value pair. Now for this domain and path, we only need one value, the shopping cart number, so the name is redundant, but we set it anyway. If you look back at the top of Listing 6.8, service, we created our cookie as "cart_number=<X>" where x is the ID of a **ShoppingCart** object in the **Hashtable shoppingCarts**. So within **GetCart**, we need to root out the shopping cart ID from the Cookie object by calling **Cookie.getValues("cart_number")**. This returns a comma-delimited **String** containing all the values for **cart_number** in this Cookie. We will only ever have one value, so we treat it as such.

The shopping cart itself, **shoppingCarts**, is a Java **Hashtable**. A **Hashtable** is simply a **Vector** where each item is identified by a key. You add items to a **Hashtable** with **put**, and retrieve existing items with **get**. In the case of shoppingCarts, the cookie value is the key, so to retrieve a particular shopping cart, we call **shoppingCarts.get** with the cookie cart_number value as the key. The item associated with that key is a **Vector** of **ShoppingCartItems** that we've created previously. Listing 6.22 shows the source for the **ShoppingCartItem** class.

Listing 6.22 The ShoppingCartItem encapsulates the user's shopping cart.

```
/** A class for encapsulating the data items that make up
an item in the shopping cart.
*/
class ShoppingCartItem {
  /** The catalog id. */
  public String catalog_id;
  /** The imprint. */
  public String imprint;
  /** How many? */
  public String quantity;

  /** Set the public strings to the supplied values. */
  public ShoppingCartItem( String cid, String q, String imp ) {
    catalog_id = new String( cid );
    imprint = new String( imp );
    quantity = new String( q );
    }
  }
```

ShoppingCartItem is little more than a structure containing the three strings we need to identify a purchase, the **catalog_id**, the **imprint**, and the **quantity**.

Anyway, back in **AddTheCart**, once we have the shopping cart from **GetCart**, it's a simple matter to roll through this **Vector**, pulling the product record from the catalog table and formatting a table row with the appropriate data. We've already written a similar table back in **DisplayCatalog**, so I won't belabor the obvious. There are, however, a few items of interest here.

First of these is the price. In this application, prices are all listed in pennies. So we have to go through the method **formatPrice**, shown in Listing 6.23, to create a **String** representation of any price.

Listing 6.23 FormatPrice creates a string representation of a price.

```
/** Given an integer penny price, return a String dollars and cents
    price.
@param iprice The price in pennies.
@return The price formatted as $00.00.
*/
String formatPrice( int iprice ) {
            String siprice = (new Integer(iprice/100)).toString();
            String sfprice = (new Integer( iprice%100)).toString();
            if( sfprice.length() == 1 )
              sfprice = new String( "0"+sfprice );
            else {
              if( sfprice.length() != 2 )
                sfprice = new String("00" );
              }
            String sprice = new String( "$"+siprice+"."+sfprice );
            return( sprice );
            }
```

The second item of interest is the **TotalShipping**: the calculated shipping cost of this shipment. The application is designed to calculate shipping dynamically based on the total weight of items and the ship-to zip code. So in **TotalShipping**, we run through the shopping cart, retrieving the unit weight of each item, multiplying that by the quantity ordered, and adding that to the total ship weight. When we have the total weight, we retrieve the actual shipping cost by calling **HowMuchToShip** with the total weight and ship-to ZIP code. In real-life, **HowMuchToShip** would be an interaction with a shipper-supplied application, but since we don't have a shipper lined up yet, we simply use $20. Listing 6.24 shows the methods TotalShipping and HowMuchToShip.

Listing 6.24 TotalShipping and HowMuchToShip.

```
/** Calculate the shipping cost of this order by totalling the weights
    of all the items and asking the shipper-specific algorithm how much
    it costs to ship this weight to the customer's zip code.
@param cookie   This customer's shopping cart.
@return The total cost of shipping this order.
*/
int TotalShipping(HttpServletRequest req, Cookie cookie) {
  int totalwt = 0;
    String zip = req.getParameter("zip");

    Vector v = GetCart(cookie);
    for( int i = 0; i < v.size(); i++ ) {
      try {
        ShoppingCartItem scit = (ShoppingCartItem)v.elementAt(i);
        String ssql = new String(
            "select ship_wt from catalog where catalog_id="+
            scit.catalog_id );
        ResultSet rs = SQLExecSelect( ssql );
        if( rs.next() == false )
          break;
        int quantity = (new Integer(scit.quantity)).intValue();
        totalwt += quantity*rs.getInt( "ship_wt" );
        rs.close();
        }
      catch( SQLException sqe ) {
          System.out.println("add error "+sqe );
          }
      }
    int bigsum = HowMuchToShip( totalwt, zip );
    return( bigsum );
  }

/** Assume for now that shipping is always $20  In operation, this would
    be replaced by a call to a shipper-specific table of rates, or some
    weight/price based algorithm.
@param The total weight of items to be shipped.
@param The zip code it's being shipped to.
@return Price in pennies to ship the specified weight to the specified
  zip code.
*/
```

```
int HowMuchToShip( int wt, String zip ) {
  return( 2000 );
  }
```

The last odd element of **AddTheCart** is the Clear button. We've run into this before without really explaining it. The user might want to empty his cart and start all over again. It happens. So we give him a button for just that purpose. The **HtmlForm**, buyForm, contains only a single button, labeled Clear. This form has as its action a call back into **CategoryServlet** with operation set to "clear." Figure 6.4 shows the "show shopping cart" page.

Clear is a simple branch of the application that we can deal with right here. When the user presses the clear button, he hyperlinks to:

```
http://207.31.195.11/servlet/CategoryList?operation=clear
```

So, **CategoryServlet.service** gets called with operation set to clear. We fall into the giant **if-else** block and end up calling **ClearCart**, shown in Listing 6.25.

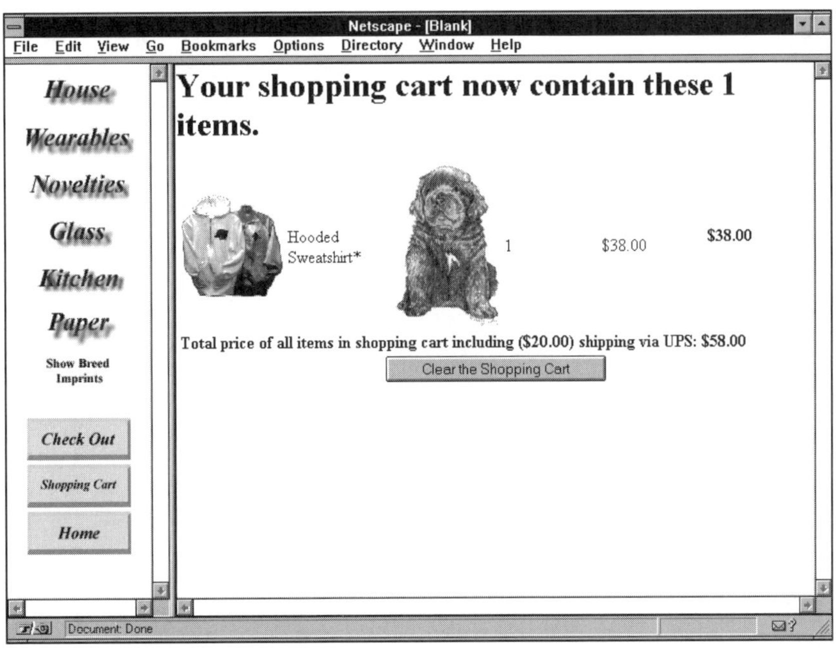

Figure 6.4 The ShowCart page.

Listing 6.25 ClearCart clears the shopping cart.

```
/** Clear the shopping cart, and display the new empty cart.
@param req  The HTTP request.
@param cookie   The user's cookie.
@return The HTML page created by ShowCart on the empty cart.
*/
HtmlPage ClearCart(HttpServletRequest req, Cookie cookie) {
    Vector v = GetCart( cookie );
    while( v.size() > 0 )
      v.removeElementAt(0);
    return( ShowCart( req, cookie ));
  }
```

ClearCart retrieves the shopping cart via **GetCart**, removes all the elements from it via **Vector.removeElementAt**, then displays the newly emptied cart via **ShowCart**. The end result of the user pressing Clear is that a page is displayed saying "Your shopping cart is empty.", the same page that would appear if a new user pressed "Show Shopping Cart" from the action page without putting any items in his cart.

Adding Items To The Shopping Cart

We've covered a lot of ground so far. We've seen how to display the catalog, the list of imprints and the shopping cart. We've also shown how to clear the shopping cart. What we need to do now is work through the process of adding items to the shopping cart.

As we've already seen, Doggie Diamonds business consists of putting breed-specific imprints on existing items. So, the process of adding an item to our cart here is more complicated than in a store where you simply pick an item off the shelf and buy. Here, putting an item in the cart is actually a two-part process. First you pick the item, then you pick the imprint and quantity.

How do you actually get an item into the cart using this application? Back in **DisplayCatalog**, each product line item has a button on it labeled Customize. Hitting this button sends off an HTTP request to CategoryServlet. This HTTP request includes the variables operation which is set to customize, and **catalog_id** which is set to the **catalog_id** of the specific item. So, to add the item to his cart, the user hits the customize button. This hyperlinks back to our servlet, and into **service** with operation set to customize. **Service**, in turn, calls **CustomizeItem**, shown in Listing 6.26.

Listing 6.26 CustomizeItem allows us to customize the product with an imprint.

```
/** Create a page that allows the user to customize the product that
    he has selected from the catalog.  Put the product image on the
    left side of the screen, and the customization applet on the right
    side.
@param req The HTTP request.
@return An HtmlPage that contains the product image and applet.
*/
HtmlPage CustomizeItem(HttpServletRequest req) {
    String lastname = new String( "" );
    String scatalog_id = req.getParameter("catalog_id");

    Vector retval;

    HtmlPage htmlp = new HtmlPage( "Added item "+scatalog_id );
    htmlp.setBodyAttributes( "BGCOLOR=\"white\"" );

    String ssql = new String( "select * from catalog where catalog_id="+
        scatalog_id );
    try {
      ResultSet rs = SQLExecSelect( ssql );
      if( rs.next() != false ) {
        HtmlTable htmlt = new HtmlTable("BORDER=0");
        HtmlRow htmlr = new HtmlRow();
      htmlr.addData(
            "<P>You have selected the following.<BR>Item: <B>"+
            rs.getString("name")+"</B><BR>Style:<B> "+
            rs.getString("style2")+"</B><BR>Unit price: <B>"+
            formatPrice(rs.getInt("price"))+"</B></P>",
            "COLSTART=1 WIDTH=200 ALIGN=TOP" );
        htmlr.addData( "<P>Now customize it by selecting an imprint and \
          a quantity.  Select one print from the list, or browse the \
          list by hitting next/previous.  When you find the one you \
          want, \
          hit Done.</P>", "COLSTART=2 WIDTH=300 ALIGN=TOP" );
        htmlt.addRow(htmlr);
        htmlr = new HtmlRow();
        htmlr.addData(
           "<IMG WIDTH=200 SRC=\""+DoggieDiamondsDirectory+
            rs.getString("image_url")+"\">",
            "COLSTART=1 WIDTH=200 ALIGN=TOP" );
        HtmlApplet htmla = new HtmlApplet( "Customize.class",
            "CODEBASE=\""+AppletDirectory+"\"",300,300 );
```

```
        htmla.addParameter( "server", Server );
        htmla.addParameter( "catalog_id", scatalog_id );
        htmlr.addData( "<P>"+htmla+"</P>",
            "COLSTART=2 WIDTH=300 ALIGN=TOP" );
        htmlt.addRow(htmlr);

        htmlp.add( htmlt );
        }
      rs.close();
      }
    catch( SQLException se ) { }

  return( htmlp );
  }
```

CustomizeItem creates an **HtmlPage** with a single **HtmlTable** containing two rows of two columns each. The first column shows the image and description of the product the user selected. The second column contains an applet. The data retrieval and page creation here is nothing we haven't seen before. The fun part is the applet. Figure 6.5 shows the page in action.

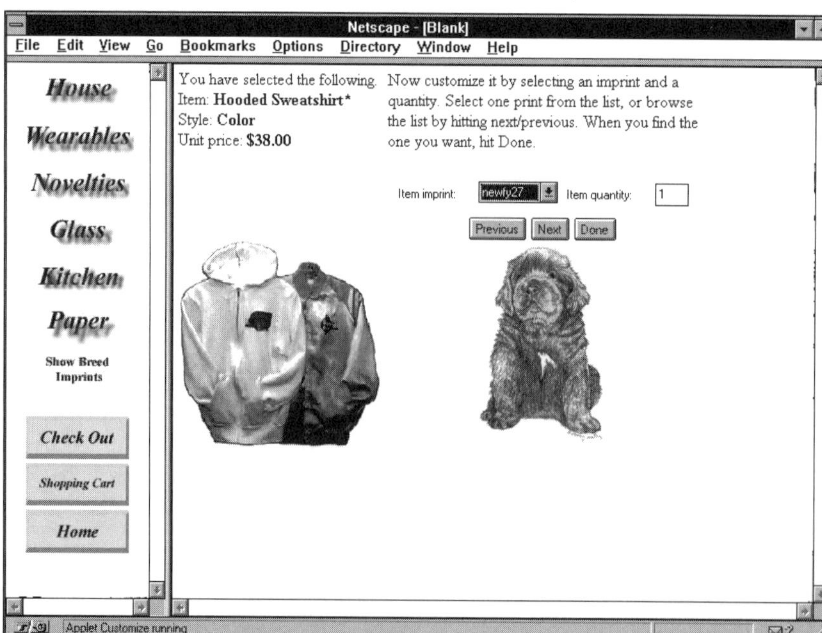

Figure 6.5 The CustomizeItem page in action.

The reason I created an applet rather than use a straight HTML solution to imprint picking is that the straight HTML solutions are extremely awkward. With the Customize applet, the user can quickly look through the imprint names, and view the likely candidates without jumping to a new page. Listing 6.27 shows the source for the Customize applet.

Listing 6.27 The Customize applet.

```
import java.applet.*;
import java.io.*;
import java.net.*;
import java.awt.*;
import java.sql.*;

/** A class for presenting the price of a stock as a bar graph
    with a numeric value that follows the top of the bar.  The ticker
    symbol and current price are also displayed centered over the
    top of the bar graph.  The scale on the left of the graph changes
    based on the current price, showing only 12 points at a time.
@see Applet
*/
public class Customize extends Applet {
//    static String Server="207.31.195.11:8080";
    static String Server="katie";

    /** The ip port the Stocker Java server is listening to.  We'll
        open this port on the host, write our symbol of interest into
        it then read it for the price messages. */
    public int port;

    /** The name of the host the Stocker Java server is running on. */
        public String host;

    /** We sit in a loop running until this boolean is set to false. */
        public boolean bRun = false;

    /** The button that we use to change ticker symbols. */
    Button useButton;
    Button nextButton;
    Button previousButton;

    /** The text field where we enter the new ticker symbol. */
    TextField quantityText;
    /** The area where our bar graph appears. */
```

```
public CustomizeGraphCanvas gp;
/** The Panel that organizes the button and text field
    changing the ticker symbol. */
Panel controlPanel;
/** The panel at the top where the ticker symbol and the
    current price appear. */
Panel BigPanel;

String scatalog_id;

public Image currentImage;

Choice ch;  // The list of available imprints

/** Boolean set when Applet.init runs. */
boolean bInited = false;

/** Called once to create a socket reader thread. */
public void init() {
    if( bInited == false ) {
        firstTime();
    }
}

/** Called once to create visual elements, as well as the
    port reader thread.  */
public void firstTime() {
    try {
    scatalog_id = getParameter("catalog_id");
    if( scatalog_id == null ) {
        System.out.println( "catalog_id parameter not set "+
            "(<param name=catalog_id value=XXXX>" );
        return;
        }

    setLayout( new BorderLayout());
    BigPanel = new Panel();
    Panel panel1 = new Panel();
    Label chl = new Label( "Item imprint: " );
    chl.setBackground( Color.white );
    panel1.add( chl );
    Panel panel2 = new Panel();
    ch = new Choice();
    panel1.add( ch );
    ch.addItem( "affen1" );
```

```
ch.addItem( "afghan1" );
ch.addItem( "akita1" );
ch.addItem( "almal1" );
ch.addItem( "amstaff1" );
ch.addItem( "ardale1" );
ch.addItem( "ausshep1" );
ch.addItem( "austcat1" );
ch.addItem( "austter1" );
ch.addItem( "basenji1" );
ch.addItem( "beagle1" );
ch.addItem( "bedling1" );
ch.addItem( "bermtn1" );
ch.addItem( "bichon1" );
ch.addItem( "bldhnd1" );
ch.addItem( "borcol1" );
ch.addItem( "borter1" );
ch.addItem( "boston1" );
ch.addItem( "bouvier1" );
ch.addItem( "boxer1" );
ch.addItem( "brdcol1" );
ch.addItem( "briard1" );
ch.addItem( "britspn1" );
ch.addItem( "brssgrf1" );
ch.addItem( "btcoon1" );
ch.addItem( "bulldog1" );
ch.addItem( "bullmas1" );
ch.addItem( "bullter1" );
ch.addItem( "cairn1" );
ch.addItem( "canaan1" );
ch.addItem( "cardigan1" );
ch.addItem( "chesbay1" );
ch.addItem( "chihua1" );
ch.addItem( "chow1" );
ch.addItem( "clumber1" );
ch.addItem( "cocker1" );
ch.addItem( "collie1" );
ch.addItem( "crest1" );
ch.addItem( "curlret1" );
ch.addItem( "dach1" );
ch.addItem( "dalma1" );
ch.addItem( "dobie1" );
ch.addItem( "ecocker1" );
ch.addItem( "engspr1" );
ch.addItem( "epoint1" );
ch.addItem( "esetter1" );
```

```
ch.addItem( "fbulldog1" );
ch.addItem( "foxtsm1" );
ch.addItem( "fxterwr1" );
ch.addItem( "generic1" );
ch.addItem( "golden1" );
ch.addItem( "gordon1" );
ch.addItem( "grhnd1" );
ch.addItem( "gschnz1" );
ch.addItem( "gshep1" );
ch.addItem( "gtdane1" );
ch.addItem( "ibizan1" );
ch.addItem( "isetter1" );
ch.addItem( "iterrier1" );
ch.addItem( "itlgrey1" );
ch.addItem( "iwolf1" );
ch.addItem( "iwspan1" );
ch.addItem( "japchin1" );
ch.addItem( "keesh1" );
ch.addItem( "komondr1" );
ch.addItem( "lab1" );
ch.addItem( "lemon1" );
ch.addItem( "lhasa1" );
ch.addItem( "maltese1" );
ch.addItem( "mastiff1" );
ch.addItem( "minpin1" );
ch.addItem( "minschn1" );
ch.addItem( "mterrier1" );
ch.addItem( "neomstf1" );
ch.addItem( "newfy1" );
ch.addItem( "newfy10" );
ch.addItem( "newfy11" );
ch.addItem( "newfy12" );
ch.addItem( "newfy13" );
ch.addItem( "newfy14" );
ch.addItem( "newfy15" );
ch.addItem( "newfy16" );
ch.addItem( "newfy17" );
ch.addItem( "newfy18" );
ch.addItem( "newfy19" );
ch.addItem( "newfy2" );
ch.addItem( "newfy20" );
ch.addItem( "newfy21" );
ch.addItem( "newfy22" );
ch.addItem( "newfy23" );
ch.addItem( "newfy24" );
```

```
ch.addItem( "newfy25" );
ch.addItem( "newfy26" );
ch.addItem( "newfy27" );
ch.addItem( "newfy3" );
ch.addItem( "newfy4" );
ch.addItem( "newfy5" );
ch.addItem( "newfy6" );
ch.addItem( "newfy7" );
ch.addItem( "newfy8" );
ch.addItem( "newfy9" );
ch.addItem( "norelk1" );
ch.addItem( "norter1" );
ch.addItem( "oldeng1" );
ch.addItem( "pap1" );
ch.addItem( "pbgv1" );
ch.addItem( "peke1" );
ch.addItem( "pembrok1" );
ch.addItem( "pharhnd1" );
ch.addItem( "pom1" );
ch.addItem( "poodle1" );
ch.addItem( "prtwtr1" );
ch.addItem( "pug1" );
ch.addItem( "pyr1" );
ch.addItem( "pyr2" );
ch.addItem( "ridge1" );
ch.addItem( "rottie1" );
ch.addItem( "saluki1" );
ch.addItem( "samoyed1" );
ch.addItem( "scottie1" );
ch.addItem( "sharpei1" );
ch.addItem( "sheltie1" );
ch.addItem( "shiba1" );
ch.addItem( "shihtzu1" );
ch.addItem( "sibhsk1" );
ch.addItem( "silky1" );
ch.addItem( "skye1" );
ch.addItem( "spinone1" );
ch.addItem( "stbern1" );
ch.addItem( "tervuren1" );
ch.addItem( "tibetan1" );
ch.addItem( "vizsla1" );
ch.addItem( "weimr1" );
ch.addItem( "welsh1" );
ch.addItem( "westie1" );
ch.addItem( "wheaton1" );
```

```
        ch.addItem( "whippet1" );
        ch.addItem( "yorkie1" );
        ch.select( "affen1" );

        nextButton = new Button( "Next" );
        previousButton = new Button( "Previous" );
        useButton = new Button( "Done" );
        panel2.add( previousButton );
        panel2.add( nextButton );
        panel2.add( useButton );
        nextButton.show();
        useButton.show();
        previousButton.show();
        quantityText = new TextField("1",2);
        quantityText.setBackground( Color.white );
        Label ql = new Label(" Item quantity: " );
        ql.setBackground( Color.white );
        panel1.setBackground( Color.white );
        panel2.setBackground( Color.white );
        panel1.add( ql );
        panel1.add( quantityText );
        quantityText.show();

        BigPanel.setLayout( new BorderLayout());
        BigPanel.add( "North", panel1 );
        BigPanel.add( "South", panel2 );
        add( "North", BigPanel );
        gp = new CustomizeGraphCanvas(this);
        BigPanel.setBackground( Color.white );
        add( "Center", gp );
        gp.show();
        BigPanel.repaint();
        try {
            currentImage = getImage( new URL( "http://"+Server+
            ":8080/DoggieDiamonds/images/"+ch.getSelectedItem()+".gif" ));
            }
        catch( MalformedURLException e ) {
            System.out.println( "couldn't get image" );
            }
        layout();
        }
    catch( Exception e ) {
        System.out.println( "exception in init "+e );
        }
    bInited = true;
    }
```

```
public synchronized boolean imageUpdate(Image img,
        int infoflags, int x, int y, int width, int height)
    {
    System.out.println( "img "+img+" update" );
    return( true );
    }

    public synchronized void paint( Graphics g ) {
        if( !bInited )
            return;
        Dimension d = size();
        g.setColor( Color.white );
        g.fillRect( 0,0,d.height, d.width );
    }


/** Startup the socket reader thread. */
    public void start() {
        System.out.println( "start" );
        if( bInited == true ) {
            System.out.println( "already inited" );
        }

    }

/** Kill the socket reader socket. */
    public void stop() {
    }

public boolean action( Event e, Object o ) {
        if( !bInited )
            return false;
        System.out.println( "action "+e+" o = "+o );
        if( e.target instanceof java.awt.Choice ) {
            return( false );
            }
    return( false );
    }


/** Handle UI events, the only one of which is the
    change symbol button.  */
    public boolean handleEvent(Event e) {
        if( !bInited )
            return false;
```

```
if( e.target instanceof java.awt.Choice && e.id == 1001 ) {
      try {
           currentImage = getImage( new URL( "http://"+Server+
           ":8080/DoggieDiamonds/images/"+
           ch.getSelectedItem()+".gif" ));
          }
      catch( MalformedURLException mfe ) {
          System.out.println( "couldn't get image" );
          }
      gp.repaint();
      }
else {
    if( e.target instanceof Button && e.id ==
                              Event.ACTION_EVENT ) {
        int i;
        if( ((Button)e.target).getLabel().compareTo( "Next" )
                                                   == 0 ) {
            i = ch.getSelectedIndex();
            if( i < ch.countItems())
                i++;
            ch.select( i );
            try {
                currentImage = getImage( new URL(
                   "http://"+Server+
                   ":8080/DoggieDiamonds/images/"+
                   ch.getSelectedItem()+".gif" ));
                }
            catch( MalformedURLException mfe ) {
                System.out.println( "couldn't get image" );
                }
            gp.repaint();
            }
        if( ((Button)e.target).getLabel().compareTo( "Previous" )
                                                   == 0 ) {
            i = ch.getSelectedIndex();
            if( i > 0 )
                i--;
            ch.select( i );
            try {
                currentImage = getImage( new URL( "http://"+
                Server+":8080/DoggieDiamonds/images/"+
                ch.getSelectedItem()+".gif" ));
                }
            catch( MalformedURLException mfe ) {
                System.out.println( "couldn't get image" );
```

```
                        }
                    gp.repaint();
                    }
                if( ((Button)e.target).getLabel().compareTo( "Done" )
                                                            == 0 ) {
                    AppletContext ac = getAppletContext();
                    try {
                        URL servlet = new URL( "http://"+Server+
                        ":8080/servlet/CategoryList?"+
                        "operation=customizeditem&catalog_id="+
                        scatalog_id+"&quantity="+quantityText.getText()+
                        "&imprint="+ch.getSelectedItem() );
                        ac.showDocument( servlet, "Body" );
                        }
                    catch( Exception ex )
                        { System.out.println( "can't finalize "+ex ); }
                    }
                }
            }

        return false;
    }
}


/** A class for displaying imprint image.  */
class CustomizeGraphCanvas extends Canvas {
    Customize sw;
    public Dimension dim = new Dimension( 200, 200 );
    public int offset;
    Image lastImage = null;


    public CustomizeGraphCanvas( Customize s ) {
        sw = s;
    }
    public Dimension preferredSize() {
        return( dim );
    }
    public Dimension minimumSize() {
        return( dim );
    }

    public synchronized void update(Graphics g) {
        Dimension d = size();
```

```
        if( lastImage != sw.currentImage ) {
            g.setColor( Color.white );
            g.fillRect( 0, 0, d.width, d.height );
            lastImage = sw.currentImage;
            }
    int width = sw.currentImage.getWidth(sw);
    int xoffset = (d.width-width)/2;
    g.drawImage( sw.currentImage, xoffset, 0, this );
    }

    public synchronized void paint(Graphics g) {
        Dimension d = size();
            g.setColor( Color.white );
            g.fillRect( 0, 0, d.width, d.height );
    int width = sw.currentImage.getWidth(sw);
    int xoffset = (d.width-width)/2;
    g.drawImage( sw.currentImage, xoffset, 0, this );
   }
}
```

Since this is not strictly an applet book, I won't waste a lot of time picking this code apart. What this applet needs to do is show the current imprint image, and allow the user to see the next and previous images in the imprint table. So, we split the applets window into two **Panels**. The top **Panel** contains a bunch of controls. On the first line of this panel is a list box listing all the imprints, and a text entry field for entering the quantity desired. The next line shows three **Buttons**: next, previous, and done. The bottom panel displays the selected imprint image. When the applet starts up, we display the first imprint image in the list. If the user selects next, the next image comes up. Hit previous, and the previous image comes up. The user can also move randomly around by selecting an imprint from the list box.

Though there's plenty of code here, it's actually a very simple applet. The **firstTime** method creates the top **Panel**, then it creates the listbox, text field, and buttons, and adds them to the **Panel**. Then, we create the bottom **Panel** and a **CustomizeGraphCanvas** (our own class) and add that to the bottom **Panel**.

Further down in **firstTime**, we select affen1 (the first item) as the selected item in the list box and set currentImage to the image file corresponding to affen1. We create that **Image** by calling **Applet.getImage** with the image file's URL. That URL in turn is created by appending ".gif" to the selection, "affen1", then appending all that to a hardwired prefix "http://207.31.195.11/DoggieDiamonds/images/". The function of actually displaying this imprint image is entirely encapsulated in the **CustomizeGraphCanvas** class, so we'll talk about that a little later. Suffice to say that **CustomizeGraphCanvas** displays this image when it comes up.

Having created our visual elements via the call to **firstTime**, our applet is now sitting around with the default image displayed, waiting for something to happen. That something is a button press, or a list selection. The entire point of the buttons and the list box is to set the variable currentImage. **CurrentImage** is Java **Image** object corresponding to this imprint.

Dealing with "something" happening is the job of **Applet.handleEvent**. Any event such as a menu selection, mouse move, or button press is passed to **Applet.handleEvent** by Java. There are four events we need to handle: selecting an item from the list, and pressing the next, previous, or done button.

Within **handleEvent**, we test if the target of the event is a **Choice** (our list box) and the ID is 1001 (select item), then we know the user has selected an item. In that case, we get the selected item and set currentImage to a new **Image**, which we get via **getImage**, creating the URL the same way we did back in **firstTime**.

If the target is a **Button**, we figure out which button it is by comparing the label. If it's a Next button, we move the selected item in the list box to the next item, then treat it exactly as if the user had selected an item from the list box. The previous button works the same way, only decrementing the selected item.

Once the list box, or next/previous buttons have changed the currentImage, they all make a call to **gp.repaint**. This call causes Java eventually to call the method **CustomizeGraphCanvas.paint** which handles actually displaying the **Image** in the bottom panel.

The final section of **handleEvent** deals with the Done button. What we want to accomplish with the Done button is to actually add the newly customized item to the shopping cart. So, we create a URL that calls back into our **CategoryServlet**, with operation set to **customizeditem**, **catalog_id** set to the **catalog_id** of the customized item, **imprint** set to the name of the imprint the user selected in the applet, and quantity set to the quantity the user entered in the applet text field. Then we get an **AppletContext** from Java by calling **Applet.getAppletContext**. Finally, we actually make our link to **CategoryServlet** by calling **AppletContext.showDocument** with this **CategoryServlet** URL as the argument.

That's it for the applet itself. All we have left is the **CustomizeGraphCanvas** class. We create one **CustomizeGraphCanvas** and place it in the bottom **Panel**. Its sole function is to display the **Image** specified by currentImage centered in that **Panel**. In order to do that, it needs to implement two override methods of its superclass **Panel** (via its superclass, **Component**): **paint** and **update**.

Since they're so similar, we'll just look at **update** for now. **Update** first checks to see if **currentImage** has changed. If so, it clears the window to white. Then it figures out how to center the item along the x-axis by subtracting the image width from the window width and dividing by 2. Finally, it draws the image at the appropriate offset. **Paint** works exactly the same way, except that it clears the window to white whether the image has changed or not.

That's it for the Customize applet. Easy, wasn't it? That's also it for the customize page. When the user hits the Done button in our Customize applet, he hyperlinks back into **CategoryServlet** with operation set to **customizeditem**.

With operation set to **customizeditem**, **CategoryServlet.service** calls **ShowFinalizedItem**. The page that **ShowFinalizedItem** creates is mostly a way-station, where the user can see the results of his customization. If he still wants to buy the item, with the customization and quantity he specified, then he hits a button at the bottom of this page. Listing 6.28 shows the source for **ShowFinalizedItem**.

Listing 6.28 ShowFinalizedItem shows the results of customization.

```
/** Create a page that contains a complete description of the
    item that the user has just customized, including unit price,
    subtotal price, quantity, imprint image, and product image.
@param req The HTTP request.
@return An HtmlPage that contains the customized product.
*/
```

```
HtmlPage ShowFinalizedItem(HttpServletRequest req) {
    String lastname = new String( "" );
    String scatalog_id = req.getParameter("catalog_id");
    String squantity = req.getParameter( "quantity" );
    String imprint = req.getParameter( "imprint" );

    Vector retval;

    HtmlPage htmlp = new HtmlPage("");
    htmlp.setBodyAttributes( "BGCOLOR=\"white\"" );

    String ssql = new String( "select * from catalog where catalog_id="+
        scatalog_id );
    try {
      ResultSet rs = SQLExecSelect( ssql );
      if( rs.next() != false ) {
        HtmlTable htmlt = new HtmlTable("BORDER=0");
        HtmlRow htmlr = new HtmlRow();
        int price = rs.getInt("price");
        int quantity = (new Integer(squantity)).intValue();
        int totalprice = price*quantity;
      htmlr.addData( "<P>You have selected the following.<BR>Item: <B>"+
            rs.getString("name")+"</B><BR>Style:<B> "+
            rs.getString("style2")+"</B><BR>Unit price: <B>"+
            formatPrice(rs.getInt("price"))+"</B><BR>Quantity: <B>"+
            quantity+"</B><BR>Total price: <B>"+formatPrice(totalprice)+
            "</B></P>", "COLSTART=1 WIDTH=200 ALIGN=TOP" );
        htmlr.addData( "<P>It will be imprinted with this logo:\
          <BR><BR><BR><BR><BR><BR><BR></P>", "COLSTART=2 WIDTH=300
          ALIGN=TOP" );
        htmlt.addRow(htmlr);
        htmlr = new HtmlRow();
        htmlr.addData( "<IMG WIDTH=200 SRC=\""+DoggieDiamondsDirectory+
            rs.getString("image_url")+"\">",
            "COLSTART=1 WIDTH=200 ALIGN=TOP" );
        htmlr.addData( "<IMG SRC=\""+DoggieDiamondsDirectory+"images/"+
            imprint+".gif\">", "COLSTART=2 WIDTH=300 ALIGN=CENTER" );
        htmlt.addRow(htmlr);

        String actionurl = new String(ServletDirectory+"CategoryList");
        HtmlForm buyForm = new HtmlForm(actionurl,"GET");
        buyForm.addSubmitButton( "Value=\"Add To Shopping Cart\"" );
        buyForm.addHiddenField( "operation","addtocart");
        buyForm.addHiddenField( "catalog_id",scatalog_id);
        buyForm.addHiddenField( "quantity",squantity);
        buyForm.addHiddenField( "imprint",imprint);
```

```
        htmlr = new HtmlRow();
        htmlr.addData( buyForm,
            "ALIGN=CENTER COLSTART=1 COLSPAN=2 HEIGHT=75" );
        htmlt.addRow( htmlr );

        htmlp.add( htmlt );
        }
      rs.close();
      }
    catch( SQLException se ) { }

  return( htmlp );
  }
```

This method is very much like the other display pages so, again, we won't belabor the obvious. One thing to note is how the parameters get from the applet to the servlet. The applet creates a URL with the parameters embedded just like a CGI call, and within **ShowFinalizedItem**, these parameters are pried out via **HttpServletRequest.getParameter**. Another item of note is how this page passes parameters on to the next page in the chain. We create a form, buyForm, that has a single button labeled "Add to ShoppingCart", and a bunch of hidden fields. These hidden fields contain the operation, **catalog_id**, **quantity**, and **imprint**. Thus, when the user hits the "Add to" button, the servlet URL that we link to contains these parameters, which the servlet in turn can pry out with **getParameter**.

The ShowFinalizedItem page's "Add to ShoppingCart" button calls back to our servlet with operation set to **addtocart**. **CategoryServlet.service** calls **ShowCart**, a method which probably sounds familiar. In fact, we've already covered **ShowCart** in excruciating detail back in Listing 6.19. What we want to happen when the user hits the "Add to" button is for a page to appear showing all the items in the shopping cart. So, all we need to do in this call to **ShowCart**, is to add the newly finalized item to the cart, and then show the cart. We need the same functionality we used earlier with a little prefix that adds the item to the cart. Looking back at Listing 6.19, you can see that if the **catalog_id** parameter is not null, then we get the other parameters (imprint and quantity), create a ShoppingCartItem, and add that item to our cart. That's our hook. We set **catalog_id** to our items catalog ID. With the new item added to the cart, we then display the cart just as if we'd just pressed "Show Shopping Cart" from the action frame. Figure 6.6 shows the page created by CustomizedItem.

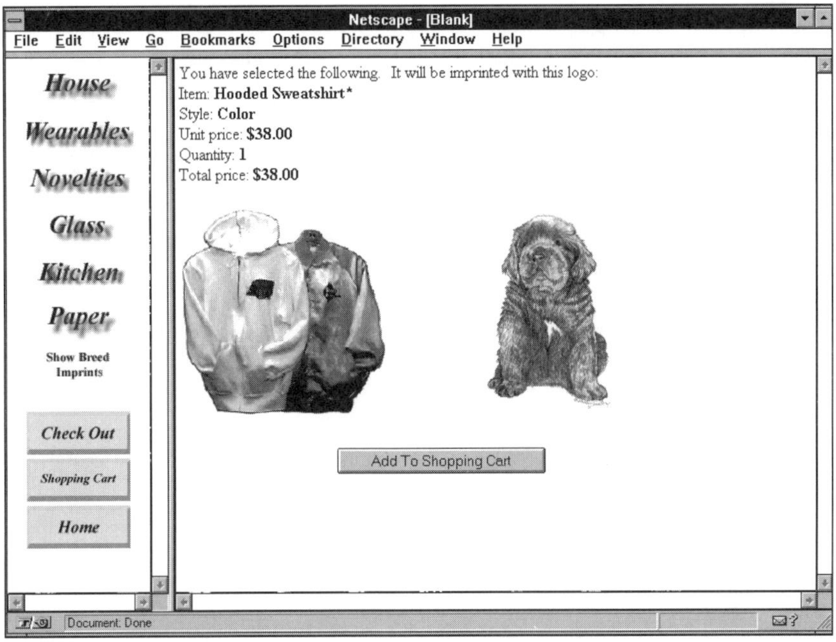

Figure 6.6 The CustomizedItem page.

The Checkout Process

We're positively zooming along now, and there's only one application branch left for us to deal with: **Checkout**. There's only one way to get to **Checkout** and that's by hitting the Checkout button on the action frame. That button links to our servlet with operation set to checkout. **CategoryServlet.service** passes that request to the method **Checkout**, shown in Listing 6.29.

Listing 6.29 Checkout collects credit card information for purchase.

```
/** Return an HTML page that contains a giant query form for
    getting the user's personal and credit card information.
@param req The HTTP request.
@param cookie The cookie which identifies the shopping cart.
@return An HtmlPage with the form inside.
*/
HtmlPage Checkout(HttpServletRequest req, Cookie cookie) {
  int bigsum = 0;
```

```
HtmlPage htmlp = new HtmlPage(
    "Buy The Stuff In Your Doggie Diamonds Shopping Cart" );
htmlp.setBodyAttributes( "BGCOLOR=\"white\"" );
htmlp.add( "<H1>Credit card entry form.</H1>" );

String actionurl = new String( ServletDirectory+"CategoryList" );
HtmlForm buyForm = new HtmlForm(actionurl,"GET");
HtmlTable htmlt = new HtmlTable("BORDER=0");
HtmlRow htmlr = new HtmlRow();
htmlr.addData( "<P>name_first</P>", "COLSTART=1" );
htmlr.addData( "<INPUT  name=name_first size=20 maxlength=20>",
  "COLSTART=2" );
htmlt.addRow( htmlr );

htmlr = new HtmlRow();
htmlr.addData( "<P>name_middle</P>", "COLSTART=1" );
htmlr.addData( "<INPUT  name=name_middle size=1 maxlength=1>",
  "COLSTART=2" );
htmlt.addRow( htmlr );

htmlr = new HtmlRow();
htmlr.addData( "<P>name_last</P>", "COLSTART=1" );
htmlr.addData( "<INPUT  name=name_last size=30 maxlength=30>",
  "COLSTART=2" );
htmlt.addRow( htmlr );

htmlr = new HtmlRow();
htmlr.addData( "<P>street</P>", "COLSTART=1" );
htmlr.addData( "<INPUT  name=street size=40 maxlength=40>",
  "COLSTART=2" );
htmlt.addRow( htmlr );

htmlr = new HtmlRow();
htmlr.addData( "<P>street1</P>", "COLSTART=1" );
htmlr.addData( "<INPUT  name=street1 size=40 maxlength=40>",
  "COLSTART=2" );
htmlt.addRow( htmlr );

htmlr = new HtmlRow();
htmlr.addData( "<P>city</P>", "COLSTART=1" );
htmlr.addData( "<INPUT  name=city size=40 maxlength=40>",
  "COLSTART=2" );
htmlt.addRow( htmlr );

htmlr = new HtmlRow();
htmlr.addData( "<P>state</P>", "COLSTART=1" );
```

```
htmlr.addData( "<INPUT  name=state size=2 maxlength=2>",
  "COLSTART=2" );
htmlt.addRow( htmlr );

htmlr = new HtmlRow();
htmlr.addData( "<P>zip</P>", "COLSTART=1" );
htmlr.addData( "<INPUT  name=zip size=10 maxlength=10>",
  "COLSTART=2" );
htmlt.addRow( htmlr );

htmlr = new HtmlRow();
htmlr.addData( "<P>phone</P>", "COLSTART=1" );
htmlr.addData( "<INPUT  name=phone size=10 maxlength=10>",
  "COLSTART=2" );
htmlt.addRow( htmlr );

htmlr = new HtmlRow();
htmlr.addData( "<P>extension</P>", "COLSTART=1" );
htmlr.addData( "<INPUT  name=extension size=5 maxlength=5>",
  "COLSTART=2" );
htmlt.addRow( htmlr );

htmlr = new HtmlRow();
htmlr.addData( "<P>fax</P>", "COLSTART=1" );
htmlr.addData( "<INPUT  name=fax size=15 maxlength=15>",
  "COLSTART=2" );
htmlt.addRow( htmlr );

htmlr = new HtmlRow();
htmlr.addData( "<P>email</P>", "COLSTART=1" );
htmlr.addData( "<INPUT  name=email size=60 maxlength=60>",
  "COLSTART=2" );
htmlt.addRow( htmlr );

htmlr = new HtmlRow();
htmlr.addData( "<P>Charge type:</P>", "COLSTART=1" );
String s = new String( "<select name=charge_type><option>Visa\
  </option><option>MasterCard</option></select>" );
htmlr.addData( s, "COLSTART=2" );
htmlt.addRow( htmlr );

htmlr = new HtmlRow();
htmlr.addData( "<P>Card number:</P>", "COLSTART=1" );
htmlr.addData( "<INPUT name=charge_id SIZE=20 MAXLENGTH=20>",
  "COLSTART=2" );
htmlt.addRow( htmlr );
```

```
    htmlr = new HtmlRow();
    htmlr.addData( "<P>Expiration:</P>", "COLSTART=1" );
    htmlr.addData( "<INPUT name=expiration SIZE=5 MAXLENGTH=5>",
      "COLSTART=2" );
    htmlt.addRow( htmlr );

    buyForm.add( htmlt );
    buyForm.addSubmitButton( "Value=\"Charge these items to \
    this card NOW.\"" );
    buyForm.addHiddenField( "operation","dotransaction");

    htmlp.add( buyForm );
    AddTheCart( req, htmlp, cookie );

  return( htmlp );
  }
```

Like many of these page creation methods, **Checkout** looks more complicated than it really is. A pseudo-code analog shows how simple it is:

```
Create a blank page.
Create a form.
Create a table.
For each of the items in the customer and transaction records.
   Create a row.
   Add the label of the field as the first cell in the row.
   Add a text field as the second cell in the row.
   Add the row to the table.
Add the table to the form.
Add a submit button to the form.
Display the current state of the shopping cart.
```

Most of the tedium in this method comes from the data entry code, which has to get name, address, phone...and credit card information. The only really interesting part of this method is how it links back into **CategoryServlet**. The button at the bottom of the page labeled "Charge the items in the cart to this card NOW" hyperlinks back to our **CategoryServlet** via the action attribute of the form. So we end up back at **CategoryServlet** with operation set to dotransaction and a huge pile of other parameters set to transaction-specific values. Figure 6.7 shows the customer information form page.

We've entered the home stretch now. All we need to do is close the deal. What we need to do is actually charge the user's credit card, enter his

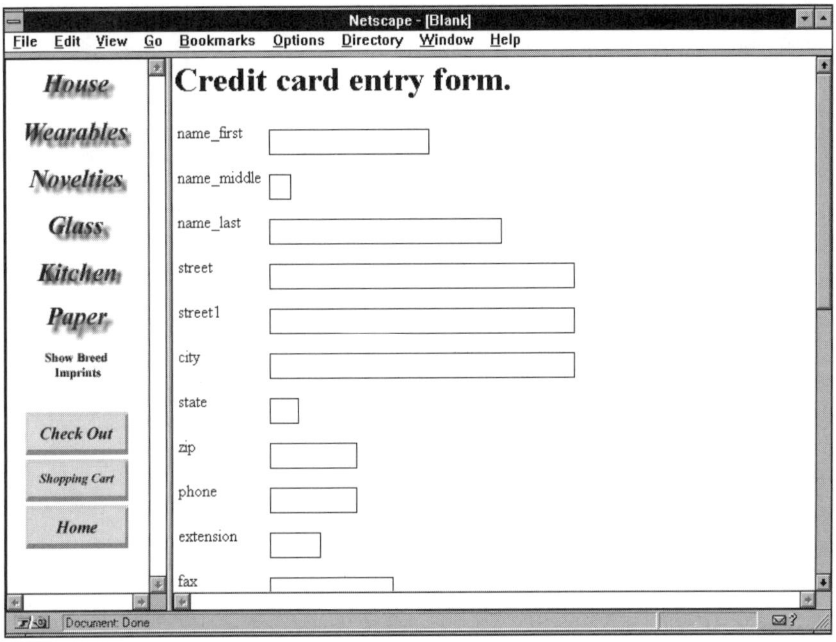

Figure 6.7 The customer information page.

personal information in the customer table, enter the order in the transaction table, and put all the shopping cart items into the ship_items table. When we're done with all that, we need to display a page that tells the user whether or not the charge was authorized.

When the user presses "Charge the items...," we hyperlink back into **CategoryServlet** with operation set to **DoTransaction**. This results in a call to **DoTransaction**, shown in Listing 6.30.

Listing 6.30 DoTransaction makes the sale.

```
/** Try to accomplish this transaction.  Authorize the tx by
    calling the credit institution, record the transaction, add
    all the items to the ship_items database, and clear the cart
    after it's all over.
@param req The HTTP request.
@param cookie The shopping cart.
@return An HtmlPage that describes how the transaction went.
*/
HtmlPage DoTransaction(HttpServletRequest req, Cookie cookie) {
    HtmlPage htmlp = new HtmlPage(
        "Buy The Stuff In Your Doggie Diamonds Shopping Cart" );
```

```
    htmlp.setBodyAttributes( "BGCOLOR=\"white\"" );
    htmlp.add( "<H1>Check authorization.</H1>" );

// Call the credit institution to authorize.
    Authorization auth = getAuthorization( req, cookie );
// Add the customer.
    int customer_id = AddCustomer( req, cookie );
// Add the transaction.
    AddTransaction( customer_id, req, cookie, auth );
    String s;
// Tell the user what happened.
    if( auth.bAuthorized == true ) {
     s = new String("Your purchase of "+formatPrice(TotalCart(cookie))+
   " has been authorized.  Thank you for shopping at Doggie Diamonds.");
        }
    else {
        s = new String( "We're sorry, your purchase of "+
          formatPrice(TotalCart(cookie))+
          " cannot be processed at this time." );
        }
    htmlp.add( "<P>"+s+"</P>" );
// Clear the shopping cart.
    ClearCart( req, cookie );
    return( htmlp );
}
```

DoTransaction itself is quite simple, relying on helper methods to do most of the work. Its first task is to get authorization for the credit transaction, via **getAuthorization**. The Authorization class, and **getAuthorization** method are shown in Listing 6.31.

Listing 6.31 The Authorization class and getAuthorization.

```
/** A class defining a credit authorization.
*/
class Authorization {
  public String id;
  public boolean bAuthorized;
}

/** Get the authorization for this transaction from the credit
    institution.  In operation, we'd be making a phone call or net
    connection out to an online authorization service, supplying
    the name, card number, expiration and total price.  For now
    randomly deny half the transactions.
```

```
@param req The HTTP request.
@param cookie The shopping cart we're buying.
@return The authorization information from credit inst.
*/
Authorization getAuthorization(HttpServletRequest req, Cookie cookie) {
  Authorization a = new Authorization();
  long x = System.currentTimeMillis();
  a.id = new String( (new Long(x)).toString());
  if( x%2 == 0 )
    a.bAuthorized = true;
  else
    a.bAuthorized = false;
  return( a );
  }
```

This method is a shell. In practice, it would include a call out to an online credit authorization service, which would return an authorization code for this transaction. For now, we simply create a string from the current time, and randomly decide to authorize, or reject, the transaction. We fill in an Authorization object and send it back to **DoTransaction**.

When **getAuthorization** returns, we have the go-ahead to record the transaction and ship the items. So we move along and add the customer to the database via **AddCustomer** shown in Listing 6.32.

Listing 6.32 AddCustomer adds the customer to the database.

```
/** Add the customer named in request to the customers table.
@param req The HTTP request, contains the customer info.
@param cookie The shopping cart for this customer.
@return The customer id.
*/
int AddCustomer( HttpServletRequest req, Cookie cookie ) {
  int customer_id = 0;
  java.util.Date d = new java.util.Date();
  String sd = new String( (d.getMonth()+1)+"/"+d.getDate()+
    "/"+d.getYear()+" "+d.getHours()+":"+d.getMinutes() );

  Vector v = new Vector(1);
  String ssql = new String( "select distinct customer_id from customers" );
  try {
    ResultSet rs = SQLExecSelect( ssql );
    while( true ) {
      try {
```

```
        if( rs.next() == false )
          break;
        v.addElement( new Integer( rs.getInt("customer_id")));
        }
      catch( SQLException se ) {
        System.out.println( "No max available "+se );
        customer_id = 1;
        }
      }
    rs.close();
    }
  catch( SQLException se ) {
    System.out.println( "Couldn't get max "+se );
    customer_id = 1;
    }

  for( customer_id = 1; customer_id < 10000; customer_id++ ) {
    boolean bFound = false;
    for( int i = 0; i < v.size(); i++ ) {
      if( customer_id == ((Integer)(v.elementAt(i))).intValue() ) {
        System.out.println( "skipping used id "+customer_id );
        bFound = true;
        }
      }
    if( bFound == false ) {
      System.out.println( "id "+customer_id+" not in use" );
      break;
      }
    }
  ssql = new String( "insert into customers ("+
  "customer_id, created, name_first, name_middle, name_last,"+
  "street, street1, city, state, zip, phone, extension, fax, email )"+
  "values ("+
    customer_id+","+
    "'"+sd+"',"+
    "'"+req.getParameter( "name_first" )+"',"+
    "'"+req.getParameter( "name_middle" )+"',"+
    "'"+req.getParameter( "name_last" )+"',"+
    "'"+req.getParameter( "street" )+"',"+
    "'"+req.getParameter( "street1" )+"',"+
    "'"+req.getParameter( "city" )+"',"+
    "'"+req.getParameter( "state" )+"',"+
    "'"+req.getParameter( "zip" )+"',"+
    "'"+req.getParameter( "phone" )+"',"+
    "'"+req.getParameter( "extension" )+"',"+
```

```
    "'"+req.getParameter( "fax" )+"',"+
    "'"+req.getParameter( "email" )+"')"
    );
    System.out.println( ssql );
  try {
    SQLExecUpdate( ssql );
    }
  catch( SQLException se ) {
    System.out.println( "add customer exception "+se );
    }
  return( customer_id );
}
```

This method is a fairly straightforward insert of form data into the database. We run through the database to find an unused ID, then create an insert statement from the values that the user entered into the form. The interesting thing to note about this code is that it doesn't pay any attention to maintaining some sort of customer "account." Each time a customer purchases something, he gets assigned a new record in the customer table. Why is that?

Maintaining customer accounts, especially via an anonymous medium like the Web, is nearly impossible. Trying to ferret out the right record by matching name and address is notoriously unreliable. Customers move, spell their names with and without a middle initial, and all sorts of other variations that make matching a royal pain in the neck. Assigning new customers an ID that they then have to remember to get back into the site also has a very low success rate. People don't want to do that. If we linked the customer record to the cookie, we could match that way, but multiple people often use one machine, cookies expire and get flushed, and to be honest, people find it downright spooky when the computer seems to know things that they can't remember telling it.

Consider, too, that the main use for maintaining customer accounts is marketing: to make sure that we mail one flyer and one flyer only to each customer. The way to deal with this is to install a separate periodic process that runs through the table figuring out which records are dupes and consolidating them in a new, marketing-oriented table. For now, Doggie Diamonds makes a new customer for each transaction.

AddCustomer returns a **customer_ID**. This ID is used to link the transaction in the transaction table to the customer it needs to be shipped to. With the **customer_ID** in hand, **DoTransaction** calls **AddTransaction**, shown in Listing 6.33, to put the transaction in the transactions table.

Listing 6.33 AddTransaction creates a new transaction.

```
/** Make a new transaction in the transaction table from the items
    in the specified shopping cart.  If the transaction has not been
    authorized, set the void flag so that the transaction doesn't get
    shipped.
@param customer_id The shopping cart that contains the transaction
items.
@param req The HTTP request.
@param cookie The cookie.
@param authorization The authorization number from our credit inst.
@return The transaction id.
*/
int AddTransaction( int customer_id, HttpServletRequest req, Cookie
  cookie,
                    Authorization auth ) {
  int transaction_id = 0;
  java.util.Date d = new java.util.Date();
  String sd = new String( (d.getMonth()+1)+"/"+d.getDate()+
    "/"+d.getYear()+" "+d.getHours()+":"+d.getMinutes() );

  Vector v = new Vector(1);
  String ssql = new String(
    "select distinct transaction_id from transactions" );
  try {
    ResultSet rs = SQLExecSelect( ssql );
    while( true ) {
      try {
        if( rs.next() == false )
          break;
        v.addElement( new Integer( rs.getInt("transaction_id")));
        }
      catch( SQLException se ) {
        System.out.println( "No max available "+se );
        transaction_id = 1;
        }
      }
    rs.close();
    }
  catch( SQLException se ) {
    System.out.println( "Couldn't get max "+se );
```

```
    transaction_id = 1;
    }

  for( transaction_id = 1; transaction_id < 10000; transaction_id++ ) {
    boolean bFound = false;
    for( int i = 0; i < v.size(); i++ ) {
      if( transaction_id == ((Integer)(v.elementAt(i))).intValue() ) {
        System.out.println( "skipping used id "+transaction_id );
        bFound = true;
        }
      }
    if( bFound == false ) {
      System.out.println( "id "+transaction_id+" not in use" );
      break;
      }
    }

  int subtotal_price = TotalCart(cookie);
  int shipping = TotalShipping(req, cookie);
  int total_wt = TotalWeight(req,cookie);
  int total_price = subtotal_price+shipping;
  int voided;
  if( auth.bAuthorized = true )
    voided = 0;
  else
    voided = 1;

   ssql = new String( "insert into transactions ("+
  "transaction_id, transaction_date, customer_id, web_id, void,"+
  "subtotal_price, total_weight, shipping, total_price, charge_type,"+
  "charge_id, expiration, authorization, ship_to_customer_id ) "+
  "values ("+
    transaction_id+","+
    "'"+sd+"',"+
    customer_id+","+
    (new Integer(cookie.getValues("cart_number"))).intValue()+","+
    voided+","+
    subtotal_price+","+
    total_wt+","+
    shipping+","+
    total_price+","+
    "'"+req.getParameter( "charge_type" )+"',"+
    "'"+req.getParameter( "charge_id" )+"',"+
    "'"+req.getParameter( "expiration" )+"',"+
    "'"+auth.id+"',"+
    customer_id+")"
```

```
    );
    System.out.println( ssql );
  try {
    SQLExecUpdate( ssql );
    }
  catch( SQLException se ) {
    System.out.println( "add transaction exception "+se );
    }

    v = GetCart( cookie );
    for( int i = 0; i < v.size(); i++ ) {
      ShoppingCartItem sci = (ShoppingCartItem)v.elementAt(i);
      ssql = new String( "insert into ship_items "+
        "(transaction_id, catalog_id, imprint, shipment_id, number ) "+
        "values ("+transaction_id+","+
        (new Integer(sci.catalog_id)).intValue()+
        ",'"+sci.imprint+"',0,"+
        (new Integer( sci.quantity)).intValue()+")");
      System.out.println( ssql );
      try {
        SQLExecUpdate( ssql );
        }
      catch( SQLException se ) {
        System.out.println( "add ship item exception "+se );
        }
      }

  return( transaction_id );
}
```

AddTransaction has two functions: to create a single record in the **transaction** table for this transaction and one record in the **ship_items** table for each item in the shopping cart. Before we can create the transaction record, there are three fields we need to calculate: the total weight of the shipment, the total price of the items without shipping, and the total price with shipping. We create a helper method for each.

Subtotal_price is provided by **TotalCart**, shown in Listing 6.34.

Listing 6.34 TotalCart sums the price of the items in the cart.

```
/** Return the price in pennies of all the items in the user's
    shopping cart.
@param cookie The cookie specifying the cart to be totalled.
@return The price in pennies of items in cart.
```

```
*/
int TotalCart(Cookie cookie) {
  int bigsum = 0;

    Vector v = GetCart(cookie);
    for( int i = 0; i < v.size(); i++ ) {
      try {
        ShoppingCartItem scit = (ShoppingCartItem)v.elementAt(i);
        String ssql = new String(
            "select * from catalog where catalog_id="+scit.catalog_id );
        ResultSet rs = SQLExecSelect( ssql );
        if( rs.next() == false )
          break;
        int quantity = (new Integer(scit.quantity)).intValue();
        int price = rs.getInt( "price" );
        int subtotalprice = price*quantity;
        bigsum += subtotalprice;
        rs.close();
        }
      catch( SQLException sqe ) { System.out.println("add error "+sqe );}
      }
    return( bigsum );
  }
```

TotalCart gets the shopping cart via **GetCart**, then runs through that **Vector** of **ShoppingCartItems**, getting their unit price from the database and multiplying by the quantity. Very straightforward. **TotalWeight**, shown in Listing 6.35, is very similar, running through the list of items and multiplying quantity by unit weight.

Listing 6.35 TotalWeight calculates the total weight of this transaction.

```
/** Calculate the shipping weight of this order by totalling the weights
    of all the items.
@param cookie   This customer's shopping cart.
@return The total weight of this order.
*/
int TotalWeight(HttpServletRequest req, Cookie cookie) {
  int totalwt = 0;
    String zip = req.getParameter("zip");

    Vector v = GetCart(cookie);
    for( int i = 0; i < v.size(); i++ ) {
      try {
```

```
        ShoppingCartItem scit = (ShoppingCartItem)v.elementAt(i);
        String ssql = new String(
            "select ship_wt from catalog where catalog_id="+
            scit.catalog_id );
        ResultSet rs = SQLExecSelect( ssql );
        if( rs.next() == false )
          break;
        int quantity = (new Integer(scit.quantity)).intValue();
        totalwt += quantity*rs.getInt( "ship_wt" );
        rs.close();
        }
      catch( SQLException sqe ) { System.out.println("add error "+sqe );}
      }
    return( totalwt );
  }
```

After **AddTransaction** calculates these values, it has enough information to create the transaction record. Then we run through the shopping cart, adding a single record to the **ship_items** table for each item in the shopping cart. Finally, **AddTransaction** returns the total shipping weight to **DoTransaction**.

That takes care of all the back office work of recording a transaction. All **DoTransaction** needs to do now is create a page that tells the user how the transaction went. If the transaction was authorized, we pat the user on the back and bid him good-day. If the transaction was rejected we just say there was an unspecified problem. In either case, we clear the shopping cart. Figure 6.8 shows the transaction authorized page.

What Remains To Be Done

What we haven't done is implement the back office interfaces that would make this a complete Internet business application. Specifically we'd need password-protected interfaces that would allow us to:

- Edit the catalog.
- Edit the imprints list.
- Print out shipping invoices and labels.
- Print out packing lists.
- Void transactions.

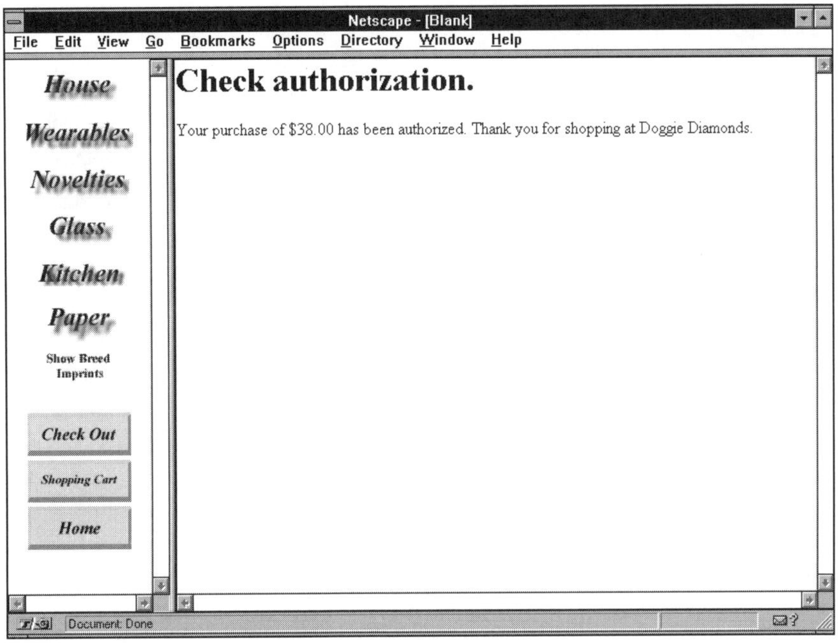

Figure 6.8 The transaction authorized page.

- Roll out old transactions.
- Report receipts for the period.
- Analyze sales data.

We also left some areas for improvement in the functionality we did implement. Specifically, were I to take this project to the next level I'd want to:

- Find a better (faster) way to generate unique customer and transaction IDs.
- Implement connection pooling.
- Implement persistent shopping carts. Take the **shoppingCarts hashTable** and store it in the database.
- Add a checkout button to the ShowFinalized page.
- Add "next" and "previous" navigation buttons to the purchase branch.
- Consolidate duplicate customer records.

These functions are left as an exercise for the reader.

Conclusion

In this chapter, we implemented the entire customer side of an Internet shopping site. The customer has full access to our entire line of products and services, and can order up, and pay for, anything we make. We've also implemented a database structure and application code that saves and links together all the data we need to fulfill those orders in the back office.

Along the way, we dealt in detail with one of the bedrock issues in Web application development: how to maintain state via the essentially stateless HTTP protocol. Using hidden fields and cookies, we passed information from one HTTP request to another to keep our application updated on what items the user had selected and what he or she wanted done with them.

We also saw a lot more JDBC, as well as an entirely new bit of Web server technology, JavaSoft's Jeeves. Using Jeeves servlets, we created a fully CGI-capable program that combines NSAPI's speed with Java's portability and ease of use. Writing only the most minimal bits of code, we created a site that produces very polished output.

Webliography

- http://home.netscape.com/newsref/std/cookie_spec.html — Netscape's cookie documentation.
- www.rodley.com:8080/DoggieDiamonds — The location of this sample application.
- www.javasoft.com/jeeves — JavaSoft's Jeeves Web server.
- www.weblogic.com — Weblogic for JDBC drivers.

part three

Chapter 7

Security

CHAPTER

7

Security

In the first six chapters, we've focused single-mindedly on providing more and better functionality to the users of our Web database applications. In this chapter, we'll step back and look at one of the key elements of providing a useful, non-stop, publicly accessible application: security. Thorough coverage of Web server security is beyond the scope of this book. You could easily write a very large book on that topic alone. Instead, this chapter points out areas for Web administrators to focus on, and addresses in detail some of the ways that Web application-writers can bulletproof their work.

Security means different things to different people. We'll define security in its broadest sense: ensuring that our application looks and acts the way we intended at all times, that our data is not altered in ways we didn't intend, that our information cannot be stolen, and that our Web machine is not used in any manner other than to serve our application.

We'll start off looking at the topography of our application (*where* different components like the Web server and database are located) and how we can modify it to achieve better security. Then we'll look at each of the components—operating system, Web server, database server, and application—to see how the peculiar vulnerabilities of each can be minimized or even eliminated.

Topology

The first thing we need to think about when it comes to security is where the pieces of our Web solution—Web server and database—reside in relation to our corporate LAN. The public access-point for our application is our Web server, and we assume that the Web server is insecure. The aim of secure topology, then, is to isolate the Web server, which is assumed to be insecure, from the corporate LAN, which must be kept secure. Only a few topologies are worth discussing:

- *Orphan.* This topology, shown in Figure 7.1, places the Web server and database on a machine completely unconnected to the corporate LAN. In this configuration, the corporate LAN and Web server machine are

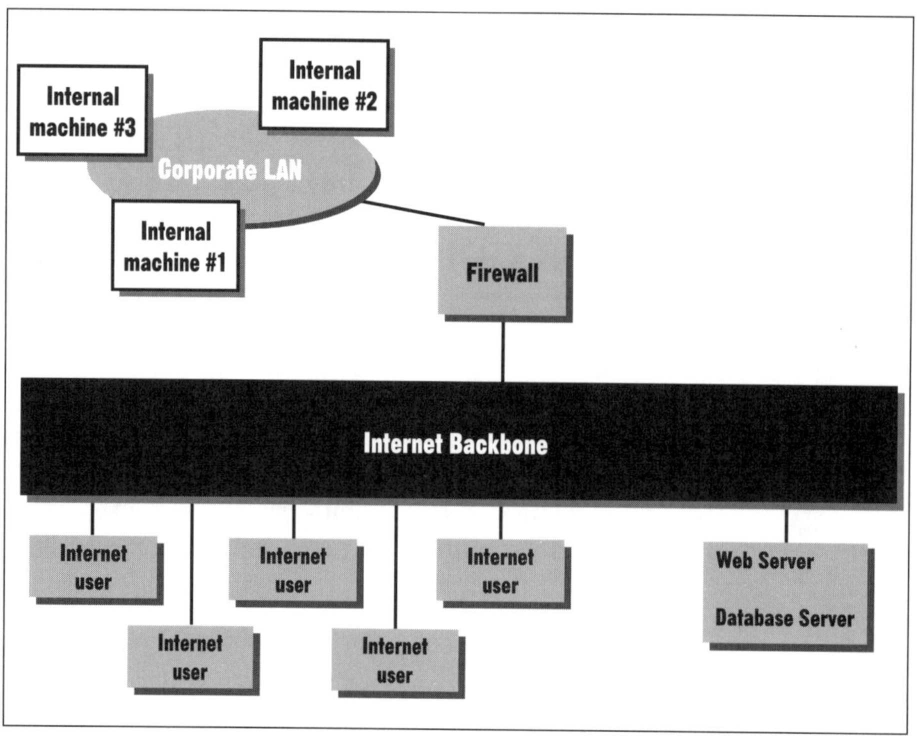

Figure 7.1 The orphan topology is the safest security option.

no more related to one another than any two other machines on the Internet. This is the safest option of all, allowing you to build a fortress around the corporate LAN without worrying about letting Web traffic through. With the increasing availability and affordability of Web serverco-location (where you "locate" a standalone server at a service provider's site and on their local network), you should think long and hard before discarding this option.

- *Sacrificial lamb.* This topology, shown in Figure 7.2, places both the Web server and database on a machine outside the corporate LAN, with the firewall between them and the corporate LAN. With the exception of the orphan option, this is probably the safest topology. The firewall can be very restrictive on inbound packets without crippling either the Web server or the corporate LAN.

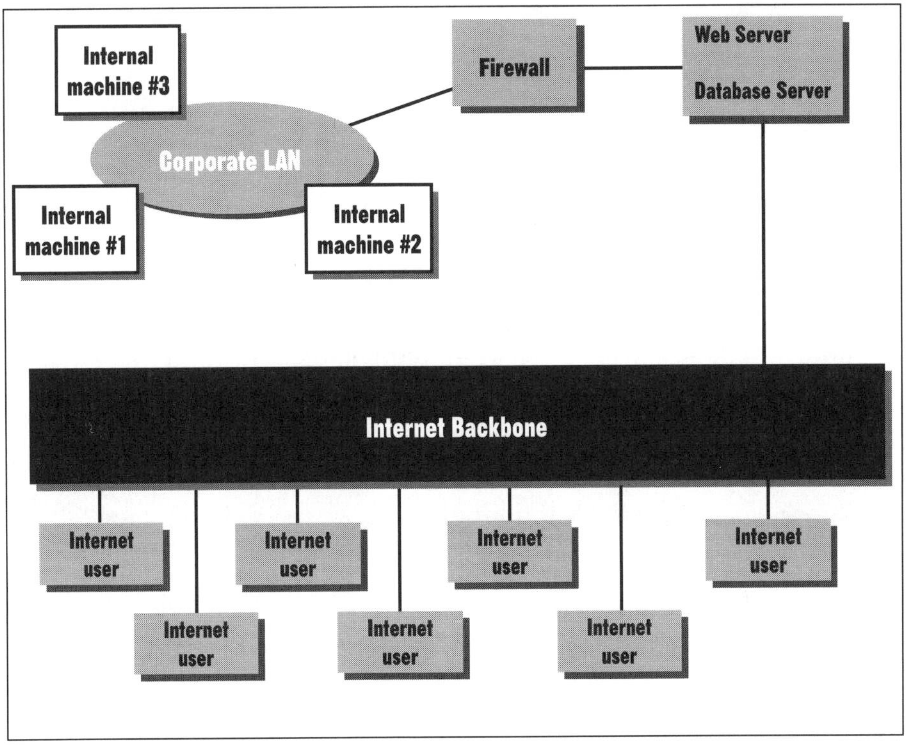

Figure 7.2 The sacrificial-lamb topology is not as safe as the orphan topology, but can still be quite restrictive.

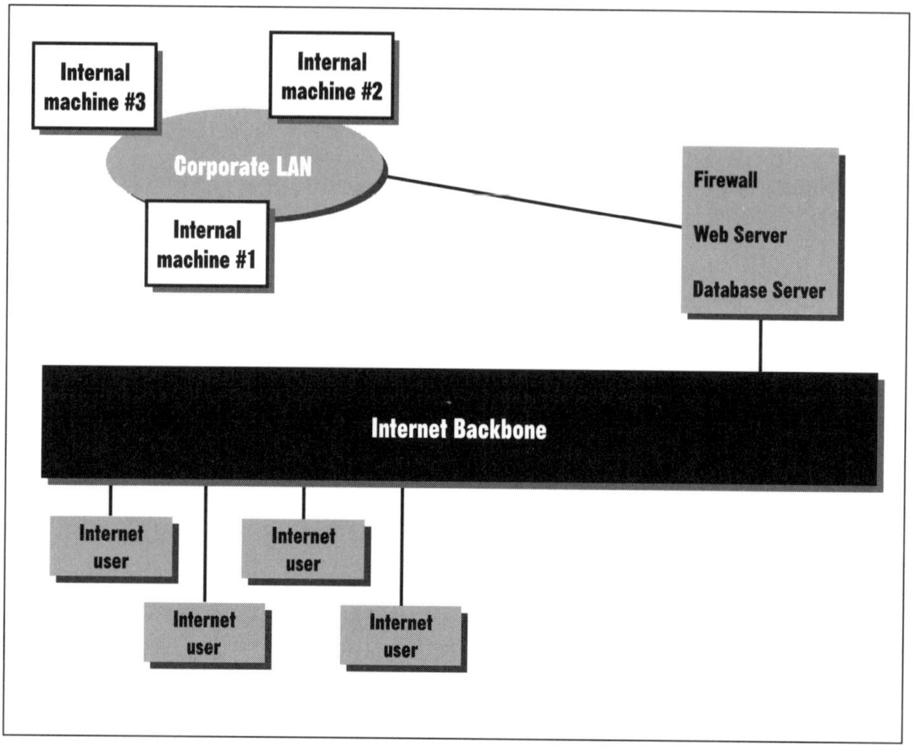

Figure 7.3 The firefence topology is common but controversial.

- *Firefence.* This topology, shown in Figure 7.3, puts the Web server and database *on* the firewall machine. This practice is both extremely common and extremely controversial. While it saves the cost of a separate firewall machine, it is significantly less safe than the separate firewall options. Why? In this topology, anyone who breaks into the Web server has, by definition, also broken into the firewall. From there, the leap into the corporate LAN is quite short.
- *Inaccessible.* This topology, shown in Figure 7.4, puts the Web server and database inside the firewall. This protects the Web server all right—by making it completely inaccessible to the outside world. While fine for intranets, this topology is not useful for publicly accessible sites.

There are infinite variations on these topologies. Many variations rely on "tunneling" techniques. In one typical tunneling topology, shown in Figure 7.5, the Web server is configured as a sacrificial lamb, but then we install a

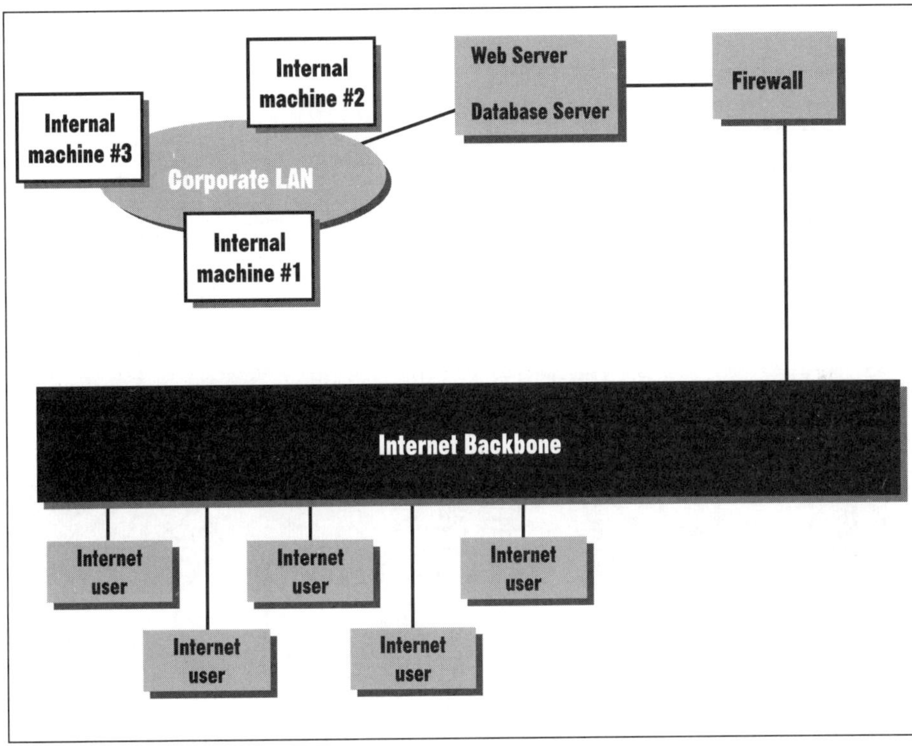

Figure 7.4 This topology is impractical for publicly accessible sites.

"tunnel" through the firewall to a database server machine on the corporate LAN inside the firewall. This tunnel configures the firewall to ignore database network traffic while maintaining the same restrictions on other traffic.

There are situations where tunneling is an attractive option. Consider, for instance, the case where our database contains mission-critical data that must be maintained by users within the corporate LAN. We could hardly stick this database out on an orphan or sacrificial lamb machine (without becoming sacrificial lambs ourselves). A tunnel is virtually the only halfway secure option.

Keep in mind, though, that when you open a tunnel you can never be certain what traffic is going to go through it. By definition, a tunnel is a security risk. It also violates the KISS rule ("keep it simple, stupid"). Adding a tunnel to an already complex firewall adds a mechanism that might be exploited by intruders.

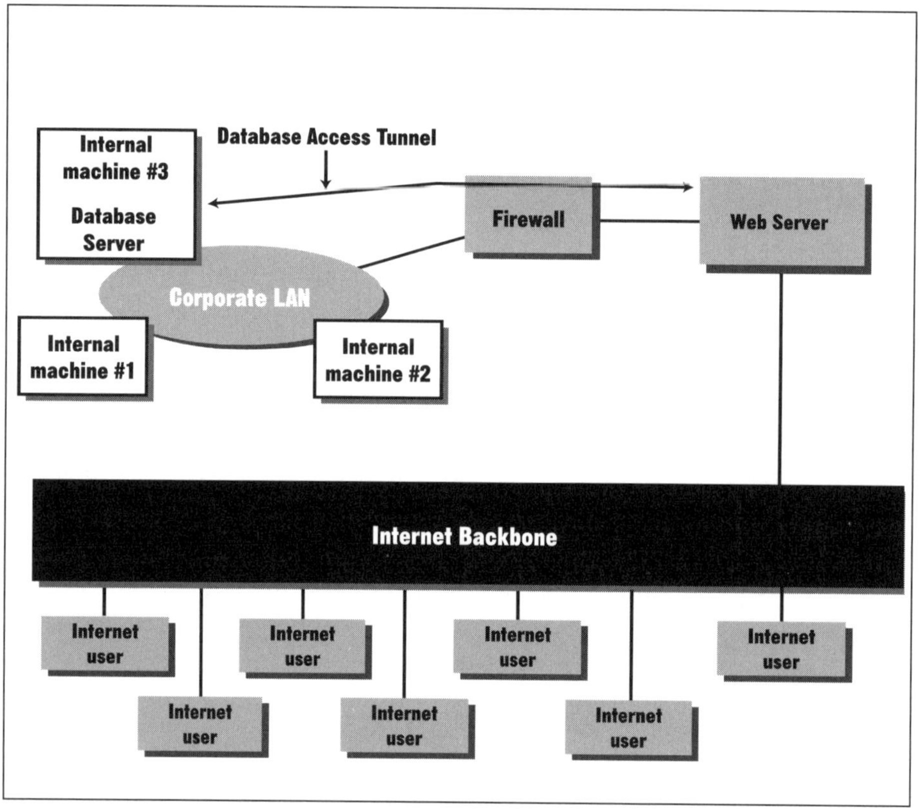

Figure 7.5 This is a typical tunneling topology.

So tunnels are useful, but problematic. Is there any way to protect the mission-critical database while still making it available on the Web? Many sites have adopted the drastic but effective strategy of maintaining mirror databases. One database lives on a machine within the firewall and serves as the record copy, while the mirror database lives on the Web server machine outside the firewall. The success of this strategy hinges on having some reliable and secure mechanism of keeping the internal and external databases in sync. The same strategy can be applied to the Web server itself, keeping internal and external copies of the entire Web site. Mirrors, of course, can turn into a huge operational nightmare.

This brief discussion of the topology problem shows why network administrators don't smile much. It's never a question of whether a site is secure or insecure, but what compromises we make to gain certain bits of security. None of the solutions are very good. They are all just more or less unsatisfactory.

Operating System And Network OS Security

A comprehensive discussion of security under any particular OS would take up an entire volume of its own, and we don't have that kind of space here. What we can talk about, though, are common multiuser system administration issues. No discussion of security would be complete without mentioning a few commonsense rules for baseline security. If you have any system administration experience (or a modicum of common sense), you should probably skip to the next section before I insult your intelligence.

- Do not run unnecessary network daemons. The most common open-door daemons are FTP and Telnet, but many other programs, including most network administration tools, also monitor IP ports. Any daemon accepting connections on an IP port is a security risk. Thus, hackers will often try to connect on every port on a system just to discover which daemons are running. A tool that logs attempted port connections is an absolute must for a secure Web site.
- Do not define unnecessary users. A login that sits around unused and unnoticed is an invitation to abuse.
- Enforce strict password security, including non-word passwords and frequent password changes.
- Monitor your log files. Nothing will lose you your job faster than a break-in that got logged, but ignored. Most operating systems and applications log unusual events. Windows NT's event logs, server access logs, and error logs contain a lot of good information. Use it.

These are just a few of the basic rules of network system administration. Depending on how popular and public your system is, you will probably need to pay much more attention to OS and NOS security issues.

Database Security

Like most database systems, SQL Server provides its own user-authentication system entirely distinct from the operating system's username/password authentication system. It does this primarily because the notion of a "database connection" is not built into most local or network operating systems. For instance, a program on one machine can open a connection to a database on another machine simply by referencing that machine's name and the database name. This is why, in all our database access code so far, we've always provided a machine name to the database connection call.

A user making a database connection to a database on our machine does not exist as a local user on our machine. All he has is a network pipeline to the instance of SQL Server running on our machine. Thus, SQL Server has to provide a method to authenticate that user and restrict his activities.

SQL Server provides two styles of authentication, *standard* and *integrated.* Standard security implements a set of usernames and passwords entirely separate from Windows NT's usernames and passwords. Integrated security uses Windows NT's usernames and passwords to authenticate database connections. The thing to remember about integrated security is that it only uses NT's authentication services to determine that a particular username/password combination is valid. After that rather cursory check, all the security issues are handled by SQL Server, not NT. So the difference between integrated and standard security is simply whether SQL Server or Windows NT authenticates the username/password combination. After that authentication, which occurs just once when you make the connection to the database, all security checks are handled by SQL Server.

Once you're past the authentication step at connection time, what defenses does SQL Server provide? For each database table there are four types of access: insert, update, select, and delete. For each user, you can specify whether or not each of these SQL statements can be run against the table. For example, if user webster has insert, select, and delete permission on table shortdog, he or she can run this statement:

```
insert into shortdog values ( 'RIN TIN TIN', ….
```

However, the user cannot run the statement

```
update shortdog set NAME='RIN TIN TIN' where NAME='RIN TIN TON'
```

because update permission against that table has not been granted.

The same sort of permission applies to columns within tables. For each column in the table, two types of access—select and update—can be granted or revoked. If, for example, webster has update but not select permission on the NAME column, then the statement

```
update shortdog set NAME='RIN TIN TIN' where SNAME='CHARLIE'
```

will run, but the statement

```
select * from shortdog where NAME='RIN TIN TIN'
```

will not run because it requires selecting the row based on the NAME column.

That's a brief overview of SQL Server's security system. Now, let's look at how it applies to our applications. Back in the Newfoundland Dog Database, we embedded a username and password in our HTML code. Our CGI code read these values from the GET or POST arguments and used them to create the database connection. While handy for test and debugging purposes, in an operational system, this method is an invitation to disaster.

Remember that simply by knowing the machine name, username, and password, we can create an ODBC connection to the database. Thus, publishing them in the HTML source is truly dopey. With these values in hand, an intruder can write his own program that makes the ODBC connection and wreaks havoc on our database. So, we have to take those values out of the HTML source and hide them back on the server. We'll look at our source modified to do this later on.

The next thing to look at is what username and password we're using. For test purposes, we used the reserved value **sa** (which stands for *system administrator*). By default, **sa** has all permissions on all objects in the SQL Server system. Again, this is fine for a test, but highly irresponsible for actual operations. We need a new user who has only the permissions that are

Table 7.1 These are the permissions in the Newfoundland Database.

Table name	Select	Insert	Update	Delete
usage		X		
shortdog	X			
newdog	X	X		

absolutely necessary for the CGI programs to run. Table 7.1 shows the permissions our Newfoundland Dog Database CGI program needs to do its job.

As you can see, given the nature of what we're trying to accomplish in the CGI programs, we can be extremely restrictive in granting table-level permissions. We could be even more restrictive, by specifying column-level permissions on shortdog and newdog. In that case, we'd grant our user no update permission and select permission only on the columns QUOTENO, NAME, SNAME, DNAME, AFFIX, and COUNTRY. For our purposes, though, column-level permissions are overkill and not likely to be worth the trouble.

We've created a very restricted user, and hidden the username and password from prying eyes. What other steps can we take to keep the database safe? One of the easiest steps is to *not* create an ODBC data source attached to the database. Without a defined ODBC data source, remote users can't make an ODBC connection to the database even if they do have the machine name, username, and password.

I would also recommend *not* using an integrated login for web database CGI access. Remember that an integrated login is a username/password that is valid both for an operating system login *and* a database connection. If an intruder manages, somehow, to pry the username and password out of our CGI executable, we don't want the intruder to be able to use this to log into the machine and get a command prompt. This is the essence of defense in depth—avoiding administrative shortcuts that make the intruder's job easier.

Can People Steal My Data?

Whether people can steal your data is an interesting question, because when you put a database up on the Web, you're actually asking people to steal your data. Consider the Newfoundland Dog Database of Chapters 2 through 4. The data is there, and we present people with an easy way to get it. Obviously, the question is not whether we want people to take data, but to what purpose?

Users should be allowed to run queries for their own information, but we don't want people downloading the entire database through the query facility, then opening their own site using our data. This problem illustrates one of the basic principles of security, namely, that absolute security is not an achievable goal. What you want to do is to increase the cost of theft to the point where it is not worth the effort.

For the Newfoundland Dog Database, this requires taking a hard look at the queries we support, to make sure that they don't inadvertently facilitate large-scale data theft. Within the database, we supply the following queries:

- All dogs by sire
- All dogs by dame
- All dogs by kennel
- All dogs by exact name
- All dogs by name-fragment
- Family tree by exact name

The first problem we notice is that none of these queries limit the number of records they return. While no query *should* return a huge number of records, putting a hard limit on the number of records returned is an absolute prerequisite for a secure site. This is accomplished easily enough, by putting a simple counter into our fetch loop and exiting the loop if the counter is exceeded, as in Listing 7.1.

Listing 7.1 This is an example of simple response-limiting in the Newfoundland Dog Database.

```
/* Query - Run the actual query to retrieve data
from the db and emit HTML results based on that
data.
*/
#define MAX_RECORDS 200
void Query(int style) {
  int i = 0;
```

```
int numcolumns;
int count = 0;

// Prepare the statement and open a cursor
EXEC SQL PREPARE stmt1 FROM :select_cmd;
EXEC SQL OPEN C1;

// Records from shortdog (VERIFIED) have one more
// field (the update button) than records from
// newdog. This sets up an array of table column
// data fields for our HTML output function to use.
// The HTML row output function uses the values
// in the variables pointed to by the cols array
// to fill in the table. So here, we set up the
// array to point to our host variables.
if( style == VERIFIED )
 cols[i++] = update_link;
cols[i++] = plink;
cols[i++] = description;
cols[i++] = headstone;
cols[i++] = slink;
cols[i++] = dlink;
cols[i++] = BREEDER;
cols[i++] = OWNER;
cols[i++] = REGNO;
cols[i++] = COUNTRY;
cols[i++] = TITLES;
cols[i++] = CHDATE;
cols[i++] = JWOB;
cols[i++] = JWDATE;
cols[i++] = DOB2;
cols[i++] = RECESSIVE;
cols[i++] = kennel_link;
cols[i++] = REMARKS;
cols[i++] = HIPTOT;
cols[i++] = HIPR;
cols[i++] = HIPL;
cols[i++] = DOB;
cols[i++] = DIED;
cols[i++] = HDCERT;
cols[i++] = HIPS;
cols[i++] = OFANO;
cols[i++] = OVCNO;
cols[i++] = KCBVAEYE;
cols[i++] = TATTOO;
cols[i++] = HEARTGRADE;
```

```
cols[i++] = SOURCE;
cols[i++] = SB;
cols[i++] = WORKAREA;
cols[i++] = CHANGEDATE;
cols[i++] = CHANGETEXT;
cols[i++] = SEX;
cols[i++] = COLOUR;
cols[i++] = QUOTENO;
numcolumns = i;

// Make all column data centered.
for( i = 0; i < MAX_COLUMNS; i++ )
 alignments[i] = "CENTER";

// Go through all the rows, fetching the data
// and outputting HTML to represent it.
rownum = 0;
while (1) {
 if( count++ >= MAX_RECORDS )
   break;
 EXEC SQL FETCH C1 INTO
...
```

We define a maximum number of records that can be returned, 200. We increment it in the **fetch** loop, and break out of the **fetch** loop if the counter is exceeded. In reality, waiting for even a 200-record table to come over the wire at 28,800bps is excruciating. The average user should not be unduly inconvenienced by this limitation.

With that safeguard in place, we can analyze our queries and see if we left any openings for a data thief. Since sire, dame, kennel, and exact name are all implemented using the SQL construct "WHERE <field_name>=<value>", a thief would have to run a huge number of such queries to steal any amount of data, and could not possibly know what query values to use to get the whole database. Thus, those queries seem safe. The family-tree-by-exact-name query doesn't return individual records, so it wouldn't be useful to a data thief.

That leaves us with the all-dogs-by-name-fragment query. Back in Chapter 3, we discussed limiting the number of responses to this query by requiring users to enter at least six characters of the dog's name. By itself, this is a very effective restriction. To download the entire database, a data thief would have to construct 26^6 individual queries, clearly a prohibitively expensive (though not impossible) adventure. The real problem with this query, though, lies in the implementation of the SQL query itself.

Simplified, the actual SQL statement says

```
SELECT * FROM SHORTDOG WHERE NAME LIKE %<value>%
```

where *<value>* is whatever value the user entered in the query criteria form. So, for instance, if the user enters NAUTILUS in the query criteria form, the query comes out as:

```
SELECT * FROM SHORTDOG WHERE NAME LIKE %NAUTILUS%
```

The percent signs that bracket the user's search criteria tell SQL Server to return all records that have the string NAUTILUS preceded by any value (the leading percent sign) and/or followed by any value (the trailing percent sign). This is all well and good, a neat bit of functionality. What happens, though, if the user enters the value %%%%%%?

Oops. Using ISQLW, try entering this query against your copy of the Newfoundland Dog Database:

```
SELECT * FROM SHORTDOG WHERE NAME LIKE %%%%%%
```

As you might expect, SQL Server blithely returns all the records in the database. This is, of course, unacceptable.

Our response-limiting code in Listing 7.1 is a good start toward thwarting this kind of theft. What this analysis reveals, though, is a bigger problem. We're allowing users to write their own SQL statement in a very limited way, by giving them unchecked control over the value that appears between the percent signs in the query. What we really ought to do is strip that value of any and all non-alphabetic characters, just to be sure that users can't slip some bit of SQL past us. Listing 7.2 shows the original version of NormalizeName and a new version modified to do just that.

Listing 7.2 The insecure NormalizeName and a version modified to strip non-alphabetic characters.

```
/* The insecure version. */
void NormalizeName( char *OutputName, char *InputName ) {
   int i, k;
```

```
   k = 0;
   for( i = 0; InputName[i] != '\0'; i++ ) {
      if( InputName[i] == '\'' )
         continue;
      OutputName[k++] = toupper( InputName[i] );
      }
   }

/* The insecure version modified to strip non-alpha chars. */
void NormalizeName( char *OutputName, char *InputName, int length ) {
  int i, k;

  if( strlen( InputName ) >= length ) {
   OutputName[0] = '\0';
   fprintf( errfp, "INPUT BUFFER OVERFLOW ATTACK\
   NormalizeName( --,%s,%d)\n", InputName, length );
   return;
   }

  k = 0;
  for( i = 0; InputName[i] != '\0'; i++ ) {
     if( InputName[i] == '\'' )
        continue;
     if( !isalpha( InputName[i] ))
                                    continue;
   OutputName[k++] = toupper( InputName[i] );
   }
  }
```

Back in **ProcessArgs**, **NormalizeName** is called to set **sought_name**, which, in turn, is the variable that gets copied into the SQL statement that runs the search.

This gives you an idea of how to think about the ways in which you present data on the Web. With a couple of simple modifications, we've secured the Newfoundland Dog Database against the most simple forms of large-scale data theft. Such data theft is the easiest and most common form of Web attack. It is not, however, the only danger our Web applications face.

Web Server Security

The Web server software is the point of public access to our application. Thus, it is usually, though not always, the starting point for any sort of attack. Web servers are also fairly complex programs, designed to provide (to the right people), precisely the sort of access that hackers seek to abuse. On top of that, with the wild proliferation of Web servers (470,000 according to the October 1996 NetCraft Web Server Survey), we now have a huge set of novice Web server administrators. These administrators often have no experience in fending off the kinds of attacks that military and university network administrators have been dealing with for years. A new systems administrator versus an experienced and determined hacker is a very unequal match.

The assumption I've made all through this book is that our database application is the only application running on this Web server. This Web server installation exists solely to present our application to the world. This model fits a lot of situations in the world today, and fails to fit a lot of others. If our Web server is dedicated solely to our application, then there are a number of steps we can take to limit our vulnerability to attack:

- Remove unused associations. Most Web servers (though not some versions of Netscape) use the operating system's application associations to decide what program to run when a CGI script is called. For example, what happens if a Web user invokes the script http://www.myhome.com/cgi-bin/xyz.pl? The Web server first asks the operating system what application the file extension .pl is associated with. The operating system typically has a perl interpreter associated with pl files. If the operating system has that association, the Web server invokes the perl interpreter with xyz.pl as the only argument. If we don't configure our operating system with that application-file extension association, then either that CGI invocation fails, or it returns the file xyz.pl as a byte stream (which does a hacker no good at all).
- Remove unused programs, especially interpreters and command shells. A hacker can't abuse an application that doesn't exist on your machine.

These steps are problematic if you're administering a machine that serves more than one application. You can still take them, but they're more difficult and time-consuming, and less effective. There are, however, a few precautions that more complex Web servers can take to make hacking more difficult:

- Keep all CGI executables in one directory. There is usually a configuration option in the Web server to either have a single CGI directory or to allow CGIs in any directory. Keeping all CGIs in one directory makes watching it easier, and thus more likely.

- Only allow CGIs to which you have the source. This will deter malicious CGIs and allow you to inspect for obvious "hack-ability."
- Run the Web server in a **chroot** environment. On Unix systems, **chroot** changes the application's notion of what the root directory of the file system is. Thus, if we say "chroot /usr/" and then run the Web server, the Web server itself and any CGI program it executes will see /usr as /. It will be unable to see any directory above /usr.
- Disallow server-side includes. We'll talk a little more about server-side includes later on. For now, suffice to say that SSIs allow HTML authors to execute programs from within their HTML source. The SSI program itself is CGI-compliant and generates HTML that gets plopped into the spot in the original HTML file where the include statement was invoked. Especially on systems where shell scripting is the favored programming mode, SSIs can be a significant risk.

Buffer Overflow

One of the most popular methods of attacking a Web server is to try to overflow the input buffer of a CGI program. The point is to try to crash the CGI program. Why bother crashing the CGI program? What often happens on Unix systems when you crash a CGI program is that you're left at a command shell running with whatever privileges the Web server has (or better). This command-shell access is the goal of hackers. Once they can run programs on your machine, you are a very short step away from disaster. At the very least, an intruder with this kind of access to your Web server can reconfigure your Web site (as hackers have done to the CIA and the Department of Justice) to display whatever they want the public to see and put you out of business for as long as it takes to discover the problem.

What do we mean by overflowing input buffers? Again, let's look back at the Newfoundland Dog Database. Where does it get user input from? The only user input to the database comes via the GET and POST arguments. The original version of the function **PostArguments**, shown again in Listing 7.3, reads **stdin** to get the user's input.

Listing 7.3 PostArguments reads stdin for user input.

```
/************** ARGUMENT PROCESSING CODE ****************/

// The maximum number of arguments we'll accept
#define MAX_ARGS        50

/* Grab all the input we can from standard input, stuff it
into a string, then pass that string to ProcessArgs. */
void PostArguments() {
   int length;
   char *qs;
   char buffer[1024];
   int i;

   // Find the length of the stream coming in over stdin
   qs = getenv( "CONTENT_LENGTH" );
   if( qs == NULL )
      return;
   length = atoi( qs );

   // Read the appropriate number of bytes from stdin
   for( i = 0; i < length; i++ )
      buffer[i] = getchar();
   // Don't forget to null terminate the string.
   buffer[i] = '\0';

   // Now buffer looks just like it would have if
   // we had gotten it via getenv("QUERY_STRING")
   // so send it to ProcessArgs.
   ProcessArgs( buffer );
}
```

What happens if the variable length is greater than 1,024? Under Windows NT, we'll most likely throw an exception in the loop that reads characters into a buffer. That, however, is not guaranteed, and we could just as easily crash the machine or end up at a command prompt. The correct way to do this is shown in Listing 7.4.

Listing 7.4 This is the right way to read POST arguments from stdin.

```
/* Grab all the input we can from standard input, stuff it
into a string, then pass that string to ProcessArgs. */
void PostArguments() {
```

```
    int length;
    char *qs;
    char *buffer;
    int i;

    // Find the length of the stream coming in over stdin
    qs = getenv( "CONTENT_LENGTH" );
    if( qs == NULL )
       return;
    length = atoi( qs );

    // Allocate a buffer big enough to hold the arguments
    if(( buffer = malloc( length+1 )) == NULL )
                                 return;
    // Null terminate the string
    buffer[length] = '\0';

    // Read the appropriate number of bytes from stdin
    for( i = 0; i < length; i++ )
       buffer[i] = getchar();
    // Don't forget to null terminate the string. Redundant.
    buffer[i] = '\0';

    // Now buffer looks just like it would have if
    // we had gotten it via getenv("QUERY_STRING")
    // so send it to ProcessArgs.
    ProcessArgs( buffer );
    // Free the dynamically allocated string
    free( buffer );
}
```

Instead of using a statically sized character array, we allocate a buffer from free memory to hold exactly the number of characters we read from **stdin**. This protects us from a buffer overflow attack that simply provides a giant, nonsensical POST argument. Our argument processing contains another, more serious version of the buffer overflow problem in **ProcessArgs**. Listing 7.5 shows **ProcessArgs** up to the point where it saves the argument, **QUOTENO**.

Listing 7.5 ProcessArgs gets the argument, QUOTENO.

```
/* Process the string of arguments passed in via the qs
  argument. */
void ProcessArgs( char *qs ) {
   char *key[MAX_ARGS];
   char *ptr, *ptr1, *qs1;
```

```
char *value[MAX_ARGS];
char achar[3];
int srcindex = 0;
int destindex = 0;
int i,j,k;
int index = 0;

// Convert all the special chars into their actuals
ptr1 = FixString( qs );
if( ptr1 == NULL ) {
   fprintf( errfp, "bad strdup\n" );
   exit( 1 );
   }

qs1 = ptr1;

// Null out the entire value array.
for( i = 0; i < MAX_ARGS; i++ )
   value[i] = NULL;

// March through the name/value pair string replacing
// any instance of '&' or '=' with a string terminator.
// Since the string is of the form:
//    key=value&key1=value1&key2=value2
// this algorithm can quickly turn the string into
// two arrays of character pointers, one array for keys
// and one for values.
for( i = 0; i < MAX_ARGS; i++ ) {
   key[i] = qs1;
   ptr = strchr( qs1, '=' );
   if( ptr == NULL )
      break;
   *ptr = '\0';
   ptr++;
   value[i] = ptr;

   ptr = strchr( ptr, '&' );
   if( ptr == NULL )
      break;
   *ptr = '\0';
   ptr++;
   qs1 = ptr;
   }

index = 0;
for( j = 0; j < MAX_ARGS; j++ ) {
   if( key[j] == NULL || (value[j] == NULL ))
```

```
          continue;
       if( strlen( value[j] ) == 0 )
          continue;

       if( strcmp( value[j], "any" ) == 0 )
          continue;

       // The application enforces certain rules for dog
       // names, so we call NormalizeName to deal with
       // the incoming dog name.
       if( strcmp( key[j], "dog.text" ) == 0 ) {
          NormalizeName( sought_name, value[j] );
       continue;
       }
    if( strcmp( key[j], "NAME" ) == 0 ) {
          NormalizeName( NAME, value[j] );
          strcpy( sought_name, NAME );
          StripChar( NAME, '\'' );
          continue;
          }

       if( strcmp( key[j], "QUOTENO" ) == 0 ) {
          strcpy( QUOTENO, value[j] );
          continue;
          }
```

Let's ignore the **NAME** argument for now, and consider the simpler case of **QUOTENO**. By now, you should already be suspicious of any call to **strcpy**, and this one is no exception. **QUOTENO** is a statically sized SQL host variable, while **value[j]** is just a piece of the dynamically sized string argument, **qs**. There is no guarantee that **value[j]** will fit into **QUOTENO**. If you look back at Listing 2.8, you'll see that we use this construction for all the possible arguments, thus presenting the persistent intruder with innumerable opportunities to try the buffer-overflow hack. To deal with this, we need to compare the string length of **value[j]** to the size of the host variable we're copying it into. Listing 7.6 shows the new version of **ProcessArgs**.

Listing 7.6 Here is the fixed version of ProcessArgs.

```
#define STRCPY(d,s)if(strlen(s)<sizeof(d)){strcpy(d,s);}\
else{fprintf(errfp,"BUFFER OVERFLOW ATTACK %s=%s\n",key[j],value[j]);}

/* Process the string of arguments passed in via the qs
   argument. */
```

```
void ProcessArgs( char *qs ) {
   char *key[MAX_ARGS];
   char *ptr, *ptr1, *qs1;
   char *value[MAX_ARGS];
   char achar[3];
   int srcindex = 0;
   int destindex = 0;
   int i,j,k;
   int index = 0;

   // Convert all the special chars into their actuals.
   ptr1 = FixString( qs );
   if( ptr1 == NULL ) {
      fprintf( errfp, "bad strdup\n" );
      exit( 1 );
      }

   qs1 = ptr1;

   // Null out the entire value array.
   for( i = 0; i < MAX_ARGS; i++ )
      value[i] = NULL;

   // March through the name/value pair string replacing
   // any instance of '&' or '=' with a string terminator.
   // Since the string is of the form
   //    key=value&key1=value1&key2=value2,
   // this algorithm can quickly turn the string into
   // two arrays of character pointers, one array for keys
   // and one for values.
   for( i = 0; i < MAX_ARGS; i++ ) {
      key[i] = qs1;
      ptr = strchr( qs1, '=' );
      if( ptr == NULL )
         break;
      *ptr = '\0';
      ptr++;
      value[i] = ptr;

      ptr = strchr( ptr, '&' );
      if( ptr == NULL )
         break;
      *ptr = '\0';
      ptr++;
      qs1 = ptr;
      }
```

```
index = 0;
for( j = 0; j < MAX_ARGS; j++ ) {
   if( key[j] == NULL || (value[j] == NULL ))
      continue;
   if( strlen( value[j] ) == 0 )
      continue;

   if( strcmp( value[j], "any" ) == 0 )
      continue;

   // The application enforces certain rules for dog names, so we call
   // NormalizeName to deal with the incoming dog name.
   if( strcmp( key[j], "dog.text" ) == 0 ) {
      NormalizeName( sought_name, value[j], sizeof(sought_name) );
      continue;
      }
   if( strcmp( key[j], "NAME" ) == 0 ) {
      NormalizeName( NAME, value[j],sizeof(NAME) );
      strcpy( sought_name, NAME );
      StripChar( NAME, '\'' );
      continue;
      }

   if( strcmp( key[j], "QUOTENO" ) == 0 ) {
       STRCPY( QUOTENO, value[j] );
       continue;
       }
   if( strcmp( key[j], "CHANGEDATE" ) == 0 ) {
       STRCPY( CHANGEDATE, value[j] );
       continue;
       }
   if( strcmp( key[j], "CHANGETEXT" ) == 0 ) {
       STRCPY( CHANGETEXT, value[j] );
       continue;
       }
   if( strcmp( key[j], "REGNO" ) == 0 ) {
       STRCPY( REGNO, value[j] );
       continue;
       }
   if( strcmp( key[j], "COUNTRY" ) == 0 ) {
       STRCPY( COUNTRY, value[j] );
       continue;
       }
   if( strcmp( key[j], "TITLES" ) == 0 ) {
       STRCPY( TITLES, value[j] );
       continue;
       }
```

```
if( strcmp( key[j], "CHDATE" ) == 0 ) {
    STRCPY( CHDATE, value[j] );
    continue;
    }
if( strcmp( key[j], "JWOB" ) == 0 ) {
    STRCPY( JWOB, value[j] );
    continue;
    }
if( strcmp( key[j], "JWDATE" ) == 0 ) {
    STRCPY( JWDATE, value[j] );
    continue;
    }
if( strcmp( key[j], "DOB" ) == 0 ) {
    STRCPY( DOB, value[j] );
    continue;
    }
if( strcmp( key[j], "DOB2" ) == 0 ) {
    STRCPY( DOB2, value[j] );
    continue;
    }
if( strcmp( key[j], "SEX" ) == 0 ) {
    STRCPY( SEX, value[j] );
    continue;
    }
if( strcmp( key[j], "SNAME" ) == 0 ) {
  NormalizeName( SNAME, value[j],sizeof(SNAME) );
  StripChar( SNAME, '\'' );
    continue;
    }
if( strcmp( key[j], "DNAME" ) == 0 ) {
   NormalizeName( DNAME, value[j],sizeof(DNAME) );
   StripChar( DNAME, '\'' );
   continue;
   }
if( strcmp( key[j], "COLOUR" ) == 0 ) {
   STRCPY( COLOUR, value[j] );
 if( strcmp( COLOUR, "Landseer" ) == 0 )
   STRCPY( COLOUR, "WH&BL" );
   continue;
   }
if( strcmp( key[j], "RECESSIVE" ) == 0 ) {
   STRCPY( RECESSIVE, value[j] );
   continue;
   }
if( strcmp( key[j], "OWNER" ) == 0 ) {
   STRCPY( OWNER, value[j] );
```

```
continue;
   }
if( strcmp( key[j], "AFFIX" ) == 0 ) {
   NormalizeName( AFFIX, value[j],sizeof(AFFIX) );
   StripChar( AFFIX, '\'' );
   continue;
   }
if( strcmp( key[j], "BREEDER" ) == 0 ) {
    STRCPY( BREEDER, value[j] );
    continue;
    }
if( strcmp( key[j], "REMARKS" ) == 0 ) {
    STRCPY( REMARKS, value[j] );
    continue;
    }
if( strcmp( key[j], "HIPTOT" ) == 0 ) {
    STRCPY( HIPTOT, value[j] );
    continue;
    }
if( strcmp( key[j], "HIPR" ) == 0 ) {
    STRCPY( HIPR, value[j] );
    continue;
    }
if( strcmp( key[j], "HIPL" ) == 0 ) {
    STRCPY( HIPL, value[j] );
    continue;
    }
if( strcmp( key[j], "DIED" ) == 0 ) {
    STRCPY( DIED, value[j] );
    continue;
    }
if( strcmp( key[j], "HDCERT" ) == 0 ) {
    STRCPY( HDCERT, value[j] );
    continue;
    }
if( strcmp( key[j], "HIPS" ) == 0 ) {
    STRCPY( HIPS, value[j] );
    continue;
    }
if( strcmp( key[j], "OFANO" ) == 0 ) {
    STRCPY( OFANO, value[j] );
    continue;
    }
if( strcmp( key[j], "OVCNO" ) == 0 ) {
    STRCPY( OVCNO, value[j] );
```

```
        continue;
        }
    if( strcmp( key[j], "KCBVAEYE" ) == 0 ) {
        STRCPY( KCBVAEYE, value[j] );
        continue;
        }
    if( strcmp( key[j], "TATTOO" ) == 0 ) {
        STRCPY( TATTOO, value[j] );
        continue;
        }
    if( strcmp( key[j], "HEARTGRADE" ) == 0 ) {
        STRCPY( HEARTGRADE, value[j] );
        continue;
        }
    if( strcmp( key[j], "SOURCE" ) == 0 ) {
        STRCPY( SOURCE, value[j] );
        continue;
        }
    if( strcmp( key[j], "SB" ) == 0 ) {
        STRCPY( SB, value[j] );
        continue;
        }
    if( strcmp( key[j], "WORKAREA" ) == 0 ) {
        STRCPY( WORKAREA, value[j] );
        continue;
        }
    if( strcmp( key[j], "SRCADDRESS" ) == 0 ) {
        STRCPY( SRCADDRESS, value[j] );
        continue;
        }
    if( strcmp( key[j], "SRCEMAIL" ) == 0 ) {
        STRCPY( SRCEMAIL, value[j] );
        continue;
        }
    if( strcmp( key[j], "FAMILIAR" ) == 0 ) {
       STRCPY( FAMILIAR, value[j] );
       continue;
       }
    if( strcmp( key[j], "SITE" ) == 0 ) {
       STRCPY( SITE, value[j] );
       continue;
       }
    if( strcmp( key[j], "URL" ) == 0 ) {
       STRCPY( URL, value[j] );
       continue;
       }
```

```
        if( strcmp( key[j], "COMMENTS" ) == 0 ) {
           STRCPY( COMMENTS, value[j] );
           continue;
           }
        if( strcmp( key[j], "QueryType" ) == 0 ) {
//            fprintf( errfp,  "found query type (%s)\n", value[j] );
           if( strcmp( value[j], "update" ) == 0 ) {
              sprintf( table_caption, "updating " );
              QueryType = QUERY_UPDATE;
              }
           if( strcmp( value[j], "insert" ) == 0 ) {
              sprintf( table_caption, "adding " );
              QueryType = QUERY_INSERT;
              }
           if( strcmp( value[j], "Dam" ) == 0 ) {
              sprintf( table_caption, "All dogs from dam " );
              QueryType = BY_DAM;
              }
           if( strcmp( value[j], "Pedigree" ) == 0 ) {
              sprintf( table_caption, "Pedigree chart for " );
              QueryType = BY_PEDIGREE;
              }
           if( strcmp( value[j], "Sire" ) == 0 ) {
              sprintf( table_caption, "All dogs from sire " );
              QueryType = BY_SIRE;
              }
           if( strcmp( value[j], "Kennel" ) == 0 ) {
              sprintf( table_caption, "All dogs from kennel " );
              QueryType = BY_KENNEL;
              }
           if( strcmp( value[j], "Name" ) == 0 ) {
              sprintf( table_caption, "All dogs named " );
              QueryType = BY_NAME;
              }
           if( strcmp( value[j], "partial" ) == 0 ) {
              sprintf( table_caption, "All dogs named " );
              QueryType = BY_NAME_PARTIAL;
              }
           if( strcmp( value[j], "new" ) == 0 ) {
              sprintf( table_caption, "New dogs " );
              QueryType = QUERY_NEW;
              }
           if( strcmp( value[j], "rbinsert" ) == 0 ) {
              sprintf( table_caption, "Newf Lawn " );
              QueryType = QUERY_RBINSERT;
              }
```

```
        }
    if( strcmp( key[j], "base" ) == 0 )
       STRCPY( documentbase, value[j] );
    if( strcmp( key[j], "server" ) == 0 )
       STRCPY( servername, value[j] );
    if( strcmp( key[j], "cgi" ) == 0 )
       STRCPY( cgi_directory, value[j] );
    if( strcmp( key[j], "db" ) == 0 )
       STRCPY( dbname, value[j] );
    if( strcmp( key[j], "country" ) == 0 )
       STRCPY( country, value[j] );
    if( strcmp( key[j],"user" ) == 0 )
       STRCPY( username, value[j] );
    if( strcmp( key[j], "tbl" ) == 0 ) {
       STRCPY( tblname, value[j] );
      }
    }
  sprintf( table_caption, sought_name );
  free( ptr1 );
  }


void NormalizeName( char *OutputName, char *InputName, int length ) {
  int i, k;

  if( strlen( InputName ) >= length ) {
     OutputName[0] = '\0';
     fprintf( errfp, "INPUT BUFFER OVERFLOW ATTACK\
     NormalizeName( --,%s,%d)\n", InputName, length );
     return;
     }

  k = 0;
  for( i = 0; InputName[i] != '\0'; i++ ) {
     if( InputName[i] == '\'' )
        continue;
     OutputName[k++] = toupper( InputName[i] );
     }
  }
```

Notice that we define **STRCPY(d,s)** as a new macro that only copies the string if the length of the string is less than the size of the destination buffer. We also report any occurrence of this problem. Combining this report with the corresponding entry in the server access log gives us evidence of the hacker's attack and a trail back to the attacker's ISP.

ProcessArgs contains two other variations on the buffer overflow problem—the calls to **NormalizeName** and **sprintf**. We modify **NormalizeName** to compare the destination size with the source length and report any problems. The calls to **sprintf** are just lazy, and should have been calls to **strcpy** right from the start. We change those into calls to our new macro **STRCPY**.

This has been a long and tedious exercise simply to close one door that might not have been open in the first place. It was, however, well worth it from a security standpoint. Intruders will employ the same plodding tenacity and attention to detail when attacking your system. As any hacker will readily confess, the vast majority of successful hacks are enabled by sloppy coding on the target system.

Knowledge Is Power

Knowledge is power. The more knowledge an intruder has about your system, the more power he or she has over it. We touched on this equation just a little when we looked at ways of misleading the hacker through the fake command shell. The weaknesses of various Web servers, the operating systems they run under, and their myriad versions are often quite well documented. The easiest form of hard-shell defense is to strictly limit the information that your system provides about itself to the public. There are two bits of extremely useful information that your Web server gives away that it really doesn't have to:

- Web server software name and version. Think about it. If a Web server tells you that it's a Microsoft Internet Information Server, what operating system do you think it's running on?
- Directory listings.

Many Web servers provide a directory listing whenever a user provides a directory URL and the directory has no index or default HTML file. So, for example, if I point my Web browser at the URL http://www.channel1.com/users/ajrodley/Scituate, where Scituate is a directory that has no index or default HTML file, then the Web server might serve me a directory listing of that directory. The existence of a file named .cshrc, for example, tells the hacker that she's looking at a Unix system. An EXE file says that it's a DOS/Windows/NT box. One way to deal with this is to provide an index.html (or default.html) file that only shows the files you want browsers to see. A better way is to simply not put any files in your HTML tree that would provide any useful information to hackers. The presumption should always be that any file in the HTML directory tree will be visible to hackers.

Never Publish Your Source

In writing this book, I've violated one of the primary tenets of security: I've given away the source to my CGI executables. Think about it. Once you knew to look for **strcpy** of input variables into statically sized buffers, how long did it take you to find those errors in the original implementation of newfq.exe? Not very long, I'd imagine.

Not only does this information increase the chance of a hacker hitting you successfully, it reduces his risk in doing so. An intruder who has to sit online, testing your defenses without knowing how they'll react, is taking a risk (small though it might be) that someone, somewhere, is tracking those packets back through the Internet. The more the hacker hits your machine, and the longer she stays on, the higher the risk. A hacker with your source knows exactly how to hit you and can do it in the minimum amount of time.

There is another side to the "never publish" debate too, though. Really popular public-domain software tends, at a certain point, to be much more thoroughly debugged, simply because of all the different programmers who've looked at, and mucked with, the code. As is almost always the case, you have to evaluate individual programs on their own merits.

Hard-Shell Vs. Defense-In-Depth

There are two approaches to security: so-called *hard-shell* security and *defense-in-depth.* The hard-shell approach seeks to keep unauthorized users out of the system by extremely strict authentication (username and password) combined with frequent, mandatory password changes—presenting a "hard shell" to the outside world. Once inside the hard shell, users are generally not watched or restricted in any meaningful way.

Hard-shell security isn't really an option for us because our Web server is open to the public. Users are already inside the system. What we need to employ is a defense-in-depth strategy. This approach assumes that every line of defense will, at some point, be breached, and attempts to extract the maximum penalty from intruders at every stage.

Thus, we close all the buffer-overflow holes, but still assume that somehow a hacker can get access to a command prompt. What happens then, and what can we do about it? Well, if you leave a completely capable command shell lying around for hackers to use, then you get whatever the hacker feels like inflicting on you. An easy and effective defense against a hacker who gets access to a command shell is to replace the command shell itself with a program of our own making. In our case, we would replace the normal command shell, CMD.EXE.

What would our replacement shell look like? At the very least, we **must** log the date and time of any occurrence of this shell, which we do with our quick hit to shell.log. This log, combined with our server-access log and any logging that our CGI programs do, should be enough to quickly point to the security hole our intruder climbed through.

What else should we do in the fake command shell? That's a tougher question than it might seem. The easy thing to do is simply exit, closing the door in the intruder's face. That, however, is hard-shell thinking. A determined intruder will simply look for another hole.

One of the basic premises of hacking is that all systems can be cracked. They only differ in the amount of time it takes to get the job done. This is where defense-in-depth derives its power. It seeks to increase the time it takes to accomplish every step in the hacking process to the point where the whole process becomes prohibitively expensive.

If we simply bounce the intruder at our fake command shell, we've protected ourselves without costing the intruder anything. He simply moves on to try the next door (or window). Instead, we could implement a number of strategies that would cost real time, and perhaps mislead the hacker into wasting a lot more time:

- Display a fake welcome message. If you're a Windows machine, display a Unix welcome message, like "Welcome to SCO Unix Version 3.2." This should prompt the intruder to dig out a book of SCO 3.2 hacks and try them all, one by one.

- Implement fake versions of standard commands, such as **dir**, **ls**, **sh**, **csh**, **finger**, **whois**, and **ping**. For the directory listing commands, you should print out as long and realistic a list as possible. Remember that the point is to waste as much of the hacker's time as humanly possible.
- When displaying messages from the fake shell, place a long (but not too long) delay between each character. Remember, there is a long chain of links between your machine and the hacker, and she can't know for sure where any delay is being introduced. Simply waiting a couple of seconds between character outputs is a cheap and effective method of wasting time. If you're lucky, you might keep the hacker interested and online long enough for your ISP to track her down.

The whole point is to waste hackers' time and make them think they know more about your server than they really do. There is a fine line however, between misleading the hacker and daring him to beat you. It's really a judgment call that depends entirely on your own assessment of the kind of threat your system faces. If your intruders are teenage pranksters with only mildly malicious intent, then you might be better off just logging the incident and exiting. If, however, potential intruders are more intent on destroying or stealing your property, then you might want to engage in this more involved sort of grappling. You have to assess the threat, and tailor your response accordingly.

Eavesdropping And Secure Socket Connections

Eavesdropping is the giant red herring of the Web security debate. It keeps the uninitiated awake at night, worrying about how some wily hacker might "tap the connection" when they type their VISA numbers into the order-entry screens of commercial Web sites. What they envision, with help from the media, is some sort of wiretap, where the contents of their socket connections from browser to server are diverted to evil purposes.

At least today, this kind of hacking is so unlikely that, as a programmer, defending against it often feels like a stupid waste of time. It is much easier to break into a Web site or corporate LAN and steal the data out of one of the applications running there than it would ever be to divert the socket

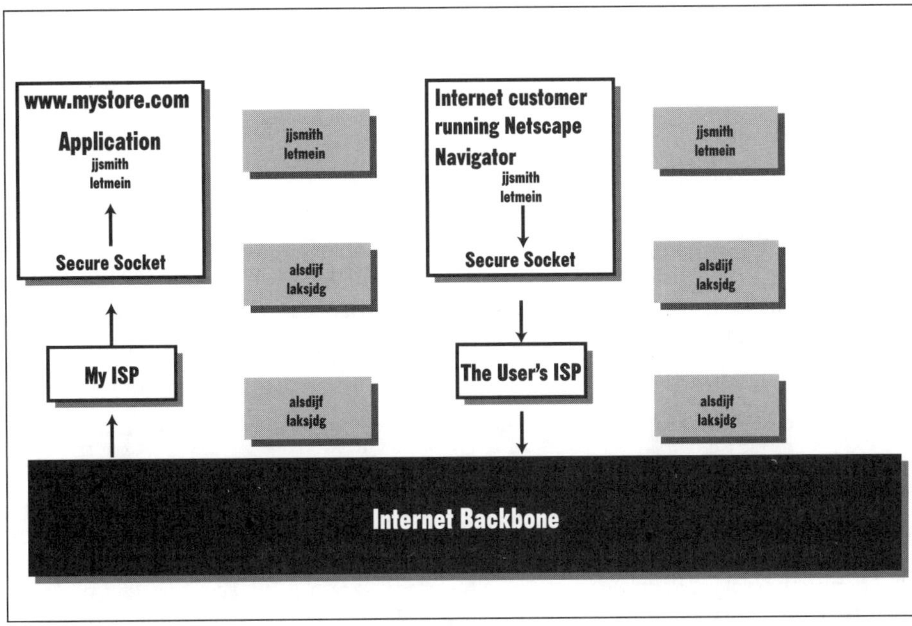

Figure 7.6 A username and password travel over a secure connection.

connection and steal the data from the byte stream. However, public confidence is critically important in Internet commerce, and if secure socket connections promote that confidence, then they're worth doing for that alone.

There is also a kernel of truth in the mostly hysterical secure-connection business. Data theft is a business. Today, the profit-to-risk ratio in that business favors the tactic of breaking into servers, not tapping the connection. However, Web servers, database servers, FTP servers, and firewalls will all eventually mature. Breaking into them will become much riskier and much less profitable. At some point, tapping the connection will become a viable option for data thieves. That is when encryption becomes necessary.

A secure connection is one where the data is encrypted from the point where a user enters it on the browser, to the point where the Web server software reads it into memory on the other side. Any eavesdropper tapping such a connection would see only garbled bytes. Figure 7.6 illustrates the concept.

The user enters the username/password combination of *jjsmith/letmein* from a browser. When the browser sends those two phrases through the secure socket, they become the gobbledy-gook, *alsdijf/laksjdf.* That nonsense phrase travels over the network and is not converted back into its plain-English meaning until it passes through the secure socket on the server. Note that, even in this simplified diagram, there are two actual physical points where the data stream from the user's browser to the Web server could be intercepted: at My ISP and at the user's ISP. The threat of eavesdropping is not theoretical, it's just exaggerated.

A Web application on its own cannot provide a secure link of its own making, unless, like our Stocker applet, it creates an independent socket connection and controls both sides. Secure connections require cooperation between the browser and server. These two entities have to agree on the encryption method, as well as the key they'll use to encrypt a particular connection. Netscape, which makes both browsers and servers came up with the solution, it's *Secure Sockets Layer,* or *SSL,* which most servers and browsers today support. SSL 3.0 also includes authentication, where the client and server present each other with certificates that identify them absolutely.

SSL is actually quite complex, and its internal workings are beyond the scope of this book. Fortunately, we don't need to look that deeply to be able to use SSL in our Web database applications.

How do we make a secure connection? Let's look at an example. Say our server is at www.myserver.com. To get our home page, users connect to http://www.myserver.com. Suppose now that we have an order-entry form located at Order.html. We can see this form at http://www.myserver.com/Order.html. However, if we connect to https://www.myserver.com/Order.html, then we'll get an SSL connection where all the data transferred over the wire is encrypted.

The key is the protocol specification, HTTPS as opposed to HTTP. Most Web servers that support SSL do so through a separate IP port, 443, as opposed to port 80, which is the unsecured HTTP port. A connection to http://www.myserver.com connects to port 80 on myserver.com, while the connection to https://www.myserver.com connects to port 443 on myserver.com.

Now, suppose we have a CGI application, cgi-bin/TakeMyCreditCard.exe. Our order form processes the credit card by using this CGI program as the ACTION of its HTML <FORM> element. When the user hits the Submit button on this form, our CGI program will be called. We need to make a secure connection to the CGI program, so we specify it in the ACTION statement as https://www.myserver.com/cgi-bin/TakeMyCreditCard.exe. This way, the data is encrypted as it travels over the wire, but unencrypted by the time TakeMyCreditCard.exe either reads the POST data or accesses the environment variables in a GET transaction.

Conclusion

In this chapter, we've looked at the risks associated with a Web presence. Each of the various pieces of our application—the CGI executable, Web server, database server, operating system, network operating system, and the network itself—all have peculiar vulnerabilities. Using network topology, good system-administration practices, and some common sense, we can make it much more difficult for hackers to compromise any of these pieces, or, having compromised one of them, to injure us.

We also looked in detail at some of the "ancient and honorable" mistakes that people typically make in writing CGI executables and corrected them in our own CGI executable for the Newfoundland Dog Database. We also looked at the design of our application to see where we might be giving data away when we probably didn't want to. And finally, we looked at the mostly theoretical risk of eavesdropping and saw how we can use secure connections to eliminate that threat.

Security in a Web site is not one thing, but many. A secure Web site relies on defense-in-depth, where each element assumes that the other elements can't be trusted and acts accordingly. When each element itself is secure, together they make a secure site.

Webliography

- http://www.genome.wi.mit.edu/WWW/faqs/www-security-faq.html — Lincoln Stein's excellent FAQ on Web security issues. Lincoln has also authored a book, *How to Set Up and Maintain a World Wide Web Site: The Guide for Information Providers*, that covers these issues in more detail.

• http://www.netscape.com/newsref/std/SSL.html	Netscape's SSL documentation.
• http://www.somarsoft.com	Windows NT Server security discussion.
• http://www.bombnet.com/Chapter9/	More Windows NT Server security.
• http://www.sophist.demon.co.uk/ping/	Denial-of-service-attack description.
• http://www.consensus.com/security/ssl-talk-faq.html	More SSL and proxy talk.

Chapter 8

Operational Issues

CHAPTER 8

Operational Issues

In previous chapters, we covered a wide spectrum of Web database applications, from the straight lookup-style Newfoundland Dog Database of Chapter 2, to the push-model StockWatch application of Chapter 5, to the Web shopping site of Chapter 6. Along the way, we concentrated, successfully, on getting the applications to work right. To keep that winning streak going, though, we need to navigate a minefield of operational issues—any one of which could spell the difference between a site that is merely interesting and one that is a business success.

Our site is like a horse-drawn wagon. The horse, in our case, is the database. Like a horse that needs to be fed and watered, this engine has needs that have to be met to keep the wagon moving forward.

You can think of a database server as a machine that turns raw disk space into usefully-organized information. In order to keep it going, we need to ensure that there is a supply of raw disk space. In SQL Server, that means dealing with transaction logging and backup.

As we discussed back in Chapter 1, SQL Server logs all transactions so that an unsaved database can be recovered using the log records for transactions that happened since the last backup. That feature makes the database extremely robust, but it comes at a fairly high cost. The log itself takes up a lot of valuable disk space. We need to allocate disk space to the log, and make sure that the log doesn't overflow. Should the log overflow, all update/insert/delete statements will fail until new log space is freed up.

Up to now, we've danced around this issue. In applications like Doggie Diamonds, we've merely truncated any log file that overflows during normal operation. This keeps the application running, but it's a terrible way to run an operational database because it leaves us without any evidence of what users have been doing. Should the system crash, all that work may be lost.

Regular Backup

The first thing to understand about SQL Server backup is that the Microsoft term for backup is **dump**. This truly counter-intuitive choice of terms seems to imply throwing the data out, rather than saving it, but I've chosen some pretty funky terms in my day, so I can't complain too much. Because dump is really backup, this gives us a fresh look at how we've been treating transaction logs up to this point. When we say "dump transaction shoppe with no_log" what we're really saying is "backup the transaction log for the Doggie Diamonds database". The simplest form of the syntax for the dump transaction command is:

```
dump transaction database_name
   [TO device]
   [WITH {truncate_only|no_log|no_truncate}]
```

Whenever the transaction log is backed up, SQL Server copies the completed transactions (the inactive portion of the transaction log) to the backup device. Then it frees up the space in the transaction log that those completed transactions were using. This is why we use the "dump transaction" statement to free up space in the transaction log. But what the heck does that "with no_log" clause do for us?

The transaction log keeps a record for each transaction that modifies the database. This includes the "dump transaction" statement itself. If we issue a dump statement, SQL Server first tries to add a record to the transaction log that describes this dump statement. If the transaction log is full, adding this dump transaction to the log will fail, and the whole dump statement will fail. If we specify "with no_log", that tells SQL Server to NOT log this dump statement. Using this clause, we can successfully dump a transaction log even if the log is already full.

Another interesting thing to note about our emergency dump statement (dump transaction shoppe with no_log) is that it doesn't tell SQL Server where to backup the transaction log. Where (to which device) does it get backed up when we issue this statement? Nowhere. In essence, when we issue this statement without a backup device, we're telling SQL Server just to free up the log space used by the completed transactions.

There are three variations of the **with** clause: **no_log**, **truncate_only**, and **no_truncate**. We've already talked about **no_log**-free the inactive space and no transaction log record for the dump statement. **Truncate_only** is identical to **no_log** with the exception that a transaction log record is generated. **No_truncate** copies the log and does not free the inactive space in the log file. It is mostly useful in building one big transaction log from an existing log plus other backed-up ones in order to rebuild a corrupted database.

There are two cases that we need to cover when it comes to managing the transaction log via the backup process. The first is the normal operating case where we want to try to maintain a reasonable level of free space in the transaction log. In this case, we probably want to back up the transaction log to tape on a regular schedule, say once a day. If we back up the whole database once a week, we can combine that backup with the daily transaction log backups to rebuild the database.

The other case we need to account for is the unexpected, where somehow the transaction log has filled up (or nearly filled up) in the time between our regular transaction log backups. In relatively less active databases, this condition usually indicates a poorly-designed ("runaway") application. In more active databases, how often to back up the transaction log will be one of those items that need to be tuned fairly frequently. Either way, we need to know when the transaction log is running out of space and we need to do something about it.

Our original solution to this problem, detecting the "log full" error programmatically and dumping the log with no_log, is a last-ditch, emergency, worst-case, don't-try-this-at- home solution, unsuitable for production systems. We can leave that code in there, but we need something better.

Before we deal with the emergency situations, we need to get the database and transaction log periodic backups done. The preferred solution is to back these things up to a tape that is regularly rotated. The first thing to do then is to add the tape device to Windows NT via Control Panel. Simply bring up the Tape Device applet and have it auto-detect the attached drive. Figure 8.1 shows the tape device applet after we've added our tape device.

Having installed the device in NT, it's a good idea to test it using NT's backup utility before trying to use it in SQL Server. Bring up NT's backup and pick a directory as shown in Figure 8.2 and 8.3.

Having picked the directory nttools, we slap a tape in the drive, select backup as in Figure 8.4.

Set if off, and with any luck we'll get the successful completion, shown in Figure 8.5.

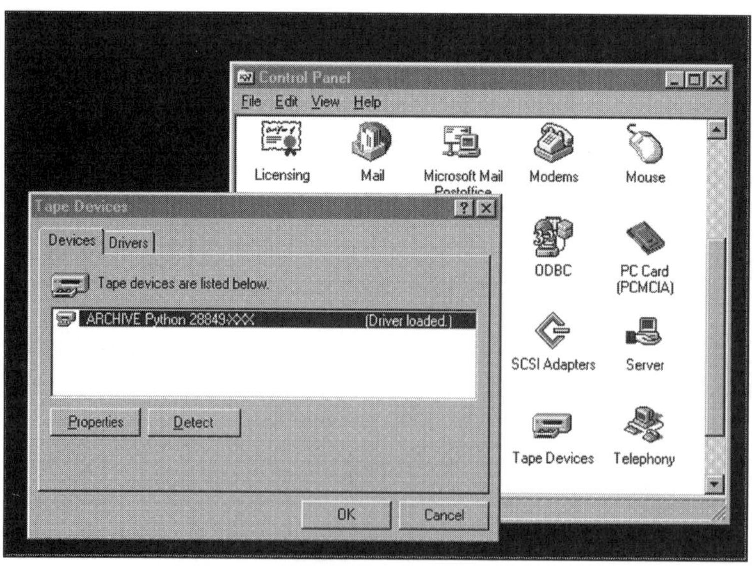

Figure 8.1 The tape device applet adds our tape.

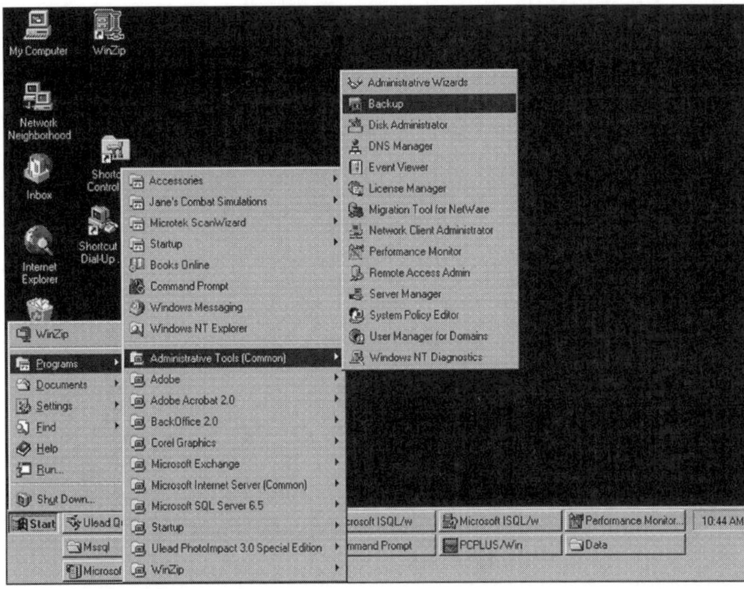

Figure 8.2 Bringing up NT backup.

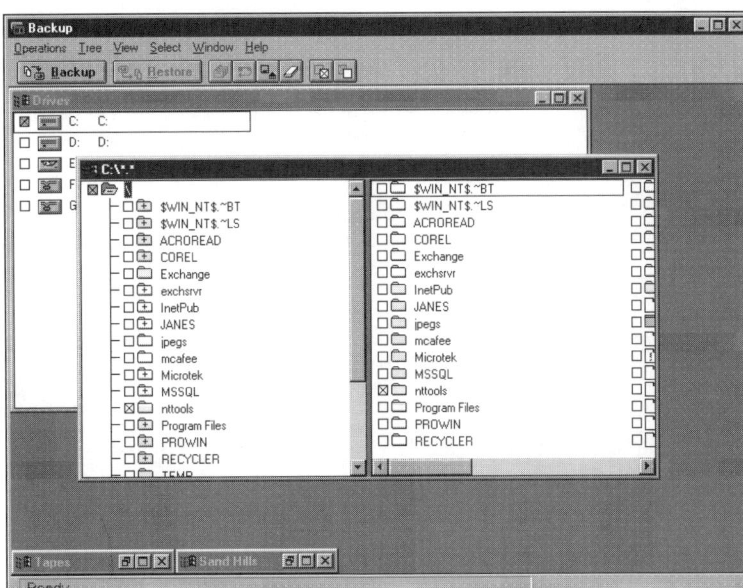

Figure 8.3 Picking a directory in NT backup.

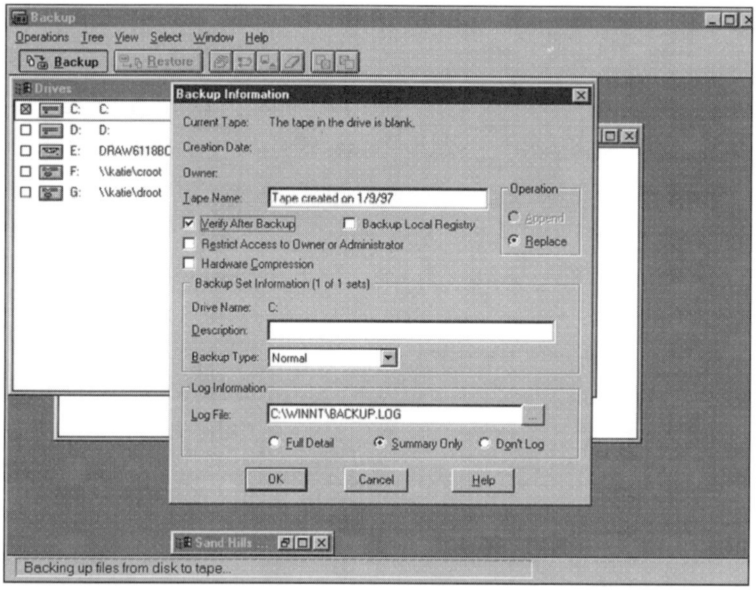

Figure 8.4 Backup information dialog.

With the device successfully defined in NT, we need to add it to SQL Server. Within Enterprise Manager select Tool|Database Backup|New as shown in Figure 8.6.

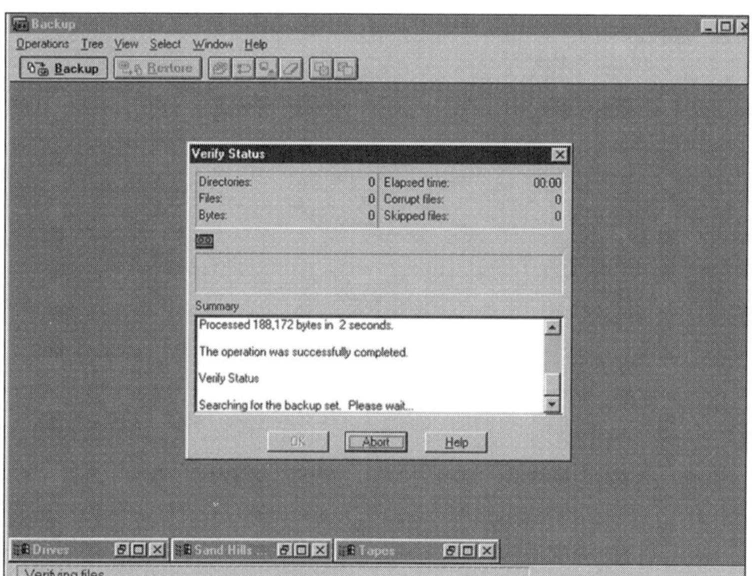

Figure 8.5 Successful backup via NT backup.

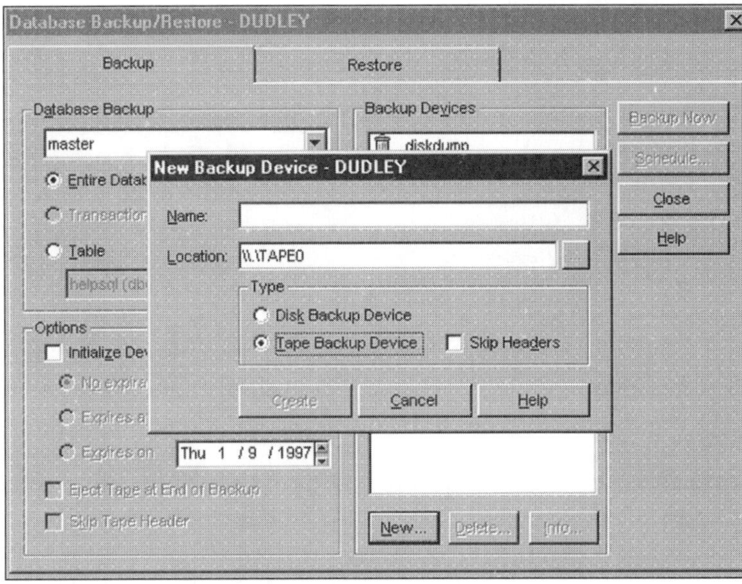

Figure 8.6 Adding the new tape device to SQL Server.

When we're done, we should end up with both the default diskdump device and the new tape device in the Backup Devices column as in Figure 8.7.

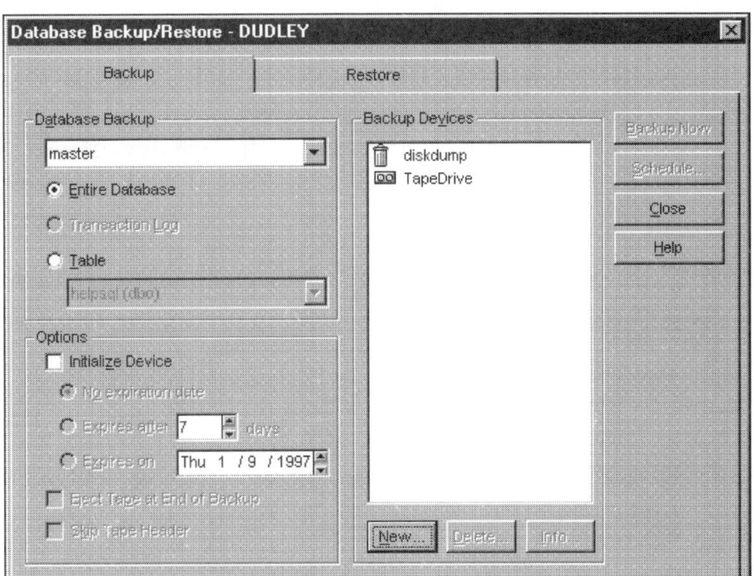

Figure 8.7 The device successfully added to SQL Server.

Test the device under SQL Server by selecting the master database, and initialize device, and hitting backup-now.

With the device installed and tested in NT, then added to SQL Server and tested there, we can go ahead and implement the backup strategy for our databases. We have three databases to worry about: Newf, Shoppe, and Stock, each of which has its own peculiar needs. Newf has massive updates every three or four months, and in the interim adds a few records per day. The data added on a daily basis is not critical: it has very little monetary value. In Newf, lost data is unfortunate, but not a crisis. For Newf then, we can do a full backup of the database once a month, append a backup of the transaction log once a day, and probably get adequate coverage.

Shoppe has a massive catalog update a couple of times a year, but also has hundreds of purchase records added every day. Each of these purchase records is critical, with a finite monetary value and an even higher replacement cost. Losing data from Shoppe could be a life-threatening crisis for the business. For Shoppe, we'll back up the entire database once a week, and we'll back up the transaction log every hour.

Stock, on the other hand, has a fairly fixed set of records that are updated on a minute-by-minute basis. The set of records is important, but the up-to-date price is relatively unimportant, since it gets updated almost the instant the application is re-started. Here, we back up the full database once a month. We need to back up the transaction log much more frequently in order to keep it from overflowing, but we don't really want to waste tape saving it, so we remove the to-device clause from the backup statement.

There's one more database that needs to be backed up - master. SQL Server stores tons of interesting information in master, including database and device definitions, user login information, and extended stored-procedure definitions. Fortunately, the master database is usually not that big in relative terms, nor is it updated that frequently. For the purposes of this book, the set of users is constant, the structure of the databases doesn't change much, and I'm constantly updating a set of utilities that allow me to rebuild all the databases from scratch (including user-logins) so the master database is not as critical as it might be in other applications. Thus, I'll back up the master weekly and leave it at that. The master database stores data and transaction log records on the same device, so separate transaction log backups are not allowed.

That gives us our backup profile. Let's walk through scheduling the two Doggie Diamonds backup jobs. First, we crank up Enterprise Manager, then select Tools-Backup, which displays the dialog box of Figure 8.8.

To set up a weekly full backup of the entire database, within the backup dialog of Figure 8.8, select Shoppe from the database list, set the entire database flag, and select the tape device from the device list, as shown in Figure 8.9. We want to schedule it for once a week, so we hit the schedule button, click through the volume label dialog, and end up at the schedule dialog of Figure 8.9.

The default schedule is once a week, Sunday at midnight, which is fine for this application. With that in place, we then need to define the hourly transaction log backups, so we go back to the backup dialog and set the transaction log flag as in Figure 8.10.

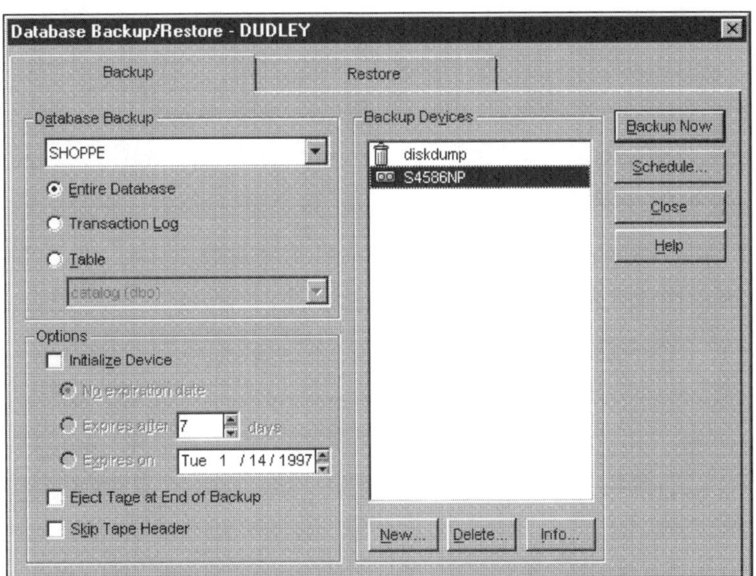

Figure 8.8 The backup dialog for Shoppe.

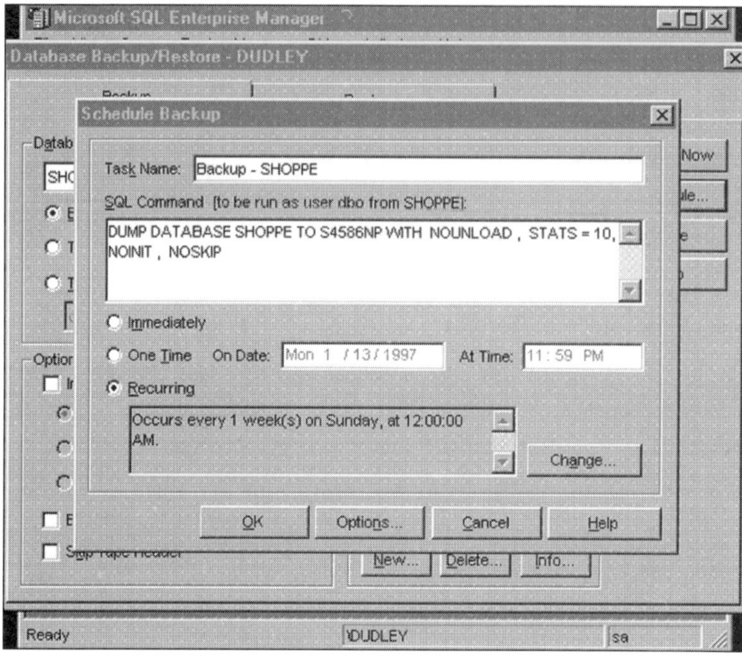

Figure 8.9 The schedule backup dialog for Shoppe's weekly backup.

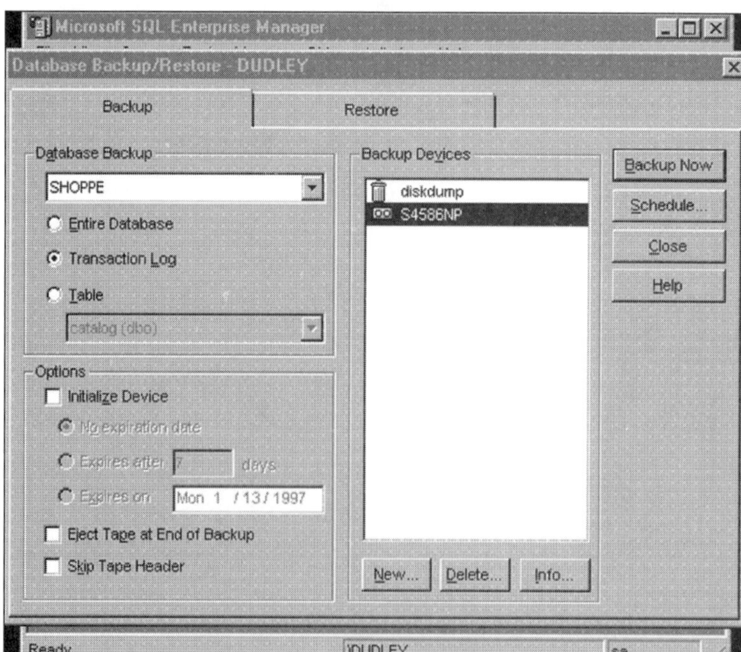

Figure 8.10 Setting up the hourly transaction log backup.

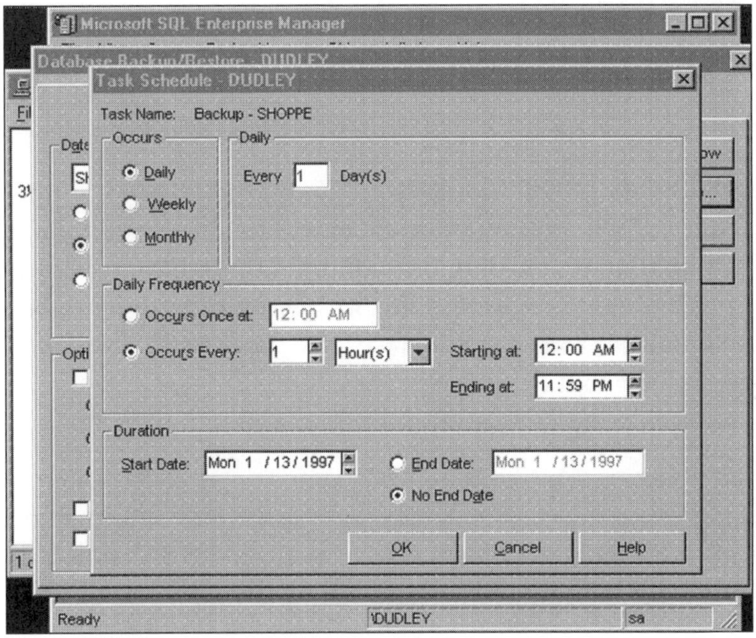

Figure 8.11 Changing the schedule to once per hour every day.

As before, we go to schedule, clicking through the volume label box. Instead of the default weekly scheduling, we click on change which brings up the scheduling dialog of Figure 8.11.

We select a daily backup and set the daily frequency at every hour, on the hour. With that, we have a reasonable backup plan for the Shoppe database. As discussed above, we need to repeat this process for each of the other databases in order to completely cover ourselves. And as with any backup plan, a plan that is not tested is no plan at all. When implementing a plan like this, build full-scale tests of the plan into the schedule.

Alerts And The Unexpected

The backup plan we've just defined should assure a reasonable supply of disk space in normal operation. However, systems do not always operate normally. This industry's massive horde of beeper-clad sysops can testify to that. The usual solution to dealing with the unexpected is to physically have somebody watching the system at all times, testing response, watching critical measurements, and waiting for his shift to end.

Windows NT, SQL Server, and the net provide us with a mechanism for a better solution. Via SQL Server alerts and Performance Monitor alerts, we can put boundaries on the performance of the system. If the application crosses those boundaries, we can fire off email or corrective actions.

There are a bunch of database issues that we need to monitor during normal operation. We want to be sure that we have a big enough pipe to our data, i.e., that we have sufficient throughput. Back in Chapter 1, we jumped through lots of huge hoops to predict throughput and the number of concurrent connections we'd need. Here, in operation, is where we can put those predictions to the test.

SQL Performance Monitor gives us a huge number of performance variables that we can watch. For the throughput/concurrent-connection question, there are three in particular to which we should pay attention: concurrent connections, transactions per second, and CPU time. Using these variables, we can look at both types of throughput—average and peak.

1. Number of concurrent connections. Every open connection to SQL Server increments this value.

2. Transactions per second (TPS). This is purely a load indicator that tells us how many SQL statements are being run per second. For the most part, there's a one-to-one correspondence between SQL statements and user interactions. In the Newfoundland Database, for example, the user issues a query, we turn it into formal SQL and return the result. One user-request leads to one CGI program execution which leads to one SQL statement. The big exception to this rule is the pedigree search where we perform a recursive search with a maximum of 63 individual queries. Given this exception, we need to combine TPS with concurrent connections to figure out when there's a problem.

3. CPU Time. This is the amount of time that a connection remains open. For the Newfoundland Database, this is also the transaction duration. Greater than 60 seconds probably indicates an application bug, or a poorly designed query. Frequent transactions lasting greater than 30 seconds indicate poor performance that may require either an application tuneup or a hardware upgrade. In a NSAPI, or Jeeves application like Doggie Diamonds, which opens

the connection and keeps it open over a number of transactions, this measure is not the same as transaction duration. The problem with a CPU Time alert is that it must be assigned to a particular connection. You can't assign a global alert that goes off whenever any connection exceeds a particular duration.

Let's go through, end to end, the exercise of adding an alert to the number of concurrent connections. In order to determine a "panic" value for the number of concurrent connections, we need to determine a baseline for that variable with none of our processes running. Figure 8.12 shows SQL Performance Monitor displaying the number of connections to the database.

As you can see, without any of our database access processes running, there are still seven open connections. Let's crank up Jeeves, query the Doggie Diamonds catalog, and see what we get then in Figure 8.13.

Again, as you might expect, querying the Doggie Diamonds database loads the CategoryServlet which opens a single connection and leaves it open. We're left with eight open connections. If we then load up all the other connected examples from the book, Stocker and it's data feed, we get two more connections for a baseline of ten open connections without any user activity.

Thus, 15 connections is cause for concern because that means there are five simultaneous Newfoundland Database processes. This requires an email to the DBA and some corrective action.

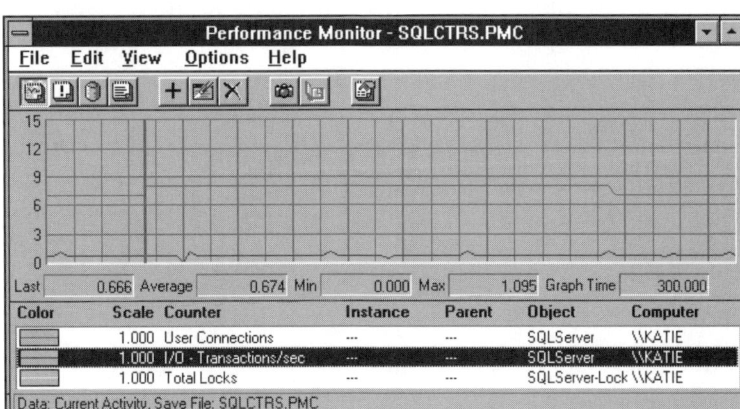

Figure 8.12 Open connections to the database.

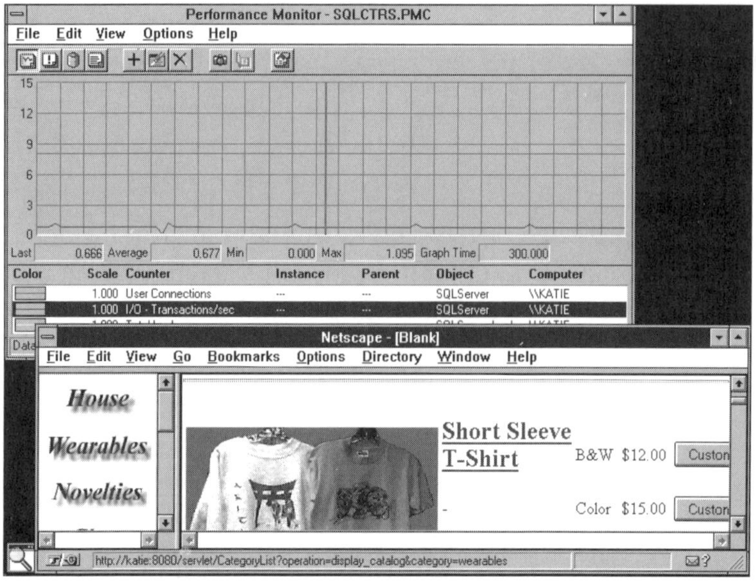

Figure 8.13 CategoryServlet adds a connection.

What should that corrective action be? If the system had an operator chained to it, we could raise an alert and disable the database until the operator fixed the error. Unfortunately, the operator for a Web database is typically remotely located, and not at the machine's beck and call. The ideal solution would be to find the processes that are holding the open connections and kill them. However, that would take quite a bit of programming for a situation that really requires manual analysis and correction. What we'll do here is to email the alert, then simply reboot the machine. This should terminate all the open processes relatively gracefully and restart us in a useable state. With the machine back up, the operator can analyze the logs to his heart's content.

In order to hook an SQL performance alert defined in Performance Monitor to an action like rebooting the system, we need to go through two steps:

1. Define a new alert with associated action (reboot) in SQL Server.
2. Define a new alert in Performance Manager and hook it to the SQL Server alert.

Let's define our 15 open connections alert in SQL Server first. We want to reboot the system whenever the alert goes off, so we have to define a task that tells SQL Server how to reboot the system. Select Server-Scheduled Tasks|New Task. Figure 8.14 shows the new task dialog.

Our task is to be executed on-demand, rather than one-time, or recurring, and it requires a command shell, so we set the type to CmdExec. In the Command field, we need to tell SQL Server the exact program to execute (including any parameters). To reboot the system, I use a utility called "Reboot.exe" from Cohesion Software Benelux (Gert E. R. Drapers) that will reboot a Windows NT machine. Enter a full path to the executable so that we're not dependent on the state of the PATH environment variable.

Now that we've defined the task that our alert will run, we need to define the alert itself and hook it to that task. From Enterprise Manager, select Server-Alerts|New Alert. Figure 8.15 shows SQL Server's New Alert dialog with our 15-connection alert defined.

The first thing we need to do here is define an SQL error message to be written to the SQL error log when the alert goes off. From the New Alert dialog, select Error-Number| Add Error. From there, define a new error message numbered greater than 50,000. Figure 8.16 shows our new error message.

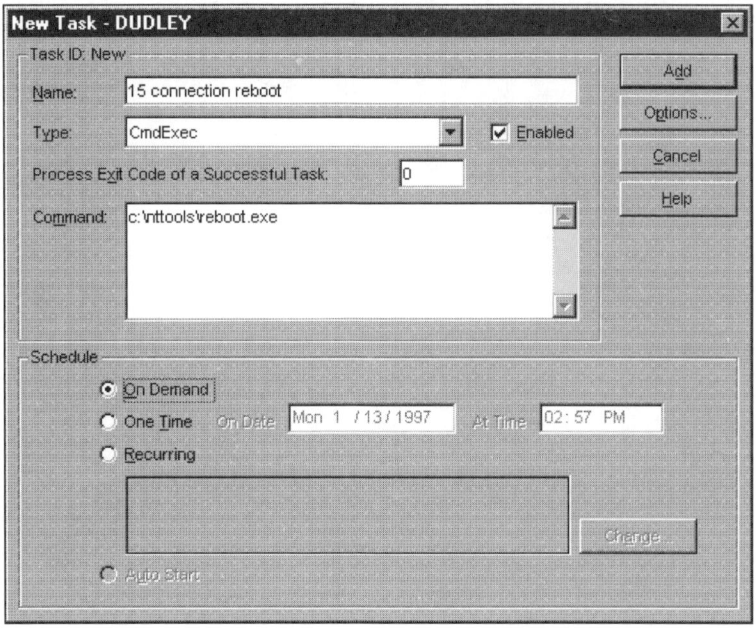

Figure 8.14 The new task dialog with our task defined.

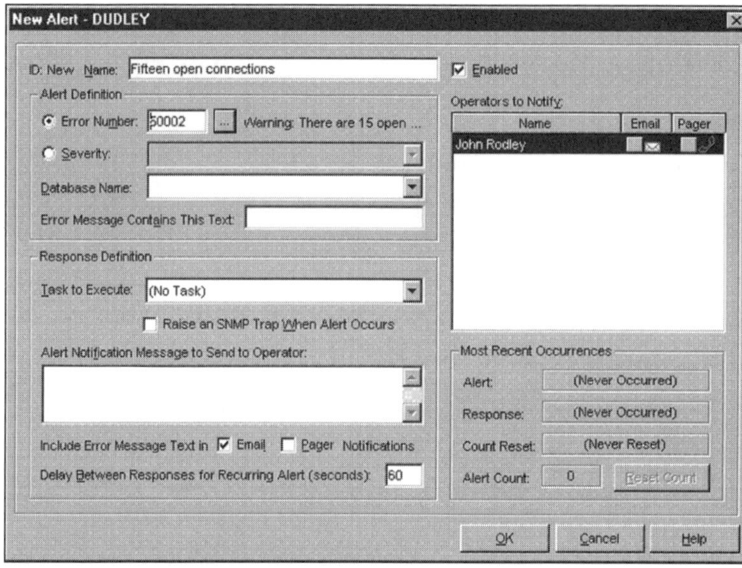

Figure 8.15 The 15 connection alert defined in SQL Server.

In addition to the new error message, we select a user from the operators list who will receive email when the alert goes off—in this case, me. We also select our new reboot task from the list of possible tasks to execute.

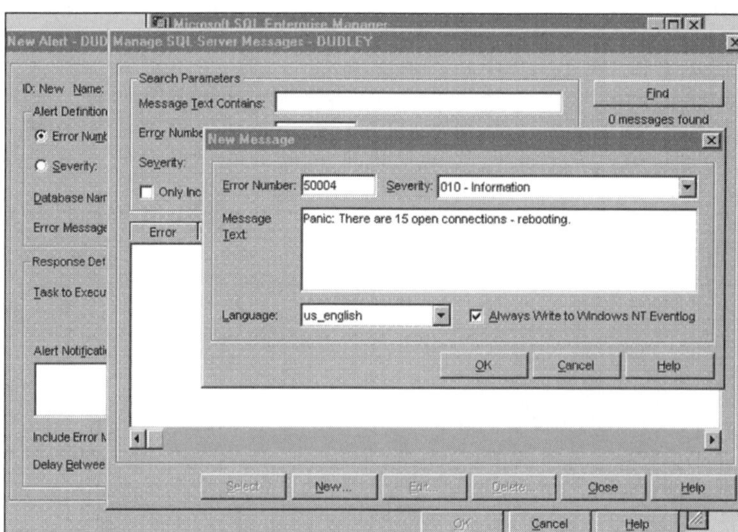

Figure 8.16 Our new error message.

Now that we've defined the SQL Server side of this alert process, we can define the Performance Monitor alert that actually watches the database. To get this going, start up SQL Performance Monitor and select View Alert, then Edit|Add_To_Alert. Figure 8.17 shows Performance Monitor's new alert dialog.

Select SQLServer as the object we want to monitor. That fills the counter list box with all the counters that SQLServer provides. Select User Connections as the counter, and set the Alert-If value to over 15.

That determines when this alert will trigger. We want to hook this alert back to the SQL Server alert, so we set the "Run Program on Alert" value as follows:

```
c:\mssql\binn\sqlalrtr /E50004
```

Sqlalrtr is an executable that sets off an exception in SQL Server. The exception that gets set off is the one named in the /E argument. In this case, error number 50004, the one we just defined, which in turn calls Reboot.exe.

Making Performance Alerts Persistent

We've defined a set of performance alerts, but it only persists for as long as this instance of perfmon is running. We need to save our alerts in a file. This is easy enough via file/save-as. Our performance alerts are all stored in a file called rodley.pma.

What happens when the system is rebooted? When the system comes back up, these alerts are not active. We need to start up perfmon with our alerts file as its only argument. We could add the following command line to our startup folder:

```
perfmon c:\rodley.pma
```

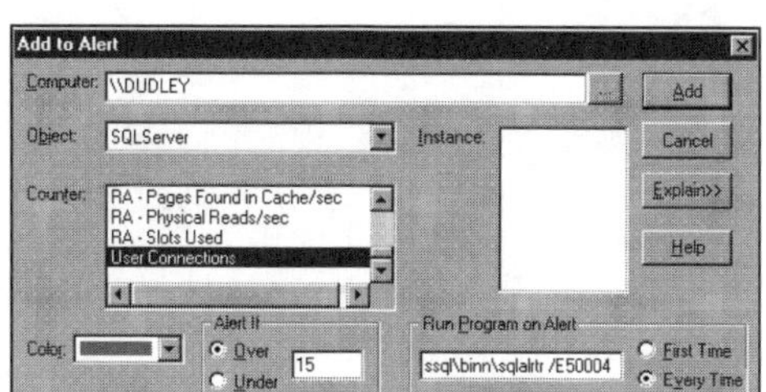

Figure 8.17 Defining a new Performance Monitor alert.

This would start up performance monitor loaded with our alert set active whenever we logon. What we really want though, is for the performance monitor to start up with our alert set whenever the system is rebooted—whether or not anyone is logged on.

Adding Performance Monitor Alert As A Service

In order to have our performance monitor alert activated automatically whether we're logged in or not, we need to install perfmon.exe as a Windows NT service. The Microsoft Developer's Kit includes a utility called SRVANY.EXE. This program allows you to install any executable as a service. Srvany is just a shell that handles communication with the Windows Service Manager.

Use the accompanying utility INSTSRV to add SRVANY to the list of services:

```
INSTSRV SQLPerformance c:\reskit\srvany.exe
```

This will bring up the screen of Figure 8.18. Now start up Control Panel and crank up the Services applet as in Figure 8.19.

Mark the SQLPerformance service as Automatic startup and log on as an account that has the ability to run Reboot.exe. Close the services applet. At this point, there is a service called SQLPerformance that will run SRVANY under the system account automatically on system boot. What we need to do now is configure SRVANY to run our application, perfmon c:\rodley.pma.

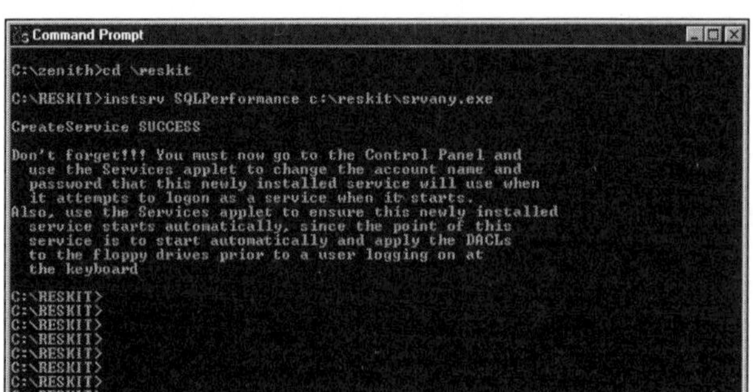

Figure 8.18 Running INSTSRV to install our service.

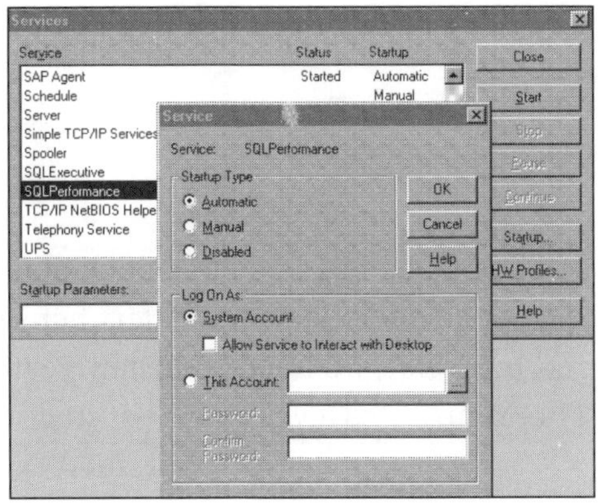

Figure 8.19 Services applet configuring our performance alert.

SRVANY determines which application to run by checking a set of registry variables. To set these variables, start up the registry editor, regedt32. Select HKEY_LOCAL_MACHINE, SYSTEM, CurrentControlSet, Services. At that point, you'll see a list of the installed services. That list should include our newly created service, SQLPerformance. Select SQLPerformance, then edit/add-key, and enter Parameters as the key name, as in Figure 8.20.

With that done, Parameters should appear in the list of keys for SQLPerformance. Select Parameters, then edit/add-value, and enter Application as the name, and perfmon.exe as the value. Figure 8.21 illustrates.

Finally, we need to point perfmon at our alerts file. So we need to add one more value to the Parameters key. Select the Parameters key. Then select

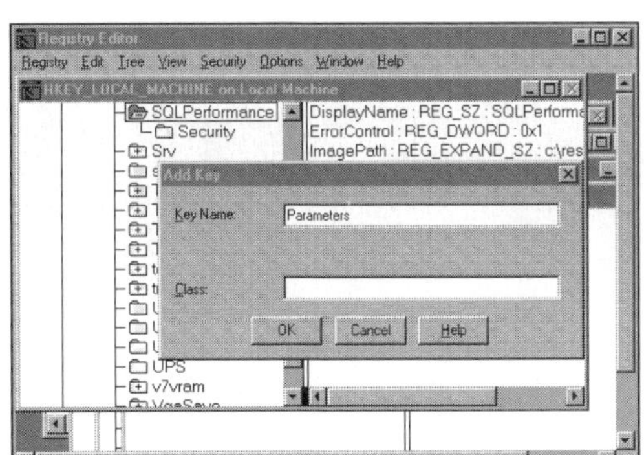

Figure 8.20 Adding the Parameters key to our service.

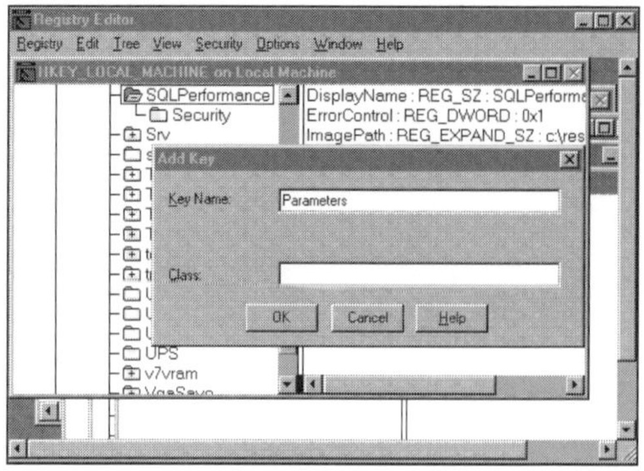

Figure 8.21 Adding the application value.

edit/add-value, and enter AppParameters as the name, and our alerts file, c:\rodley.pma, as the value. Figure 8.22 illustrates.

That finishes up the installation of our performance alerts as a service. With any system that is this complicated to configure it's always a good idea to test it right away. For us, this just means rebooting, logging in, and starting up a bunch of instances of ISQLW, the interactive query manager. After the fourth instance, the system should reboot.

Conclusion

In this chapter, we covered the bare necessities of Web database administration: regular backup and performance alerts. We saw how to think through a backup plan and how to implement it in SQL Server. For each

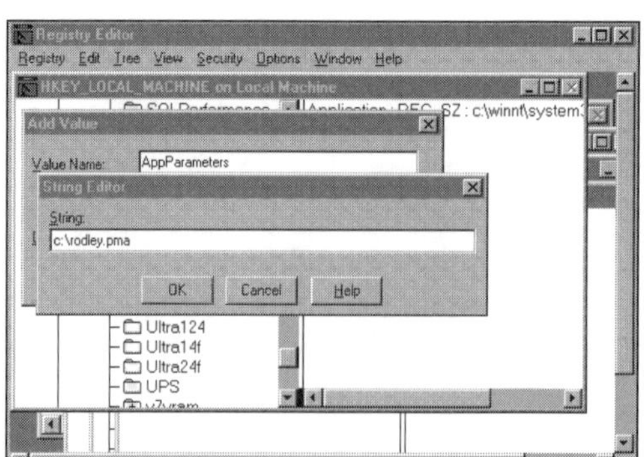

Figure 8.22 Adding the alerts file as the application parameter.

database, we decided on a schedule for both full database backups and incremental, transaction log backups. We also looked at the issue of performance monitoring. Using a single variable, concurrent connections, we worked through determining reasonable values. Then we went step by step through the process of attaching an alert to a particular value and executing our chosen program when that value is exceeded. Hopefully, these two exercises can get you well on the way to putting up your own non-stop Web database application.

This book has covered three fairly complicated applications in serious detail. If you've worked through these applications as you went along, then you have a good grounding in many of the basics required of Web database developers today. The field is rapidly changing, but not as rapidly as you might imagine. The basic technologies—SQL, HTTP, HTML, and CGI, for example—are evolving much more slowly than the huge raft of tools that sit atop them. Mastering the applications in this book should give you a headstart no matter what tool set you end up using for your particular application.

Index

Note: Page numbers in boldface type refer to program code listings.

A

B

C

G

H

I

O

S

T

U

V

W